MostUsedWords.com presents

C000135755

French Frequency Dictionary

Intermediate Vocabulary

2501-5000 Most Common French Words

Book 2

First Printing, 2018

Jolie Laide LTD
12/F, 67 Percival Street, Hong Kong

www.MostUsedWords.com

Contents

Why This Book?

Hello, dear reader.

Thank you for purchasing this book. We hope it serves you well on your language learning journey.

Not all words are created equal. The purpose of this frequency dictionary is to list the most used words in descending order, to enable you to learn a language as fast and efficiently as possible.

First, we would like to illustrate the value of a frequency dictionary. For the purpose of example, we have combined frequency data from various languages (mainly Romance, Slavic and Germanic languages) and made it into a single chart.

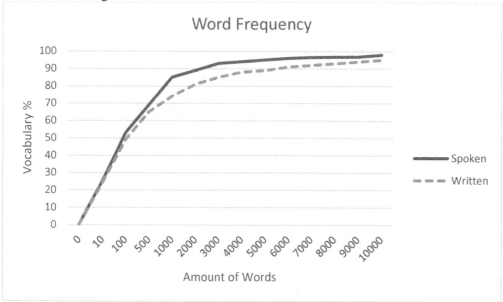

The sweet spots, according to the data seem to be:

Amount of Words	Spoken	Written
• 100	53%	49%
• 1.000	85%	74%
• 2.500	92%	82%
• 5.000	95%	89%
• 7.500	97%	93%
• 10.000	98%	95%

Above data corresponds with Pareto´s law.

Pareto's law, also known as the 80/20 rule, states that, for many events, roughly 80% of the effects come from 20% of the causes.

In language learning, this principle seems to be on steroids. It seems that just 20% of the 20% (95/5) of the most used words in a language account for roughly all the vocabulary you need.

To put his further in perspective: The Concise Oxford Hachette French Dictionary lists over 175.000 words in current use, while you will only need to know 2.9% (5000 words) to achieve 95% and 89% fluency in speaking and writing. Knowing the most common 10.000 words, or 5.6%, will net you 98% fluency in spoken language and 95% fluency in written texts.

Keeping this in mind, the value of a frequency dictionary is immense. Study the most frequent words, build your vocabulary and progress naturally. Sounds logical, right?

How many words do you need to know for varying levels of fluency?

While it's important to note that it is impossible to pin down these numbers and statistics with 100% accuracy, these are a global average of multiple sources.

According to research, this is the amount of vocabulary needed for varying levels of fluency.

1. 250 words: the essential core of a language. Without these words, you cannot construct any sentence.
2. 750 words: those that are used every single day by every person who speaks the language.
3. 2500 words: those that should enable you to express everything you could possibly want to say, although some creativity might be required.
4. 5000 words: the active vocabulary of native speakers without higher education.
5. 10,000 words: the active vocabulary of native speakers with higher education.
6. 20,000 words: what you need to recognize passively to read, understand, and enjoy a work of literature such as a novel by a notable author.

Caveats & Limitations.

A frequency list is never "The Definite Frequency List."

Depending on the source material analyzed, you may get different frequency lists. A corpus on spoken word differs from source texts based on a written language.

That is why we chose subtitles as our source, because, according to science, subtitles cover the best of both worlds: they correlate to both spoken and written language.

The frequency list is based on analysis of roughly 20 gigabytes of French subtitles.

Visualize a book with almost 16 million pages, or 80.000 books of 200 pages each, to get an idea of the amount words that have been analyzed for this book. A large base text is vital in order to develop an accurate frequency list.

The raw data included over 1 million entries. The raw data has been lemmatized; words are given in their root form.

Some entries you might find odd, in their respective frequency rankings. We were surprised a couple of time ourselves. Keep in mind that the frequency list is compiled from a large amount of subtitle data, and may include words you wouldn't use yourself.

You might find non-French loanwords in this dictionary. We decided to include them, because if they´re being used in subtitle translation, it is safe to assume the word has been integrated into the French general vocabulary.

We tried our best to keep out proper nouns, such as "James, Ryan, Alice as well as "Rome, Washington" or "the Louvre, the Capitol".

Some words have multiple meanings. For the ease of explanation, the following examples are given in English.

"Jack" is a very common first name, but also a noun (a jack to lift up a vehicle) and a verb (to steal something). So is the word "can" It is a conjugation of the verb "to be able" as well as a noun (a tin can, or a can of soft drink).

This skews the frequency rankings slightly. With the current technology, it is unfortunately not possible to rightly identify the correct frequency placements of above words. Luckily, these words are very few, and thus negligible in the grand scheme of things.

If you encounter a word you think you won't need in your vocabulary, just skip learning it. The frequency list includes 25 extra words to compensate for any irregularities you might encounter.

The big secret to learning language is this: build your vocabulary, learn basic grammar and go out there and speak. Make mistakes, have a laugh and learn from them.

We hope you enjoy this frequency dictionary, and that it helps you in your quest of speaking French.

How To Use This Dictionary

abbreviation	*abr*
adjective	*adj*
adverb	*adv*
article	*art*
auxiliary verb	*av*
conjunction	*con*
interjection	*int*
noun	*f(eminine), m(asculine)*
numeral	*num*
particle	*part*
phrase	*phr*
prefix	*pfx*
preposition	*prp*
pronoun	*prn*
suffix	*sfx*
verb	*vb*
singular	*sg*
plural	*pl*

Word Order

The most common translations are generally given first. This resets by every new respective part of speech. Different parts of speech are divided by ";".

Translations

We made the decision to give the most common translation(s) of a word, and respectively the most common part(s) of speech. It does, however, not mean that this is the only possible translations or the only part of speech the word can be used for.

International Phonetic Alphabet (IPA)

The pronunciation of foreign vocabulary can be tricky. To help you get it right, we added IPA entries for each entry. If you already have a base understanding of the pronunciation, you will find the IPA pronunciation straightforward. For more information, please visit www.internationalphoneticalphabet.org

French English Frequency Dictionary

Rank	French	English Translation(s)
	Part of Speech	French Example Sentence
	[IPA]	-English Example Sentence
2501	**établir**	**establish**
	vb	Elle a notamment pu établir que son effectif est actuellement de 6 241 personnes.
	[etabliʁ]	-The current strength of the police force has been established at 6,241 officers.
2502	**touche**	**key**
	f	Maintenez la touche (Option) (Alt) enfoncée et appuyez sur la touche fléchée vers la droite.
	[tuʃ]	-Hold down the (Option) (Alt) key, and press the right arrow key.
2503	**profil**	**profile**
	m	J'essaie de faire profil bas.
	[pʁɔfil]	-I try to keep a low profile.
2504	**budget**	**budget**
	m	Il faut saluer ce budget, c'est le dernier budget heureux, le dernier budget tranquille.
	[bydʒɛ]	-We must welcome this budget, it is the last easy budget, the last simple budget.
2505	**panneau**	**panel|sign**
	m	La cartouche ne doit pas être plus large que le panneau de signalisation.
	[pano]	-The additional board must be no broader than the signal board.
2506	**lame**	**blade**
	f	Les gardiennes trouvèrent une lame de scie à métaux dans la poche de la prisonnière.
	[lam]	-The guards found a hacksaw blade in the prisoner's pocket.
2507	**disponible**	**available; on call**
	adj; adv	(Le rapport est imprimé en annexe aux pages 913 à 921 (disponible dans le format imprimable PDF).)
	[dispɔnibl]	-(The report is printed as an appendix at pages 913-921 (available in print format PDF).)
2508	**illusion**	**illusion**
	f	Il était possible que tout était une illusion, ou pire, une illusion satanique?
	[ilyzjɔ̃]	-It was possible that everything was illusion, or worse, satanic illusion?
2509	**caravane**	**caravan|trailer**
	f	Une caravane de cinquante chameaux se dirigeait lentement à travers le désert.
	[kaʁavan]	-A caravan of fifty camels slowly made its way through the desert.
2510	**pacifique**	**peaceful|pacific**
	adj	Je suis pacifique.
	[pasifik]	-I am a peace loving person.
2511	**scotch**	**Scotch tape|whisky**
	m	Ce scotch ne colle pas.
	[skɔtʃ]	-This tape isn't sticky.
2512	**mystérieux**	**mysterious**

adj
[misteʁjø]

Le mystérieux décès d'activistes politiques reste inexpliqué 10 ans après.
-The mysterious deaths of political activists remain unexplained 10 years later.

2513 **concevoir**

vb
[kɔ̃səvwaʁ]

design|conceive

Peut-on concevoir un autre «rêve européen» pour une Europe davantage plurale ?
-Dare one dream a different European dream, a dream of a more pluralistic Europe?

2514 **historique**

adj
[istɔʁik]

historical

L'historique, la structure et le contenu de la nomenclature y étaient expliqués.
-The background, organization and content of the publication were presented.

2515 **régiment**

m
[ʁeʒimɑ̃]

regiment

En 1954 au centre de régiment Secunderabad.
-In 1954... at the Secunderabad Army Regiment Centre.

2516 **missile**

adj; m
[misil]

missile; missile

L'attaque par missile a pris un grand nombre de vies.
-The missile attack took a heavy toll of lives.

2517 **boucher**

m; vb
[buʃe]

butcher; plug

Leur boucher cet horizon, c'est maintenir là une poudrière.
-If we slaughter this prospect, we shall be storing up a powder keg.

2518 **niquer**

vb
[nike]

fuck

Je devrais aussi niquer mon prof d'Anglais...
-Although I might have to bang my English teacher as well.

2519 **légitime**

adj
[leʒitim]

legitimate

Dans la culture de certains peuples, s'est inscrit, de manière indélébile, un sentiment de supériorité tel, qu'il les rend capables de totalement déshumaniser les autres peuples, au point que toute torture, tout viol, tout assassinat de masse leur apparaît légitime.
-In the cultures of certain peoples, a marked feeling of superiority has developed, so much so that it makes them capable of completely dehumanizing other peoples, to the point that that any kind of torture, rape, or mass murder seems acceptable to them.

2520 **cuit**

adj
[kɥi]

cooked|baked

Et pour ce qui est de la préparation, le poisson est déjà cuit.
-And when it comes to cooking, the fish are already cooked.

2521 **pilote**

m
[pilɔt]

pilot

Jack n'a pas l'étoffe d'un pilote de course.
-Jack doesn't have what it takes to be a race car driver.

2522 **épuiser**

vb
[epɥize]

exhaust|drain

Nous savons qu'on a laissé venir de gros chalutiers qui ont épuisé les stocks de poisson.
-We know how the large trawlers have been allowed to come in and deplete the fishing stocks.

2523 **former**

vb
[fɔʁme]

form|train

Michael m'a autorisé à former un commando anti-exhibitionnistes.
-Michael has authorized me to form an emergency anti-flashing task force.

2524 **sucer**

vb
[syse]

suck|suck out

Tu me demandes si j'ai essayé de me sucer moi-même ?
-You're asking me if I ever tried to suck my own penis?

2525	**considérer**	**consider**
	vb[kɔ̃sideʀe]	La vérité, c'est qu'aujourd'hui, nous pouvons considérer cela comme un succès. -The truth is that today we can consider this to be a success.

2526	**héroïne**	**heroin**
	f [eʀɔin]	Le roman se termine par la mort de l'héroïne. -The novel ends with the heroine's death.

2527	**bruit**	**noise|sound**
	m [bʀɥi]	Le bruit des voitures et des camions est la principale source de bruit. -Of all noise sources, the noise generated by cars and lorries is the most crucial one.

2528	**tendance**	**trend|movement**
	f [tɑ̃dɑ̃s]	Ce professeur a tendance à être partial envers les étudiantes de sexe féminin. -That teacher tends to be partial to female students.

2529	**serviteur**	**servant**
	m [sɛʀvitœʀ]	L'argent est un bon serviteur, mais un mauvais maître. -Money is a good servant, but a bad master.

2530	**revancher**	**requite**
	vb [ʀəvɑ̃ʃe]	S'ils persistent en revanche, contactez immédiatement votre médecin. -If these side effects continue, however, contact your doctor immediately.

2531	**décrire**	**describe|depict**
	vb [dekʀiʀ]	Cependant, il ne suffit pas de les décrire pour encourager les parties prenantes. -However, simply describing these will not, in itself, encourage the stakeholders.

2532	**répétition**	**repetition|rehearsal**
	f [ʀepetisjɔ̃]	C'est une bonne chose que ce soit survenu au cours de la répétition et non de la représentation ! -It's a good thing that this happened during the rehearsal and not the performance!

2533	**punition**	**punishment**
	f [pynisjɔ̃]	Il doit aussi être assuré que la punition n'excède pas le crime. -It must also be assured that the punishment does not exceed the crime.

2534	**assistant**	**assistant; assistant**
	adj; m [asistɑ̃]	Un assistant administratif et un assistant au programme compléteraient le secrétariat. -An administrative and a programme assistant would support the secretariat.

2535	**apparence**	**appearance**
	f [apaʀɑ̃s]	Les fichiers images se caractérisent par un format et une apparence stables. -Document images provide stability in terms of document format and appearance.

2536	**effectivement**	**effectively**
	adv [efɛktivmɑ̃]	Les Verts veilleront à ce que ces ajustements soient effectivement mis en œuvre. -The Greens will ensure that these adjustments are actually implemented.

2537	**honorable**	**honorable**
	adj[ɔnɔʀabl]	L'honorable sénateur Lang a remplacé l'honorable sénateur Frum (le 16 mai 2012). -The Honourable Senator Lang replaced the Honourable Senator Frum (May 16, 2012).

2538	**minimum**	**minimum; minimum**

adj; m
[minimɔm]

Je n'ai fait que le strict minimum.
-I only did the bare minimum.

2539 absent — **absent; absentee**

adj; m
[apsɑ̃]

Je suis le chef absent d'une très petite entreprise familiale établie à Londres.
-I am the absentee boss of a very small enterprise, our family business in London.

2540 vachement — **really**

adv
[vaʃmɑ̃]

OK, ça maintenant ! La combinaison de ceci et ça pourrait être vachement sexy !
-OK, this next! The combination of this and this might be way sexy!

2541 quêter — **take collection**

vb
[kete]

Ce qui est sur la table, c'est le fait qu'il faut arrêter que les gens soient obligés de quêter pour avoir leur propre argent.
-The issue is the fact that people must no longer be forced to beg to collect their own money.

2542 possession — **possession**

f
[pɔsesjɔ̃]

Comment es-tu entré en possession de ce tableau ?
-How did you come by owning this painting?

2543 chanteur — **singer**

m
[ʃɑ̃tœʁ]

Le défunt Freddie Mercury, ancien chanteur principal de Queen, avait une tessiture de quatre octaves.
-The late Freddie Mercury, former lead singer of Queen, had a vocal range of four octaves.

2544 colonne — **column**

f
[kɔlɔn]

Insérer une nouvelle colonne, avant la colonne pour la Division 1.1, comme suit :
-Insert a new column before the current column for Division 1.1, as follows:

2545 évacuer — **evacuate**

vb
[evakɥe]

Plusieurs participantes ont mentionné que cela leur avait permis d'évacuer leur colère.
-Several participants mentioned that it had allowed them to vent their anger.

2546 confortable — **comfortable**

adj
[kɔ̃fɔʁtabl]

Demain, la Commission remaniée pourra compter avec une majorité très confortable.
-Tomorrow, the modified Commission will be able to count on a very comfortable majority.

2547 héritage — **heritage|legacy**

m
[eʁitaʒ]

Ils défendent leurs erreurs comme s'ils défendaient leur héritage.
-They defend their errors as if they were defending their inheritance.

2548 atterrir — **touch down**

vb
[ateʁiʁ]

Un vol de l'ECHO devait atterrir sur la piste de cet aérodrome le 12 mai.
-An ECHO flight had been expected to land at the airstrip on 12 May.

2549 troupeau — **herd|flock**

m[tʁupo]

L'artiste est un mouton qui se sépare du troupeau. -An artist is a sheep that strays from the flock.

2550 vaisselle — **dishes**

f
[vɛsɛl]

Ils feront la vaisselle.
-They will wash dishes.

2551 photographe — **photographer**

	m/f [fɔtɔgʁaf]	Le photographe a été transporté dans un hôpital de Jérusalem puis rapatrié en France. -The photographer was taken to a Jerusalem hospital and then repatriated to France.
2552	**ambassade** f [ãbasad]	**embassy** Il est diplomate à l'ambassade américaine. -He is a diplomat at the American Embassy.
2553	**engin** m [ãʒɛ̃]	**machine | engine** Lorsque Jack s'est arrêté au stop, son engin a calé. -When Jack stopped for a stop sign, his engine stalled.
2554	**âne** m [an]	**donkey** C'est parce que l'âne a cassé sa mâchoire. -That's 'cause the donkey busted her jaw.
2555	**clef** f; adj [kle]	**key; pivotal** La clef de la chambre, s'il vous plaît. -The room key, please.
2556	**villa** f [vila]	**villa** Il est résolu à faire l'acquisition de la villa au bord de mer. -He is bent on buying the seaside villa.
2557	**réussite** f [ʁeysit]	**success** Ma réussite est improbable. -There is little prospect of my success.
2558	**muscle** m [myskl]	**muscle** Le plus gros muscle du corps humain est le grand fessier. -The largest muscle in the human body is the gluteus maximus.
2559	**selle** f [sɛl]	**saddle** Ne mets pas la selle sur le mauvais cheval. -Don't put the saddle on the wrong horse.
2560	**négocier** vb [negɔsje]	**negotiate** Les représentants des employés pourront négocier directement avec l'employeur. -Employee representatives will be able to bargain directly with the employer.
2561	**noyer** m; vb [nwaje]	**walnut; drown** Jack est en train de se noyer. -Jack's drowning.
2562	**nage** m [naʒ]	**swim** Je nage dans le lac. -I am swimming in the lake.
2563	**psychiatre** m/f [psikjatʁ]	**psychiatrist** Les pilules viennent de sa copine psychiatre. -The pills come from a girlfriend who's a shrink
2564	**survivant** m; adj[syʁvivã]	**survivor; surviving** Il n'y avait qu'un survivant à l'accident. -There was only one survivor of the accident.
2565	**profession** f [pʁofesjõ]	**profession** Il y avait une profession, celle des charpentiers de marine, fière d'elle - même. -There was a profession, that of boat-builder, which was a proud profession.
2566	**déesse**	**goddess**

	f [deɛs]	Dans l'antiquité, la justice est représentée par une déesse : Justitia. -Justice is classically represented as a female goddess: Justitia.
2567	**conscient** adj [kɔ̃sjɑ̃]	**aware|conscious** Le Bangladesh est conscient de la situation et appuie sans réserve la résolution. -Bangladesh is aware of the situation and extends full support to the resolution.
2568	**bloquer** vb [blɔke]	**block|lock** Je ne comprends pas pourquoi, au Conseil, on a voulu bloquer cette possibilité. -I really do not understand what it is in the Council that it makes it want to block this possibility.
2569	**allure** f [alyʁ]	**look|pace** Mr. Bingley plaisait dès l'abord par un extérieur agréable, une allure distinguée, un air avenant et des manières pleines d'aisance et de naturel. -Mr. Bingley was good-looking and gentlemanlike; he had a pleasant countenance, and easy, unaffected manners.
2570	**thérapie** f [teʁapi]	**therapy** Je suggère que tu entames une thérapie comportementale afin de te guérir de ton obsession des virgules. -I suggest that you start a behavioral therapy in order to cure yourself of your obsession with comas.
2571	**expédition** f [ɛkspedisjɔ̃]	**shipment|expedition** NASA dit qu'elle possède assez d'information pour affirmer qu'une expédition humaine vers Mars serait possible. -NASA says it has sufficient information to say that a human visit to the red planet is feasible.
2572	**curer** vb [kyʁe]	**muck out** Ces mains font tout à part te curer le nez. -Man, these hands do everything but pick your nose.
2573	**ambiance** f [ɑ̃bjɑ̃s]	**ambience|environment** Le dialogue avec le Comité s'est déroulé dans une ambiance franche et constructive. -The dialogue with the Committee took place in an open and constructive atmosphere.
2574	**festival** m [fɛstival]	**festival|celebration** Chaque année, il y a un festival d'hiver, un festival pour enfants et un festival cinématographique. -Every year, there is a winter festival, a kids' festival and a film festival.
2575	**thème** m [tɛm]	**theme** Pourquoi avez-vous choisi ce thème particulier ? -Why did you choose that particular subject?
2576	**gentiment** adv[ʒɑ̃timɑ̃]	**kindly|gently** Je me comporte gentiment. -I'm being friendly.
2577	**marchand** m; adj [maʁʃɑ̃]	**dealer|seller; mercantile** Le riche marchand sentait l'heure de sa mort approcher. -The rich merchant felt the hour of his death approaching.
2578	**aussitôt** adv [osito]	**immediately** L'équipe a aussitôt visité l'endroit sans aucune escorte. -The team at once visited the location without escort.
2579	**protégé**	**protected**

	adj	S'il est arrivé à cette position, c'est principalement parce qu'il était le protégé d'hommes d'affaires de Djibouti.
	[pʁɔteʒe]	-He was able to accomplish this feat mainly as a protégé of Djibouti businessmen.
2580	**pan**	**panel; bang!**
	m; int	Les bandes de pan de corps avant et arrière comprennent un laminé de film élastomère.
	[pɑ̃]	-The front and back body panel webs comprise an elastomeric film laminate.
2581	**lutter**	**fight|combat**
	vb	Monsieur le Président, le Parlement européen doit lutter pour ses droits démocratiques.
	[lyte]	-Mr President, the European Parliament must fight for its democratic rights.
2582	**péter**	**fart**
	vb	Tu peux aller péter devant elle.
	[pete]	-Now you can go and fart in front of her.
2583	**apercevoir**	**see|perceive**
	vb	Le premier européen à apercevoir le Samoa était un hollandais, Jacob Roggeveen.
	[apɛʁsəvwaʁ]	-The first European to sight Samoa was a Dutchman, Jacob Roggeveen.
2584	**défaut**	**fault|failing**
	m	Un petit engrenage fait défaut ici.
	[defo]	-A small gear is missing here.
2585	**réduire**	**reduce|decrease**
	vb	Les faveurs de la présidence contribuent pour beaucoup à réduire les coûts d'exploitation.
	[ʁedɥiʁ]	-Presidential favour is an important ingredient in cutting operational costs.
2586	**homo-**	**homo-**
	pfx	C'est cette curiosité qui a engagé Homo sapiens dans la voie de l'évolution.
	[omo-]	-It is this curiosity that propelled Homo sapiens up the slope of evolution.
2587	**taureau**	**bull**
	m	Le taureau est plus fort que le toréador, mais il perd quasiment à chaque fois.
	[tɔʁo]	-The bull is stronger than the bullfighter, but he almost always loses.
2588	**constamment**	**constantly**
	adv	L'Union européenne s'est constamment opposée aux exécutions extrajudiciaires.
	[kɔ̃stamɑ̃]	-The European Union has consistently opposed extrajudicial killings.
2589	**poli**	**polished|polite**
	adj[pɔli]	Je pense donc, pour être poli, qu'il s'agit d'un malentendu de sa part. -So I think that is a misunderstanding on his part - to be polite to him.
2590	**pénible**	**painful|hard**
	adj	Le Gouvernement soutient les femmes fonctionnaires qui font un travail pénible.
	[penibl]	-The RGC provides grant support to women civil servants doing difficult work.
2591	**Brésil**	**Brazil**
	m	Il a immigré au Brésil à la recherche d'une vie meilleure.
	[bʁezil]	-He immigrated to Brazil in search of a better life.
2592	**coke**	**coke**

m
[kok]
Vous voyez, les lignes de coke.
-You know, the lines of coke.

2593 saisir
vb
[sezartʁ]
seize|grasp
Comment pouvons-nous saisir cette occasion, si nous sommes dans une impasse ?
-How can we be given that opportunity if it is a Catch-22?

2594 cognac
m
[kɔɲak]
cognac
Jack a besoin d'un cognac.
-Jack needs a cognac.

2595 spécialiste
m/f
[spesjalist]
specialist
Consulter un spécialiste après l'autre, ce n'est pas recevoir de bons soins.
-Going from specialist to specialist to specialist is not good care.

2596 raccrocher
vb
[ʁakʁɔʃe]
hang up
Il est parfois difficile aux personnes âgées de raccrocher le téléphone.
-It is difficult for senior citizens to hang up sometimes.

2597 accorder
vb
[akɔʁde]
grant|award
Bavadra's nominee on Deuba Accord Committee, participant and signatory to the Accord.
-Bavadra au Comité sur l'Accord de Deuba participant et signataire de l'Accord.

2598 routine
f
[ʁutin]
routine
Je suis fatigué de la routine quotidienne de la vie.
-I am tired of the day-to-day routine of life.

2599 Bang!
int
[bɑ̃:g!]
Pow!
Il viole en outre quotidiennement l'espace aérien libanais, terrorisant la population avec le « bang » de ses avions supersoniques.
-It infiltrates on a daily basis Lebanese air space, terrorizing the population with its aircrafts' sonic booms.

2600 soda
m
[sɔda]
soda
Ravina ressemble à un soda européen.
-Ravina sounds like a European soda.

2601 douzaine
f
[duzɛn]
dozen
Comparer les pratiques de communication dans une douzaine de cultures.
-Comparing the communication practices in a dozen of cultures.

2602 dépenser
vb
[depɑ̃se]
spend|outlay
Il est facile de dépenser de l'argent, le tout est de le dépenser utilement.
-It is easy to spend money, the trick is to spend it sensibly.

2603 majorité
f[maʒɔʁite]
majority
Vous avez la majorité des deux tiers au parlement et c'est une majorité légitime. -You have a two-thirds majority in parliament and it is a legitimate majority.

2604 instrument
m
[ɛ̃stʁymɑ̃]
instrument|implement
La Commission a alors créé le petit instrument qu'est l'instrument ICI.
-The Commission then created the little instrument that is the ICI Instrument.

2605 angoisse
f
[ɑ̃gwas]
anguish
Son visage marqua la peur et l'angoisse.
-His face registered fear and anxiety.

2606 serveur
m
[sɛʁvœʁ]
waiter
Je travaille comme serveur depuis trois ans.
-I've worked as a waiter for three years.

2607 **infiniment**   **infinitely**

adv

[ɛ̃finimɑ̃]

Et Dieu est infiniment honnête, infiniment intelligents, infiniment pur, infiniment Love.
  -And God is infinitely honest, infinitely intelligent, infinitely pure, infinitely Love.

2608 **dinde**   **turkey**

f

[dɛ̃d]

Puisqu'elle est végétarienne, elle a mangé du tofu au lieu de la dinde.
  -She's vegetarian, so she ate tofu instead of turkey.

2609 **canal**   **channel|canal**

m

[kanal]

Un canal coule entre deux rangées de maisons.
  -A canal flowed between two rows of houses.

2610 **janvier**   **January**

m

[ʒɑ̃vje]

Présidente de l'Association des juristes maliennes, janvier 1988 à janvier 1995
  -President of the Malian Women Jurists' Association, January 1988 to January 1995.

2611 **coma**   **coma**

m

[kɔma]

If the disease is not treated, the patient goes into a coma and inevitably dies.
  -Si la maladie n'est pas soignée, le patient tombe dans le coma et décède inévitablement.

2612 **mériter**   **deserve|earn**

vb

[meʁite]

C'est le minimum que l'on est en droit d'attendre d'un Parlement qui veut mériter son nom.
  -That is the least that can be expected of a parliament worthy of the name.

2613 **batte**   **bat**

f

[bat]

Troisièmement, nous sommes préoccupés de constater que la KEDO a la batte mais n'a pas de balle.
  -Thirdly, we are concerned about the fact that KEDO is a bat without a ball.

2614 **formule**   **formula|form**

f

[fɔʁmyl]

Connaissez-vous la formule chimique du phénol ?
  -Do you know the chemical formula of phenol?

2615 **jules**   **stud**

m

[ʒyl]

A-t-elle un jules ?
  -Does she have a boyfriend?

2616 **probable**   **likely**

adj

[pʁɔbabl]

la gravité probable de violences à venir ou d'une future situation de négligence.
  -the probable severity of a future incident of abuse or condition of neglect.

2617 **manager**   **manager**

m

[manadʒɛʁ,manadʒœʁ]

Ils ont nommé M. White manager.
  -They appointed Mr. White as manager.

2618 **exciter**   **excite|arouse**

vb

[ɛksite]

Éteignez toutes ces choses qui vont exciter votre cerveau.
  -Turn off all of those things that are also going to excite the brain.

2619 **vertu**   **virtue**

f

[vɛʁty]

Il n'est plus possible d'échapper à la réalité ou à la vertu du multilatéralisme.
  -There is no escape from the reality or the virtue of multilateralism.

2620 chiffrer — number|cipher
vb
[ʃifʁe]
Il n'est pas possible de chiffrer ces économies, mais elles en valent la peine.
-Although no firm figure could be put on such savings, the action was worth taking.

2621 irlandais — Irish; Irish
adj; m|mpl
[iʁlɑ̃dɛ]
Les Irlandais pensaient que le gouvernement britannique contrôlait Equitable Life.
-The Irish thought that the British Government was checking on Equitable Life.

2622 équilibre — balance
m
[ekilibʁ]
Ces systèmes incitent les partis à équilibrer leurs listes électorales.
-Proportional representation systems motivate parties to balance their electoral tickets.

2623 amateur — amateur; amateur
adj; m
[amatœʁ]
Il n'est qu'un amateur.
-He is just an amateur.

2624 désordre — disorder
m
[dezɔʁdʁ]
Il y a un désordre social et politique et le désordre monétaire est à notre porte.
-There is social and political disorder and monetary disorder is knocking at the door.

2625 marchandise — commodity
f
[maʁʃɑ̃diz]
La marchandise arrive par mer.
-The goods arrive by sea.

2626 gênant — embarrassing
adj
[ʒɛnɑ̃]
On n'ose pas parler du gouvernement du Québec, parce que ce serait trop gênant.
-To turn to the Government of Quebec is out of the question; it would be too embarrassing.

2627 galerie — gallery
f
[galʁi]
Qui est cette mignonne fille avec laquelle je vous ai vues à la galerie commerciale ?
-Who's that cute girl I saw you with at the mall?

2628 navette — shuttle
f[navɛt]
Autant arrêter une navette spatiale avec un élastique. -Its like trying to stop a space shuttle with a rubber band.

2629 résidence — residence
f
[ʁezidɑ̃s]
Nous n'avons pu trouver son lieu de résidence.
-We couldn't find out her whereabouts.

2630 ressource — resource
f
[ʁəsuʁs]
Cette ressource présentera un intérêt inestimable pour la communauté internationale.
-This resource will be of invaluable use to the international community.

2631 muet — silent; mute
adj; m
[mɥɛ]
Le pauvre enfant était né sourd-muet.
-The poor child was born deaf and dumb.

2632 tissu — fabric|tissue
m
[tisy]
De quel tissu est faite cette veste ?
-What stuff is this jacket made of?

2633 foudre — lightning
f
[fudʁ]
La foudre a frappé sa maison.
-Lightning struck his house.

2634	**engagement**	**commitment|engagement**
	m	Nous prenons cet engagement au sérieux.
	[ãgaʒmã]	-It is a commitment that we take seriously.
2635	**moustache**	**mustache|whiskers**
	f	Jack s'est rasé la moustache.
	[mustaʃ]	-Jack shaved off his mustache.
2636	**filet**	**net|fillet**
	m	J'ai attrapé des papillons avec un filet.
	[filɛ]	-I captured butterflies with a net.
2637	**parrain**	**sponsor**
	m	Alors, qualifier Museveni de parrain est une accusation très, très grave.
	[paʁɛ̃]	-Therefore, to call President Museveni a godfather is a very, very serious matter.
2638	**nièce**	**niece**
	f	Pourquoi avez-vous amené votre nièce vivre ici?
	[njɛs]	-Why did you bring on your niece to live here?
2639	**exposition**	**exposure|exhibition**
	f	Quelques heures d'exposition ne représentent aucun risque.
	[ɛkspozisjõ]	-A few hours of exposure shouldn't pose a risk.
2640	**coiffure**	**hairdressing|coiffure**
	f	J'ai changé de coiffure, mais il n'a pas aimé.
	[kwafyʁ]	-I changed my hair, but he didn't like it.
2641	**baignoire**	**bath**
	f	Jack sortit de la baignoire et se sécha.
	[bɛɲwaʁ]	-Jack got out of the bathtub and dried himself off.
2642	**cachette**	**hiding place|cache; hideaway**
	f; adj	., âgé de 52 ans, a été témoin du pillage à partir de sa cachette.
	[kaʃɛt]	-The 52-year-old K.P. witnessed the looting from his hiding place.
2643	**cavalier**	**rider; cavalier**
	m; adj	À l'heure actuelle, les États-Unis ont décidé de faire cavalier seul.
	[kavalje]	-At present the Unites States have decided to ride alone.
2644	**intervention**	**intervention|speech**
	f	Jack a décidé de subir l'intervention.
	[ɛ̃tɛʁvãsjõ]	-Jack has decided to have the surgery.
2645	**peintre**	**painter**
	m	Une toile (« Pigeons d'Orient ») du peintre anglais Alfred Elmore datant de 1880 (endommagée).
	[pɛ̃tʁ]	-A painting entitled "Doves of the East" by the English painter Alfred Elmore and dated 1880, damaged.
2646	**balancer**	**swing**
	vb	But that international city must balance five centuries of imbalance.
	[balãse]	-Mais cette ville internationale doit rééquilibrer cinq siècles de déséquilibre.
2647	**capacité**	**capacity|ability**
	f	On leur nie toute capacité d'apprentissage et même la capacité d'innover.
	[kapasite]	-Their ability to learn and even their ability to innovate are denied.
2648	**violon**	**violin**
	m	Pourquoi n'achètes-tu pas un violon à Jack ?
	[vjɔlõ]	-Why don't you buy Jack a violin?
2649	**lent**	**slow**

adj
[lã]

Le système de recrutement actuel est trop lent et n'est pas suffisamment dynamique.
-The current recruitment process was too slow and not sufficiently proactive.

| 2650 | **visite** | **visit** |

f
[vizit]

Je ne peux pas te dire combien j'attendais ta visite avec impatience.
-I can't tell you how much I've been looking forward to your visit.

| 2651 | **montage** | **mounting** |

m
[mɔ̃taʒ]

Le montage est ainsi considérablement simplifié.
-This causes a considerable simplification of the mounting.

| 2652 | **acide** | **acid|sour; acid** |

adj; m
[asid]

La pluie acide n'est pas un phénomène naturel.
-Acid rain is not a natural phenomenon.

| 2653 | **correction** | **correction|patch** |

f
[kɔʁɛksjɔ̃]

Merci pour la correction.
-Thanks for the correction.

| 2654 | **sèche** | **fag; dry** |

f; adj
[sɛʃ]

Ma chemise n'est pas encore sèche.
-My shirt isn't dry yet.

| 2655 | **rebelle** | **rebel; rebellious** |

m/f; adj
[ʁəbɛl]

L'agriculture a toujours été par le passé un secteur rebelle, non soumis à des règles commerciales.
-Agriculture has been one of those mavericks that have not been under trade rules in the past.

| 2656 | **verdict** | **verdict** |

m
[vɛʁdikt]

Finalement, le jour du procès arrive et la verdict tombe.
-Finally, the trial takes place and a verdict is rendered.

| 2657 | **bénédiction** | **blessing** |

f
[benediksjɔ̃]

Vénérables Frères, chers Fils et Filles, salut et Bénédiction Apostolique !
-Venerable Brothers and dear sons and daughters, greetings and the apostolic blessing.

| 2658 | **racheter** | **redeem** |

vb
[ʁaʃte]

Les fillettes sont réduites en esclavage pour racheter les péchés de parents de sexe masculin.
-Young girls are enslaved to atone for the sins of a male relative.

| 2659 | **brut** | **gross; crude** |

adj; m
[bʁyt]

Le produit national brut est la somme de la production totale de biens et de services en valeur financière.
-Gross national product is a nation's total output of goods and services as measured in monetary value.

| 2660 | **intime** | **intimate** |

adj
[ɛ̃tim]

J'ai donc voté contre ce rapport par intime conviction.
-I voted against out of my innermost conviction.

| 2661 | **prétendre** | **claim|pretend** |

vb
[pʁetɑ̃dʁ]

Les victimes ne disposent donc pas d'un recours utile et ne peuvent prétendre à réparation.
-Victims thus have no effective remedy and cannot claim reparation.

| 2662 | **marteau** | **hammer** |

m
[maʁto]

Ne casse pas une noix avec un marteau de forgeron.
-Don't crack a nut with a sledgehammer.

| 2663 | **conducteur** | **driver|conductor** |

	m	C'est un mauvais conducteur.
	[kɔ̃dyktœʁ]	-He is bad at driving.
2664	**douloureux**	**painful**
	adj	Srebrenica n'a pas seulement un passé douloureux: le présent aussi y est
	[duluʁø]	douloureux.
		-Srebrenica not only has a painful past, it also has a painful present.
2665	**héritier**	**heir|heirdom**
	m	La fortune de M. Bennet consistait presque entièrement en une terre de
	[eʁitje]	deux mille livres sterling de rente, qui, malheureusement pour ses filles,
		était substituée, au défaut d'héritier mâle, à un parent éloigné.
		-Mr. Bennet's property consisted almost entirely in an estate of two
		thousand a year, which, unfortunately for his daughters, was entailed, in
		default of heirs male, on a distant relation.
2666	**brillant**	**brilliant|bright; gloss**
	adj; m	Sami était un jeune homme avec un brillant avenir devant lui.
	[bʁijã]	-Sami was a young man with a bright future ahead of him.
2667	**mafia**	**mafia**
	f	Pendant ce temps, les chefs de la mafia des mendiants vivent dans des
	[mafja]	villas luxueuses.
		-Meanwhile, the heads of the mob are living in luxurious mansions.
2668	**révéler**	**reveal|tell**
	vb	L'élaboration d'indicateurs de progrès à cet égard peut se révéler une bonne
	[ʁevele]	idée.
		-The elaboration of indicators of progress in this respect might turn out to
		be good idea.
2669	**repérer**	**spot**
	vb	Ces bombettes non explosées sont petites, souvent difficiles à repérer et très
	[ʁəpeʁe]	instables.
		-These unexploded bomblets are small, often difficult to spot and highly
		volatile.
2670	**quantité**	**amount|number**
	f[kɑ̃tite]	Il ne mesure pas la quantité de poisson prise il ne fait que mesurer la
		quantité de poisson débarquée. -It does not measure the amount of fish
		caught; it only measures the amount of fish landed.
2671	**frire**	**fry**
	vb	Pourquoi pas les faire frire tout de suite et les servir avec des frites.
	[fʁiʁ]	-Why don't we fry them up now and serve them with chips?
2672	**fermeture**	**closing|closure**
	f	La fermeture-éclair est coincée.
	[fɛʁmətyʁ]	-The zipper is stuck.
2673	**tatouage**	**tattoo**
	m	Il y a à peine 55 ans, une méthode similaire de tatouage existait en Europe.
	[tatwaʒ]	-It was only 55 years ago that a similar tattooing procedure existed in
		Europe.
2674	**comique**	**comic; comic**
	adj; m/f	Chichester pourrait-il faire fonction de comique aussi bien que de
	[kɔmik]	parlementaire européen.
		-Perhaps Mr Chichester could double as a stand-up comedian as well as an
		MEP.
2675	**compassion**	**compassion**
	f	Ils choisissent soigneusement les personnes auxquelles va leur compassion
	[kɔ̃pasjɔ̃]	politique.

-They pick and choose those to whom they award their political compassion.

2676	**silencieux**	**silent; silencer**
	adj; m	Tout était silencieux dans la maison.
	[silɑ̃sjø]	-All was silent in the house.
2677	**confirmer**	**confirm**
	vb	Toutefois, l'équipe chargée de l'enquête n'a pas pu confirmer ces affirmations.
	[kɔ̃fiʁme]	-The investigation team was not able to confirm these representations, however.
2678	**renversé**	**reversed**
	adj	Il a en outre déclaré que le gouvernement serait renversé par la violence.
	[ʁɑ̃vɛʁse]	-He stated further that violence would be used to secure a change of Government.
2679	**pneu**	**tire**
	m	Je suppose que je saurais changer un pneu s'il me le fallait.
	[pnø]	-I suppose I could change a tire if I had to.
2680	**pâle**	**pale**
	adj	Lorsque je suis sorti de la réunion, je vous jure, mon garde du corps m'a regardé et m'a demandé pourquoi j'étais si pâle.
	[pal]	-When I finished my meeting with him, I swear to you, my bodyguard looked at me and asked why I was pale-faced.
2681	**boiter**	**limp**
	vb	J'ai toujours rêvé de boiter.
	[bwate]	-I've always wanted a limp.
2682	**grange**	**barn**
	f	Les « effaceurs » ont fait irruption dans le champ et ont entraîné les parents dans une grange voisine, à laquelle ils ont mis le feu.
	[gʁɑ̃ʒ]	-The effaceurs came to the field and dragged the parents to a nearby barn.
2683	**atterrissage**	**landing**
	m	Ils disent que la plupart des accidents d'avion ont lieu à l'atterrissage ou au décollage.
	[ateʁisaʒ]	-They say most airplane accidents occur at landing or takeoff stages.
2684	**punir**	**punish|discipline**
	vb	Les objectifs des sanctions ne sont pas de punir ou d'imposer un châtiment.
	[pyniʁ]	-The objectives of sanctions are not to punish or otherwise exact retribution.
2685	**galaxie**	**galaxy**
	f	Les trous de vers permettent aux vaisseaux spatiaux de voyager à travers toute la galaxie.
	[galaksi]	-Wormholes allow spaceships to travel throughout the galaxy.
2686	**messe**	**mass**
	f	Elle allait tous les jours à la messe.
	[mɛs]	-She went to mass every day.
2687	**stratégie**	**strategy**
	f	L'honnêteté, je pense, est la meilleure stratégie.
	[stʁateʒi]	-Honesty, I believe, is the best policy.
2688	**flash**	**flash|flashlight**
	m	Parfois un petit flash est nécessaire.
	[flaʃ]	-Sometimes a little flash is what's required.
2689	**comptable**	**accounting; accountant**

	adj; m/f [kɔ̃tabl]	Si l'expert-comptable révoque son avis, ce dernier ne devra plus être utilisé. -If the Wirtschaftsprüfer revokes the auditor's report, it may no longer be used.
2690	**descente** f [desɑ̃t]	**descent** La descente est dangereuse. -The descent is dangerous.
2691	**international** adj; m [ɛ̃tɛʁnasjɔnal]	**international; international** On prévoit que Kiwanis International continuera à soutenir l'élimination durable des TCI. -It is expected that Kiwanis International will continue to provide support to IDD elimination and sustainability.
2692	**plafond** m [plafɔ̃]	**ceiling|plafond** J'ai vu une araignée qui se baladait sur le plafond. -I saw a spider walking on the ceiling.
2693	**planquer** vb [plɑ̃ke]	**hide** On allait se planquer avec une cochonne et pour 25 cents, elle montrait la marchandise. -We had to go behind the barn with the dirty girl and pay her a quarter so she could show us her goodies.
2694	**papillon** m [papijɔ̃]	**butterfly** Papillon est un très joli mot. -Butterfly is a very nice word.
2695	**intimité** f [ɛ̃timite]	**privacy** Le droit à l'intimité, à la liberté et au secret des communications est garanti. -The right to privacy, freedom and confidentiality of communications is guaranteed.
2696	**jalousie** f[ʒaluzi]	**jealousy** Il n'y a point d'amours sans jalousie. -There's no love without jealousy.
2697	**jumeau** adj; m [ʒymo]	**twin; twin** J'ai un frère jumeau. -I have a twin brother.
2698	**individu** m [ɛ̃dividy]	**individual** Il est évident que chaque individu doit être traité précisément comme un individu. -Each individual will of course be treated precisely as an individual.
2699	**démocratie** f [demɔkʁasi]	**democracy** Nous défendons la démocratie. -We stand for democracy.
2700	**tranquillement** adv [tʁɑ̃kilmɑ̃]	**quietly** And yet there are some who would like to stir up the tranquil waters. -Mais certains aimeraient bien troubler les eaux tranquilles.
2701	**grec** adj; m [gʁɛk]	**Greek; Greek** Je ne suis ni Athénien, ni Grec, mais un citoyen du monde. -I am neither an Athenian nor a Greek, but a citizen of the world.
2702	**interne** adj; m/f [ɛ̃tɛʁn]	**internal; intern** En particulier, un interne a été chargé d'aider à la réalisation de l'évaluation postformation. -In particular, an intern has been selected to assist in the post-training evaluation.
2703	**potentiel**	**potential; potential**

	adj; m	Jack a un énorme potentiel.
	[pɔtɑ̃sjɛl]	-Jack has enormous potential.
2704	**agneau**	**lamb**
	m	Elle aime jouer avec cet agneau.
	[aɲo]	-She likes to play with this lamb.
2705	**danseur**	**dancer**
	m	Là, au milieu de ces centaines de danseuses, l'unique danseur masculin apparaît.
	[dɑ̃sœʁ]	-There, in the middle of these hundred dancers, the only male dancer appeared.
2706	**rechercher**	**search|look for**
	vb	Rechercher la vérité est facile. Accepter la vérité est difficile.
	[ʁəʃɛʁʃe]	-Searching for the truth is easy. Accepting the truth is hard.
2707	**sauvetage**	**rescue|salvage**
	m	Où sont les canots de sauvetage ?
	[sovtaʒ]	-Where are the lifeboats?
2708	**hommage**	**tribute**
	m	Les gens se rendent au cimetière, aujourd'hui, afin de rendre hommage à leurs chers disparus.
	[ɔmaʒ]	-People are going to the cemetery today to pay respect to their deceased loved ones.
2709	**steak**	**steak**
	m	Prenez-moi en photo avec le steak.
	[stik]	-Get a picture of me with this steak.
2710	**hurler**	**scream|howl**
	vb[yʁle]	La jeune fille craqua et se mit à courir en hurlant et en déchirant ses vêtements. -The girl was overwhelmed and began to run and howl and tear her garments.
2711	**stress**	**stress**
	m	Jack dit qu'il a du mal à supporter le stress.
	[stʁɛs]	-Jack says he's having trouble coping with the stress.
2712	**augmenter**	**increase|raise**
	vb	La conséquence logique de tout cela est que la pollution va augmenter dans la région.
	[ɔgmɑ̃te]	-The logical consequence of this is that pollution will increase in the region.
2713	**duel**	**duel**
	m	Son fils fut tué en duel.
	[dɥɛl]	-His son had been killed in a duel.
2714	**rideau**	**curtain**
	m	Elle leva le rideau.
	[ʁido]	-She drew up the curtain.
2715	**berger**	**shepherd**
	m	Jack est berger.
	[bɛʁʒe]	-Jack is a shepherd.
2716	**poursuite**	**pursuit|prosecution**
	f	Saignant du petit doigt, la nymphomane entama une course poursuite avec la police à bord d'un radeau volé.
	[puʁsɥit]	-Bleeding from her little finger, the nymphomaniac started a hot pursuit with the cops on a stolen raft.
2717	**carnet**	**book**

m
[kaʁnɛ]

Notre vie est comme un carnet de notes dont les pages sont pleines de tous les événements, les bons comme les mauvais, les hauts et les bas.
-Our life is like a notebook of which pages are covered with all the moments, both the goods and bads, the ups and downs.

2718 légume — **vegetable**

m
[legym]

Comment appelez-vous ce légume en anglais ?
-What do you call this vegetable in English?

2719 voter — **vote**

vb
[vɔte]

Remplacer, dans la première phrase, les mots "doivent voter" par "sont habilités à voter".
-In the first sentence, change the reference to "required to vote" to "entitled to vote".

2720 dynamiter — **dynamite**

vb
[dinamite]

Nous avions été engagés par un fermier pour dynamiter la glace sur son étang.
-Well, we were hired by a farmer to dynamite the ice off a stock pond.

2721 fée — **fairy; pixy**

f; adj
[fe]

La fée des dents enseigne aux enfants qu'ils peuvent monétiser des parties de leurs corps.
-The tooth fairy teaches children that they can sell body parts for money.

2722 communiquer — **communicate | transmit**

vb[kɔmynike]

Je suis en train d'étudier 31 langues, parce que je voudrais connaître mieux le monde que j'évite, par exemple, lire les textes mal traduits et communiquer avec mes amis qui parlent les autres langues maternelles, la plupart d'entre eux ne sont pas capables de parler en anglais ou, s'ils le font, ne pourraient pas exprimer ce qu'ils ressentent ou pensent exactement. -I am studying 31 languages because I want to know better the world in which I live. This helps me avoid, for example, reading faulty translations. It also helps me communicate with my friends in their native languages, seeing that some of them don't speak English or, if they do, are unable to express what they actually feel or think.

2723 grotte — **cave**

f
[gʁɔt]

C'est l'histoire de Platon et de la grotte, c'est le signifiant et non pas le signifié.
-It is like the story of Plato and the cave; it is the signifier, not the signified.

2724 troubler — **disturb | trouble**

vb
[tʁuble]

d) Ne doit pas troubler l'ordre public ou le fonctionnement normal du service public de l'éducation.
-(d) must not disturb public order or the normal functioning of the public education system.

2725 vulgaire — **vulgar**

adj
[vylgɛʁ]

Je vote contre cette récupération vulgaire d'une bonne idée.
-I shall vote against this crude hijacking of what was a good idea.

2726 jet — **jet | stream**

m
[ʒɛ]

The pipeline iswas used exclusivelydedicated to for the supply of Jet A-1 fuel.
-La conduite servait exclusivement à l'approvisionnement en carburant Jet A-1.

2727 tournoi — **tournament**

m
[tuʁnwa]

Il a emporté le premier prix du tournoi d'échecs.
-He won the first prize at the chess tournament.

2728	**développement**	**development**
	m	Le développement économique est important pour l'Afrique.
	[devlɔpmɑ̃]	-Economic development is important for Africa.
2729	**évasion**	**evasion**
	f	Al Capone fut finalement jeté en prison pour évasion fiscale.
	[evazjɔ̃]	-Al Capone was finally sent away for tax evasion.
2730	**signaler**	**report|point out**
	vb	Women in Ukraine made a signal contribution to the formation of a democratic civil society.
	[siɲale]	-Les femmes en Ukraine apportent une contribution remarquable à l'instauration d'une société civile démocratique.
2731	**poumon**	**lung**
	m	Cela peut provoquer un cancer du poumon, aussi.
	[pumɔ̃]	-It may cause lung cancer, too.
2732	**rocher**	**rock; spit**
	m; vb	Je suis en train de déplacer le rocher.
	[ʁɔʃe]	-I'm moving the rock.
2733	**cuire**	**cook**
	vb[kɥiʁ]	Cuire au four à 100 °C jusqu'à arriver à une température de 56 °C au cœur.
		-Cook in an oven at 100°C until it reaches a temperature of 56°C at the centre.
2734	**priorité**	**priority|preference**
	f	J'ai la priorité sur vous.
	[pʁijɔʁite]	-I outrank you.
2735	**Maya**	**Maya; Maya**
	m; adj	Les deux premières traductions ont été réalisées dans les langues maya et huasteca hidalgense mexicaine.
	[maja]	-The first two translations were in the Maya and Mexican Huasteca Hidalgense languages.
2736	**boucler**	**buckle|fasten**
	vb	Nous sommes convaincus que nous pourrons boucler ce projet rapidement et à un coût peu élevé.
	[bukle]	-We are confident that this project can be completed quickly and quite cheaply.
2737	**assassinat**	**assassination**
	m	Cet assassinat souligne la radicalisation croissante de la société pakistanaise.
	[asasina]	-This assassination underlines the growing radicalisation of Pakistani society.
2738	**structure**	**structure**
	f	Toute la structure du pouvoir vacille.
	[stʁyktyʁ]	-The whole power structure is tottering.
2739	**innocence**	**innocence**
	f	Je continue de clamer mon innocence, mais personne ne m'écoute.
	[inɔsɑ̃s]	-I keep saying that I'm innocent, but no one will listen.
2740	**aspect**	**aspect|appearance**
	m	Jack porte un chapeau à l'aspect étrange.
	[aspɛ]	-Jack is wearing a strange-looking hat.
2741	**faiblesse**	**weakness**
	f	Même à la fin du dix-neuvième siècle, les marins de la marine britannique
	[fɛblɛs]	n'étaient pas autorisés à utiliser des couteaux et des fourchettes parce que

c'était considéré comme un signe de faiblesse.
-Even at the end of the nineteenth century, sailors in the British Navy were not permitted to use knives and forks because using them was considered a sign of weakness.

2742	**mont**	**mount**
	m	Le mont Fuji est extraordinaire.
	[mɔ̃]	-Mt. Fuji was very fantastic.
2743	**deuil**	**mourning**
	m	Son deuil était trop profond pour les larmes.
	[dœj]	-Her grief was too acute for tears.
2744	**euro**	**euro**
	m	Réponse : Le taux de change de l'euro est le suivant : 1 euro = 2,20371 florins
	[øʀo]	-Answer: The rate of exchange for the euro is: 1 euro = 2.20371 guilders.
2745	**hôte**	**host**
	m[ot]	Cette cérémonie a eu lieu en l'honneur de l'hôte venu de Chine. -The ceremony was held in honor of the guest from China.
2746	**bandit**	**bandit|gangster**
	m	Le FBI a secrètement truffé de micros le repaire du bandit.
	[bɑ̃di]	-The FBI secretly bugged the mobster's hangout.
2747	**étage**	**floor|stage**
	m	Jack est à l'étage dans sa chambre.
	[etaʒ]	-Jack is upstairs in his bedroom.
2748	**insecte**	**insect**
	m	Il écrasa l'insecte du talon.
	[ɛ̃sɛkt]	-He squashed the insect with the heel of his foot.
2749	**complice**	**accomplice**
	m/f	Monsieur le Président, comme l'a dit mon complice, Monsieur Nordmann, les rapports Ford et Nordmann sont de retour!
	[kɔ̃plis]	-Mr President, as my partner in crime, Mr Nordmann, said, the Ford and Nordmann reports are back!
2750	**soûl**	**drunk**
	adj	Ce n'est pourtant pas un con, mais quand il est soûl, il est pas possible.
	[sul]	-It's not that he's an idiot, but when he's drunk, he's impossible.
2751	**archives**	**archives**
	fpl	On pourrait gagner un temps fou si l'on mettait en place une classification méthodique de nos archives.
	[aʀʃiv]	-Putting in place a systematic classification of our archives could be a great time saver.
2752	**malentendu**	**misunderstanding**
	m	Le Gouvernement estime que cette question est le résultat d'un malentendu.
	[malɑ̃tɑ̃dy]	-The government believes that this question is the result of a misunderstanding.
2753	**drame**	**drama**
	m	J'ai regardé un drame américain.
	[dʀam]	-I watched an American drama.
2754	**local**	**local**
	adj	Les travaux de l'Ombudsman local sont régis par la loi sur les collectivités locales.
	[lɔkal]	-Work of the local-level Ombudsman is governed by the Local Self-Government Law.

2755	**robe**	**dress|gown**
	f	Cette robe vous va à la perfection !
	[ʁɔb]	-This dress fits you to perfection!
2756	**veine**	**vein|luck**
	f	Peut-être êtes-vous encore en veine. L'anesthésique n'entre pas dans la veine.
	[vɛn]	-You may still be in luck. The anesthetic isn't entering the vein.
2757	**col**	**collar|pass**
	m	Il n'y a qu'un col qui franchit la montagne.
	[kɔl]	-There is only one pass over the mountain.
2758	**tester**	**test|try**
	vb[tɛste]	Il a été conçu pour tester certaines charges utiles et logiciels expérimentaux. -The satellite has been designed to test some experimental payloads and software.
2759	**extrême**	**extreme; extreme**
	adj; m	La participation de la population de Vieques dans les études environnementales scientifiques revêt une extrême importance.
	[ɛkstʁɛm]	-The role of the population of Vieques in conducting the scientific environmental research was of very great importance.
2760	**bougie**	**candle|spark plug**
	f	J'allumai la bougie.
	[buʒi]	-I lit the candle.
2761	**ultime**	**ultimate**
	adj	Une ultime remarque : nous voulons aider la Tunisie, cela ne fait aucun doute.
	[yltim]	-One last comment: we want to help Tunisia, about that there can be no doubt.
2762	**vainqueur**	**winner|conqueror; winning**
	m; adj	Jack a été déclaré vainqueur par abandon.
	[vɛ̃kœʁ]	-Jack was declared the winner by forfeit.
2763	**concierge**	**concierge**
	m/f	Allons au poste chercher les antécédents du concierge.
	[kɔ̃sjɛʁʒ]	-Let's go the precinct and run a background on the janitor.
2764	**dépôt**	**deposit|filing**
	m	As-tu besoin d'un dépôt ?
	[depo]	-Do you need a deposit?
2765	**fuser**	**gush**
	vb	Le prix de la terre va fuser.
	[fyze]	-The price of land will skyrocket.
2766	**facture**	**invoice|statement**
	f	J'ai reçu ma facture d'électricité.
	[faktyʁ]	-I received my electricity bill.
2767	**réagir**	**react**
	vb	Il était impossible de réagir autrement que de la manière dont j'ai réagi.
	[ʁeaʒiʁ]	-There was no alternative but to react in the way that I did.
2768	**marais**	**marsh**
	m	Le projet aurait eu pour conséquence la destruction du marais.
	[maʁɛ]	-The project would have destroyed the marsh.
2769	**grain**	**grain**
	m	Le seigle était appelé le grain de la pauvreté.
	[gʁɛ̃]	-Rye was called the grain of poverty.

2770	**bip**	**beep|beeper**
	m	Ils peuvent commencer à parler durant le bip.
	[bi]	-They might start talking during the beep.
2771	**différemment**	**differently**
	adv	J'aurais certes formulé différemment certains points de la Constitution
	[difeʁamã]	hongroise.
		-I would have framed some of the points in the Hungarian constitution
		differently.
2772	**libération**	**release|releasing**
	f[libeʁasjɔ̃]	On dit que c'est une meneuse au sein du mouvement de libération des
		femmes. -She is said to be a leader in the women's liberation movement.
2773	**violer**	**violate|breach**
	vb	Il est vrai que l'introduction de nouveaux éléments pourrait violer le
	[vjɔle]	consensus.
		-It is true that the introduction of new elements could violate the
		consensus.
2774	**délit**	**offense|misdemeanor**
	m	Elles ont été prises en flagrant délit.
	[deli]	-They were caught red-handed.
2775	**noce**	**nuptials**
	f	Chhoti aussi aura une noce magnifique.
	[nɔs]	-Chhoti will have just as fine a wedding...
2776	**renard**	**fox**
	m	Un renard naïf n'existe pas, un homme sans faute il n'y en a pas.
	[ʁənaʁ]	-There is no such thing as a naïve fox, nor a man without faults.
2777	**orient**	**east**
	m	Voilà le Moyen-Orient d'aujourd'hui, le Moyen-Orient dont on ne parle pas.
	[ɔʁjã]	-This describes the Middle East of today, the Middle East that we do not
		discuss.
2778	**ring**	**ring**
	m	Vous transformez mon resto en ring!
	[ʁiŋ]	-You turn my place into boxing ring!
2779	**fédéral**	**federal**
	adj	Il ne faut pas oublier que la Constitution fédérale confère l'autonomie aux
	[fedeʁal]	unités fédérées.
		-It is important not to forget that the Federal Constitution grants autonomy
		to the federated units.
2780	**biscuit**	**biscuit**
	m	Les bretzels salés étaient le biscuit apéritif préféré des enfants.
	[biskɥi]	-Salted pretzels were the favourite snack of the kids.
2781	**cache**	**cover**
	m	Elle ne porte que des cache-tétons et un string.
	[kaʃ]	-She's wearing only pasties and a G-string.
2782	**barrage**	**dam**
	m	Il y avait un moulin à eau sous le barrage.
	[baʁaʒ]	-There was a watermill under the dam.
2783	**profondeur**	**depth|hollowness**
	f	La profondeur des sculptures doit être d'au moins 80 % de la profondeur
	[pʁɔfɔ̃dœʁ]	d'origine.
		-The minimum tread depth shall be at least 80 per cent of the full tread
		depth.

2784	**moine**	**monk**
	m [mwan]	Quoi ? Tout ce que j'ai, c'est une petite soupe et du céleri ? Je ne suis pas un moine Zen, je ne peux pas survivre à un régime d'austérité comme celui-ci. -What? A little soup and celery is all I get? I'm not a Zen monk. I can't survive on an austerity diet like this.

2785	**longueur**	**length**
	f[lɔ̃gœʁ]	Jack a toujours une longueur d'avance sur nous. -Jack is always one step ahead of us.

2786	**philosophie**	**philosophy**
	f [filɔzɔfi]	Le premier sujet qui a attiré mon attention était la philosophie. -The first subject that attracted my attention was philosophy.

2787	**compromis**	**compromise**
	m [kɔ̃pʁɔmi]	Après moult négociations, les deux parties sont parvenues à un compromis. -After much negotiation, the two sides in the dispute reached a compromise.

2788	**alpha**	**alpha**
	m [alfa]	Apprenez à bouger comme un mâle alpha. -You have to learn how to walk like the alpha male.

2789	**évolution**	**evolution**
	f [evɔlysjɔ̃]	Je m'intéresse beaucoup à l'évolution des dinosaures. -I'm very interested in the evolution of the dinosaurs.

2790	**invention**	**invention**
	f [ɛ̃vɑ̃sjɔ̃]	L'idée de légalité internationale est une invention des démocraties. -The concept of international legality is the invention of democracies.

2791	**insensé**	**senseless; madman**
	adj; m [ɛ̃sɑ̃se]	Ce que tu dis est insensé. -What you say makes no sense.

2792	**banc**	**bench|bank**
	m [bɑ̃]	Il s'est cru obliger de me parler du moratoire sur le banc Georges. -He felt compelled to comment, in his letter to me, on the George's Bank moratorium issue.

2793	**tiroir**	**drawer**
	m [tiʁwaʁ]	Je flanque d'habitude ma petite monnaie dans mon tiroir de bureau. -I usually toss my loose change into my desk drawer.

2794	**accrocher**	**hang**
	vb [akʁɔʃe]	Un des cinq membres finira par avoir honte de s'accrocher à cette notion archaïque. -Eventually any of the Five will feel ashamed to cling to this archaic notion.

2795	**défaire**	**undo|defeat**
	vb [defɛʁ]	Une panne ultérieure du système ne devrait pas "défaire" ce qui s'est déjà produit. -Subsequent failure of the system should not `undo' what has already occurred.

2796	**facturer**	**charge**
	vb [faktyʁe]	Les renseignements supplémentaires demandés par les utilisateurs seront facturés. -Additional information asked by users will be produced on an invoice basis.

2797	**intervenir**	**intervene**

vb
[ɛ̃tɛʁvəniʁ]

Ce n'est qu'au moment où il comparaît devant le juge qu'un avocat peut intervenir.
-It is only when defendants appear before a judge that their solicitor can intervene.

2798 championnat

m[ʃɑ̃pjɔna]

championship

Le boxeur a dû perdre du poids pour le combat du championnat. -The boxer had to lose weight for the championship fight.

2799 citron

adj; m
[sitʁɔ̃]

lemon; lemon

Ajoutez la saveur du citron au thé.
-Please add lemon flavor to the tea.

2800 désespoir

m
[dezɛspwaʁ]

despair

Quand il y avait du désespoir dans les régions atteintes par la sécheresse et la crise économique à travers le pays, elle a vu une nation qui conquérait la peur elle-même avec un New Deal, de nouveaux emplois et d'un nouveau sens d'un but commun. Oui, nous pouvons.
-When there was despair in the dust bowl and depression across the land, she saw a nation conquer fear itself with a New Deal, new jobs, a new sense of common purpose. Yes, we can.

2801 ivrogne

m/f; adj
[ivʁɔɲ]

drunkard; drunken

Un ivrogne m'a dévalisé.
-A drunk robbed me.

2802 montre

f
[mɔ̃tʁ]

watch

J'ai été tenu par une interview sur ce rapport et ma montre n'était pas à l'heure.
-I was held up by an interview on this report and my watch was wrong.

2803 visiteur

m
[vizitœʁ]

visitor

Par la suite, en cas de besoin, un visiteur de santé se rend à son domicile.
-Thereafter, if it appears necessary, home visits are made by a Health Visitor.

2804 défoncer

vb
[defɔ̃se]

smash

La police a utilisé un bélier pour défoncer la porte.
-The police used a battering ram to break down the door.

2805 raser

vb
[ʁaze]

raze|brush

Des centaines de chars ont bombardé la ville pendant des mois, jusqu'à la raser complètement.
-Hundreds of tanks pounded the town for months, razing it to the ground.

2806 osé

adj
[oze]

bold|racy

C'est osé mais je vais essayer.
-It's bold, but I'll run with it.

2807 automatique

adj
[ɔtɔmatik]

automatic

Elle a une machine à laver automatique.
-She has an automatic washing machine.

2808 aiguiller

vb
[egɥije]

switch

Peuvent être en mesure de vous donner de l'information et de vous aiguiller vers des services utiles.
-May be able to provide information and refer you to helpful services.

2809 conclusion

f
[kɔ̃klyzjɔ̃]

conclusion

Ta conclusion est hautement polémique.
-Your conclusion is highly arguable.

2810 plonger

vb
[plɔ̃ʒe]

dive|plunge

Croyez bien que je vais m'y plonger avec toute l'attention que ce problème mérite.

-Be assured that I am going to give it all the attention that the problem deserves.

2811	**facteur**		**factor|mailman**
	m[faktœʁ]		Le facteur est-il déjà passé ? -Has the mailman already come?
2812	**carburer**		**carburize| thrive**
	vb [kaʁbyʁe]		Pour travailler dans une telle équipe, il faut aimer l'action, carburer aux défis et surtout ne jamais être à court d'idées. -To handle this kind of work, you have to love action, thrive on challenge, and above all, never be short of ideas.
2813	**fauché**		**broke|hard**
	adj [foʃe]		Je reviendrai quand je serai fauché. -I'll come back for help when I'm broke.
2814	**grille**		**grid|gate**
	f [gʁij]		Vous pouvez activer la grille de capture " magnétique " avec cette grille. -You can also set this grid in line with the " magnetic " snap grid.
2815	**concept**		**concept**
	m [kɔ̃sɛpt]		Quel concept ridicule ! -What a ridiculous concept!
2816	**maigre**		**lean|meager; lean**
	adj [mɛgʁ]		La proposition du Luxembourg était déjà maigre et à la limite de l' acceptable. -The Luxembourg proposal was already scarce and at the limits of acceptability.
2817	**cheminer**		**plod**
	vb [ʃəmine]		Et puis, vous nous avez expliqué comment vous entendiez cheminer sur le chemin de la paix. -And then you explained how you intended to progress along the road to peace.
2818	**positif**		**positive; positive**
	adj; m [pozitif]		Tu devrais refaire le test. Le résultat peut avoir été un faux positif. -You should have the test done again. The result may have been a false positive.
2819	**candidat**		**candidate; elect**
	m; adj [kɑ̃dida]		Pourquoi ne vous portez-vous pas candidat au conseil des étudiants ? -Why don't you run for student council?
2820	**février**		**February**
	m [fevʁije]		Janvier, février, mars, avril, mai, juin, juillet, août, septembre, octobre, novembre et décembre sont les douze mois de l'année. -January, February, March, April, May, June, July, August, September, October, November and December are the twelve months of the year.
2821	**coiffeur**		**hairdresser|barber**
	m [kwafœʁ]		Avez-vous été chez le coiffeur? -Have you been to the barber?
2822	**chômage**		**unemployment**
	m [ʃomaʒ]		Je pensais qu'ils étaient au chômage. -I thought they were unemployed.
2823	**gin**		**gin**
	m [dʒin]		Gin n'est pas mon ami. -Gin is not my friend.
2824	**traire**		**milk**

	vb	D'autres veulent la traire continuellement sans la nourrir.
	[tʁɛʁ]	-Others want to milk it constantly without feeding it.
2825	**balai**	**broom**
	m	Saisissez un balai et aidez-nous à nettoyer !
	[balɛ]	-Grab a broom and help us clean.
2826	**plomb**	**lead | plumb**
	m	C'est aussi lourd que du plomb.
	[plɔ̃]	-This is as heavy as lead.
2827	**paysan**	**peasant; peasant**
	adj; m	Cela n'a pas de sens de vouloir mettre en concurrence directe le paysan
	[peizɑ̃]	tchadien et le farmer du Minnesota, le berger des Andes et les latifundia de Nouvelle-Zélande.
		-There is no sense in trying to have direct competition between the small farmer in Chad and the big farmer in Minnesota, or between the shepherds of the Andes and the latifundia of New Zealand.
2828	**sénat**	**senate**
	m	Le Sénat ordonna qu'un nouveau Consul soit choisi et que le pays soit libéré de ses ennemis.
	[sena]	-The Senate decreed that a new consul be chosen and the country be delivered from the enemies.
2829	**cracher**	**spit | cough up**
	vb	Plus tard, il a constaté la présence de sang dans son urine, et s'est mis à cracher du sang.
	[kʁaʃe]	-Later, he discovered blood in his urine, and he started to spit blood.
2830	**tordre**	**twist | wring**
	vb	Autour de ces nobles caractères tordre un scénario de l'amour et de tristesse en même temps.
	[tɔʁdʁ]	-Around these noble characters twist a scenario of love and sadness at the same time.
2831	**apparaître**	**appear**
	vb	C'est ici qu'apparaissent le rôle et la signification du conseil transatlantique.
	[apaʁɛtʁ]	-This is where the role and significance of the Transatlantic Council become apparent.
2832	**jazz**	**jazz**
	m	Je ne comprends pas le jazz moderne.
	[dʒaz]	-I don't get modern jazz.
2833	**recette**	**recipe**
	f	Si ça te plaît, je te donne la recette.
	[ʁəsɛt]	-If you like it, I'll give you the recipe.
2834	**grimper**	**climb | soar**
	vb	Le nombre d'arrestations de jeunes pour crime violent a par conséquent continué de grimper.
	[gʁɛ̃pe]	-As a consequence, juvenile arrests for violent crimes have continued to climb.
2835	**char**	**tank**
	m	Je vais prendre mon char.
	[ʃaʁ]	-I'm going to take my car.
2836	**altitude**	**altitude | height**
	f	geostationary altitude (ZGEO) = 35,786 km (the altitude of the geostationary Earth orbit).
	[altityd]	-altitude géostationnaire (Z GEO) = 35 786 km (altitude de l'orbite terrestre géostationnaire)

2837	**coq**	**rooster**
	m[kɔk]	Jack doit être fier comme un coq. -Jack must be very proud.
2838	**domestique**	**domestic; domestic**
	adj; m/f [dɔmɛstik]	Elle avait également travaillé comme domestique et avait été très maltraitée par son employeur. -She had also been working as a child maid and had been treated very badly by her employer.
2839	**cinquième**	**fifth**
	adj [sɛ̃kjɛm]	Le cinquième Amendement interdit ainsi l'exploitation des déclarations involontaires. -The Fifth Amendment thus prohibits the use of involuntary statements.
2840	**coton**	**cotton**
	m [kɔtɔ̃]	Les producteurs de coton espagnols veulent - nous voulons - continuer à produire du coton. -The Spanish cotton growers want - we want - to continue growing cotton.
2841	**Hourra!**	**Hurrah!**
	int [uʁa!]	Nous pourrions nous écrier: "Hourra ! -We could say "Hurrah!
2842	**répliquer**	**reply**
	vb [ʁeplike]	Ce à quoi celui-ci et les Chinois auront beau jeu de répliquer: "sauf là où vous ne la formez pas!" -Mr Putin and the Chinese will counter: except for where you are not!
2843	**décor**	**decor**
	m [dekɔʁ]	J'ai pensé qu'un changement de décor pourrait nous faire du bien. -I figured a change of scenery might do us good.
2844	**drôlement**	**funnily**
	adv [dʁolmɑ̃]	Premièrement, il est apparemment drôlement pénible de réaliser vraiment le marché unique. -Firstly, it is clearly insanely difficult really to make a reality of the Single Market.
2845	**élection**	**election**
	f [elɛksjɔ̃]	L'élection du Parlement était une élection ouverte. -The election in Parliament was an open election.
2846	**insulter**	**insult|offend**
	vb [ɛ̃sylte]	Il est scandaleux d'insulter ainsi la mémoire des millions de victimes de l'Holocauste. -It is wrong to insult the memory of so many victims of the holocaust in this way.
2847	**refuge**	**refuge|shelter**
	m [ʁəfyʒ]	La violence est le dernier refuge des incompétents. -Violence is the last refuge of the incompetent.
2848	**moucher**	**snuff**
	vb [muʃe]	Se moucher sans cesse le nez pendant la saison des allergies. -Constantly blowing his nose in allergy season.
2849	**mannequin**	**model|dummy**
	m [mankɛ̃]	Un mannequin se doit d'avoir une belle voiture. -A fashion model must have a good carriage.
2850	**danse**	**dance**
	f[dɑ̃s]	Pour une danse de mariage spéciale. -You could give us a special wedding dance.
2851	**disposition**	**provision|disposal**

	f	J'ai ma voiture à sa disposition.
	[dispozisjɔ̃]	-I put my car at his disposal.
2852	**garantir**	**ensure|insure**
	vb	Deuxièmement, la stratégie de la Cour devrait garantir que justice soit effectivement rendue.
	[gaʁɑ̃tiʁ]	-Secondly, the Court's strategy should ensure that justice is actually done.
2853	**reporter**	**reporter; postpone**
	m; vb	Était-ce votre idée de reporter la réunion ?
	[ʁəpɔʁte]	-Was it your idea to postpone the meeting?
2854	**maîtrise**	**control|proficiency**
	f	Elle maîtrise le français.
	[mɛtʁiz]	-She is proficient in French.
2855	**désespéré**	**desperate|hopeless**
	adj	Il est désespéré car la Russie est dans une situation désespérée.
	[dezɛspeʁe]	-He is desperate, because Russia's situation is desperate.
2856	**glisser**	**slip|run**
	vb	Tu l'as laissé te glisser entre les doigts.
	[glise]	-You let him slip through your fingers.
2857	**musicien**	**musician**
	m	Jack est un peu musicien.
	[myzisjɛ̃]	-Jack is something of a musician.
2858	**express**	**express**
	m	Prenez-vous la carte American Express ?
	[ɛkspʁɛs]	-Do you take American Express?
2859	**radar**	**radar**
	m	Connaissance des règles du CEVNI concernant la navigation au radar.
	[ʁadaʁ]	-Knowledge of regulations of CEVNI relating to radar navigation by radar.
2860	**pop**	**pop; pop**
	adj; m	Ma musique préférée est la pop.
	[pɔp]	-My favourite genre of music is pop.
2861	**fumé**	**smoked**
	adj	Oui, j'ai fumé du crack.
	[fyme]	-Yes, I have smoked crack cocaine.
2862	**discret**	**discreet**
	adj	Elle m'a pour ma part extrêmement satisfait, mais je suis délibérément resté plutôt discret.
	[diskʁɛ]	-I, for one, was very happy with it, but deliberately did not say very much.
2863	**entrepôt**	**warehouse|store**
	m	Rendez-vous à l'entrepôt !
	[ɑ̃tʁəpo]	-Go to the store!
2864	**sacrifier**	**sacrifice**
	vb	Faire respecter les premiers impliquerait d'être disposé à sacrifier les seconds.
	[sakʁifje]	-Upholding the former would imply a readiness to sacrifice the latter.
2865	**tube**	**tube|hit**
	m[tyb]	Je ne serais pas très surpris si cette chanson devenait un tube. -I wouldn't be too surprised if this song became a hit.
2866	**fermier**	**farmer**
	m	Jill n'avait jamais soupçonné l'amour du jeune fermier, elle l'aimait comme un frère.
	[fɛʁmje]	

-Jill had not suspected that the young farmer liked her; she loved him as a brother.

2867	**actuel** adj [aktɥɛl]	**current** La seule solution à long terme au conflit actuel serait un accord de paix final. -The only long-term solution to the ongoing conflict is a final peace agreement.
2868	**haricot** m [aʁiko]	**bean** Le haricot magique contre nos vies. -The magic bean in exchange for our lives.
2869	**proie** f [pʁwa]	**prey|decoy** Les émeutiers étaient comme des animaux en proie à une frénésie primitive. -The rioters were like animals in the grip of a primitive frenzy.
2870	**obséder** vb [ɔpsede]	**obsess** Il continuera encore à obséder tous ceux qui ont littéralement bafoué le droit international ici. -It will now continue to haunt all of you who have literally massacred international law here.
2871	**sueur** f [sɥœʁ]	**sweat|sweating** Supprimer une monnaie, c'est supprimer, nier toute cette époque de sueur et de sacrifice. -To do away with a currency is to suppress, to deny this time of sweat and sacrifice.
2872	**contrairement** adv [kɔ̃tʁɛʁmɑ̃]	**counter** « En droit civil, contrairement à ce qui prévaut en common law, le fait que la jouissance d'un bien soit accordée d'une manière exclusive ou pas ne change rien à la qualification du contrat. -In civil law, contrarily to what prevails in common law, the fact that use of a property is granted exclusively or not changes nothing to the qualification of the agreement.
2873	**mouillé** adj [muje]	**wet** La 4-nitrophénylhydrazine est fabriquée dans un état mouillé avec de l'eau. -The 4-Nitrophenylhydrazine is manufactured in a water wet condition.
2874	**fiction** f [fiksjɔ̃]	**fiction** Aimez-vous les films de science-fiction ? -Do you like SF movies?
2875	**complot** m [kɔ̃plo]	**conspiracy** Par exemple la prévarication peut être un élément constitutif du délit de complot. -For example, bribery may be indicative of the tort of conspiracy.
2876	**latin** adj [latɛ̃]	**Latin** Mármora, Lelio (2003), Mutually agreed migration policies in Latin America. -Mutually agreed migration policies in Latin America.
2877	**perle** f[pɛʁl]	**pearl|jewel** Comme secrétaire, c'est une perle. -As a secretary she is a prize.
2878	**organe** m [ɔʁgan]	**organ** L'OMI, organe maritime de l'ONU, l'a remarqué au cours de la dernière décennie. -Over the last decade, this has been observed by the UN's maritime body, the IMO.

2879 **dénoncer**
vb
[denɔ̃se]

denounce

En outre, conformément à la loi No 1 de 1973 relative au Code de procédure pénal, toute personne peut dénoncer une infraction pénale.
-I of 1973 on the Criminal Procedural Code anyone can denunciate the commission of a criminal offense.

2880 **explosif**
adj; m
[ɛksplozif]

explosive; explosive

Les démineurs ont enlevé l'explosif.
-No! The bomb squad took out the explosive.

2881 **tronche**
f
[tʁɔ̃ʃ]

face

Ce coup-là en pleine tronche l'aurait tué.
-Good thing I didn't hit him in the face. He'd be dead now.

2882 **cheviller**
vb
[ʃəvije]

pin

Barillet: sélectionner la partie centrale pour ouvrir toutes les chambres et la cheviller comme indiqué ci-dessus;
-Revolver cylinder: central section to be cut away to open up all chambers and to be pinned as above;

2883 **décharger**
vb
[deʃaʁʒe]

discharge|unload

Ça prendra du temps pour finir de décharger le camion.
-It'll take some time to finish unloading the truck.

2884 **rapprocher**
vb
[ʁapʁoʃe]

bring closer

Ainsi, les amendements 6, 11 et 16 semblent ignorer les règles nationales que le texte de la position commune tente justement de rapprocher.
-For example, Amendments Nos 6, 11 and 16 appear to pass over the existing national provisions that the text of the common position is in fact trying to bring closer together.

2885 **capturer**
vb
[kaptyʁe]

capture|take

Il est possible de perturber, de capturer ou de tuer des terroristes individuels.
-It is possible to disrupt, capture or kill individual terrorists.

2886 **coordonner**
vb
[kɔɔʁdɔne]

coordinate

Les Premiers ministres et les présidents doivent coordonner leurs campagnes.
-The prime ministers and presidents must coordinate their campaigns.

2887 **encre**
f
[ɑ̃kʁ]

ink

Encre : encre réactive aux solvants et extirpateurs et encre antiphotographique;
-Inks: ink reactive to the use of solvents and ink removers and ink resistant to photographic reproduction.

2888 **divorcé**
adj; m
[divɔʁse]

divorced; divorcee

Dans une affaire de divorce, le juge responsable doit remplir un formulaire de divorce.
-A judge who administers divorce case is obliged to fill out a divorce form.

2889 **louche**
f; adj[luʃ]

ladle; shady

Il se passe quelque chose de louche. -There's something fishy going on.

2890 **mouiller**
vb
[muje]

wet|anchor

Nous nous arrangeons tous pour ne pas nous mouiller, pour ne pas avoir à faire quelque chose.
-We are all covering our own butts so we do not have to do something about it.

2891 **soviétique**

Soviet

	adj	Le modèle centralisateur soviétique est largement responsable de cette désinformation.
	[sɔvjetik]	-The Soviet centralist model is largely responsible for this misinformation.
2892	**tactique**	**tactical; tactics**
	adj; f	La tactique a fonctionné.
	[taktik]	-The tactic worked.
2893	**humble**	**humble**
	adj	C'était là ma première apparition, humble mais déterminée, sur la scène diplomatique.
	[ɛ̃bl]	-That was my first humble but determined emergence on the diplomatic scene.
2894	**artistique**	**artistic**
	adj	Les groupements d'inspiration culturelle et artistique sont toujours très demandés.
	[aʁtistik]	-The groups of cultural and artistic orientations continues to be highly demanded.
2895	**camionnette**	**van**
	f	Une des balles a traversé la porte de la camionnette et atteint M. Quintana.
	[kamjɔnɛt]	-One of the bullets went through the door of the van and wounded Mr. Quintana.
2896	**interrogatoire**	**examination|questioning**
	m	Je n'aime pas faire l'objet d'un interrogatoire.
	[ɛ̃tɛʁɔgatwaʁ]	-I don't like being interrogated.
2897	**saoul**	**drunk**
	adj	Avant, il criait après Sophie et battait sa mère quand il était saoul.
	[saul]	-He used to yell at Sabrina and beat up her mom when he got drunk.
2898	**regret**	**regret**
	m	Je suis au regret de vous informer qu'elle est décédée.
	[ʁəgʁɛ]	-I am very sorry to inform you that she died.
2899	**défiler**	**pass**
	vb	Activez cette option pour faire défiler le texte à l' arrière-plan de l' objet.
	[defile]	-Mark this option to have the text wrap through the background of an object.
2900	**trouble**	**disorder|trouble; dim**
	m; adj	On parle parfois d'«autisme infantile» ou de «trouble autistique».
	[tʁubl]	-It is sometimes referred to as "infant autism" or "autistic disorder."
2901	**roue**	**wheel**
	f	La roue commença à tourner.
	[ʁu]	-The wheel began to turn.
2902	**copine**	**girlfriend; pally**
	f; adj	Sa petite copine ne le soutenait pas.
	[kɔpin]	-His girlfriend was not supportive.
2903	**inspirer**	**inspire**
	vb	Espérons que ce que nous faisons au Sénat pourra inspirer les enfants en ce sens.
	[ɛ̃spiʁe]	-We can only hope that what we do here in this place will inspire all children to do just that.
2904	**élite**	**elite**
	f	Le Saint-Laurent accueille une clientèle d'élite...
	[elit]	-The St. Laurent caters to an elite clientele…
2905	**périmètre**	**perimeter**

	m	Quiconque approche le périmètre sera abattu.
	[peʁimɛtʁ]	-Anything approaching the perimeter is to be fired upon.
2906	**escroc**	**crook**
	m	Comment est-il possible que la photo d'un escroc soit toujours accrochée au mur ?
	[ɛskʁo]	-A known crook still has his picture in the frame outside the Chamber!
2907	**quelconque**	**any; some or other**
	adj; prn	Or, rien n'indique qu'une telle protection ait été assurée à un quelconque moment.
	[kɛlkõk]	-However, there is no indication that such protection was provided at any time.
2908	**fournir**	**provide|afford**
	vb	En outre, dans certains cas, le PIB peut fournir des informations inexactes ou trompeuses.
	[fuʁniʁ]	-Moreover, in certain cases, GDP may provide inaccurate and misleading information.
2909	**bataillon**	**battalion**
	m	Le bataillon nigérian de Freetown sera le dernier à partir.
	[batajõ]	-The Nigerian battalion in Freetown will be the last battalion to depart.
2910	**spécialement**	**specially|notably**
	adv	Le yankee du Connecticut ne se souciait pas spécialement des règles de concurrence.
	[spesjalmã]	-The Connecticut Yankee was not particularly concerned about competition rules.
2911	**graviter**	**gravitate**
	vb	Lors de ces débats, le Conseil semblait graviter vers d'autres domaines comme par hasard au lieu de suivre une démarche stratégique.
	[gʁavite]	-In convening thematic debates, the Council appears to be gravitating to other areas by default and without a strategic approach.
2912	**bec**	**beak|spout**
	m	Ils ont eu une prise de bec, hier.
	[bɛk]	-They had a spat yesterday.
2913	**dernièrement**	**recently|at last**
	adv	Dernièrement, les incitations des pouvoirs publics ont aussi joué un rôle clef.
	[dɛʁnjɛʁmã]	-More recently, the encouragement provided by the Government has also played a key role.
2914	**cavalerie**	**cavalry**
	f	Lord Raglan ordonne que la cavalerie attaque immédiatement.
	[kavalʁi]	-Lord Raglan's orders are that the cavalry should attack immediately.
2915	**intense**	**intense**
	adj[ɛ̃tãs]	Une douleur intense est comprise comme une douleur vive, violente ou intense. -Intense suffering is defined by doctrine as being vivid, violent or intense.
2916	**grossier**	**coarse|rude**
	adj	Il semble grossier, mais au fond il est très doux.
	[gʁosje]	-He seems rough, but at heart he is very gentle.
2917	**franchir**	**cross|pass**
	vb	Nous sommes devant le Rubicon, et aucun de nous ne peut le franchir seul.
	[fʁãʃiʁ]	-We are at the Rubicon, and no one of us can cross it alone.
2918	**chrétien**	**Christian; Christian**

adj; m
[kʁetjɛ̃]

Cette proposition a été faite par Mme Oomen, au nom du groupe chrétien-démocrate.
-The proposal was submitted by Mrs Oomen, on behalf of the Christian-Democrats.

2919 **correspondre** — **correspond**

vb
[kɔʁɛspɔ̃dʁ]

Or, la notion « d'appui » peut correspondre en partie à celle de complicité.
-However, the notion of "support" may correspond in part to that of complicity.

2920 **fouet** — **whip**

m
[fwɛ]

Nous étions surveillés par un gardien, un homme détestable avec un fouet.
-We used to be watched over by a guard... who was a disagreeable fellow with a whip.

2921 **balader** — **stroll**

vb
[balade]

Si vous vous baladez dans nos villes, vous verrez que l'immigration clandestine se rapporte davantage aux employées de maison, aux personnes travaillant dans l'agriculture ou dans nos restaurants.
-If you take a walk around our cities, you will see that illegal immigration has more to do with domestic staff, people working in agriculture and people working in our restaurants.

2922 **culot** — **base|nerve**

m
[kylo]

Il a eu le culot de dire ça.
-He had the nerve to say that.

2923 **dépêcher** — **dispatch**

vb
[depeʃe]

Décide de dépêcher d'urgence une mission d'enquête de haut niveau à Beit Hanoun.
-Decides to dispatch urgently a high level fact-finding mission to Beit Hanoun.

2924 **bazar** — **bazaar**

m
[bazaʁ]

Est-il vraiment nécessaire d'acheter tout ce bazar ?
-Is it really necessary to buy all this stuff?

2925 **grenade** — **grenade**

f
[gʁənad]

Le 20 avril 2008, une grenade a explosé dans un kiosque albanais kosovar à Pec.
-On 20 April 2008, a hand grenade exploded in a Kosovo-Albanian kiosk in Pec.

2926 **cristal** — **crystal**

m
[kʁistal]

La vieille gitane bougea sa main au-dessus de la boule de cristal et, scrutant à l'intérieur, vit mon avenir.
-The old gypsy moved her hand over the crystal ball and, peering inside, beheld my future.

2927 **habituer** — **accustom|get used to**

vb
[abitɥe]

Nous devons habituer nos citoyens à penser «euro».
-We should accustom our citizens to think in euro terms.

2928 **relais** — **relay**

m
[ʁəlɛ]

Il veut diriger l'administration du relais.
-He wants to take over the relay's management.

2929 **vider** — **empty|drain**

vb
[vide]

Pour moi, ce projet de loi est une coquille vide.
-That is why I say the legislation is hollow.

2930 **ligue** — **league**

f
[lig]

Même une ligue anti-mandchoue voulait m'assassiner.
-There was even an anti-Manchurian league who wanted to assassinate me.

2931	**square**	**square**
	m	Bon. Attends-moi au square. Je te ramène ton beurre.
	[skwaʁ]	-Wait for me in the park, I'll call for you to come up.
2932	**compliment**	**compliment**
	m	J'ignore s'il s'agit d'un compliment, je laisse le Parlement seul juge.
	[kɔ̃plimã]	-I will leave it to the House to decide whether or not that is a compliment.
2933	**vaste**	**vast	wide**
	adj	Le pays exécute un vaste programme de construction de logements.
	[vast]	-A large-scale program of housing construction is proceeding in the country.
2934	**intuition**	**intuition**
	f	Que vous dit votre intuition ?
	[ɛ̃tɥisjɔ̃]	-What is your intuition telling you?
2935	**consulter**	**consult	search**
	vb	Elle a dit qu'elle devait consulter ses homologues des provinces.
	[kɔ̃sylte]	-She spoke of having to consult with her provincial counterparts.
2936	**minou**	**kitty**
	m	Pense à toutes ces femmes qui ont porté ce minou.
	[minu]	-I mean, just think of all the women who have held this kitty.
2937	**confus**	**confused**
	adj	C'est un projet de loi d'ordre administratif gros et confus qui contient beaucoup de choses réconfortantes.
	[kɔ̃fy]	-This legislation is a big fuzzy housekeeping bill that contains a lot of feel good stuff.
2938	**inverse**	**reverse; reverse**
	adj; m	La vie imite l'art plus souvent que l'inverse.
	[ɛ̃vɛʁs]	-Life imitates art more often than the other way around.
2939	**corruption**	**corruption**
	f	Le politicien fit pression pour une réforme en dénonçant la corruption des responsables gouvernementaux.
	[kɔʁypsjɔ̃]	-The politician pushed for reform by denouncing the corruption of the government officials.
2940	**cicatrice**	**scar**
	f	Où vous êtes-vous fait cette cicatrice ?
	[sikatʁis]	-Where did you get that scar?
2941	**édition**	**edition**
	f[edisjɔ̃]	Adobe et Apple ont tous deux des logiciels d'édition vidéo de toute première catégorie. -Adobe and Apple both have top-notch video editing programs.
2942	**sympathique**	**sympathetic**
	adj	J'ai écouté le sénateur Kenny dire à quel point les membres de ce comité constituaient un groupe sympathique.
	[sɛ̃patik]	-I listened to Senator Kenny saying what a congenial group this committee was.
2943	**mouchoir**	**handkerchief**
	m	Elle s'essuya la figure avec un mouchoir.
	[muʃwaʁ]	-She wiped her face with a handkerchief.
2944	**rasoir**	**razor**
	m	J'aurais dû essayer ce rasoir électrique avant de l'acheter.
	[ʁazwaʁ]	-I should have tried out this electric shaver before buying it.
2945	**vieillard**	**old man**

m
[vjɛjaʁ]

Jack est un vieillard débauché.
-Jack is a lecherous old man.

2946 confession — **confession**

f
[kɔ̃fesjɔ̃]

Il ne croit en aucune confession.
-He does not believe in any faith.

2947 arrangement — **arrangement|understanding**

m
[aʁɑ̃ʒmɑ̃]

L'arrangement floral est un élément de la culture japonaise.
-Flower arrangement is a part of Japanese culture.

2948 déchirer — **tear|rip**

vb
[deʃiʁe]

Nous devrions prendre ce projet de loi, le déchirer, le jeter et dire que ça suffit...
-We should take this legislation, tear it up, throw it away and say enough-

2949 fréquence — **frequency**

f
[fʁekɑ̃s]

À quelle fréquence utilises-tu ton téléphone ?
-How often do you use your phone?

2950 bouclier — **shield**

m
[buklije]

Le bouclier thermique est en feu.
-The heat shield is on fire.

2951 fardeau — **burden|charge**

m
[faʁdo]

Je sais que je suis un fardeau ; inutile de le répéter.
-I know that I'm a burden; you don't need to be repeating it.

2952 aîné — **eldest; senior**

adj; m
[ene]

J'ai un frère aîné et deux sœurs cadettes.
-I have one big brother and two little sisters.

2953 pathétique — **pathetic; pathos**

adj; m
[patetik]

Vous êtes si pathétique.
-You're so pathetic.

2954 affiche — **poster|public notice**

f
[afiʃ]

Il s'arrêta pour regarder l'affiche.
-He paused to look at the poster.

2955 laid — **ugly**

adj
[lɛ]

Il est peut-être gros ou considéré comme laid, et les autres ne l'aiment pas.
-Maybe he is fat and considered to be ugly or homely.

2956 nier — **deny**

vb[nje]

Le nier revient à nier leur histoire et à mettre en péril leur avenir. -To deny that was to deny their history and endanger their future.

2957 maïs — **corn**

m
[mais]

La famille entière était dehors à récolter le maïs.
-The whole family was out harvesting the corn.

2958 impressionner — **impress**

vb
[ɛ̃pʁesjɔne]

Pour reprendre les propres paroles du ministre: Ne nous laissons pas impressionner.
-I am using the minister's own words: Let us stop being bullied around.

2959 colis — **package**

m
[kɔli]

En d'autres termes, la limite par colis s'applique à chacun de ces colis.
-In other words, the package limitation applies to each such package.

2960 surnom — **nickname**

m
[syʁnɔ̃]

Votre indic mérite vraiment son surnom.
-Well, your snitch is really earning his nickname.

2961 froc — **frock|pants**

	m	
	[fʁɔk]	Je pense que je vais chier dans mon froc. -I think I'm gonna shit myself.
2962	**brosse**	**brush**
	f	J'ai passé un coup de brosse sur mon chapeau. -I gave my hat a brush.
	[bʁɔs]	
2963	**difficulté**	**difficulty**
	f	Au milieu de chaque difficulté se cache une opportunité. -In the middle of difficulty lies opportunity.
	[difikylte]	
2964	**addition**	**addition|sum**
	f	Partageons l'addition aujourd'hui. -Let's split the bill today.
	[adisjɔ̃]	
2965	**jupe**	**skirt**
	f	Pourquoi pas la jupe perlée... et le dos-nu beige en crochet ? -What about the beaded skirt with that beige...... crocheted halter you have in the closet?
	[ʒyp]	
2966	**exceptionnel**	**exceptional**
	adj	En d'autres termes, le sida est un problème exceptionnel qui exige des mesures exceptionnelles. -In short, AIDS is an exceptional problem which demands an exceptional response.
	[ɛksɛpsjɔnɛl]	
2967	**démonstration**	**demonstration|proof**
	f	C'est une démonstration qui n'aboutit à rien. -The demonstration achieved nothing.
	[demɔ̃stʁasjɔ̃]	
2968	**cloche**	**bell**
	f	Voici la cloche pour le 14ème et dernier round. -There's the bell for the 15th and final round.
	[klɔʃ]	
2969	**exécuter**	**execute**
	vb	Ce ministère est chargé d'élaborer et de faire exécuter la politique de la santé. -This Ministry is responsible for drafting and implementing the policy on health.
	[ɛgzekyte]	
2970	**craquer**	**crack|creak**
	vb	Fais une pause, ou tu vas finir par craquer. -Take a break, or you'll fall apart.
	[kʁake]	
2971	**touriste**	**tourist**
	m/f	En Thaïlande, il y a une touriste de sexe féminin pour deux touristes masculins. -In Thailand, for every female tourist there are two male tourists.
	[tuʁist]	
2972	**ressort**	**spring|resilience**
	m	Chose plus importante encore, rendons hommage au ressort de la famille. -Most important, let us honour the resilience of the family.
	[ʁəsɔʁ]	
2973	**mexicain**	**Mexican**
	adj	Lorsque l'Espagne colonisa les Philippines, celles-ci furent administrées depuis Mexico. C'est donc l'espagnol mexicain, non le castillan, qui influença le tagalog. -When Spain colonized the Philippines, they were administrated by Mexico City. So it was Mexican Spanish, not Castilian Spanish, that influenced Tagalog.
	[mɛksikɛ̃]	
2974	**phénomène**	**phenomenon**

	m	Un phénomène naturel de nature exceptionnelle, inévitable et irrésistible.
	[fenɔmɛn]	-A natural phenomenon of exceptional, inevitable and irresistible character.
2975	**homicide**	**homicide; homicidal**
	m; adj	Soixante-trois prisonniers ont été exécutés pour homicide et homicide
	[ɔmisid]	aggravé de vol.
		-Sixty-three prisoners were executed for homicide and homicide accompanied by robbery.
2976	**amende**	**fine|penalty**
	f	En conséquence, l'unanimité sera nécessaire pour amender cette directive.
	[amɑ̃d]	-Consequently, unanimity will be necessary to amend this directive.
2977	**cocktail**	**cocktail**
	m	J'envisage de me rendre à sa soirée cocktail.
	[kɔktɛl]	-I plan to go to her cocktail party.
2978	**option**	**option**
	f	Quite frankly, doing nothing is not an option and has never been an option.
	[ɔpsjɔ̃]	-Franchement, ne rien faire n'est pas une option et n'a jamais été une option.
2979	**religieux**	**religious; religious**
	adj; m	Il n'est pas religieux.
	[ʁəliʒjø]	-He is not religious.
2980	**triomphe**	**triumph**
	m	Ils étaient convaincus de leur triomphe.
	[tʁijɔ̃f]	-They felt sure of success.
2981	**convoi**	**convoy**
	m	Truang devrait bientôt atteindre ce convoi.
	[kɔ̃vwa]	-Truang should reach that convoy in a bit.
2982	**décoller**	**take off**
	vb	Celui-ci n'a pas été endommagé et a pu décoller quatre heures plus tard.
	[dekɔle]	-The aircraft did not sustain any damage, and was allowed to take off after four hours of delays.
2983	**économique**	**economic|thrifty**
	adj	La structure du bilan énergétique ukrainien n'a pas de justification économique.
	[ekɔnɔmik]	-The structure of the fuel-energy balance in Ukraine is not economically viable.
2984	**femelle**	**female; female**
	adj; f	Pourquoi y a-t-il des différences entre le mâle et la femelle ?
	[fəmɛl]	-Why are there differences between the male and the female?
2985	**chirurgie**	**surgery**
	f	On devrait retourner à la chirurgie.
	[ʃiʁyʁʒi]	-We should get you back to the surgery.
2986	**photographier**	**photograph**
	vb	Il est difficile de photographier la consolidation de la paix.
	[fɔtɔgʁafje]	-It is hard to photograph peacebuilding.
2987	**crack**	**crack|wiz**
	m	Êtes-vous drogué au crack ?
	[kʁak]	-Are you high on crack?
2988	**domicile**	**home|residence**
	m	Le domicile civil n'a rien de commun avec le domicile politique.
	[dɔmisil]	-Civil domicile has nothing in common with political domicile.

2989 pull
m
[pyl]
sweater
Jack portait un pull de Noël affreux.
-Jack wore an ugly Christmas sweater.

2990 typique
adj
[tipik]
typical
Ce rapport est typique de l'approche socialisante si chère au présent Parlement.
-This report is typical of the socialistic approach so beloved of this Parliament.

2991 rempli
adj; m
[ʁɑ̃pli]
filled|full; tuck
Le garage de Jack est rempli de choses qu'il n'utilise jamais.
-Jack's garage is filled with things that he never uses.

2992 grillé
adj
[gʁije]
grilled
Il a commandé un poisson grillé pour le dîner.
-He ordered one grilled fish dinner.

2993 taupe
f; adj
[top]
mole; taupe
Il est myope comme une taupe.
-He's as blind as a mole.

2994 grouiller
vb
[gʁuje]
hurry|swarm
Tu m'avais dit de me grouiller.
-You were the one who told me to hurry.

2995 outre
prp; f
[utʁ]
besides; skin
Outre le fait de gagner de l'argent, je n'ai aucun intérêt dans l'immobilier.
-Apart from earning money, I have no interest in real estate.

2996 relevé
m; adj
[ʁələve]
statement; raised
La banque a confirmé que seul le relevé sur papier avait valeur légale.
-The bank concurred that the hard-copy statement is the only legal bank statement.

2997 solaire
adj
[sɔlɛʁ]
solar
Les déserts comme sources d'énergie solaire Les technologies éliothermiques disponibles
-Deserts as sources of solar energy Available solar thermal power technologies.

2998 raccompagner
vb[ʁakɔ̃paɲe]
see off
Je vais maintenant suspendre brièvement la séance, le temps de raccompagner notre invité. -I will suspend this meeting briefly while I escort our distinguished guest out of the hall.

2999 âgé
adj
[aʒe]
old
L'un des kidnappeurs était apparemment un adolescent bira âgé de 18 ans.
-One of the kidnappers was reportedly an adolescent of Bira ethnicity, aged 18.

3000 aérien
adj
[aeʁjɛ̃]
air| aerial
Cuba avait entrepris en 1956-1958 un relevé panchromatique aérien du pays.
-Cuba had started with an aerial panchromatic survey of the country in 1956-1958.

3001 ver
m
[vɛʁ]
worm
Un homme peut pêcher avec le ver qui a mangé d'un roi, et manger le poisson qui s'est nourri de ce ver.
-A man may fish with the worm that hath eat of a king, and eat of the fish that hath fed of that worm.

3002 trembler
tremble|shake

	vb [tʁãble]	Nous sommes confrontés à une vérité que ineffables enchante et nous fait trembler. -We are facing an ineffable truth that enchants and makes us tremble.
3003	**chantier** m [ʃãtje]	**site|yard** C'est là sans doute que commence pour nous le chantier de demain. -This is undoubtedly where the building site of tomorrow commences.
3004	**polonais** adj; m|mpl [pɔlɔnɛ]	**Polish; Polish** Je vous parle en tant que Polonais et résident de la voïvodie de Grande Pologne. -I am addressing you as a Pole and as a resident of the Wielkopolska voivodship.
3005	**barrière** f [baʁjɛʁ]	**barrier|fence** Visible depuis l'espace, la Grande Barrière de Corail est la plus grande structure sur Terre construite par des organismes vivants. -Visible from space, the Great Barrier Reef is the largest structure on Earth made by living organisms.
3006	**fiançailles** fpl [fjãsaj]	**engagement** Les fiançailles n'ouvrent pas le droit d'exiger que le tribunal ordonne le mariage. -Betrothal does not give the right to demand that marriage be concluded through court.
3007	**institut** m [ɛ̃stity]	**institute** Le Ministère de la Justice des États-Unis et le Bureau fédéral d'investigation (FBI) ont pris pour cible des musulmans américains lors d'opérations d'infiltration abusives menées dans le cadre de la lutte antiterroriste et basées sur des critères d'identité religieuse et ethnique, ont affirmé Human Rights Watch et l'Institut des droits de l'homme. -The US Justice Department and the Federal Bureau of Investigation (FBI) have targeted American Muslims in abusive counterterrorism "sting operations" based on religious and ethnic identity, Human Rights Watch and Human Rights Institute said.
3008	**autobus** m[otobys]	**bus** C'est trop loin pour aller à pied à la gare, aussi prenons l'autobus. -It's too far to walk to the station, so let's take a bus.
3009	**séduire** vb [sedɥiʁ]	**seduce|attract** Vous n'êtes pas obligés de les séduire. -You do not have to charm them.
3010	**terrestre** adj [teʁɛstʁ]	**terrestrial|earthly** Écosystème terrestre pris dans sa globalité ou sous-compartiments terrestres ? -Whole terrestrial ecosystem or terrestrial subcompartments?
3011	**jumelle** adj; f [ʒymɛl]	**twin; twin** Bien entendu, c'est ce qui arrive lorsqu'on ne m'appelle pas Ione Christensen, ma jumelle. -Of course, that is not when they are calling me Ione Christensen, my twin.
3012	**vomi** m [vɔmi]	**vomit** Thomas a vomi toute la nuit. -Thomas has been vomiting the entire night.
3013	**travailleur** m; adj [tʁavajœʁ]	**worker|employee; industrious** Le peuple chinois est très travailleur. -The Chinese are a hard-working people.
3014	**éternellement**	**eternally**

	adv	Pour cette seule raison, notre peuple vous sera éternellement reconnaissant.
	[etɛʁnɛlmɑ̃]	-For that reason alone, our people will be eternally grateful to you.

3015 célébrer — **celebrate**

vb
[selebʁe]

En nous tournant vers le passé, nous devons célébrer nos réalisations et nous en réjouir.
-As we look back along the heritage path, let us celebrate and rejoice in our achievements.

3016 épouvantable — **terrible | appalling**

adj
[epuvɑ̃tabl]

Je trouve épouvantable que le gouvernement n'ait aucun plan de réduction de la dette.
-I find it atrocious that the government has absolutely no plan to reduce the debt.

3017 sublime — **sublime**

adj
[syblim]

Cliquez ici pour obtenir la sublime figure de la Vierge Marie des Anges?
-Look at the sublime figure of the Virgin Mary of the Angels?

3018 lard — **bacon**

m
[laʁ]

Est-ce que ça ne sent pas comme du lard grillé ?
-Doesn't it smell like bacon?

3019 atroce — **atrocious**

adj
[atʁɔs]

Le manque atroce de ressources lie nos mains dans notre lutte contre la pauvreté.
-An agonizing lack of resources amidst poverty ties our hands.

3020 gage — **pledge**

m
[gaʒ]

Jack a dû mettre sa guitare en gage pour payer ses factures.
-Jack had to pawn his guitar so he could pay his bills.

3021 canne — **cane**

f
[kan]

La mobilisation des acteurs de la filière canne à sucre n'a pas été vaine.
-The mobilisation of the players in the sugar-cane sector has not been in vain.

3022 agression — **aggression**

f
[agʁesjɔ̃]

Lola, pardonne ma typique agression alcoolique.
-Lola, please forgive... my typically alcoholic aggression.

3023 concentration — **concentration | focus**

f
[kɔ̃sɑ̃tʁasjɔ̃]

C'est le genre de travail qui requiert un niveau élevé de concentration.
-It's the sort of work that calls for a high level of concentration.

3024 inscrit — **registered voter/student; enrolled**

m/f; adj
[ɛ̃skʁi]

La Commission indépendante vérifie que chaque électeur inscrit peut participer librement et équitablement au scrutin, à titre d'électeur ou de candidat.
-The Independent Electoral Commission (IEC) oversees the free and fair participation of every registered voter in the election, either to vote or to stand for election.

3025 séparation — **separation**

f
[sepaʁasjɔ̃]

La séparation de l'Église et de l'État est l'un des principes fondamentaux de la constitution.
-The separation of church and state is one of the fundamental principles of the Constitution.

3026 crayon — **pencil**

m
[kʁɛjɔ̃]

Puis-je utiliser ton crayon ?
-Can I use your pencil?

3027 oreiller — **pillow**

m
[ɔʁeje]

Les salles sont pourvues d'un lit avec un matelas, un oreiller, une taie d'oreiller, des draps et une alèse.
-The rooms contain a bed with a mattress, pillow, pillow case, sheets and a mattress protector.

3028 **dramatique** — **dramatic**

adj
[dʁamatik]

Dans cette situation dramatique et difficile, il n'y a pas de solution facile.
-In this dramatic and difficult situation, there is no easy solution.

3029 **allumette** — **match**

f
[alymɛt]

Notre fille s'est brûlée le doigt avec une allumette.
-Our daughter burned her finger with a match.

3030 **dessiner** — **draw | design**

vb
[desine]

L'élaboration de ce statut, longue à se dessiner, résultait d'un compromis.
-That statute took a long time to draw up and was the result of a compromise.

3031 **soudainement** — **suddenly**

adv
[sudɛnmã]

Soudainement, l'enfant avait été tué et le père blessé et en état de choc.
-Suddenly the child was shot dead and the father was wounded, in a state of shock.

3032 **paysage** — **landscape**

m
[peizaʒ]

De jolies maisons à colombages parsemaient le paysage.
-Some lovely half-timbered houses dotted the landscape.

3033 **patate** — **potato (chip)**

f
[patat]

La patate était tellement chaude que ça m'a brûlé la bouche.
-The potato was so hot that it burned my mouth.

3034 **fouille** — **search**

f[fuj]

Les procédures de fouille des enfants et des jeunes par palpation, scanner ou fouille à corps. -Procedures for searching children and young people by a pat down, scanner or strip search .

3035 **ruiner** — **ruin | wreck**

vb
[ʁɥine]

Il est plus facile de ruiner un pays que de le reconstruire.
-It is easier to ruin a country than to rebuild it.

3036 **chantage** — **blackmail**

m
[ʃãtaʒ]

Il exerce sur elle du chantage.
-She is being blackmailed by him.

3037 **loyal** — **loyal | fair**

adj
[lwajal]

Ils offrent un service professionnel, loyal et dévoué à l'école et à la GRC.
-They provide a professional, loyal and dedicated service to the depot and the force.

3038 **laser** — **laser**

m
[lazɛʁ]

Les imprimantes laser sont généralement meilleur marché à entretenir que les imprimantes à jet d'encre.
-Laser printers are generally cheaper to maintain than inkjet printers.

3039 **indépendance** — **independence**

f
[ɛ̃depãdãs]

Notre peuple a soif d'indépendance.
-Our people thirst for independence.

3040 **académie** — **academy**

f
[akademi]

Il fréquenta une académie des beaux-arts afin d'étudier la peinture et la sculpture.
-He went to art school to study painting and sculpture.

3041 **récolte** — **harvest | crop**

	f	"Partez tôt à votre champ si vous voulez le récolter".
	[ʁekɔlt]	-"Hurry to your cultivated land if you mean to harvest (its produce)!"
3042	**aigle**	**eagle**
	m/f	L'aigle américain a dû aller voir le Viet Cong et parler avec lui.
	[ɛgl]	-The American eagle had to go to see the Viet Cong and talk to them.
3043	**piqûre**	**sting|puncture**
	f	Une piqûre d'abeille peut être fort douloureuse.
	[pikyʁ]	-A bee sting can be very painful.
3044	**allonger**	**lengthen**
	vb	La plupart des Canadiens jugent que les périodes d'attente ne font que s'allonger.
	[alɔ̃ʒe]	-Most Canadians have indicated that they feel waiting times are only getting worse.
3045	**exposer**	**expose|exhibit**
	vb	Cela pourrait exposer l'ONU à des risques financiers, opérationnels et autres.
	[ɛkspoze]	-This may further expose the United Nations to financial, operational and other risks.
3046	**trajet**	**path**
	m	Le graphique montre le trajet suivi le plus souvent par les projets de loi présentés par le gouvernement aux Communes.
	[tʁaʒɛ]	-The chart shows the usual path followed by government bills introduced in the House of Commons.
3047	**fusillade**	**shooting**
	f[fyzijad]	La fusillade s'est arrêtée. -The shooting has stopped.
3048	**transmettre**	**transmit|convey**
	vb	Ce droit comprend le droit de recevoir et de transmettre des informations et des idées.
	[tʁɑ̃smɛtʁ]	-This right shall include freedom to seek, receive and impart information and ideas.
3049	**pressé**	**pressed**
	adj	Le service correctionnel a été pressé comme un citron.
	[pʁese]	-It has squeezed Correctional Service Canada.
3050	**toubib**	**doctor|medic**
	m	Vous étiez en train de mourir mais le toubib vous a sauvé la vie.
	[tubib]	-You were dying, but the doctor saved your life.
3051	**définitivement**	**definitively**
	adv	L'entrée en vigueur de la Convention a consacré définitivement cette orientation.
	[definitivmɑ̃]	-With the entry into force of the Convention, that is now definitively the case.
3052	**explorer**	**explore**
	vb	Envoyons un robot pour l'explorer.
	[ɛksplɔʁe]	-Let's send a robot to explore it.
3053	**brique**	**brick**
	f	Quelqu'un a lancé une brique à travers ma fenêtre.
	[bʁik]	-Somebody threw a brick through my window.
3054	**yankee**	**Yankee**
	adj	Le yankee du Connecticut ne se souciait pas spécialement des règles de concurrence.
	[jɑ̃ki]	

-The Connecticut Yankee was not particularly concerned about competition rules.

3055	**Bouddha**		**Buddha**
	m		Selon Bouddha, «Les parents sont les premiers guides de l'enfant».
	[buda]		-According to the Buddha's teaching, "The parents are the first mentors of a child".
3056	**étouffer**		**stifle|smother**
	vb		Le futur gouvernement de l'Afghanistan ne doit plus être soumis à l'unilatéralisme qui l'a étouffé si longtemps.
	[etufe]		-The future Government of Afghanistan must not be subjected any more to the unilateralism that has smothered it for so long.
3057	**désagréable**		**unpleasant**
	adj		Un cas de ce genre est désagréable et mauvais pour nous, au Canada.
	[dezagʁeabl]		-A case such as this is disagreeable and bad for us in Canada.
3058	**honorer**		**honor**
	vb		On a donc décidé qu'il fallait vraiment y aller pour honorer cet arrangement avec l'Australie.
	[ɔnɔʁe]		-So now we've just decided we really have to go to honor this arrangement with Australia.
3059	**réserve**		**reserve|reservation**
	f[ʁezɛʁv]		Les fondements de la réserve portugaise ne sont pas les mêmes que ceux de la réserve grecque. -The Portuguese reservation is not based on the same grounds as the Greek reservation.
3060	**artifice**		**artifice|trick**
	m		Le vérificateur général appelle cela un artifice comptable, et c'est exactement cela.
	[aʁtifis]		-The Auditor General called it an accounting trick, which is exactly what it was.
3061	**rassembler**		**gather|collect**
	vb		La commission du commerce voudrait rassembler cela sous une seule et même ligne.
	[ʁasɑ̃ble]		-The Trade Committee would like this to be unified into one single budget line.
3062	**grandeur**		**size|magnitude**
	f		La quantification paraissait souhaitable afin de délimiter un ordre de grandeur.
	[gʁɑ̃dœʁ]		-Quantification appeared desirable from the standpoint of indicating an order of magnitude.
3063	**mis**		**placed**
	adj		Nous espérons que cet engagement du Gouvernement sera rapidement mis en pratique.
	[mi]		-We hope that this commitment by the Government will be swiftly put into practice.
3064	**fondation**		**foundation**
	f		Je ne les ai pas achetés, mais après quelqu'un a amené trois chatons à la fondation Gorira.
	[fɔ̃dasjɔ̃]		-Well, I didn't buy them, but later someone brought three baby kittens to the Gorilla Foundation.
3065	**barman**		**bartender**
	m		À une époque, il était barman à la taverne Freddie's à Tempe, en Arizona.
	[baʁmɑ̃]		-At one point he was a bartender at Freddie's Tavern in Tempe, Arizona.
3066	**authentique**		**authentic|genuine**

	adj [otãtik]	Enfin, ils aspirent à la proclamation d'un véritable et authentique État indépendant. -Finally, they aspire to the proclamation of a true and genuine independent State.
3067	**vase** m; f [vaz]	**vase; mud** Le fond est constitué de vase, de sable et de coquillages. -The bottom consists of mud, sand and shells.
3068	**matelas** m [matla]	**mattress** La victime est morte après que l'accusé eût mis le feu à son matelas. -The victim died after his mattress was set on fire by the accused.
3069	**fixer** vb [fikse]	**set|fix** Il conviendra donc de fixer une limite minimale pour la durée des visites. -A suitable solution would be to fix a minimum entitlement in this respect.
3070	**transporter** vb [tʁɑ̃spɔʁte]	**transport|move** Le cas échéant, le nombre maximal de voyageurs debout que peut transporter le véhicule; -The maximum number of standing places, if any, the vehicle is designed to carry;
3071	**racler** vb [ʁakle]	**scrape** Ils sont trop nombreux à racler leurs fonds de tiroirs pour vivre dans une mansarde digne de La Bohème . -Too many continue to scrape together a living in a kind of La Bohème garret.
3072	**ruine** f [ʁɥin]	**ruin|doom** Cela signifierait la ruine totale du royaume. -It would mean the total ruin of the kingdom.
3073	**inévitable** adj [inevitabl]	**inevitable** Un phénomène naturel de nature exceptionnelle, inévitable et irrésistible. -A natural phenomenon of exceptional, inevitable and irresistible character.
3074	**gâchis** m [gaʃi]	**mess** Quel gâchis de tes compétences de juriste ! -What a waste of your lawyer qualifications!
3075	**immobilier** adj [imɔbilje]	**immovable** Ce pourrait être le secteur des assurances, l'immobilier ou l'industrie automobile. -It could be in the insurance industry, in real estate or in the automobile industry.
3076	**pic** m [pik]	**peak|woodpecker** Fais attention à la marche, les escaliers sont à pic. -Watch your step. The stairs are steep.
3077	**faillite** f [fajit]	**bankruptcy** De nombreuses petites entreprises ont fait faillite. -Many small companies went bankrupt.
3078	**couvent** m [kuvã]	**convent** Demandez à être conduite au couvent. -Ask to be shown to the convent.
3079	**anonyme** adj [anɔnim]	**anonymous** À l'heure actuelle, les demandes d'accouchement anonyme sont extrêmement rares. -At present, there are minimal requests for anonymous childbirth.

3080 **éditeur** — editor
m
[editœʁ]
Éditeur de China and World Economy, éditeur adjoint d'Asian Economic Policy Review.
-Editor of China and World Economy, associate editor, Asian Economic Policy Review.

3081 **privilège** — privilege
m
[pʁivilɛʒ]
Quoi qu'il en soit, la question de privilège ne me semble pas fondée.
-As a question of privilege I would judge it is not a question of privilege.

3082 **sauveur** — savior
m
[sovœʁ]
Femmes, soyez soumises à vos maris, comme au Seigneur; car le mari est le chef de la femme, comme Christ est le chef de l'Église, qui est son corps, et dont il est le Sauveur.
-Wives, submit yourselves to your own husbands as you do to the Lord. For the husband is the head of the wife as Christ is the head of the church, his body, of which he is the Savior.

3083 **drogué** — drugged; junkie
adj; m
[dʁɔge]
La lettre m'a fait penser à un drogué en train de nier, accro aux subsides.
-The letter reminded me of a drug addict in denial, addicted to subsidies.

3084 **débattre** — discuss|debate
vb
[debatʁ]
Cela ne fait qu'envenimer le débat.
-All it does is incite us as we go along.

3085 **quasiment** — almost
adv
[kazimɑ̃]
La ratification universelle des trois Conventions est donc quasiment réalisée.
-Universal ratification of the three Conventions has almost been achieved.

3086 **jambon** — ham
m
[ʒɑ̃bɔ̃]
Quelques enfants ont emmené des sandwiches au beurre de cacahuètes, d'autres des sandwiches au jambon ou au fromage.
-Some children brought peanut butter sandwiches, some ham, and others cheese.

3087 **échanger** — exchange|trade
vb
[eʃɑ̃ʒe]
Coopérer et échanger des informations en cas d'activités de courtage illicites.
-Cooperate and exchange information on matters relating to illicit brokering.

3088 **parer** — parry|ward off
vb
[paʁe]
L'Europe veut se parer des atours d'un État.
-Europe wants to adorn itself with the regalia of a state.

3089 **entourer** — surround|enclose
vb
[ɑ̃tuʁe]
Le signal Galileo va entourer le signal américain et ne sera plus juxtaposé.
-The Galileo signal will surround the US signal and will no longer be overlaid.

3090 **rupture** — break|rupture
f
[ʁyptyʁ]
De plus en plus de gens sont en rupture de paiement de leurs emprunts.
-More and more people are falling behind in their mortgage payments.

3091 **jouir** — enjoy
vb
[ʒwiʁ]
Le droit à un recours effectif en matière pénale fait partie des droits fondamentaux protégés, c'est-à-dire des «droits-garanties» jouissant d'une portée universelle.
-The right to an effective remedy in criminal proceedings is a protected fundamental right, i.e. a universal "right-cum-guarantee".

3092 **quarante** — forty

	num	
	[kaʁɑ̃t]	Je lui donnai quarante ans. -I guessed her to be 40.
3093	**pyjama**	**pajamas**
	m	Je vais mettre mon pyjama.
	[piʒama]	-I'll just put on my pajamas.
3094	**tacher**	**stain|spot**
	vb	Cette composition est sensiblement dépourvue de substances susceptibles de souiller ou de tacher le tissu.
	[taʃe]	-The composition is essentially free of any material that would soil or stain fabric.
3095	**réchauffer**	**warm|heat up**
	vb	L'Ontario surchauffait, et le reste commençait à peine à se réchauffer.
	[ʁeʃofe]	-When Ontario was overheating, the rest was just beginning to warm up a little.
3096	**standard**	**standard; standard**
	adj; m[stɑ̃daʁ]	D'ailleurs, la différence entre l'anglais et l'anglo-américain est probablement plus importante qu'entre le flamand standard et le néerlandais standard des Pays-Bas. -In fact, the difference between Bristish English and American English is more important than between standard Flemish and the standard Dutch of the Netherlands.
3097	**entreprise**	**business**
	f	Je serais très reconnaissant si je pouvais effectuer une réservation d'une chambre qui a un accès facile à votre entreprise.
	[ɑ̃tʁəpʁiz]	-I'd be very thankful if I could make a reservation for a room that has good access to your company.
3098	**tango**	**tango**
	m	J'aimerais très beaucoup danser le tango.
	[tɑ̃go]	-I very much would like to dance the tango.
3099	**insupportable**	**unbearable|insupportable**
	adj	Pour Penny, c'était insupportable.
	[ɛ̃sypɔʁtabl]	-For a girl like Penny, that was unbearable.
3100	**paille**	**straw**
	f	Il fallait examiner le traitement de la paille en liaison avec le chapitre 1002.
	[paj]	-Treatment of straw would have to be considered in connection with chapter 1002.
3101	**tomate**	**tomato**
	f	Strictement parlant, la tomate est un fruit.
	[tɔmat]	-Strictly speaking, the tomato is a fruit.
3102	**glace**	**ice|mirror**
	f	Refroidis-la sur un lit de glace !
	[glas]	-Chill it on ice.
3103	**embarquer**	**embark**
	vb	Il s'est retourné vers moi avant d'embarquer dans l'avion.
	[ɑ̃baʁke]	-He looked back at me before he went on board the plane.
3104	**mairie**	**town hall**
	f	Les vitres de la mairie et d'autres bâtiments adjacents ont volé en éclats.
	[mɛʁi]	-The windows at the Town Hall and other adjacent buildings were shattered.
3105	**parcourir**	**travel|run through**
	vb	On a acheté ces appareils, par exemple, pour que le premier ministre puisse se rendre en Afrique où, lors de son récent voyage, il a parcouru un total de 25 000 kilomètres.
	[paʁkuʁiʁ]	

-They were purchased, for example, so the Prime Minister would have such a plane to travel all over Africa, as he did in his recent trip, a total of 25,000 kilometres.

3106	**gym** f [ʒɛ̃]	**gym** Il te faut aller à la gym. -You need to hit the gym.
3107	**néanmoins** con; adv [neãmwɛ̃]	**however; withal** Ce mécanisme renforcerait néanmoins considérablement la confiance dans le Conseil. -However, such a mechanism would greatly strengthen confidence in the Council.
3108	**judiciaire** adj; m/f[ʒydisjɛʁ]	**judicial; judiciary** Nous encouragerons un activisme judiciaire à tout crin. -We will be encouraging a judicial activism free for all.
3109	**choper** vb [ʃɔpe]	**bust** Je signe, si on peut choper ces salauds. -I'll give you one if it can bust these sons of bitches.
3110	**richesse** f [ʁiʃɛs]	**wealth|richness** Même avec toute sa richesse, il n'est point heureux. -With all his wealth, he is not happy.
3111	**nettoyage** m [netwajaʒ]	**cleaning|scrub** Aujourd'hui, nous ferons un grand nettoyage ! -Today, we're doing a big cleanup.
3112	**valable** adj [valabl]	**valid** En pareil cas, les termes « valable/non valable » semblaient plus appropriés. -In such cases, the terms "valid/invalid" seemed more appropriate.
3113	**augmentation** f [ɔgmãtasjɔ̃]	**increase|rise** Cette augmentation est directement liée à l'augmentation des postes proposés. -The increase is also directly associated with the increase in posts proposed.
3114	**assembler** vb [asãble]	**assemble** Il faut aussi beaucoup de créativité et d'innovation pour assembler des paquets de financement. -It also takes a very great deal of creativity and innovation to assemble funding packages.
3115	**certificat** m [sɛʁtifika]	**certificate|degree** Pourriez-vous remplir le certificat médical pour l'école de mon fils ? -Could you fill out the medical certificate for my son's school?
3116	**valet** m [valɛ]	**valet** Tu devrais renvoyer ton valet pour son incompétence. -You ought to fire your valet for being so careless.
3117	**maillot** m [majo]	**shirt** Mon maillot te plaît-il ? -Do you like my T-shirt?
3118	**foirer** vb [fwaʁe]	**misfire** L'équipe de tournage en est à sa cinquième prise parce que l'actrice n'arrête pas de foirer son texte. -The film crew is on their fifth take because the actress keeps flubbing her lines.

3119	**province**	**province**
	f	
	[pʁɔvɛ̃s]	Comprend la province de Lima et la province constitutionnelle du Callao.
		-Includes the province of Lima and the constitutional province of Callao.

3120	**refus**	**refusal|rejection**
	m	Le protectionnisme, c'est le refus de la mondialisation et de l'Union
	[ʁəfy]	européenne.
		-Protectionism is a denial of globalisation and a denial of the European
		Union.

3121	**souhait**	**wish**
	m	Il est devenu chanteur contre le souhait de ses parents.
	[swɛ]	-He became a singer against his parents wishes.

3122	**cape**	**mantle**
	f[kap]	Government of Cape Verde and UNICEF, Children and Women in Cape
		Verde. -Gouvernement du Cap-Vert et UNICEF, L'enfant et la femme au
		Cap-Vert.

3123	**chauve**	**bald**
	adj	La seule chose qu'elles puissent faire, c'est de se contenter de chahuter,
	[ʃov]	comme le fait le député chauve.
		-The only thing they can do is sit over there and heckle like my bald-
		headed friend.

3124	**futé**	**smart**
	adj	Un voyageur futé prévoit le moindre retard.
	[fyte]	-A smart traveler always allows for unexpected delays.

3125	**bracelet**	**bracelet|strap**
	m	Il possède une montre-bracelet de grande valeur.
	[bʁaslɛ]	-He owns a very valuable wristwatch.

3126	**bizarrement**	**oddly|peculiarly**
	adv	Bizarrement, le Hamas a même bombardé le passage frontalier de Khani.
	[bizaʁmɑ̃]	-Bizarrely, Hamas has even been shelling the border crossing at Khani.

3127	**duchesse**	**duchess**
	f	Kate Middleton est désormais Son Altesse Royale la princesse William
	[dyʃɛs]	Arthur Philip Louis, duchesse de Cambridge, comtesse de Strathearn,
		baronne de Carrickfergus, maître ès arts.
		-Kate Middleton is now Her Royal Highness Princess William Arthur
		Philip Louis, Duchess of Cambridge, Countess of Strathearn, Baroness
		Carrickfergus, Master of Arts.

3128	**tripler**	**triple**
	vb	D'ici à 2030, la proportion de Singapouriens âgés de plus de 65 ans va
	[tʁiple]	tripler.
		-By the year 2030, the proportion of Singaporeans aged 65 and above
		would triple.

3129	**démolir**	**demolish|destroy**
	vb	En veillant sur le "dépôt" révélé, le Magistère ne veut donc pas démolir,
	[demɔliʁ]	mais redresser pour édifier.
		-Watching over the revealed "deposit", the Magisterium does not seek to
		tear down, but rather to straighten and thus to build up.

3130	**arc**	**arc|longbow**
	m	L'arc me ressemble, et je ressemble à l'arc.
	[aʁk]	-The bow resembles me, and I resemble the bow.

3131	**massage**	**massage**
	m	La plaignante avait suivi un cours de massage sportif dirigé par le
	[masaʒ]	défendeur.

-The female complainant attended a sports massage course run by the male defendant.

3132	**familier**	**familiar; familiar**
	adj; m	Ça te semble familier ?
	[familje]	-Sound familiar?
3133	**réservoir**	**tank**
	m	Le réservoir d'eau grouille de larves de moustiques.
	[ʁezɛʁvwaʁ]	-The water tank teems with mosquito larvae.
3134	**cogner**	**knock|bang**
	vb[kɔɲe]	Je viens de me cogner la tête dans un truc. -I just banged my head on something.
3135	**cachet**	**stamp|cachet**
	m	Il faut 1,13 kg de pression pour un cachet parfait.
	[kaʃɛ]	-2.5 pounds of pressure is what you need to get the perfect stamp.
3136	**bouquin**	**book**
	m	Elle passe juste prendre un bouquin.
	[bukɛ̃]	-She's just coming by to pick up a book.
3137	**égard**	**respect**
	m	A cet égard, il a subi un dommage.
	[egaʁ]	-In that respect he suffered damage.
3138	**pister**	**track**
	vb	J'ai toutefois l'impression que dans ce domaine, la Commission a choisi la mauvaise piste.
	[piste]	-I get the impression, though, that this is where the Commission has chosen the wrong track.
3139	**stable**	**stable|steady**
	adj	Toutes ces catégories de personnes doivent vivre dans la sécurité et être protégées, ce qui n'est pas toujours facile même dans des pays à l'économie plus stable.
	[stabl]	-It is necessary to provide for all mentioned categories the security and protection level, which is not always easy even for economically more stabile countries.
3140	**publier**	**publish|publicize**
	vb	Publier une convention au Journal officiel la rend applicable.
	[pyblije]	-The publication of a convention in the Gazette makes it enforceable.
3141	**marron**	**brown; brown**
	adj; m	Lequel est marron ?
	[maʁɔ̃]	-Which is brown?
3142	**clou**	**nail**
	m	Je crois avoir trouvé notre clou.
	[klu]	-I think I may have found our nail, sir.
3143	**nain**	**dwarf; dwarf**
	adj; m	Qu'un nain se tienne sur une montagne, il n'en sera pas pour autant plus grand.
	[nɛ̃]	-A dwarf may stand on a mountain, but it will not make him tall.
3144	**marijuana**	**marijuana**
	f	Ce projet de loi prévoit une amende pour simple possession de marijuana.
	[maʁiʁwana]	-This bill is intended to seek a fine for those who are found with simple possession of marihuana.
3145	**appât**	**bait**

	m	En effet, seuls les canneurs à appât continuent de bénéficier des anciennes dérogations.
	[apa]	-Indeed, only bait boats still benefit from previous derogations.
3146	**fourmi**	**ant**
	f	Sysko fait un travail de fourmi.
	[fuʁmi]	-Sysko works like an ant.
3147	**attentat**	**attempt|attack|bombing**
	m	C'était un attentat-suicide.
	[atɑ̃ta]	-It was a suicide bombing.
3148	**colonie**	**colony**
	f	Gibraltar est en fait un territoire d'outre-mer et non une colonie du Royaume-Uni.
	[kɔlɔni]	-Gibraltar is actually an overseas territory and not a colony of the United Kingdom.
3149	**gentillesse**	**kindness**
	f	Votre amitié, votre professionnalisme et votre gentillesse sont légendaires.
	[ʒɑ̃tijɛs]	-You are known for your friendship, professionalism and kindness.
3150	**reportage**	**report**
	m	Depuis ce reportage, Paul Hauser a disparu.
	[ʁəpɔʁtaʒ]	-Since this report was filed, Paul Hauser has disappeared.
3151	**gripper**	**seize**
	vb	Bref, la machine est grippée et - j'use là d'un euphémisme, gentil - il faut la relancer, pour entrer - il est temps - dans un temps et dans des cercles vertueux.
	[gʁipe]	-In short, the machinery is jammed and - to put it nicely and euphemistically - we have to get it started again, because it is time to get into a virtuous circle.
3152	**prostituer**	**prostitute**
	vb	Les enfants des rues, faute d'autres moyens d'existence, sont parfois contraints de se prostituer.
	[pʁɔstitɥe]	-Street children are sometimes forced to prostitute themselves if they have no other means of survival.
3153	**constitution**	**constitution|incorporation**
	f	La nouvelle constitution ne résoudra pas les problèmes de l'Égypte.
	[kɔ̃stitysjɔ̃]	-The new constitution will not solve the problems of Egypt.
3154	**précédent**	**previous; precedent**
	adj; m	Auquel cas vos possibilités se ramènent au cas précédent.
	[pʁesedɑ̃]	-In which case your options reduce to the previous case.
3155	**badge**	**badge**
	m	Ils me dépouilleraient de mon badge.
	[badʒ]	-They would strip me of my badge in leatherwork.
3156	**boxeur**	**boxer**
	m	Le boxeur fut contraint de s'allonger.
	[bɔksœʁ]	-The boxer was pressured to throw the fight.
3157	**flipper**	**pinball; freak out**
	m; vb	Il est difficile de trouver un flipper entièrement mécanique. De nos jours, ils sont tous électroniques.
	[flipe]	-It's hard to find a totally mechanical pinball machine. These days, they're all electronic.
3158	**renverser**	**reverse|turn**

	vb	Nous nous efforçons de renverser la politique européenne en matière de recherche.
	[ʁɑ̃vɛʁse]	-We are striving to overturn the EU's research policy.
3159	**orbiter**	**orbit**
	vb	Neptune met 165 ans à orbiter autour du soleil.
	[ɔʁbite]	-It takes 165 years for Neptune to orbit around the sun.
3160	**farce**	**farce|joke**
	f[faʁs]	La menstruation m'apparaissait comme une horrible farce. -The idea of menstruation seemed like such a horrifying and macabre joke.
3161	**armure**	**armor**
	f	Mais son armure ne brillait pas.
	[aʁmyʁ]	-Except that his armor really didn't shine very much.
3162	**marée**	**tide**
	f	Monsieur le Président, il semble que la marée politique ait changé au Tadjikistan.
	[maʁe]	-Mr President, the political tide in Tajikistan seems to be turning.
3163	**autographe**	**autograph**
	m	J'ai eu l'autographe d'un chanteur célèbre.
	[ɔtɔgʁaf]	-I got a famous singer's autograph.
3164	**delta**	**delta**
	m	J'exécute une approche delta dans 3...
	[dɛlta]	-I'm going to backtrack using a delta approach in three... two... one.
3165	**commentaire**	**comment|commentary**
	m	Tel est mon commentaire et le commentaire repris dans notre rapport.
	[kɔmɑ̃tɛʁ]	-That is my comment and that is the comment included in our report.
3166	**campus**	**campus**
	m	Je l'ai rencontrée sur le campus hier.
	[kɑ̃pys]	-I met her on campus yesterday.
3167	**grenier**	**attic|granary**
	m	Ils étaient cachés dans un grenier, portes verrouillées, il leur est apparu.
	[gʁənje]	-They were hiding in an attic, the doors locked, and he appeared to them.
3168	**sensé**	**sensible**
	adj	Nous allons agir d'une manière sensée et équilibrée pour le bien de tous les Canadiens.
	[sɑ̃se]	-We will act in a balanced and sane way for the benefit of all Canadians.
3169	**délai**	**period|delay**
	m	J'aimerais m'y mettre sans délai.
	[delɛ]	-I'd like to get started right away.
3170	**billard**	**billiards**
	m	Ceux-ci se rassemblent dans les endroits où l'on joue au billard, aux flippers et à des jeux électroniques.
	[bijaʁ]	-These children congregate in places where billiards, pinball games and electronic games are played.
3171	**grenouille**	**frog**
	f	Sinon je te changerai en grenouille.
	[gʁənuj]	-Otherwise I'll turn you into a frog.
3172	**atomique**	**atomic**
	adj	Source : Agence de l'énergie atomique, World Energy Investment Outlook (2003).
	[atɔmik]	-Source: International Energy Agency, World Energy Investment Outlook (2003).

3173 **voire** — **indeed**
adv
[vwaʁ]

Des journalistes indépendants sont agressés, congédiés, voire éliminés physiquement.
-Independent journalists are attacked, dismissed and even physically eliminated.

3174 **horizon** — **horizon**
m
[ɔʁizɔ̃]

La mort n'est qu'un horizon. Et un horizon n'est qu'une frontière de notre champ de vision.
-Death is only a horizon. And a horizon is just the edge of our field of view.

3175 **détenir** — **hold|detain**
vb
[detniʁ]

"Les conducteurs des véhicules transportant des marchandises dangereuses doivent détenir un certificat".
-"Drivers of vehicles carrying dangerous goods shall hold a certificate."

3176 **mou** — **soft; slack**
adj; m
[mu]

C'est mou au toucher.
-It's soft to the touch.

3177 **conviction** — **conviction|belief**
f
[kɔ̃viksjɔ̃]

Notre responsabilité collective est de réagir avec conviction et détermination.
-It is our collective responsibility to respond with conviction and resolve.

3178 **formé** — **formed|trained**
adj
[fɔʁme]

Après ces élections, un gouvernement de coalition Alliance-Parti travailliste a été formé.
-Following this election, a Labour-Alliance coalition Government was formed.

3179 **féliciter** — **congratulate**
vb
[felisite]

Monsieur le Président, Mesdames et Messieurs, je voudrais féliciter Mme Ana de Palacio.
-Mr President, ladies and gentlemen, I must congratulate Mrs Ana de Palacio.

3180 **persuader** — **persuade**
vb
[pɛʁsɥade]

Nous avons fait le maximum afin de persuader le Conseil du bien-fondé de nos idées.
-We have made a huge effort to persuade the Council that our positions are correct.

3181 **gêner** — **hinder**
vb
[ʒene]

Ces limites ne doivent pas gêner l'exécution de l'obligation.
-Such limitations should not be allowed to hinder compliance with the obligation.

3182 **hockey** — **hockey**
m
[ɔkɛ]

Qui joue au hockey ce soir ?
-Who's playing hockey tonight?

3183 **pharmacie** — **pharmacy|dispensary**
f
[faʁmasi]

Assistant en pharmacie; préparateur en pharmacie; infirmier diplômé d'Etat.
-Pharmacy assistant; Pharmaceutical dispenser; State-registered nurse.

3184 **mentionner** — **mention**
vb
[mɑ̃sjɔne]

Quatrièmement, et pour finir, je dois mentionner le cancer qu'est la corruption.
-Fourthly and finally, I must mention the cancer of corruption.

3185 **flingue** — **gun|shooter**

	m	Jack a sorti son flingue.
	[flɛ̃g]	-Jack pulled out his gun.
3186	**épicerie**	**grocery**
	f	Nous trouvions aussi chez les Américains une petite épicerie et un petit bar.
	[episʁi]	-The Americans provided us with a little grocery store and a little bar.
3187	**familial**	**family**
	adj	Elle reste une entreprise familiale, qui n'est cotée sur aucun des marchés des titres mondiaux.
	[familjal]	-It remains a family-owned company and is not listed on any of the world's stock exchanges.
3188	**romain**	**Roman**
	adj	Dans l'Empire Romain, le temps était marqué en référence au souverain de l'époque.
	[ʁɔmɛ̃]	-In the Roman Empire, time was marked in reference to the ruler at the time.
3189	**saké**	**sake**
	m	Mon père ne boit pas trop de saké.
	[sake]	-My father doesn't drink so much sake.
3190	**observation**	**observation|comment**
	f	Je voudrais ajouter une autre observation.
	[ɔpsɛʁvasjɔ̃]	-There is another observation I would like to make.
3191	**briquet**	**lighter**
	m	Avez-vous un briquet ?
	[bʁikɛ]	-Have you got a lighter?
3192	**description**	**description|depiction**
	f	Pour une description détaillée de la procédure, voir par. 82 du présent document.
	[dɛskʁipsjɔ̃]	-For a detailed outline of the process, see paragraph 82 of the present document.
3193	**maîtriser**	**control|master**
	vb	Il faut fixer une période de transition pour maîtriser la durée du règlement.
	[metʁize]	-There has to be a transitional period to control the tempo of the settlement.
3194	**bulletin**	**newsletter**
	m	Le bulletin météo est mauvais.
	[byltɛ̃]	-The weather report is bad.
3195	**renseigner**	**inform**
	vb	On peut établir des indicateurs qui renseigneront sur l'activité, les priorités, la productivité et la couverture des besoins.
	[ʁɑ̃seɲe]	-Indicators can be constructed that will give information on the activity, priority, productivity and coverage of needs.
3196	**ficher**	**file**
	vb	La vieille toupie n'attend que de me ficher à la porte.
	[fiʃe]	-That old bag's just dying for a chance to throw me out.
3197	**téléphone**	**phone**
	m	À qui est ce numéro de téléphone ?
	[telefɔn]	-Whose phone number is this?
3198	**applaudissement**	**cheering**
	m	(Applaudissement et rires) Je dis compagnon au sens «confraternel».
	[aplodismɑ̃]	-(Applause and laughter) I mean comrade in the 'comradely' way.
3199	**mineur**	**minor; minor**

| | | adj; m | Il y a cependant un défaut mineur. |
| | | [minœʁ] | -There is yet one minor blemish. |

3200 **office** office|pantry

m[ɔfis] Cette canette fera office de cendrier. -The can will do for an ashtray.

3201 **barbecue** barbecue

m Que dites-vous d'un barbecue dimanche prochain ?
[baʁbəky] -How about having a barbecue party next Sunday?

3202 **balcon** balcony

m L'école ne va pas allumer l'air conditionné, ainsi les étudiants vont jeter
[balkɔ̃] leurs ballons d'eau chaude par le balcon en signe de protestation.
-The school won't turn on the air conditioning, so the students are going to throw their hot water flasks off of the balcony in protest.

3203 **licence** license

f J'ai obtenu ma licence cet été.
[lisɑ̃s] -I got my license this summer.

3204 **croiser** cross|pass

vb Cela dit, les deux voies doivent se croiser, s' entrelacer.
[kʁwaze] -Having said that, the two tracks should intersect and intertwine.

3205 **mallette** briefcase

f Les réponses sont dans la mallette.
[malɛt] -Well, the answers are in the briefcase.

3206 **mat** matt; mate; morning

adj; m; abr Je me suis couchée à 5 heures du mat'.
[ma] -I went to bed at 5 o'clock in the morning.

3207 **comptoir** counter

m Le journal sera disponible sur le site Web et au comptoir des documents à
[kɔ̃twaʁ] la porte 40.
-The journal will be available on the website and at the documentation counter at door 40.

3208 **arbitre** referee

m Ce précédent projet de loi nommait un médiateur-arbitre autorisé à amener
[aʁbitʁ] les parties à conclure une entente.
-That legislation appointed a mediator-arbitrator authorized to mediate and bring about an agreement between the parties.

3209 **bœuf** beef

m À grosse maille, vous devriez prévoir une livre de bœuf pour deux invités.
[bœf] -As a rule of thumb, you should plan on one pound of beef for every two guests.

3210 **baigner** bathe|wash

vb Les habitants des régions du Nord ou non touristiques ont aussi le droit de
[beɲe] se baigner en toute sécurité.
-People in northern or non-tourist regions also have the right to bathe in safety.

3211 **aspirine** aspirin

f On ne peut pas traiter une infection sérieuse en prenant de l'aspirine.
[aspiʁin] -Nobody treats a dangerous infection with aspirin.

3212 **bacon** bacon

m Seulement deux tranches de bacon par sandwich.
[bekɔn] -And let's just use two strips of bacon per sandwich.

3213 **suggestion** suggestion

	f	This suggestion is also compatible with the proposal contained in article 3.
	[sygʒɛstjɔ̃]	-Cette proposition est également compatible avec la proposition d'article 3.
3214	**mule**	**mule**
	f	Es-tu jamais montée à dos de mule ?
	[myl]	-Have you ever ridden a mule?
3215	**rabbin**	**rabbi**
	m	Edith Stein s'est portée volontaire pour se substituer à ce rabbin dans les chambres à gaz.
	[ʁabɛ̃]	-She volunteered to substitute herself for that rabbi in the gas chambers.
3216	**district**	**district**
	m	Le procureur du district est réticent à poursuivre à cause de l'insuffisance des preuves.
	[distʁikt]	-The district attorney is unwilling to proceed due to insufficient evidence.
3217	**humide**	**wet|damp**
	adj	Les vêtements protecteurs sont chers et insupportables dans la chaleur tropicale humide.
	[ymid]	-Protective clothing is expensive and unbearable to wear in the humid tropical heat.
3218	**diabolique**	**diabolical|devilish**
	adj	Et comme je ne suis pas diabolique, j'ai voté contre.
	[djabɔlik]	-Since I am not devilish, I voted against.
3219	**rançon**	**ransom**
	f	La résurgence des enlèvements brutaux contre une rançon constitue un fait inquiétant.
	[ʁɑ̃sɔ̃]	-The resurgence of brutal kidnappings for ransom is a worrisome development.
3220	**sperme**	**sperm**
	m	Recenser le sperme de l'ensemble de l'Union européenne devrait poser quelques problèmes.
	[spɛʁm]	-Counting the sperm of the whole of the European Union would be difficult.
3221	**député**	**member|deputy**
	m	J'aimerais entendre les observations du député là-dessus.
	[depyte]	-I would like to have the member's comments on that.
3222	**prononcer**	**pronounce**
	vb	Ma délégation ne va pas se prononcer sur les différentes propositions à ce stade.
	[pʁɔnɔ̃se]	-My delegation will not pronounce itself on the various proposals at this stage.
3223	**insigne**	**badge|insignia; signal**
	m; adj	Cet insigne devrait aussi être porté en miniature.
	[ɛ̃siɲ]	-A miniature of this badge should be included in those worn from the medal bar.
3224	**calibrer**	**calibrate|grade**
	vb	Nous avons passé trois mois à calibrer des antennes à Tchalinko.
	[kalibʁe]	-We have just spent three months calibrating the new antennae at Tchalinko.
3225	**seau**	**bucket**
	m	Certains diront que c'est une goutte d'eau dans le seau de l'adaptation.
	[so]	-One might argue that this is just a drop in the adaptation bucket.
3226	**sinistre**	**sinister|grim; fire**

adj; m[sinistʁ] | La communauté internationale était appelée à remédier à cette sinistre situation. -The international community was called upon to address this bleak situation.

3227 inconscient — **unconscious; unconscious**
adj; m
[ɛ̃kɔ̃sjɑ̃] | Il était inconscient du danger.
 -He was unaware of the danger.

3228 empoisonner — **poison**
vb
[ɑ̃pwazɔne] | Tout progrès, a souligné le Président Mbeki, reposait sur la confiance mutuelle, dont l'absence « empoisonnait » les relations entre les parties.
 -Underlying any progress, President Mbeki emphasized, was the factor of mutual confidence and trust, the lack of which currently "bedevilled' relations among the parties.

3229 réaliste — **realistic; realist**
adj; m/f
[ʁealist] | Je suis suffisamment réaliste et je sais qu'il s'agit d'une évolution progressive.
 -I am enough of a realist to know that this is a gradual process.

3230 physiquement — **physically**
adv
[fizikmɑ̃] | Néanmoins, il doit être physiquement et " opérationnellement " proche de l'AESA.
 -Nevertheless it should be physically and operationally close to the EFSA.

3231 chapelle — **chapel**
f
[ʃapɛl] | Fabriqué par Big City Costumes spécialement pour cette chapelle.
 -Manufactured by Big City Costumes. Specifically designed for this chapel.

3232 marge — **margin**
f
[maʁʒ] | Il vit en marge de la société.
 -He lives off the grid.

3233 fontaine — **fountain|spring**
f
[fɔ̃tɛn] | La fontaine du village marche mal.
 -The fountain in the town has water problems.

3234 registrer — **register**
vb
[ʁəʒistʁe] | Parfois, les organisations acceptent de vous registrer dans leur nom.
 -Sometimes organisations will agree to register you in their name.

3235 plume — **feather**
f
[plym] | Cela permet aux autres intervenants qui reçoivent la plume de faire office de médiateurs.
 -This provides an opportunity for others using the feather to intervene as Mediators.

3236 développer — **develop; adopt**
vb; vb
[devlɔpe] | La révolution numérique, à l'origine de l'essor économique, a surtout profité aux pays développés.
 -The developed countries had reaped the greatest benefit from the information and communication technology revolution which had launched the economic boom.

3237 pourboire — **tip|fee**
m
[puʁbwaʁ] | Avez-vous laissé un pourboire ?
 -Did you leave a tip?

3238 présumer — **assume**
vb[pʁezyme] | Pour cela, comme je l'ai dit, il faudrait présumer de l'existence de règles du jeu équitables. -That, as I have suggested, would assume the presence of a level playing field.

3239 creux — **hollow|sunken; hollow**

	adj; m [kʁø]	Lorsqu'un livre et une tête se télescopent et qu'un bruit creux se fait entendre, faut-il que cela provienne toujours du livre ? -When a book and a head collide and a hollow sound is heard, must it always have come from the book?
3240	**perruque** f [peʁyk]	**wig** Ça prendra un peu de temps pour s'habituer à porter une perruque. -It'll take some time to get used to wearing a wig.
3241	**supermarché** m [sypɛʁmaʁʃe]	**supermarket** Le supermarché est ouvert tous les jours, sauf le dimanche. -The supermarket is open all days except Sunday.
3242	**harmonie** f [aʁmɔni]	**harmony** Mettre tout en équilibre, c'est bien ; mettre tout en harmonie, c'est mieux. -To put everything in balance is good, to put everything in harmony is better.
3243	**décollage** m [dekɔlaʒ]	**take-off** Je donne l'autorisation de décollage. -All right. I'll clear it for takeoff.
3244	**poignet** m [pwaɲɛ]	**wrist** Vous avez une cicatrice au poignet gauche. -It says you have a small scar on your left wrist.
3245	**vice** m [vis]	**vice** Un vice conduit à un autre. -One vice leads to another.
3246	**assistance** f [asistãs]	**assistance|audience** Je lui prêterai assistance. -I'll give her a hand.
3247	**céder** vb [sede]	**yield|cede** Il n'y a aucune raison de céder à la panique. -There's no reason to panic.
3248	**hésiter** vb [ezite]	**hesitate** Pas un seul libéral à la Chambre ne devrait hésiter à appuyer ce projet de loi. -There should not be a Liberal in the House who would hesitate to vote for this bill.
3249	**respectable** adj [ʁɛspɛktabl]	**respectable** C'est une opinion très respectable, mais elle ne peut pas être prise en considération. -It is a very respectable opinion, but it cannot be taken into account.
3250	**escorter** vb [ɛskɔʁte]	**escort** Je prie le Chef du protocole de bien vouloir escorter le Président jusqu'à la tribune. -I request the Chief of Protocol to escort the President to the podium.
3251	**rituel** adj; m[ʁityɛl]	**ritual; ritual** Casher - Les procédures appropriées d'abattage rituel doivent être respectées. -Kosher - appropriate ritual slaughter procedures must be satisfied.
3252	**quarantaine** f [kaʁɑ̃tɛn]	**quarantine|about forty** Espérons qu'ils lèvent bientôt la quarantaine. -No, hopefully they'll lift the quarantine soon.
3253	**caca**	**poo**

	m	Il n'a pas eu de lavement, il a fait caca partout.
	[kaka]	-He didn't have his colonic and he like pooped everywhere.
3254	**créateur**	**creator**
	m	Aux yeux du Créateur, ils sont tous égaux.
	[kʁeatœʁ]	-In the eyes of the Creator, all are equal.
3255	**confidentiel**	**confidential**
	adj	Le Haut Commissariat demeure résolu à traiter le rapport comme un document confidentiel et regrette qu'il ait été rendu public.
	[kɔ̃fidɑ̃sjɛl]	-OHCHR remains committed to treating the report as confidential and regrets its publication.
3256	**symptôme**	**symptom**
	m	C'est un symptôme de stress et le résultat prévisible d'un mauvais régime fiscal.
	[sɛ̃ptom]	-It is a symptom of stress and the predictable result of a bad tax system.
3257	**touchant**	**touching**
	adj	La jambe de force est-elle réglée en longueur de manière à ne pas toucher le plancher (compatibilité ?
	[tuʃɑ̃]	-is the support leg installed in lengths not touching the floor (compatibility?
3258	**éclat**	**eclat	brightness**
	m	La magnificence et la galanterie n'ont jamais paru en France avec tant d'éclat que dans les dernières années du règne de Henri second.
	[ekla]	-Grandeur and gallantry never appeared with more lustre in France, than in the last years of Henry the Second's reign.
3259	**évacuation**	**evacuation	draining**
	f	La poudre ainsi produite est fluidifiée au moment de son évacuation.
	[evakɥasjɔ̃]	-The resulting powder is fluidized upon its discharge.
3260	**rime**	**rhyme**
	f	Pourtant, l'AIEA prétend, sans rime ni raison, que mon gouvernement viole les accords internationaux.
	[ʁim]	-Nevertheless, with no rhyme or reason, the IAEA claims that my Government is in violation of international agreements.
3261	**slip**	**briefs	panties**
	m	Dîtes lui qu'il a oublié son slip chez moi.
	[sli]	-Tell him he left his underwear here.
3262	**distraire**	**distract**
	vb	Il ne faut pas nous laisser distraire de cela par les discours des groupes d'experts.
	[distʁɛʁ]	-Talk of expert groups must not be allowed to distract us from that.
3263	**score**	**score**
	m	Quel était le score à la mi-temps ?
	[skɔʁ]	-What was the score at halftime?
3264	**musical**	**musical**
	adj[myzikal]	Comme vous pouvez le constater, même notre moment musical émanait du monde de la francophonie. -As you can see, even the music came from the world of La Francophonie.
3265	**code**	**code**
	m	Le code complet est beaucoup trop large pour tenir dans un article ; vous pouvez le télécharger accompagné d'un Makefile pour linux à partir d'ici.
	[kɔd]	-The full code is far too large to fit in an article; you can download it along with a Makefile for Linux from here.
3266	**paisible**	**peaceful	quiet**

adj
[pezibl]

Le climat électoral avait été paisible et aucune information n'avait fait état de la moindre tentative d'intimidation de l'opinion.
-The election environment had been calm and no reports of general intimidation had been received.

3267 **prévoir** — **provide|predict**

vb
[pʁevwaʁ]

Il faut prévoir les retombées imprévues potentielles du Programme puis les gérer.
-There is a need to anticipate and manage potential unintended effects of the Program.

3268 **obstacle** — **obstacle**

m
[ɔpstakl]

Il rencontra un obstacle imprévu.
-He met an unexpected obstacle.

3269 **soulier** — **shoe**

m
[sulje]

J'ai un caillou dans mon soulier.
-There is a rock in my shoe.

3270 **apparition** — **appearance**

f
[apaʁisjɔ̃]

L'apparition de souches de falciparum résistantes est particulièrement préoccupante.
-The appearance of resistant falciparum strains is a matter of particular concern.

3271 **confusion** — **confusion**

f
[kɔ̃fyzjɔ̃]

Cet empoisonnement peut provoquer confusion et désorientation.
-This type of poisoning can cause confusion and disorientation.

3272 **ruse** — **cunning|ruse**

f
[ʁyz]

Je refuse de me laisser avoir par sa ruse.
-I refuse to be taken in by her guile.

3273 **wagon** — **car|wagon**

m
[vagɔ̃]

Je me trouve dans le wagon de queue.
-I'm in the rear car.

3274 **infection** — **infection**

f
[ɛ̃fɛksjɔ̃]

Peut-être une allergie ou une infection locale.
-Could be an allergic reaction or some kind of localized infection.

3275 **torturer** — **torture**

vb
[tɔʁtyʁe]

Les détenus sont forcés de se tuer ou de se torturer s'ils tentent de fuir.
-Prisoners are forced to kill or torture one another if they try to escape.

3276 **treize** — **thirteen**

num
[tʁɛz]

Commencez à lire à la ligne treize.
-Start reading on line thirteen.

3277 **ego** — **ego**

m[əgo]

Je voudrais simplement signaler que, comme l'a très bien dit l'un de nos collègues, il ne s'agit pas de notre ego. -I would just like to point out here that, as has been said very well by one of our colleagues, this is not about our egos.

3278 **inspection** — **inspection**

f
[ɛ̃spɛksjɔ̃]

L'inspection peut intervenir sur plainte d'une partie concernée ou être une inspection de routine.
-Inspection may be done upon complaint by an interested party or through routine inspection.

3279 **visuel** — **visual**

adj
[vizɥɛl]

Le contrôle est visuel ou s'effectue par l'analyse des données de mesure.
-These tests shall be performed visually or by evaluation of measured data.

3280	**stock**	**stock**
	m	Notre système comptabilise tout notre stock.
	[stɔk]	-Our system keeps track of every item in stock.

3281	**bavarder**	**chat|talk**
	vb	Ils sont en train de bavarder d'autre chose certainement, mais il s'agit d'un fait important.
	[bavaʁde]	-They are chatting away on some other matter no doubt, but it is an important fact.

3282	**plaie**	**wound**
	f	Vous devrez nettoyer et recouvrir la plaie.
	[plɛ]	-You'll need to clean and re-wrap the wound.

3283	**gonzesse**	**chick**
	f	Tu es une chouette gonzesse.
	[gõzɛs]	-You are a good person.

3284	**féminin**	**female|feminine**
	adj	Le personnel masculin et féminin reçoit une formation obligatoire approfondie.
	[feminɛ̃]	-Male and female staff received considerable obligatory training.

3285	**démissionner**	**resign|step down**
	vb	Trois de ses membres ont déjà dû démissionner à cause d'un conflit d'intérêts.
	[demisjɔne]	-Three of its members have already had to resign because of a conflict of interest.

3286	**rampe**	**ramp|rail**
	f	Les fusées ont été lancées depuis une rampe de lancement.
	[ʁɑ̃p]	-The rockets were fired from a launching pad.

3287	**génétique**	**genetic; genetics**
	adj; f	Grâce au génie génétique, le maïs peut produire ses propres pesticides.
	[ʒenetik]	-Through genetic engineering, corn can produce its own pesticides.

3288	**psychiatrique**	**psychiatric**
	adj	Vous êtes un patient psychiatrique maintenant.
	[psikjatʁik]	-You're a psychiatric patient now, Mr. Munk.

3289	**décédé**	**deceased; defunct**
	adj; m	Le mariage est dissous lorsque l'époux ou l'épouse décède ou que le tribunal le (la) déclare décédé(e).
	[desede]	-A marriage is dissolved when one of the spouses dies or if the court declares him/her dead.

3290	**pressentiment**	**feeling**
	m	J'ai eu le pressentiment que tu ferais ça.
	[pʁesɑ̃timɑ̃]	-I had a hunch you would do that.

3291	**continent**	**continent; continent**
	adj; m	Le continent africain est le continent le moins avancé au monde.
	[kõtinɑ̃]	-The African continent is the least developed continent in the world.

3292	**bout**	**end|toe**
	m	Il fallait donc assurer à tout prix un chiffrement de bout en bout et bidirectionnel.
	[bu]	-This indicated an absolute requirement for two-way, end-to-end encryption.

3293	**menton**	**chin**
	m	Je l'ai frappé au menton.
	[mɑ̃tõ]	-I hit him on the chin.

3294 récit — story | recital

m

[ʁesi]

Le récit est plein de lacunes.
-The story is full of holes.

3295 tsar — tsar

m

[tsaʁ]

Le tsar de l'an 2000, Guy McKenzie, un fonctionnaire au passé irréprochable, sera dorénavant dans la fonction publique.
-The year 2000 czar will now be in the public service, Mr. Guy McKenzie, who is a civil servant with an irreproachable past.

3296 dépense — expenditure | expense

f

[depãs]

Ces amendements supposent donc une dépense fiscale inconnue.
-These amendments, then, also imply an unknown tax expenditure.

3297 informatique — data processing; paperless

f; adj

[ɛ̃fɔʁmatik]

Contrôle informatique des flux migratoires par voie aérienne et terrestre;
-Computerized monitoring of air and overland migration movements.

3298 luire — gleam | glisten

vb

[lɥiʁ]

Je ne l'ai jamais vu luire comme ça.
-I've never seen it glow like that.

3299 serrure — lock

f

[seʁyʁ]

A.3 Projet de règlement technique mondial sur les serrures et les organes de fixation des portes
-Draft global technical regulation on door lock and door retention components

3300 chèvre — goat

f

[ʃɛvʁ]

La région de Finlande dont je proviens produit un délicieux fromage au lait de chèvre.
-The region that I come from in Finland produces a delicious goat's milk cheese.

3301 séduisant — attractive | seductive

adj

[sedɥizã]

De même, les plus fortes raisons d'arrêter sont en général les bénéfices à court terme (par exemple, se sentir en meilleure santé et plus séduisant).
-Similarly, the strongest reasons for stopping are usually the short-term benefits (for example, feeling healthier and more attractive).

3302 brun — brown; brown

adj; m

[bʁɛ̃]

Le brun est également à moi.
-That brown one is mine, too.

3303 mécanique — mechanical; mechanics

adj; f[mekanik]

Le sénateur Banks : Comme on l'a appris, c'est la réponse de la poupée mécanique. -Senator Banks: We have learned that that is the wind-up doll response.

3304 ciseau — chisel

m

[sizo]

Essaie de me trouver un ciseau et un marteau.
-See if you can get me a chisel and a hammer.

3305 coutume — custom | practice

f

[kutym]

Autre pays, autre coutume.
-So many countries, so many customs.

3306 inscrire — enroll | list

vb

[ɛ̃skʁiʁ]

Les délégations sont priées de s'inscrire sur la liste des orateurs le plus tôt possible.
-Delegations were urged to inscribe their names on the list of speakers as soon as possible.

3307 rejeter — reject | dismiss

vb

[ʁəʒəte]

Seulement trois députés l'ont rejeté il y a bien longtemps et sept y ont opposé leur veto hier.

-Only three members said no to it way back when and we had seven nixing the bill yesterday.

3308 prudence

f

[pʁydɑ̃s]

caution|prudence

Nous devrions au moins, par prudence, ne jamais parler de nous-mêmes, parce que c'est un sujet sur lequel nous pouvons être sûrs que les points de vue des autres gens ne sont jamais en accord avec le nôtre.

-We ought at least, for prudence, never to speak of ourselves, because that is a subject on which we may be sure that other people's views are never in accordance with our own.

3309 provision

f

[pʁɔvizjɔ̃]

provision

Une provision de ce type est prévue en 2006 concernant des affaires juridiques en instance.

-In 2006 a provision of this kind for pending legal cases is made.

3310 ballet

m

[balɛ]

ballet

J'aurais dû continuer le ballet.

-I should have continued ballet.

3311 croisé

adj; m

[kʁwaze]

cross; crusader

Je l'ai croisé par hasard hier à l'aéroport.

-I came acrross him by accident at the airport yesterday.

3312 détenu

adj; m

[detny]

detained; inmate

Le détenu l'ayant fait, le policier a jeté une tasse d'eau sur le détenu.

-After the detainee did so, the MP threw a cup of water on the detainee.

3313 enthousiasme

m

[ɑ̃tuzjasm]

enthusiasm

Poursuivez avec enthousiasme, avec dévouement votre travail apostolique.

-Continue this apostolic work of yours with enthusiasm, with commitment.

3314 parade

f

[paʁad]

parade

On a bien aimé regarder la parade de cirque.

-We enjoyed watching a circus parade.

3315 exemplaire

m; adj

[ɛgzɑ̃plɛʁ]

copy; exemplary

Jack fut un détenu exemplaire.

-Jack was a model inmate.

3316 merdique

adj[mɛʁdik]

crappy|shitty

Une ville champignon merdique comme les autres. -Just another shitty boomtown like all the others.

3317 procéder

vb

[pʁɔsede]

proceed

Il est apparu qu'il fallait procéder progressivement, de manière réaliste et pragmatique.

-It was felt that one should proceed in a gradual, realistic and pragmatic way.

3318 aire

f

[ɛʁ]

area

Trois heures de conduite m'ont épuisé. Arrêtons-nous à la prochaine aire de repos que nous voyons.

-Three hours of driving has worn me out. Let's pull over at the next rest stop we see.

3319 marquis

m

[maʁki]

marquis

De mauvaises nouvelles du marquis de Pombal.

-I fear I have bad tidings from the Marquis of Pombal.

3320 enlèvement

removal|abduction

	m	Jack a participé à l'enlèvement de la fille de Jill.
	[ãlɛvmã]	-Jack took part in the kidnapping of Jill's daughter.
3321	**extra-terrestre**	**alien; alien**
	adj; m/f	J'ai été kidnappé par des extra-terrestres.
	[ɛkstʁatɛʁɛstʁ]	-I was abducted by aliens.
3322	**racine**	**root**
	f	L'argent est la racine de tous les maux.
	[ʁasin]	-Money is the root of all evil.
3323	**mater**	**stare at**
	vb	On pourrait y aller, mater les nénettes.
	[mate]	-Thought we'd go there, check out the talent.
3324	**inhabituel**	**unusual**
	adj	Il est cependant inhabituel que ce type de comportement barbare puisse être filmé.
	[inabityɛl]	-It was unusual, however, in that this barbaric behaviour was caught on film.
3325	**ras**	**all clear|short**
	adj	Jack remplit le seau jusqu'à ras bord.
	[ʁa]	-Jack filled the bucket to the top.
3326	**comparer**	**compare|confront**
	vb	Comme Swoboda, je voudrais comparer la Croatie et la Macédoine.
	[kɔ̃paʁe]	-Mr President, like Mr Swoboda, I would like to compare Croatia and Macedonia.
3327	**porteur**	**carrier|holder; supporting**
	m; adj	Il doit être possible d'afficher à l'écran la position de son bateau porteur.
	[pɔʁtœʁ]	-It shall be possible to display the skipper's own ship's position on the screen.
3328	**béton**	**concrete**
	m	Application à une composition cimentaire et à un béton renforcé.
	[betɔ̃]	-The invention is applicable to a cement composition and a reinforced concrete.
3329	**butin**	**booty|loot**
	m	Les soldats ont pillé la maison et forcé le jeune homme à porter leur butin.
	[bytɛ̃]	-The soldiers looted the house and forced the young man to carry the loot.
3330	**saucisse**	**sausage**
	f	J'ai apporté de ma nouvelle saucisse.
	[sosis]	-I brought you some of my new sausage.
3331	**actif**	**active|working; assets**
	adj; m	Transport/interface, marchandises (entreposage actif ou passif), sécurité/sûreté.
	[aktif]	-Transport /interface, cargoes (active or passive storage), security and safety.
3332	**mousse**	**foam|moss**
	f	La sciure, la vermiculite ou la mousse de tourbe peuvent également être utilisées.
	[mus]	-Sawdust, vermiculite or peat moss may also be used.
3333	**fusion**	**fusion**
	f	Sur le point« fusion thermonucléaire contrôlée, fusion nucléaire contrôlée», nous nous abstenons.
	[fyzjɔ̃]	-We are abstaining on controlled thermonuclear fusion, controlled nuclear fusion.

3334 portail   **portal; portal**
adj; m
[pɔʁtaj]
Ferme le portail.
-Close the gate.

3335 évader   **escape**
vb
[evade]
Malheureusement, cette personne est parvenue à s'évader et à regagner le Portugal.
-Unfortunately he was able to escape from prison and make his way back to Portugal.

3336 psychopathe   **psychopath**
m/f
[psikɔpat]
C'est un psychopathe.
-Because he's a psycho.

3337 mental   **mental**
adj
[mɑ̃tal]
On sait aujourd'hui que la malnutrition peut retarder le développement mental et physique.
-We now know that malnutrition can retard mental and physical development.

3338 massacrer   **massacre|murder**
vb
[masakʁe]
Les terroristes utilisent un ensemble d'armes pour tuer, mutiler et massacrer.
-The terrorists use an array of weapons to kill, maim and slaughter.

3339 semblable   **similar; fellow creature**
adj; m
[sɑ̃blabl]
Très peu se sont levés pour dire la vérité; très peu se sont intéressés au sort effroyable de leur semblable et l'ont déclaré victime.
-Very few accepted and spoke the truth; very few considered the catastrophe of their fellow human being and declared that he was a victim.

3340 virage   **turn|shift**
m
[viʁaʒ]
Sa voiture se mit à tournoyer dans le virage.
-His car spun out of control going around the curve.

3341 casquette   **cap**
f
[kaskɛt]
À récupérer ma casquette tombée dans l'étang.
-I got it to fish my cap out of the pond.

3342 trancher   **settle|slice**
vb[tʁɑ̃ʃe]
Un couteau peut s'utiliser pour trancher notre pain quotidien mais aussi pour tuer. -A knife may be used to slice our daily bread but it may also be used to kill.

3343 farine   **flour**
f
[faʁin]
La pâte à crêpes est faite d'œufs, de farine, de beurre, de lait et de sucre.
-The batter for crepes is made of eggs, flour, butter, milk and sugar.

3344 cellulaire   **cellular**
adj
[selylɛʁ]
La durée de la détention en régime cellulaire a été réduite d'un mois à 20 jours.
-The duration of solitary confinement has been reduced from one month to 20 days.

3345 vermine   **vermin**
f
[vɛʁmin]
Les phoques ne sont pas de la vermine, mais bien une ressource précieuse qui n'a pas été reconnue à sa juste valeur.
-They are not a pest, but a valuable resource that has been undervalued.

3346 doper   **boost|dope**
vb
[dɔpe]
J'en ai acheté une pour doper tes ventes.
-I bought one to boost your sales.

3347 zone   **area**

	f	Le lieu est un petit village de montagne dans une zone perdue de la Virginie.
	[zon]	-The scene was a tiny mountain village in a remote area of West Virginia.

3348 déchet — **wretch**

m
[deʃɛ]

Une part importante du bois prélevé finit comme déchet technologique.
-A large proportion of the timber that is removed becomes technological waste.

3349 alcoolique — **alcoholic; alcoholic**

adj; m/f
[alkɔlik]

Il me reste juste assez de temps pour devenir alcoolique.
-I may have just enough time left to become an alcoholic.

3350 préserver — **preserve**

vb
[pʁezɛʁve]

Chaque groupe est libre de promouvoir et préserver sa culture et ses traditions.
-Each group is free to and does promote and preserve its culture and traditions.

3351 chauffé — **heated**

adj
[ʃofe]

En règle générale un liquide ne doit pas être chauffé audelà de son point d'éclair.
-In general, a liquid shall not be heated up to a temperature above its flashpoint.

3352 honnêteté — **honesty**

f
[ɔnɛtte]

Nous respectons tous son honnêteté.
-There are none of us who do not respect his honesty.

3353 canyon — **canyon**

m
[kanjɔn]

Nous sommes coincés dans ce canyon.
-We're stuck in the canyon with no way out.

3354 soupçon — **suspicion|soupcon**

m
[supsɔ̃]

Vous avez été lavé de tout soupçon.
-You've been cleared of all charges.

3355 torche — **torch**

f[tɔʁʃ]

Peux-tu me prêter une lampe torche ? -Do you have a flashlight I can borrow?

3356 égalité — **equality**

f
[egalite]

L'amour de la démocratie est celui de l'égalité.
-The love of democracy is that of equality.

3357 repasser — **iron|replay**

vb
[ʁəpase]

Je dois repasser ma chemise.
-I have to iron my shirt.

3358 détention — **detention|possession**

f
[detɑ̃sjɔ̃]

Notre réponse traditionnelle-détection, détention et dissuasion-n'a pas fonctionné.
-Our traditional response of detection, detention and deterrence simply has not worked.

3359 bouquet — **bouquet|bunch**

m
[bukɛ]

Si un garçon a un bouquet de fleurs à la main, cela signifie qu'il a l'intention d'étudier l'anatomie et non pas la botanique.
-If a guy has got a bunch of flowers in his hand, it means that he is going to practise not botany, but anatomy.

3360 généralement — **generally|usually**

adv
[ʒeneʁalmɑ̃]

La législation est généralement considérée accessible pour 86% des répondants.

-The legislation is generally considered to be accessible, by 86% of respondents.

3361	**gratuitement**	**free of charge**
	adv	La direction de l'éducation délivre gratuitement les fournitures scolaires.
	[gʁatɥitmɑ̃]	-Stationery for primary schools is provided free of charge by the Department.
3362	**orphelinat**	**orphanage**
	m	Sami a donné l'argent à un orphelinat.
	[ɔʁfəlina]	-Sami donated the money to an orphanage.
3363	**sacrément**	**mighty**
	adv	Dieu reste fidèle à l'alliance qu'il noue avec l'homme dans le sacrement de l'ordre.
	[sakʁemɑ̃]	-God remains faithful to his covenant with man in the Sacrament of Holy Orders.
3364	**littéralement**	**literally**
	adv	Sa définition est reprise litté-ralement dans l'article 119 du Code pénal de 1998, actuellement en vigueur.
	[liteʁalmɑ̃]	-The definition of such activities was reproduced verbatim in article 119 of the Penal Code of 1998, currently in force.
3365	**mèche**	**wick**
	f	Ils ont vendu la mèche.
	[mɛʃ]	-They gave away the wick.
3366	**quotidien**	**daily; daily**
	adj; m	Ce journal est un quotidien.
	[kɔtidjɛ̃]	-This is a daily newspaper.
3367	**prophète**	**prophet**
	m[pʁɔfɛt]	Ils sont clairement inscrits dans le Coran et dans les enseignements du prophète Mahomet. -They are clearly embodied in the Koran and the traditions of the Prophet Mohammed.
3368	**combler**	**fill in|make up**
	vb	Il incombera aux acteurs de la Conférence intergouvernementale de combler cette lacune.
	[kɔ̃ble]	-It will be up to those involved in the Intergovernmental Conference to make good that shortcoming.
3369	**débarquer**	**land|disembark**
	vb	Quelques navires de croisière tentent cependant de débarquer chaque année des passagers.
	[debaʁke]	-However, a handful of passing cruise ships do attempt to offload passengers each year.
3370	**orgueil**	**pride**
	m	Sa conduite témoigne de son orgueil.
	[ɔʁgœj]	-Her manner marks her pride.
3371	**affamer**	**starve**
	vb	L'auteur entendait affamer des civils comme méthode de guerre.
	[afame]	-The perpetrator intended to starve civilians as a method of warfare.
3372	**fichier**	**catalog|file**
	m	Un fichier MP3 est un fichier audio.
	[fiʃje]	-An MP3 file is an audio file.
3373	**entretenir**	**maintain|nurture**
	vb	Entretenir des relations étroites avec des organisations internationales et régionales;
	[ɑ̃tʁətniʁ]	-Maintain close contacts with international and regional organizations.

3374 **architecte** — **architect**
m
[aʁʃitɛkt]
Un avenant au contrat de l'architecte a été signé en conséquence en juillet 2006.
-In that connection, an amendment to the architect's contract was signed in July 2006.

3375 **tailleur** — **tailor**
m
[tajœʁ]
Mon tailleur est riche.
-My tailor is rich.

3376 **échantillon** — **sample**
m
[eʃɑ̃tijɔ̃]
L'échantillon n'est pas assez pur.
-The sample is not pure enough.

3377 **sobre** — **sober**
adj
[sɔbʁ]
Comunicado especial sobre conversión de deuda externa por inversión educativa.
-Special communiqué on the swapping of foreign debt for investment in education.

3378 **investissement** — **investment**
m
[ɛ̃vɛstismɑ̃]
Un investissement majeur a été réalisé aux dernières élections.
-We have seen a major investment going into the last election.

3379 **imaginaire** — **imaginary**
adj[imaʒinɛʁ]
Ce film part non des Evangiles, mais de cette exploration imaginaire d'un conflit spirituel de toute éternité. -This film is not based upon the Gospels but upon this fictional exploration of the eternal spiritual conflict.

3380 **identification** — **identification**
f
[idɑ̃tifikasjɔ̃]
Justement, c'est pour une parfaite identification.
-That's why we must leave it, to complete the identification.

3381 **honteux** — **shameful|ashamed**
adj
[ɔ̃tø]
Ne sommes-nous pas honteux de ce qui se passe en Afrique centrale? Nous en reparlerons aujourd'hui.
-And today, are we not ashamed about what is happening in Central Africa?

3382 **tank** — **tank**
m
[tɑ̃k]
An opening water tank is integrated into the humidifier base.
-Un réservoir d'eau ouvrant est intégré dans la base d'humidificateur.

3383 **pacte** — **pact|agreement**
m
[pakt]
De nombreux pays ont signé un pacte de désarmement nucléaire.
-Numerous countries have signed a nuclear disarmament agreement.

3384 **écho** — **echo**
m
[eko]
Programmez une écho pour confirmer le calcul.
-Schedule an ultrasound to confirm the presence of a stone.

3385 **cuisinier** — **cook**
m
[kɥizinje]
Chaque cuisinier doit garder une chose primordiale en tête...
-There's one thing that's paramount for every cook to keep in the back of their mind.

3386 **fosse** — **pit|grave**
f
[fos]
Ses murs créaient une fosse gigantesque.
-Its walls enclosed me like some gigantic pit.

3387 **rhum** — **rum**
m
[ʁɔm]
La définition du "rhum agricole" a pu être préservée lors des négociations.
-It was possible to retain the definition of 'agricultural rum' during the negotiations.

3388 **assumer** vb [asyme]

assume

Nous, les membres du Conseil de sécurité, devons assumer pleinement nos responsabilités.
-We, the members of the Security Council, must fully assume our responsibilities.

3389 **techniquement** adv [tɛknikmɑ̃]

technically

Le Comité directeur sera appuyé techniquement par un secrétariat technique.
-The Steering Committee will be technically supported by a technical Secretariat.

3390 **élégant** adj; m [elegɑ̃]

elegant; dandy

En ce qui nous concerne, il ne s'agit certainement pas du plus élégant des rapports.
-In our opinion, this is certainly not the most elegant of reports.

3391 **borne** f [bɔʁn]

terminal

Il savent que le processus de remise en cause de leurs droits n'a pas de bornes.
-They know that the process to dismantle their rights has no bounds.

3392 **coopération** f[kɔɔpeʁasjɔ̃]

cooperation

Je voulais ta coopération. -I wanted your cooperation.

3393 **cambriolage** m [kɑ̃bʁijɔlaʒ]

burglary

Il fut envoyé en prison pour le cambriolage.
-He was sent to jail for the burglary.

3394 **arche** f [aʁʃ]

ark

Maintenant je comprends pourquoi il y avait 8 personnes et 7 paires d'animaux de chaque espèce dans l'arche de Noé.
-Now I understand why there were 8 persons and 7 pairs of animals of each species in Noah's Ark.

3395 **statut** m [staty]

status

Ce contributeur a réclamé le statut de contributeur avancé. Sentez-vous libre de partager votre opinion avec nous. Envoyez-nous un message en utilisant le lien suivant.
-This contributor has asked for advanced contributor status. Please feel free to share your opinion with us. Send us a message using the following link.

3396 **pénétrer** vb [penetʁe]

enter|penetrate

J'ai vu un étranger pénétrer dans cette maison.
-I saw a stranger enter that house.

3397 **légèrement** adv [leʒɛʁmɑ̃]

slightly|lightly

Je suppose que je suis légèrement indisposé.
-I am slightly ill, I assume.

3398 **martial** adj [maʁsjal]

martial

Si nous ne voulons pas la guerre, si nous n'avons pas les moyens d'entamer une guerre, nous ne devons pas adopter un ton martial.
-If we do not want war, if we do not have the means to wage war, then we should not sound a warlike note.

3399 **tremper** vb [tʁɑ̃pe]

soak|dip

Fais tremper tes pieds de vieille femme.
-Soak those old-lady feet of yours.

3400 **détente** f [detɑ̃t]

relaxation

Enlevez votre doigt de la détente.
-Just take your finger slowly off the trigger.

3401	**obligation**	**obligation|bond**
	f	Vous n'êtes aucunement dans l'obligation de divulguer cette information.
	[ɔbligasjɔ̃]	-You are under no obligation to divulge that information.

3402	**climat**	**climate**
	m	Je crois que le climat de créativité va même au-delà du climat d'
	[klima]	innovation.
		-I believe that the climate of creativity goes even beyond the climate of innovation.

3403	**pois**	**pea**
	m	Mange tes petits pois.
	[pwa]	-Eat your peas.

3404	**poignarder**	**stab**
	vb	Il ne doit pas poignarder les forces démocratiques dans le dos.
	[pwaɲaʁde]	-It should not stab the democratic forces in the back.

3405	**faucon**	**falcon**
	m[fokɔ̃]	Le faucon attrapa une souris. -The hawk caught a mouse.

3406	**comporter**	**include|have**
	vb	L'envoi d'observateurs est par conséquent judicieux mais peut également
	[kɔ̃pɔʁte]	comporter des risques.
		-The sending of observers is therefore very useful, but can also entail risks.

3407	**bâtir**	**build|erect**
	vb	Ils doivent jeter les bases sur lesquelles les citoyens antillais peuvent bâtir
	[batiʁ]	leurs vies.
		-It must lay foundations on which Antillean citizens can build their lives.

3408	**électronique**	**electronic; electronics**
	adj; f	Le tableau de bord de cette voiture est entièrement électronique.
	[elɛktʁɔnik]	-The dashboard of this car is completely electronic.

3409	**vagin**	**vagina**
	m	Eraflures à la poitrine, légère déchirure au vagin.
	[vaʒɛ̃]	-Well, there was bruising on her breast... slight tearing around the vagina.

3410	**rive**	**bank|shore**
	f	Un problème particulier tenait à l'absence de données provenant de la rive
	[ʁiv]	gauche du Dniestr.
		-A particular problem was the lack of data from the left bank of the Dniestr river.

3411	**script**	**script**
	m	Donc Stéphanie va faxer le script...
	[skʁipt]	-We'll have Stephanie fax over a script…

3412	**seize**	**sixteen**
	num	Entre quinze et seize ans, il a grandi de trois pouces entiers.
	[sɛz]	-Between the ages of 15 and 16, he grew three whole inches.

3413	**capote**	**hood**
	f	Comment est-ce que je déploie la capote ?
	[kapɔt]	-How do I open the hood?

3414	**toutefois**	**however; nevertheless**
	con; adv	Il convient toutefois de tenir davantage compte des différences
	[tutfwa]	interrégionales.
		-Interregional differences, however, need to be taken into greater consideration.

3415	**croyant**	**believer; god-fearing**

m; adj
[kʁwajɑ̃]

Axmali voulait passer les détonateurs à un croyant.
-Axmali wanted to pass the triggers on to a believer.

3416 éveiller — **awaken**

vb
[eveje]

Le chapitre nécessaire concernant l'emploi ne doit pas éveiller de faux espoirs.
-The necessary chapter on employment must not arouse any false hopes.

3417 indispensable — **essential**

adj
[ɛ̃dispɑ̃sabl]

Dans ces entreprises, le plein appui de l'Assemblée générale sera indispensable.
-In those endeavours, the full support of the General Assembly will be much needed.

3418 SIDA — **AIDS**

abr[ɛsidea]

Selon des études sur le sida, le taux de morbidité du VIH/sida est en hausse.
-According to studies on AIDS, there has been an increase in HIV/AIDS morbidity.

3419 gravement — **seriously|gravely**

adv
[gʁavmɑ̃]

Ces conditions peuvent compromettre gravement leur santé et leur épanouissement.
-These situations might seriously hamper their health and development.

3420 investir — **invest**

vb
[ɛ̃vɛstiʁ]

À son niveau, l'Union européenne veut également investir dans l'économie européenne.
-The European Union as a whole is also seeking to invest in the European economy.

3421 politicien — **politician**

m
[pɔlitisjɛ̃]

La phrase « politicien honnête » est un oxymore.
-The phrase 'honest politician' is an oxymoron.

3422 préoccuper — **concern|preoccupy**

vb
[pʁeɔkype]

C'est cela qui devrait nous préoccuper, nous, peuples du monde.
-This is what should preoccupy us, the peoples of the world.

3423 fidélité — **loyalty|fidelity**

f
[fidelite]

Mets-tu en doute ma fidélité ?
-Are you questioning my loyalty?

3424 pauvret — **poor looking**

m/f
[povʁɛ]

Au Bangladesh, 45% des 160 millions d'habitants vivent au-dessous du seuil de pauvret.
-In Bangladesh, 45% of 160 million inhabitants still live under poverty line.

3425 soulever — **raise; bench press**

vb; m
[sulve]

Monsieur le Président, concernant ce rapport, je voudrais soulever trois questions.
-Mr President, I would like to raise three issues with regard to this report.

3426 flûte — **flute**

f
[flyt]

Ce n'est pas pour la liberté que nous avons besoin d'une flûte enchantée.
-It is not for freedom that we need a magic flute.

3427 régulièrement — **regularly**

adv
[ʁegyljɛʁmɑ̃]

Il devrait y avoir un échange de vue régulier sur l'application de ce règlement.
-There should be a regular exchange of views on the implementation of the Regulation.

3428 fourrure — **fur**

	f	Elle portait une fourrure.
	[fuʁyʁ]	-She was wearing a fur coat.
3429	**aveu**	**confession**
	m	Le silence est un aveu de culpabilité.
	[avø]	-Silence is an admission of guilt.
3430	**bac**	**tray**
	m	Un bac comprend un dessus et un dessous.
	[bak]	-A tray comprises a topside and a underside.
3431	**temporaire**	**temporary**
	adj[tɑ̃pɔʁɛʁ]	Mais cette compétence est par nature temporaire puisqu'une occupation est par définition temporaire. -But this authority is inherently temporary as occupation is by definition temporary.
3432	**graine**	**seed**
	f	Leurs pouvoirs finiront dans la seule graine restante.
	[gʁɛn]	-Their power will be amassed into the single remaining seed.
3433	**rail**	**rail**
	m	Research activity in the rail transport area is being performed for Železnicná spoločnosť a.s. by VVUŽ Žilina.
	[ʁaj]	-Des travaux de recherche portant sur le secteur des transports ferroviaires sont entrepris par VVUŽ Žilina pour le compte de la société Železnicná spoločnost' a.s.
3434	**confort**	**comfort**
	m	Cette flexibilité améliore considérablement le confort du patient.
	[kɔ̃fɔʁ]	-This flexibility provides a great deal of comfort to the patient.
3435	**lessive**	**laundry|lye**
	f	La femme est plus souvent chargée de la cuisine, de la lessive, du repassage ou des travaux dits « de routine ».
	[lesiv]	-Women deal more often with cooking, washing, ironing, or work classified as "routine".
3436	**gâchette**	**trigger**
	f	Ne m'obligez pas à tirer sur la gâchette !
	[gaʃɛt]	-Don't make me pull the trigger.
3437	**répugner**	**loathe**
	vb	La manière dont cette action est entreprise, toutefois, nous répugne.
	[ʁepyɲe]	-The way in which this is done, however, fills us with disgust.
3438	**transférer**	**transfer|switch**
	vb	Il peut transférer moins dans un programme afin de pouvoir transférer plus dans l'autre.
	[tʁɑ̃sfeʁe]	-He can transfer less under a given program in order to transfer more under another.
3439	**champignon**	**mushroom**
	m	Ces spores sont la forme hivernante du champignon.
	[ʃɑ̃piɲɔ̃]	-These spores serve as the overwintering form of the fungus.
3440	**écoute**	**listening**
	f	Une autre candidate a été jugée inapte à cause de ses très faibles habiletés d'écoute.
	[ekut]	-A third candidate was deemed unsuitable due to very poor listening skills.
3441	**pointer**	**point**
	vb	Nous ne pouvons pointer un doigt accusateur ni distribuer des réprimandes.
	[pwɛ̃te]	-We cannot point fingers or apportion blame.
3442	**gilet**	**vest**

	m	Son gilet était déboutonné.
	[ʒilɛ]	-Her cardigan was unbuttoned.
3443	**établissement**	**establishment**
	m	Le chef d'établissement serra la main à chacun des élèves reçus.
	[etablismã]	-The principal shook hands with each of the graduating pupils.
3444	**volume**	**volume|tonnage**
	m[vɔlym]	Pourriez-vous baisser le volume ? -Would you mind turning down the volume?
3445	**sixième**	**sixth**
	num	Le projet de textes pour la première année est établi et celui des deuxième et sixième années est entamé.
	[sizjɛm]	-It ahs drafted the texts of the first form of 9-year education, and it is presently working for the texts of the second and sixth form.
3446	**pitoyable**	**pitiful**
	adj	Cela en dit long sur le pitoyable système d'immigration que nous avons au Canada.
	[pitwajabl]	-That is a pathetic statement about the pathetic immigration system in Canada.
3447	**manoir**	**manor**
	m	Il dit qu'il a payé pour les nuits qu'il a passées dans le manoir en mars dernier.
	[manwaʁ]	-The minister says he paid for the nights that he spent in the mansion back in March.
3448	**accéder**	**access**
	vb	De cette façon, les élèves et les professeurs peuvent accéder à des lectures d'actualité.
	[aksede]	-This gives students and teachers a chance to access information about current affairs.
3449	**emmerder**	**bother**
	vb	Je ne voulais pas vous emmerder avec ça.
	[ãmɛʁde]	-I didn't want to bother you with it.
3450	**fiable**	**reliable**
	adj	Il est difficile d'obtenir une estimation fiable du nombre de chrétiens en Iran.
	[fjabl]	-It is difficult to obtain a reliable estimate of the number of Christians in Iran.
3451	**villageois**	**villager**
	m	De quoi un villageois africain a-t-il le plus besoin ?
	[vilaʒwa]	-What is more useful to a villager in Africa?
3452	**véhicule**	**vehicle; vehicular**
	m; adj	Véhicules conçus et construits pour le transport de voyageurs assis et de voyageurs debout.
	[veikyl]	-Vehicles designed and constructed to carry seated and standing passengers.
3453	**financier**	**financial; financier**
	adj; m	Il a amassé une fortune en bourse lors du dernier boom financier.
	[finãsje]	-He amassed a fortune in stock trading during the last financial boom.
3454	**jeep**	**jeep**
	f	Une jeep est absolument hors de question.
	[dʒip]	-A jeep is out of the question, absolutely.
3455	**connasse**	**motherfucker**

f
[kɔnas]

Nique ta mère, connasse.
-Fuck your mom, mofo.

3456 geler — **freeze**

vb
[ʒəle]

Il pourrait geler, il pourrait dégeler.
-It might freeze, it might thaw.

3457 châtiment — **punishment**

m
[ʃatimã]

La peine de mort constitue le châtiment cruel, inhumain et dégradant ultime.
-The death penalty is the ultimate cruel, inhuman and degrading punishment.

3458 martini — **martini**

m
[maʁtini]

Mais je sais qu'il confectionnait un dry martini du tonnerre.
-But I do know that he could make a terrific dry martini.

3459 cire — **wax**

f
[siʁ]

L'oreille contient beaucoup de cire.
-The ear has a lot of wax in it.

3460 distribution — **distribution|delivery**

f
[distʁibysjɔ̃]

Distribution : distribution et stockage des divers documents et publications.
-Distribution: distribution and storage of documents and publications.

3461 infini — **infinite; infinity**

adj; m
[ɛ̃fini]

Renvoie la valeur complémentaire de l' intégrale d' erreur de Gauss entre x et l' infini.
-The function returns complementary values of the Gaussian error integral between x and infinity.

3462 moulin — **mill**

m
[mulɛ̃]

On était au moulin, près de la canebière.
-We were at the mill, near the hemp field.

3463 banlieue — **suburbs**

f
[bɑ̃ljø]

En janvier 2003, elle a été transférée à Mbagathi, dans la banlieue de Nairobi.
-The Conference was transferred to Mbagathi, a suburb of Nairobi, in January 2003.

3464 salutation — **greeting**

f
[salytasjɔ̃]

Le salut en islam est synonyme de paix… LOL
-Islam is a religion of peace; its greeting is peace… LOL

3465 réflexion — **reflection|thinking**

f
[ʁeflɛksjɔ̃]

L'UNITAR poursuit une réflexion théorique et une action concrète dans ce domaine.
-UNITAR is pursuing theoretical reflection and pragmatic action in this field.

3466 graisse — **fat**

f
[gʁɛs]

Le Danemark a introduit la première taxe sur la graisse au monde.
-Denmark has introduced the world's first fat tax.

3467 effrayer — **scare|spook**

vb
[efʁeje]

L'intention des terroristes de nous effrayer n'a pas produit l'effet escompté.
-The intent of the terrorists to frighten us does not produce the desired effect.

3468 vaurien — **rascal|scoundrel**

m
[voʁjɛ̃]

Et elle a épousé un vaurien.
-Then she got married to a scoundrel and...

3469 scolaire — **school**

	adj [skɔlɛʁ]	Durant l'année scolaire 2004/05, 12 718 enfants ont bénéficié de ces programmes. -In the 2004/05 academic year, 12,718 children benefited from these programmes.
3470	**coopérer** vb [kɔɔpeʁe]	**cooperate|club up** Dans la logique de la résolution 2625 (XXV), les États doivent coopérer entre eux. -In line with resolution 2625 (XXV), States must cooperate amongst themselves.
3471	**bloqué** adj [blɔke]	**blocked** Mon pays et la France ont bloqué la libéralisation des marchés de l'énergie. -The liberalisation of the energy markets was blocked by my country and by France.
3472	**table** f [tabl]	**table|calculator** Disposez-vous d'une table sur le patio ? -Do you have a table on the patio?
3473	**gangster** m [gɑ̃gstɛʁ]	**gangster** "Hé toi, la ferme ! Tu parles trop", dit le gangster. -"Hey, you shut up! You talk too much," the gangster said.
3474	**conquérir** vb [kɔ̃keʁiʁ]	**conquer** Quelles mesures faut-il prendre pour conquérir le cœur et l'esprit des Iraquiens ? -What measures are needed to conquer the hearts and minds of the Iraqis?
3475	**révolutionnaire** adj; m/f [ʁevɔlysjɔnɛʁ]	**revolutionary; revolutionary** Abitbol est un révolutionnaire: il faut qu'il y en ait dans toutes les assemblées. -Mr Abitbol is a revolutionary of the kind that every assembly needs.
3476	**isoler** vb [izɔle]	**isolate|separate** Son Mouvement s'était efforcé d'isoler les civils du conflit. -They had tried hard to insulate civilians from the conflict.
3477	**justifier** vb [ʒystifje]	**justify** Voilà pourquoi le silence, qui n'est pas innocent, peut justifier un vote favorable. -This explains why, as silence is not innocent, it can justify a vote in favour.
3478	**clôture** f; vb [klotyʁ]	**closing|fence; conclude** Toutes les Parties avaient bien accueilli la fixation à 18 heures de la clôture des séances, qui s'appliquera aussi à Bali. -The 6 p.m. closing time has been well received by all Parties and will continue in Bali.
3479	**opposer** vb [ɔpoze]	**oppose|put up** C'est pourquoi ils ne doivent pas opposer de blocages financiers. -That is why they should not put up any financial barricades.
3480	**représentation** f [ʁəpʁezɑ̃tasjɔ̃]	**representation|performance** Le deuxième commentaire concerne la représentation des minorités dans la magistrature. -My second comment has to do with the representation of minorities in the judiciary.
3481	**morveux** adj; m [mɔʁvø]	**snotty; snot** C'est un petit morveux égoïste. -He's a selfish little snot.
3482	**croyable**	**believable**

adj[kʁwajabl] | Les termes «fabriqué, à peine croyable, incroyable ou inimaginable» sont tous presque antiparlementaires. -The words fabricated, hardly believable, unbelievable or incredible are all bordering on words that are unparliamentary.

3483 **millionnaire** **millionaire**
m/f
[miljɔnɛʁ] | Selon mes calculs, l'économie sera de 8 000 $ pour chaque millionnaire du pays.
-By my calculations every millionaire in this country will save $8,000.

3484 **herbe** **grass|herb**
f
[ɛʁb] | L'herbe ne croit pas plus vite si on tire dessus.
-Grass doesn't grow faster if you pull it.

3485 **tumeur** **tumor|growth**
f
[tymœʁ] | J'ai une tumeur cérébrale.
-I have a brain tumor.

3486 **œuvre** **work**
f
[œvʁ] | Mon mari œuvre pour la Défense.
-My husband does defense work on the premises.

3487 **conséquent** **consequent**
adj
[kõsekã] | Je suis conscient de ne pas avoir un bon niveau ; par conséquent, j'ai besoin de pratiquer plus.
-I'm aware I'm not at a good level; so consequently, I need to practice more.

3488 **réfugier** **refuge**
vb
[ʁefyʒje] | Dans sa position à lui, le Conseil essaie de se réfugier derrière des problèmes techniques.
-In its common position the Council tries to take refuge behind technical problems.

3489 **faîte** **ridge|top**
m
[fɛt] | Comment était-il possible que l'Europe, au faîte de sa civilisation, puisse commettre un tel crime ?
-How was it possible that Europe, at the peak of its civilization, could commit such a crime?

3490 **yacht** **yacht**
m
[jɔt] | J'aimerais bien affréter un yacht.
-I would like to charter a yacht.

3491 **ruban** **ribbon**
m
[ʁybã] | Les participants arborent un ruban blanc pour signifier leur engagement.
-Participants where a white ribbon to signify their commitment.

3492 **démission** **resignation**
f
[demisjõ] | Il a présenté sa démission.
-He tendered his resignation.

3493 **malle** **trunk**
f
[mal] | Cherchez la clé de cette malle, Anne.
-Look for the key to this trunk, Anne.

3494 **bowling** **bowling**
m
[bɔwliŋ] | Je ne veux pas aller faire du bowling.
-I don't want to go bowling.

3495 **cruauté** **cruelty**
f[kʁyote] | Elles prétendent qu'il s'agit d'une question de cruauté et de traitement inhumain. -They claim that this is a matter of cruelty and inhumane treatment.

3496 sanctuaire — sanctuary

m
[sɑ̃ktɥɛʁ]

Et le livre explique que, dans ce mystérieux sanctuaire de l'arche de l'alliance apparut.
-And the book says that in this mysterious Sanctuary the ark of the alliance appeared.

3497 stand — stall

m
[stɑ̃d]

Nous espérons vous accueillir sur notre stand.
-We look forward to welcoming you at our stand.

3498 orteil — toe

m
[ɔʁtɛj]

Le voleur se cogna l'orteil contre la porte.
-The thief stubbed his toe on the door.

3499 bourreau — executioner

m
[buʁo]

En d'autres termes, M. le Président, la Commission demeure juge, jury et bourreau.
-In other words, Mr President, the Commission remains judge, jury and executioner.

3500 cafard — cockroach

m
[kafaʁ]

Il y a un cafard dans la salle de bain.
-There's a cockroach in the bathroom.

3501 griffer — scratch

vb
[gʁife]

On le mettait dans un sac... pour ne pas se faire griffer de partout.
-We'd put them inside a bag... otherwise you'd get scratched all over.

3502 sherry — sherry

m
[ʃeʁi]

Faut juste y aller doucement sur le sherry.
-Just go easy on the sherry.

3503 infirmerie — infirmary

f
[ɛ̃fiʁməʁi]

Vous devriez allez à l'infirmerie.
-Maybe you should head down to the infirmary.

3504 fédération — federation

f
[fedeʁasjɔ̃]

L'association volontaire de deux associations professionnelles constitue une fédération.
-The voluntary association of two or more professional associations constitutes a federation.

3505 défunt — late; deceased person

adj; m
[defɛ̃]

Muriel avait combattu pendant la Seconde Guerre mondiale, tout comme son défunt mari, Bill.
-She was a veteran of World War II, as was her late husband, Bill.

3506 crapaud — toad

m
[kʁapo]

Elle ne voudrait coucher avec un crapaud puant.
-She would as soon have lain with a stinking toad.

3507 autel — altar

m
[otɛl]

Et vous les immolez sur l'autel des intérêts douteux des multinationales.
-And you are sacrificing it on the altar of questionable multinational interests.

3508 purée — puree

f
[pyʁe]

Voudriez-vous davantage de purée de pommes-de-terre ?
-Would you like more mashed potatoes?

3509 commode — convenient|handy; chest of drawers

adj; f
[kɔmɔd]

Elle gisait sous une commode et sa marchette.
-He was covered by a chest of drawers and his walker.

3510 infanterie — infantry

f
[ɛ̃fɑ̃tʀi]
D'ici la fin de cette année, deux bataillons d'infanterie seront opérationnels.
-By the end of this year, two infantry battalions will be operational.

3511 **grade** **grade**
m
[gʀad]
Donnez-moi votre nom, grade et matricule.
 -Just give me your name, rank, and serial number.

3512 **recours** **recourse|remedy**
m
[ʀəkuʀ]
Il croyait que les noirs pouvaient gagner leur combat pour l'égalité des droits sans avoir recours à la violence.
 -He believed that blacks could win their fight for equal rights without violence.

3513 **Fi!** **Pooh!**
int
[fi!]
Fi! I'm so sorry, Arnie.
 -Pooh! Je suis désolée Arnie.

3514 **épais** **thick|heavy**
adj
[epɛ]
Tissus conjonctifs épais (membrane du muscle) du côté ventral laissés en place ou enlevés.
 -Heavy connective tissue (silver skin) on ventral side removed or retained.

3515 **fréquenter** **patronize|frequent**
vb
[fʀekɑ̃te]
Jack a cessé de fréquenter l'école.
 -Jack has stopped going to school.

3516 **automobile** **automotive; automobile**
adj; f
[ɔtɔmɔbil]
Détroit est célèbre pour son industrie automobile.
 -Detroit is famous for its car industry.

3517 **trajectoire** **path**
f
[tʀaʒɛktwaʀ]
Les nuages bas ont empêché d'identifier le type de l'aéronef, sa nationalité et sa trajectoire de vol.
 -Low clouds prevented the identification of its type, nationality and flight path.

3518 **ciné** **pics**
m
[sine]
Les clubs ont organisé des activités sportives et créé et géré des ciné-clubs.
 -The clubs participated in organizing sports activities and initiating and managing cinema clubs.

3519 **tribord** **starboard**
m
[tʀibɔʀ]
Je confonds toujours quel côté est bâbord et quel côté tribord.
 -I always confuse which side is port and which starboard.

3520 **cuisse** **thigh**
f
[kɥis]
Je vais prendre une cuisse de grenouille pour finir.
 -I'll have one frog leg to go.

3521 **nouille** **noodle|dope; dumb**
f; adj
[nuj]
Regarde... chips, saveur nouilles spécial d'Osaka.
 -Potato chips with special Osaka-noodle flavor.

3522 **rassemblement** **gathering|rally**
m[ʀasɑ̃bləmɑ̃]
Nous avons tendu une embuscade à plusieurs centaines de leurs nouveaux robots J-37 derrière les lignes ennemies dans une zone de rassemblement et nous les avons tous détruits en envoyant un troupeau de moutons chargés d'explosifs à travers leur campement. -We ambushed several hundred of their new J-37 robots behind enemy lines in a staging area and we destroyed them all by sending a herd of explosive laden sheep through their encampment.

3523 **enfoncer** **push|sink**

	vb	Jusqu'à quelle profondeur arrives-tu à t'enfoncer le doigt dans le nez ?
	[ɑ̃fɔ̃se]	-How far can you stick your finger up your nose?
3524	**obscur**	**obscure|dim**
	adj	Le traité de Lisbonne est si obscur qu'il est pratiquement impossible à comprendre.
	[ɔpskyʁ]	-The Treaty of Lisbon is so obscure that it is almost impossible to understand.
3525	**cale**	**hold|wedge**
	f	Je vais jeter un œil à la cale.
	[kal]	-Think I better have a look at the hold.
3526	**psychologique**	**psychological**
	adj	Ils assurent une guidance individuelle médicale, psychologique, paramédicale et sociale.
	[psikɔlɔʒik]	-They provide individual medical, psychological, paramedical and social guidance.
3527	**parapluie**	**umbrella**
	f	Nous trouvâmes le parapluie de Jack.
	[paʁaplɥi]	-We found Jack's umbrella.
3528	**déprimer**	**depress|damp**
	vb	Nous sommes tous déprimés par les événements extrêmement tristes qui se sont succédés dans la région.
	[depʁime]	-It saddens me to note that, in the three short weeks since we last debated this issue, the situation has become worse, not better.
3529	**intrus**	**intruder; intruding**
	m; adj	Nous avons toujours considéré l'Afrique du Sud comme un intrus dans notre pays.
	[ɛ̃tʁy]	-We have always regarded South Africa as an intruder in our country.
3530	**pavillon**	**flag**
	m	La beauté du Pavillon d'Or dans la neige était sans pareil.
	[pavijɔ̃]	-The beauty of the Golden Pavilion covered in snow was unmatched.
3531	**immédiat**	**immediate**
	adj	Toutefois, afin de faciliter le financement immédiat dans les secteurs des ventes et du crédit-bail, il faudrait envisager une période de grâce pour l'inscription.
	[imedja]	-However, in order to facilitate on-the-spot financing in the sales and leasing sectors, a grace period for the filing should be considered.
3532	**surf**	**surf**
	m	Il est allé faire du surf.
	[syʁf]	-He went surfing.
3533	**blâmer**	**blame|censure**
	vb[blame]	En premier lieu, elles sont dues à la poursuite des combats, pour lesquels les Taliban sont seuls à blâmer. -First and foremost is the continuing fighting, for which the Taliban is to blame.
3534	**tabasser**	**beat up**
	vb	Il a des hippies à tabasser.
	[tabase]	-He's got hippies to beat up.
3535	**soulager**	**relieve|alleviate**
	vb	Nous n'hésiterons pas à faire ce qu'il faut chaque fois que nous pourrons soulager son sort.
	[sulaʒe]	-Where we can alleviate their plight, we will spare no effort.
3536	**achat**	**purchase**

m Merci de votre achat.

[aʃa] -Thank you for your purchase!

3537 barreau **bar**

m Courageuse proposition à soumettre au barreau.

[baʁo] -It's a brave proposition for any member of the bar to put.

3538 accélérer **accelerate|expedite**

vb Il était donc essentiel d'accélérer les négociations commerciales

[akseleʁe] multilatérales.

-It was therefore essential to accelerate the multilateral trade negotiations.

3539 shopping **shopping**

m Il en découle une augmentation du " shopping " de l'avortement.

[ʃɔpiŋ] -As a consequence, 'abortion shopping ' is on the increase.

3540 parvenir **get through**

vb J'espère vraiment que le Parlement et le Conseil pourront parvenir à un

[paʁvəniʁ] compromis.

-I very much hope that Parliament and the Council will be able to reach a
compromise.

3541 tapette **pansy**

f On attend, on trouvera un moyen de se faire cette tapette.

[tapɛt] -We sit on it, we gonna figure out a way to get that faggot.

3542 loterie **lottery**

f Jack a-t-il réellement gagné une loterie?

[lɔtʁi] -Did Jack really win a lottery?

3543 allergique **allergic**

adj Or, il semble que ce gouvernement est malheureusement allergique à la

[alɛʁʒik] vérité.

-So, it would appear that this government is unfortunately allergic to the
truth.

3544 spatial **spatial**

adj On doit construire un hélicoptère spatial.

[spasjal] -I think we have to build a space helicopter.

3545 générosité **generosity**

f La grande générosité du public doit être encouragée et appréciée.

[ʒeneʁozite] -The great generosity of people ought to be fostered, encouraged and
appreciated.

3546 convenir **admit|agree with**

vb[kɔ̃vəniʁ] Le chargeur et le destinataire peuvent convenir que le destinataire est la
partie contrôlante; -The shipper and consignee may agree that the
consignee is the controlling party.

3547 confirmation **confirmation|swearing**

f Bonjour, j'ai une réservation, mon nom est Kaori Yoshikawa. Voici la carte

[kɔ̃fiʁmasjɔ̃] de confirmation.

-Hello, I have a reservation, my name is Kaori Yoshikawa. Here is the
confirmation card.

3548 verser **pay|pour**

vb Je ne peux verser une larme pour cet horrible individu.

[vɛʁse] -I cannot shed a tear for that horrible man.

3549 phare **lighthouse|headlight**

m Nous avons vu luire la lueur lointaine d'un phare.

[faʁ] -We saw the gleam of a distant lighthouse.

3550 iris **iris**

	m	Il faudrait fermer l'iris manuellement.
	[iʁis]	-The only way is to manually close the iris.
3551	**primaire**	**primary; primary**
	adj	L'appel des forces odieuses du nationalisme primaire dans l'extrême droite pourrait s'étendre.
	[pʁimɛʁ]	-The appeal of the abhorrent forces of knee-jerk nationalism on the far right may widen.
3552	**suspendre**	**suspend|hang**
	vb	Le Bureau recommande à l'Assemblée de suspendre la session le mardi 5 décembre 2000 au plus tard.
	[syspɑ̃dʁ]	-The General Committee recommends to the Assembly that the fifty-fifth session recess not later than Tuesday, 5 December 2000.
3553	**bouleverser**	**upset|shake**
	vb	M. CHAMMA (Liban) dit que les attaques terroristes du 11 septembre 2001 ont porté un coup à la sécurité et à la stabilité internationales et bouleversé l'économie mondiale.
	[bulvɛʁse]	-Mr. CHAMMA (Lebanon) said that the terrorist attacks on 11 September 2001 had dealt a blow to international security and stability and convulsed the world economy.
3554	**souffler**	**breathe|whisper**
	vb	Il fit souffler sur les dés par sa petite amie, pour lui porter chance, avant qu'il les lance.
	[sufle]	-He had his girlfriend blow on the dice for luck before he threw them.
3555	**câlin**	**hugging; hug**
	adj; m	Jack s'endort presque toujours la nuit en faisant un câlin à son ours en peluche.
	[kalɛ̃]	-Jack almost always falls asleep at night hugging his teddy bear.
3556	**céleste**	**celestial|unworldly**
	adj	C'est un problème de mécanique céleste.
	[selɛst]	-It's a problem in celestial mechanics.
3557	**enchère**	**bid|raise**
	f	En supposant que vous remportiez l'enchère, bien entendu.
	[ɑ̃ʃɛʁ]	-Assuming you win the auction, of course.
3558	**impatience**	**impatience**
	f[ɛ̃pasjɑ̃s]	L' impatience légitime est perceptible, particulièrement dans la population noire. -There is a noticeable, justifiable impatience, particularly among the black population.
3559	**sonnerie**	**ring|bell**
	f	Toutefois, un matin, il y a eu une très longue sonnerie.
	[sɔnʁi]	-However one morning there was a very long ring.
3560	**nounou**	**nanny**
	f	Elle n'a pas de nounou, c'est pourquoi elle ne peut pas se rendre à la fête.
	[nunu]	-She doesn't have a babysitter, so she can't go to the party.
3561	**baise**	**fuck|sex**
	f	Je veux juste une bonne baise.
	[bɛz]	-All I want is a nice, hot fuck.
3562	**veinard**	**lucky**
	adj	Je suis veinard.
	[venaʁ]	-I'm lucky.
3563	**préfet**	**prefect**

	m	Le préfet a été impressionné par votre proposition.
	[pʁefɛ]	-Inspector Javert, the prefect was impressed by your proposal.
3564	**forteresse**	**fortress**
	f	Le siège de la forteresse dura longtemps.
	[fɔʁtəʁɛs]	-The siege of the fortress lasted a long time.
3565	**brutal**	**brutal; brute**
	adj; m	Les victimes tourmentées du terrorisme brutal sont largement oubliées.
	[bʁytal]	-The tormented victims of brutal terrorism are largely forgotten.
3566	**offenser**	**offend|insult**
	vb	C'est là une offense au Parlement de la part du Conseil et nous ne sommes pas prêts à l'accepter.
	[ɔfɑ̃se]	-This is a snub to Parliament by the Council which we are not prepared to accept.
3567	**fourgon**	**van**
	m	Laissez-les partir et revenez au fourgon.
	[fuʁgɔ̃]	-Let them go and come to the van.
3568	**égaler**	**match**
	vb	Il peut être une bonne chose quand les conditions de la concurrence sont égales.
	[egale]	-It can be a good thing when there is a level playing field.
3569	**traduire**	**translate|transpose**
	vb	Ce changement d'attitude doit se traduire par une transparence de l'administration.
	[tʁadɥiʁ]	-This change of attitude should find expression in openness of government.
3570	**dirigeant**	**leader**
	m	Pachahuti fut le neuvième dirigeant de la trilogie inca du Mexique.
	[diʁiʒɑ̃]	-Pachacuti was the ninth ruler of the Inca trilogy of Mexico.
3571	**frappe**	**strike|striking**
	f[fʁap]	Les dispositifs ou logiciels (ou espiogiciels) de reconnaissance de frappe peuvent être utilisés pour enregistrer et passer au crible chaque frappe de touche faite sur un ordinateur individuel. -"Keystroking" devices or software (or spyware) may be used to record and sift every keystroke made on personal computers.
3572	**sentence**	**sentence**
	f	Tu dois mémoriser cette sentence.
	[sɑ̃tɑ̃s]	-You have to memorize this sentence.
3573	**certitude**	**certainty**
	f	Cette façon d'obtenir la certitude est souvent désignée la technique de certitude par « cession ».
	[sɛʁtityd]	-This is often referred to as the "release, and surrender" certainty technique.
3574	**ail**	**garlic**
	m	On vous fera manger du pain frotté à l'ail. On y mettra un petit peu d'huile d'olive.
	[aj]	-You will be made to eat bread rubbed with garlic, with a little olive oil on top.
3575	**ski**	**ski**
	m	Pistes de ski, remontées mécaniques et téléphériques et aménagements associés.
	[ski]	-Ski runs, ski lifts and cable cars and associated developments.
3576	**absoudre**	**absolve**

	vb [apsudʁ]	Ne permettez-vous pas, ce faisant, aux forces destructrices de s'absoudre elles-mêmes ? -In doing so, are you not enabling the forces of destruction to absolve themselves?

3577 abeille — **bee**

f
[abɛj]

L'ambulance t'a amené directement ici après que l'abeille t'ai piquée.
 -The ambulance brought you here right out after the bee stung you.

3578 composer — **compose|make up**

vb
[kɔ̃poze]

J'aimerais composer quelques musiques pour la pièce.
 -I would like to compose some music for the play.

3579 garer — **park**

vb
[gaʁe]

Il est interdit de se garer sur un passage protégé ou la zone marquée par des lignes blanches en zigzag.
 -You MUST NOT park on a crossing or in the area covered by the zigzag lines.

3580 quatorze — **fourteen**

num
[katɔʁz]

Je pensais que nous avions jusqu'à quatorze heures trente pour terminer ceci.
 -I thought we had until 14:30 to finish this.

3581 calmement — **calmly**

adv
[kalməmɑ̃]

Les huissiers se sont comportés calmement et avec professionnalisme et méritent notre respect.
 -The ushers behave very calmly and professionally and deserve our respect.

3582 veau — **calf|veal**

m
[vo]

Le boucher dépeça la carcasse du veau.
 -The butcher cut up the calf's carcass.

3583 tâche — **task**

f[taʃ]

On nous a demandé d'accomplir une tâche, et cette tâche n'est pas encore achevée. -We have been directed to do a job, and that job is not yet complete.

3584 attraction — **attraction|pull**

f
[atʁaksjɔ̃]

On appelle cela l'attraction esthétique, parce qu'on considère que c'est similaire aux autres désirs esthétiques, tels que le désir de continuer à écouter une bonne chanson ou de continuer à regarder un beau coucher de soleil.
 -This is called aesthetic attraction because it is thought to be similar to other aesthetic desires, such as the desire to keep listening to a good song or to keep looking at a beautiful sunset.

3585 sécher — **dry|cure**

vb
[seʃe]

Couper, laver et sécher, s'il vous plaît.
 -Cut, wash and dry, please.

3586 louper — **miss out on**

vb
[lupe]

Je ne l'ai pas loupée une seule fois en 30 ans.
 -For 30 years I have made sure that I do not miss it.

3587 palace — **palace**

m
[palas]

Bienvenue à votre palace, madame.
 -Welcome back to your palace, madam.

3588 nœud — **node|knot**

m
[nø]

Par quel nœud faut-il commencer pour pouvoir défaire tous les autres ?
 -Which knot should be untangled first in order to untangle other relevant knots?

3589	**trophée**	**trophy**
	m	Il brandit bien haut le trophée.
	[tʁɔfe]	-He held the trophy up high.
3590	**compréhension**	**comprehension**
	f	Nous vous sommes reconnaissants pour votre compréhension.
	[kɔ̃pʁeɑ̃sjɔ̃]	-We appreciate your understanding.
3591	**intrigue**	**plot**
	f	Votre façon de penser m'intrigue.
	[ɛ̃tʁig]	-Your way of thinking intrigues me.
3592	**téléphonique**	**telephone**
	adj	Il assure la desserte téléphonique de tous les bâtiments se trouvant dans
	[telefɔnik]	l'enceinte du Secrétariat;
		-This facility provides telephonic services to all Secretariat area buildings.
3593	**berceau**	**cradle|bed**
	m	L'espoir est le bâton de marche, depuis le berceau jusqu'à la tombe.
	[bɛʁso]	-Hope is the walking stick, from the cradle to the grave.
3594	**mépriser**	**despise|disregard**
	vb	Personne n'a le droit de mépriser un autre être humain, surtout le plus
	[mepʁize]	faible.
		-No one has the right to despise another human being, least of all one weaker than oneself.
3595	**dément**	**demented|insane**
	adj	Seul un homme dément ferait ça, il doit donc être sain d'esprit.
	[demɑ̃]	-Only an insane man would do that, so he must have been and still is sane.
3596	**satisfaction**	**satisfaction**
	f[satisfaksjɔ̃]	La satisfaction des politiques ne devrait être que celle des peuples. - Politicians' satisfaction should be dependent on the satisfaction of the people.
3597	**déterminer**	**determine**
	vb	Ces émissions, et d'autres encore, devraient déterminer les critères de
	[detɛʁmine]	notification.
		-These and other uses should determine the character of reporting requirements.
3598	**chimique**	**chemical**
	adj	Le langage chimique est universel, chaque formule chimique est unique.
	[ʃimik]	-The language of chemistry is universal, and each chemical formula is unique.
3599	**premièrement**	**firstly**
	adv	Premièrement, renforcer la gouvernance économique et amorcer le
	[pʁəmjɛʁmɑ̃]	semestre européen.
		-Firstly, strengthening economic governance and initiating the European Semester.
3600	**préparation**	**preparation**
	f	Il a échoué à l'examen, faute de préparation.
	[pʁepaʁasjɔ̃]	-He failed the exam due to a lack of preparation.
3601	**servante**	**servant|maid**
	f	Je ne suis pas votre servante.
	[sɛʁvɑ̃t]	-I'm not your maid.
3602	**rancune**	**grudge|rancor**
	f	Je ne garde pas rancune.
	[ʁɑ̃kyn]	-I don't hold grudges.

3603	**économiser**	**save|conserve**
	vb	D'abord sur la question «économiser pour Maastricht».
	[ekɔnɔmize]	-Firstly, there is the question of having to economize because of Maastricht.
3604	**logement**	**housing|accommodation**
	m	Je veux que vous preniez votre propre logement.
	[lɔʒmã]	-I want you to get your own place.
3605	**générateur**	**generator; generating**
	m; adj	Unité d'alimentation de pile à combustible, un générateur d'électricité, sans cartouche.
	[ʒeneʁatœʁ]	-Fuel cell power unit means an electric generating device without a cartridge.
3606	**paiement**	**payment|payoff**
	m	Il exige le paiement immédiat.
	[pɛmã]	-He demands immediate payment.
3607	**semer**	**sow**
	vb	Le péché semer davantage de personnes et plus il semble tout va bien.
	[səme]	-The more people sow sin and the more it seems everything is fine.
3608	**confesser**	**confess**
	vb	Je veux me confesser.
	[kɔ̃fese]	-I want to confess.
3609	**fondu**	**molten**
	adj[fɔ̃dy]	Cette opération consiste à refroidir de manière contrôlée le chocolat préalablement fondu. -Tempering is the controlled cooling of previously melted chocolate.
3610	**solde**	**balance**
	m	Peux-tu me dire mon solde ?
	[sɔld]	-Could you tell me my balance?
3611	**grossesse**	**pregnancy**
	f	La contraception est moins chère que la grossesse.
	[gʁosɛs]	-Contraception is cheaper than pregnancy.
3612	**ghetto**	**ghetto**
	m	Ses ouvriers juifs venaient du ghetto.
	[geto]	-His Jewish workers came to work from the ghetto.
3613	**encaisser**	**cash**
	vb	Je voudrais encaisser un chèque voyageur.
	[ãkese]	-I'd like to cash a travelers' check.
3614	**banane**	**banana**
	f	As-tu déjà mangé une tarte à la banane ?
	[banan]	-Have you ever eaten a banana pie?
3615	**embuscade**	**ambush|fall**
	f	Des témoins oculaires se sont dits convaincus d'être tombés dans une embuscade.
	[ãbyskad]	-Eyewitnesses said unequivocally that they had been caught in an ambush.
3616	**sévère**	**severe|strict**
	adj	Le père de Jack est très sévère.
	[sevɛʁ]	-Jack's father is very strict.
3617	**percer**	**drill|pierce**
	vb	Elles sont comme un rayon de soleil parvenant à percer les ténèbres les plus
	[pɛʁse]	obscures.

-They are like a sun whose rays manage to break through the utmost darkness.

3618	**emballer**	**pack|package**
	vb	Voulons -nous réduire de 10 % la production industrielle totale de biens à emballer?
	[ãbale]	-Do we intend to reduce by 10 % the industrial production of goods that need to be packaged?

3619	**trousse**	**kit**
	f	Le service de police n'avait même pas une trousse d'empreintes digitales.
	[tʁus]	-The police department didn't even have a fingerprint kit.

3620	**embarrassant**	**embarrassing**
	adj	Dans un tel contexte, les conseils risquent d'être embarrassants pour toutes les parties intéressées.
	[ãbaʁasã]	-Counselling in such a setting may be awkward for all parties.

3621	**institution**	**institution**
	f	Le Sénat n'est pas une institution fédérale; c'est une institution canadienne.
	[ẽstitysjõ]	-The Senate is not a federal institution, but a Canadian institution.

3622	**chargement**	**loading|charge**
	m	Les enfants devaient faire le chargement.
	[ʃaʁʒəmã]	-The kids were supposed to do the loading.

| 3623 | **crâner** | **show off** |
| | vb[kʁane] | Pas besoin de crâner, fils. -You needn't brag, son. |

3624	**croissance**	**growth|growing**
	f	Un enfant en pleine croissance qui n'a pas beaucoup d'énergie a peut-être besoin de soins médicaux.
	[kʁwasãs]	-A growing child who doesn't seem to have much energy perhaps needs medical attention.

3625	**Ohé!**	**Yoo-Hoo!**
	int	Et tout en remerciant l'Assemblée pour son attention, il ne me reste plus qu'à crier « Ohé du navire !
	[ɔe!]	-In thanking the House for its attention, all I can say now is 'ship ahoy!'

3626	**consister**	**consist**
	vb	Le comportement attribuable à l'État peut consister en une action ou une omission.
	[kõsiste]	-Conduct attributable to the State can consist of actions or omissions.

3627	**alimentation**	**supply|food**
	f	Les fruits et les légumes sont essentiels à une alimentation équilibrée.
	[alimãtasjõ]	-Fruits and vegetables are essential to a balanced diet.

3628	**indigne**	**unworthy**
	adj	Il considère indigne de lui de traduire des phrases aussi simples.
	[ẽdiɲ]	-He finds it undignified to translate such simple phrases.

3629	**repousser**	**repel|fend off**
	vb	Nous devons vivre avec les déchets que nous produisons, et nous ne pouvons pas faire repousser rapidement les arbres que nous abattons.
	[ʁəpuse]	-We must live with the waste that we make, and we cannot quickly grow back the trees that we cut.

3630	**flanc**	**flank**
	m	Il y avait un cottage sur le flanc de la colline.
	[flã]	-There was a cottage on the side of the hill.

| 3631 | **violet** | **purple; purple** |

adj; m | Si on mélange du bleu et du rouge, on obtient du violet.
[vjɔlɛ] | -If you mix blue and red, you'll get purple.

3632 **nuque** — **neck**

f | Il a la nuque brisée.
[nyk] | -His neck is broken.

3633 **bouchon** — **plug|cork**

m | Pousse pas le bouchon !
[buʃɔ̃] | -Don't push it.

3634 **tigre** — **tiger**

m | C'est au cours de la période glaciaire que le tigre à dents de sabre s'est éteint.
[tigʁ] | -It was during the ice age that the saber-toothed tiger became extinct.

3635 **croisière** — **cruise**

f | Le bateau de croisière est en train de couler.
[kʁwazjɛʁ] | -The cruise ship is sinking.

3636 **horaire** — **schedule**

m | Nous avons soigneusement programmé nos demandes compte tenu de son horaire.
[ɔʁɛʁ] | -We have carefully scheduled our requests to work around their schedule.

3637 **reproche** — **reproach|rebuke**

m[ʁəpʁɔʃ] | Ce n'est pas un reproche à l'adresse du président Prodi ou de la Commission, puisque, assurément, la Commission travaille, ou plutôt elle s'occupe, devrais -je dire. -I do not say this as a rebuke to President Prodi or the Commission, because the Commission is most certainly working or, should I say, making itself busy.

3638 **têtu** — **stubborn|headstrong**

adj | Il est évident que les réformistes sont pour la plupart trop têtus pour abandonner jamais leur position anti-français.
[tety] | -It is clear that most Reform members are too hard-headed to ever drop their anti-French stance.

3639 **pelouse** — **lawn**

f | Il est en train de tondre sa pelouse.
[pəluz] | -He's mowing his lawn.

3640 **commencement** — **beginning|start**

m | C'est un moment historique, le commencement d'une nouvelle ère pour l'Union européenne.
[kɔmɑ̃smɑ̃] | -It is an historic moment, the start of a new era for the European Union.

3641 **parfaire** — **perfect**

vb | Ils arrivent à parfaire cette technologie, et se rapprochent de nous.
[paʁfɛʁ] | -They perfect this technology, and they can get close to us.

3642 **calcul** — **calculation|calculus**

m | J'ai fait un calcul rapide.
[kalkyl] | -I calculated hastily.

3643 **répondeur** — **answering machine**

m | S'il vous plait laissez un message sur mon répondeur.
[ʁepɔ̃dœʁ] | -Please leave your message on my answering machine.

3644 **emplacement** — **location|site**

m | Je cherche l'emplacement idéal pour accrocher ce tableau.
[ɑ̃plasmɑ̃] | -I'm looking for the perfect spot to hang this picture.

3645 **reprocher** — **reproach|blame**

	vb	C'est à tous ceux-là et à nous-mêmes qu'il faut reprocher l'état actuel des choses.
	[ʀəpʀɔʃe]	-It is they who are to blame for this state of affairs.

3646 excès — **excess; excess; debauchery**
adj; m; mpl
[ɛksɛ]
L'excès de travail l'a tué.
-Overworking was the death of him.

3647 cocaïne — **cocaine**
f
[kɔkain]
Il est dépendant à la cocaïne.
-He is addicted to cocaine.

3648 déclencher — **trigger | start**
vb
[deklɑ̃ʃe]
Les autorités envisagent-elles de déclencher des enquêtes sur ces allégations ?
-Do the authorities plan to launch investigations into these allegations?

3649 sonnette — **doorbell | buzzer**
f
[sɔnɛt]
Ils ont tiré la sonnette d'alarme afin que nous traitions ces questions plus sérieusement.
-They have given us an important wake-up call to look at these issues more seriously.

3650 ignorance — **ignorance**
f[iɲɔʀɑ̃s]
Autrement, les députés voteront en toute ignorance. -Otherwise I believe members will be voting from a base of ignorance.

3651 scoop — **scoop**
m
[skɔo]
Ce n'est quand même pas un scoop.
-It is not a scoop.

3652 qualifier — **qualify**
vb
[kalifje]
D'un autre côté, on a dit que le terme «néfaste» devrait qualifier cet impact.
-On the other hand, it was suggested that the term "adverse" should qualify such impact.

3653 dot — **dowry**
f
[dɔt]
La dot est illégale au Bangladesh depuis l'adoption de la loi sur l'interdiction de la dot en 1980.
-Dowry has been illegal in Bangladesh since the passing of the Dowry Prohibition Act in 1980.

3654 repriser — **darn | mend**
vb
[ʀəpʀize]
Je vais si bien repriser votre col que ce ne sera même plus visible.
-I will mend it so no one can see it.

3655 affirmer — **assert | assure**
vb
[afiʀme]
Affirmer que la démocratie exige une participation active des jeunes.
-Affirm that democracy demands an active participation of young people.

3656 secouer — **shake | rock**
vb
[səkwe]
Nous espérons, Monsieur Patijn, que vous saurez secouer tous les gouvernements européens.
-And Mr Patijn, we hope you will be able to shake up the European countries.

3657 vouer — **devote**
vb
[vwe]
Nous savons pourquoi le Gouvernement des États-Unis ne cesse de vouer Cuba aux gémonies.
-We know why the United States Government continues to seek to stigmatize Cuba.

3658 aviation — **aviation | air force**
f
[avjasjɔ̃]
Les soldats de la marine et de l'aviation passent par un processus de sélection.

-Soldiers in the navy and the air force go through a selection process for their service.

3659	relâche f [ʁəlaʃ]	respite Une série de mesures à court terme peuvent être prises rapidement afin de relâcher la pression. -A number of short-term measures can be taken quickly to ease the situation.
3660	tentation f [tɑ̃tasjɔ̃]	temptation Elle n'a pas pu résister à la tentation. -She could not resist the temptation.
3661	imposteur m [ɛ̃pɔstœʁ]	impostor Jack est un imposteur. -Jack is an imposter.
3662	corriger vb[kɔʁiʒe]	correct|right Face à ce crime horrible, que pouvons-nous faire pour corriger cette injustice ? -In the face of this horrific crime, what can we possibly do to right the wrong?
3663	embarquement m [ɑ̃baʁkəmɑ̃]	boarding|shipping Veuillez me présenter votre passeport et votre carte d'embarquement, s'il vous plait. -Please let me see your passport and boarding pass.
3664	défier vb [defje]	challenge|defy L'Iraq continue à défier la volonté de la communauté internationale de le voir désarmer. -Iraq continues to defy the will of the international community to see it disarmed.
3665	cerf m [sɛʁ]	deer|stag Je l'ai envoyé chercher le cerf. -I sent him to look for the deer.
3666	teindre vb [tɛ̃dʁ]	dye J'ai proposé il y a dix ans de teindre tous les produits d'origine incertaine. -My proposal ten years ago was for all products of uncertain origin to be dyed.
3667	paresseux adj; m [paʁesø]	lazy; sloth Ne sois pas si paresseux ! -Don't be so lazy.
3668	Hou! int [u!]	Boo! "Hou ! Regardez-moi, je saigne." -"Ooh, look at me, I'm bleeding."
3669	bridge m [bʁidʒ]	bridge Trop occupée à jouer au bridge. -You're too busy running around playing bridge.
3670	exercer vb [ɛgzɛʁse]	exercise|exert Toutefois, entre-temps, d'autres États devraient exercer leur droit souverain de ratifier le traité. -But meanwhile other states should exercise their sovereign right to ratify this Treaty.
3671	bouffon m; adj [bufɔ̃]	buffoon; fool Voici le bouffon qui se fait appeler le Tueur n° 2. -The buffoon who calls himself Killer 2.
3672	tendresse	tenderness|kindness

f
[tɑ̃dʁɛs]

Vous les avez remerciés avec votre tendresse et vos gâteaux Banbury.
-You thank them with your tenderness and your Banbury cakes.

3673 barque
f
[baʁk]

bark|small boat
Puis il monta vers eux dans la barque, et le vent cessa » (Marc 6 : 50-51).
-Then he climbed into the boat with them, and the wind died down." (Mark 6:50-51)

3674 peloton
m
[pəlɔtɔ̃]

pack
Réorganisez votre peloton volant avec Windridge.
-Bromhead, reorganise your flying platoon with Sgt Windridge.

3675 cycle
m[sikl]

cycle
J'espère que le décalage horaire ne va pas trop perturber mon cycle de sommeil. -I hope that the jet lag isn't going to disturb my sleep schedule too much.

3676 égout
m
[egu]

sewer|drain
La canalisation d'égout a explosé.
-The sewer pipe exploded.

3677 hanche
f
[ɑ̃ʃ]

hip
En matière d'accès aux projets, on tire incidemment à la hauteur de la hanche.
-With the intake of new projects we are shooting randomly from the hip.

3678 songer
vb
[sɔ̃ʒe]

reflect|wonder
Elle nous donne également la possibilité de songer à l'avenir de l'humanité au troisième millénaire.
-It also provides us with an opportunity to dream about the future of humanity in the third millennium.

3679 sympathie
f
[sɛ̃pati]

sympathy
Vous avez ma sympathie.
-You have my sympathies.

3680 déguiser
vb
[degize]

dissemble
Le choix d'appliquer ou non les règles n'est qu'un artifice pour déguiser cette réalité.
-The choice of whether to apply the rules is only a fig leaf to disguise that reality.

3681 terrifiant
adj
[teʁifjɑ̃]

terrifying
Le problème soulevé dans la première partie de la question est absolument terrifiant.
-The issue raised in the first part of the question is absolutely terrifying.

3682 alternative
f
[altɛʁnativ]

alternative
Vous recherchez une approche alternative plus holistique, je suppose.
-I assume you're looking for a more holistic, alternative approach.

3683 achever
vb
[aʃve]

finish|conclude
Mesures à prendre: Le SBSTA est invité à achever l'examen de ces documents.
-Action: The SBSTA is invited to complete its consideration of these documents.

3684 ironie
f
[iʁɔni]

irony
L'ironie dans tout cela c'est que le secteur public vote pour le Parti libéral.
-The irony of the whole thing is that the public sector votes Liberal.

3685 coupure
f; adj
[kupyʁ]

cut; clipping
Il y a eu une coupure d'électricité, mais maintenant c'est revenu.
-The electricity went out, but it's back on now.

3686	**céréale** f [seʁeal]	**cereal|fruit** Préparation industrielle de produits alimentaires, en particulier de grains de céréale. -The invention can be used in the industrial preparation of food products, in particular of cereal grains.
3687	**pâte** f [pat]	**paste** La pâte est cuite pour convertir la pâte en un produit intermédiaire. -The paste is cooked to convert the paste into an intermediate product.
3688	**excepté** prp[ɛksɛpte]	**except** Les mutilations génitales des femmes restent rares - excepté dans les régions côtières. -Female genital mutilation was not widely performed, except in coastal regions.
3689	**comptant** adj [kɔ̃tã]	**spot|cash** Le type le plus fréquent nécessitait un paiement au comptant. -The most frequent type of transaction required a cash purchase.
3690	**promis** adj [pʁɔmi]	**promised** On leur avait tant promis, on leur avait beaucoup promis et on n'a pas tenu beaucoup. -They were promised so much, they were promised a lot, and these promises were not kept.
3691	**ruisseau** m [ʁɥiso]	**stream|creek** Le bateau blanc a descendu le ruisseau. -The white boat went down the stream.
3692	**baratin** m [baʁatɛ̃]	**spiel|flannel** Il a vraiment fait gober son baratin à ma fille. -He did a real snow job on my daughter.
3693	**hamburger** m [ãbyʁʒe]	**hamburger** J'ai mangé un hamburger et j'en ai commandé encore un. -I ate a hamburger and ordered another.
3694	**évêque** m [evɛk]	**bishop** Les mécréants se sont gaussés de l'interprétation faite par l'évêque. -The irreligious scoffed at the bishop's interpretation.
3695	**bénéfice** m [benefis]	**profit|income** La société humaine est une fonction de toute l'humanité. Ceux qui en profitent le plus devraient payer le plus pour le bénéfice qu'ils en retirent. Bien sûr, étant cupides, ils en veulent simplement davantage. -Human society is a function of all humanity, those who profit most from it should pay the most for the benefit they gain, of course being greedy, they just want more.
3696	**recommander** vb [ʁəkɔmãde]	**recommend** À la 2e séance, le 24 avril, le Comité spécial a décidé de recommander -At the 2nd meeting, on 24 April, the Ad Hoc Committee decided to recommend that ….
3697	**légalement** adv [legalmã]	**legally** Dans de tels cas des coefficients réducteurs fixés légalement sont appliqués. -In such a case, reduction coefficients established by law will also be applied.
3698	**combattant** m; adj [kɔ̃batã]	**fighter; fighting** Il contribue à combattre la discrimination et à réduire la vulnérabilité des gens. -It contributes to combat discrimination and decrease people's vulnerability.

3699	**clochette**	**bell**
	f	Elle porte une clochette comme ça.
	[klɔʃɛt]	-She's wearing a bell like this one.
3700	**passionner**	**fascinate**
	vb[pasjɔne]	À mon avis, cette personne doit se passionner pour l'intérêt supérieur du Canada. -In my mind, this person must have a passion for what is best for Canada.
3701	**miette**	**crumb**
	f	Il y a une miette dans sa barbe.
	[mjɛt]	-There is a crumb in his beard.
3702	**olive**	**olive**
	f	Donne-moi l'huile d'olive.
	[ɔliv]	-Give me the olive oil.
3703	**dizaine**	**about ten|decade**
	f	Tout d'abord, les manifestants étaient très peu nombreux: ils n'étaient qu'une dizaine.
	[dizɛn]	-First of all, there were very few demonstrators, only about ten.
3704	**largement**	**widely**
	adv	Ces dispositions reflétaient des considérations largement admises et raisonnables.
	[laʁʒəmɑ̃]	-The provisions reflected largely accepted and reasonable considerations.
3705	**bonnet**	**cap**
	m	Et portez un bonnet de bain.
	[bɔnɛ]	-And be sure to wear a bathing cap.
3706	**dépit**	**spite**
	m	En dépit de sa dimension géographique, le message de cette campagne est universel.
	[depi]	-In spite of its geographical scope, the message of the campaign is universal.
3707	**hypothèse**	**hypothesis**
	f	On attribue la fuite à mes collaborateurs, mais ce n'est qu'une hypothèse.
	[ipɔtɛz]	-It is an assumption to say that my office staff was responsible for the leak.
3708	**fantasmer**	**fantasize**
	vb	Surtout éviter de fantasmer sur une personne qui réunit toutes ces caractéristiques.
	[fɑ̃tasme]	-And especially will not fantasize... about a particular person who embodies all these things.
3709	**loué**	**rented|leased**
	adj	Le locataire a le droit d'utiliser le logement loué conformément aux prescriptions du contrat.
	[lwe]	-For rented residence, the lessee has the right to use the rented house as stated in the contract.
3710	**hémorragie**	**hemorrhage**
	f	Le médecin fut finalement en mesure d'enrayer l'hémorragie.
	[emɔʁaʒi]	-The doctor was finally able to stanch the flow of blood.
3711	**milord**	**milord**
	m	Nous sommes presque prêts, milord.
	[milɔʁ]	-Well, we're almost ready, milord.
3712	**boom**	**boom**
	m	No one ever thought, for example, that the steel industry would suddenly boom again.
	[bum]	

-Personne n'aurait cru, par exemple, que la sidérurgie connaîtrait un nouvel essor.

3713	**abus**	**abuse**
	m[aby]	Cette catégorie de travailleurs est particulièrement vulnérable aux abus des employeurs. -I think that this category of worker is particularly vulnerable to abuse from employers.
3714	**soulagement**	**relief|solace**
	m [sulaʒmã]	Il poussa un soupir de soulagement. -He gave a sigh of relief.
3715	**célébrité**	**celebrity|stardom**
	f [selebʁite]	Les auteurs de graffitis sont clairement à la recherche de la célébrité. -The perpetrators of graffiti are clearly seeking fame and notoriety.
3716	**gaze**	**gauze; gauze**
	adj; f [gaz]	J'ai commencé à recouvrir la blessure avec de la gaze. -Just started packing the wound with gauze.
3717	**injection**	**injection**
	f [ɛ̃ʒɛksjɔ̃]	Each time all of the TBOs were given an injection in their left and right hips. -Chaque fois, chaque TBO recevait une piqûre à la hanche droite et à la hanche gauche.
3718	**générer**	**generate**
	vb [ʒeneʁe]	L'utilisation d'un système de freinage d'endurance doit générer le signal susmentionné. -Operation of an endurance braking system shall generate the signal mentioned above.
3719	**présidence**	**presidency**
	f [pʁezidãs]	Je veux être candidat à la présidence. -I want to run for president.
3720	**spectateur**	**spectator|onlooker**
	m [spɛktatœʁ]	Ou bien encore sommes-nous un spectateur qui regarde les événements sans s'y mêler ? -Or are we, perhaps, just a bystander, watching what is going on without getting involved?
3721	**soupir**	**sigh**
	m [supiʁ]	Il rendit son dernier soupir. -He breathed his last.
3722	**néant**	**nothingness**
	m [neã]	D'où la peur du néant, et les étudiants de Louvain vous l'ont dit. -Hence the fear of nothingness, as the Louvain students made clear to you.
3723	**hospitalité**	**hospitality**
	f [ɔspitalite]	Hospitalité ici, hospitalité et respect là-bas. -Hospitality over here and hospitality and respect over there.
3724	**couder**	**bend**
	vb [kude]	Les fils laminés, qu'il est possible de couder librement à la main, possèdent une résistance préétablie à la rupture par traction. -The wire rods can be bent freely by hand and has a predetermined tensile strength.
3725	**écureuil**	**squirrel**
	m [ekyʁœj]	S'il te plaît, maman ! Je veux un écureuil en pain d'épices ! -Please mom, I want a gingerbread squirrel!
3726	**arrogant**	**arrogant**

adj[aʁɔgɑ̃]   Vous êtes arrogant. -You're arrogant.

3727   **organisme**   **organization**

m

[ɔʁganism]   Cet organisme joue un rôle de premier plan dans la préservation de la vie sauvage.
-The organization plays a principal role in wildlife conservation.

3728   **revivre**   **relive**

vb

[ʁəvivʁ]   Nous devons nous rappeler les horreurs de l'histoire si nous ne voulons pas les revivre.
-We need to remember the horrors of history if we do not want to relive them.

3729   **gorille**   **gorilla**

m

[gɔʁij]   Un reporter est en train d'interviewer Docteur Patterson à propos de Koko, un gorille parlant.
-A reporter is interviewing Dr. Patterson about Koko, a talking gorilla.

3730   **morphine**   **morphine**

f

[mɔʁfin]   Maintenant, seule la morphine les aide.
-The only thing that's helping them right now is the morphine.

3731   **andouille**   **dummy**

f

[ɑ̃duj]   C'est une andouille de première classe, intrinsèquement apathique et incapable de penser rationnellement.
-She is a massive dimwit and inherently apathetic and incapable of rational thought.

3732   **redevenir**   **become again**

vb

[ʁədəvəniʁ]   Seule la Constitution permettra à l'UE de redevenir attractive aux yeux de l'opinion publique, d'être plus compréhensible et plus responsable.
-The Constitution alone will enable the EU to become, again, attractive to the public, for Europe will become more comprehensible and more responsible.

3733   **batteur**   **drummer|batter**

m

[batœʁ]   Actuellement, c'est notre meilleur batteur.
-Currently, he's our best batter.

3734   **réconfort**   **comfort|reassurance**

m

[ʁekɔ̃fɔʁ]   Ce réconfort transforme parfois notre peine en joie.
-With such a comfort, our very grief may turn to joy.

3735   **disciple**   **disciple**

m

[disipl]   Si quelqu'un vient à moi, et s'il ne hait pas son père, sa mère, sa femme, ses enfants, ses frères, et ses sœurs, et même sa propre vie, il ne peut être mon disciple.
-If any man come to me, and hate not his father, and mother, and wife, and children, and brethren, and sisters, yea, and his own life also, he cannot be my disciple.

3736   **minuscule**   **tiny|lowercase; minuscule**

adj; f

[minyskyl]   Cet exemple n'en est qu'un parmi d'autres, une minuscule composante du gouvernement du Canada.
-This is only one example, a minuscule part of the Government of Canada.

3737   **suédois**   **Swedish; Swedish**

adj; m

[sɥedwa]   Vous pouvez comprendre le suédois.
-You can understand Swedish.

3738   **présentation**   **presentation**

f[pʁezɑ̃tasjɔ̃]   Le professeur a donné une présentation sur l'histoire de France. -The professor gave a presentation on French history.

3739   **trompette**   **trumpet|trumpeter**

	f	Je l'ai souvent entendu jouer la mélodie à la trompette.
	[tʁɔ̃pɛt]	-I often heard him playing the melody on the trumpet.
3740	**disposer**	**dispose|arrange**
	vb	Échantillons de la signature des personnes autorisées à disposer des fonds.
	[dispoze]	-Specimens of the signatures of the persons authorized to dispose of the assets on the account.
3741	**baleine**	**whale**
	f	J'ai vu la queue d'une baleine, aujourd'hui.
	[balɛn]	-I saw a whale tail today.
3742	**crépuscule**	**dusk; dusk**
	adj; m	Jack et Jill firent l'amour passionnément sur la plage au crépuscule.
	[kʁepyskyl]	-Jack and Jill made love passionately on the beach at sunset.
3743	**trêve**	**truce**
	f	Nous ne voulons pas simplement une trêve provisoire, mais une trêve permanente, une trêve active.
	[tʁɛv]	-We do not simply aspire to a momentary truce, but to a continuous truce, an active truce.
3744	**inscription**	**registration|entry**
	f	Lors de votre inscription dans les universités américaines, votre note au TOEFL n'est qu'un des facteurs pris en compte.
	[ɛ̃skʁipsjɔ̃]	-When applying to American universities, your TOEFL score is only one factor.
3745	**ôter**	**remove**
	vb	Il persuada les autorités municipales d'ôter le manche de la pompe du puits.
	[ote]	-He persuaded the authorities to remove the handle from the pump on the well.
3746	**conception**	**design|designing**
	f	Les calculs de conception doivent être utilisés pour justifier que la conception est adaptée.
	[kɔ̃sɛpsjɔ̃]	-Design calculations shall be used to provide justification of design adequacy.
3747	**western**	**western**
	m	Ce matin nous tournons un western.
	[wɛstɛʁn]	-We're filming a western in the morning.
3748	**poussin**	**chick**
	m	Un oeuf a exactement 1/2 l'information génétique qu'il doit devenir un poussin.
	[pusɛ̃]	-An egg has exactly 1/2 the genetic information it needs to become a chick.
3749	**peigne**	**comb**
	m	Assieds-toi que je peigne tes cheveux.
	[pɛɲ]	-Come sit down and I'll comb your hair.
3750	**vicieux**	**vicious; lecher**
	adj; m	Je me suis retrouvé piégé dans un cercle vicieux.
	[visjø]	-I was trapped in a vicious circle.
3751	**habituel**	**usual|regular**
	adj[abityɛl]	Il n'est pas habituel pour ce Parlement de voter sur un exposé des motifs. -However, it is not customary for Parliament to vote on explanatory statements.
3752	**contenter**	**satisfy**
	vb	Nous considérons toutefois qu'il s'agit là d'un point de départ, dont nous ne pouvons nous contenter.
	[kɔ̃tãte]	

-But we see this just as a starting point and not something with which we should be content.

3753	**révolte**	**revolt|mutiny**
	f	En Argentine, c'est la révolte populaire qui a stoppé l'ultra-libéralisme.
	[ʁevɔlt]	-In Argentina, it was a popular revolt of the people that brought to a halt of ultra liberalism.
3754	**cardinal**	**cardinal; cardinal**
	adj; m	Vous pourriez éventrer ce cher cardinal.
	[kaʁdinal]	-Well, you could disembowel the dear cardinal.
3755	**sapin**	**pine**
	m	Dans notre forêt méditerranéenne, il y a beaucoup d'arbres: chêne, sapin, saule, frêne, orme, etc.
	[sapɛ̃]	-In our Mediterranean forest, there are lots of trees: oak, pine, willow, ash, elm, etc..
3756	**rein**	**kidney**
	m	Par exemple, la grande majorité des gens sur les listes attendent un rein.
	[ʁɛ̃]	-For example, the vast majority of people on the list are waiting for a kidney.
3757	**supprimer**	**remove|suppress**
	vb	Comment est-ce que je fais pour supprimer ce fichier ?
	[sypʁime]	-How do I delete this file?
3758	**paniquer**	**panic**
	vb	Maintenant, ne panique pas.
	[panike]	-Now, don't freak out.
3759	**limonade**	**lemonade**
	f	Une nouvelle maladie est apparue en Grande-Bretagne, pire que l'ESB; il s'agit de la limonade alcoolisée.
	[limɔnad]	-There is a disease now in Britain worse than BSE - it is called alcoholic lemonade.
3760	**prophétie**	**prophecy**
	f	Ils veulent que la prophétie défaitiste du choc des civilisations devienne réalité.
	[pʁɔfesi]	-They want to make the clash of civilizations a self-fulfilling prophecy.
3761	**buffet**	**buffet|dresser**
	m	Les places assises dans les wagons restaurant/buffet sont exclues
	[byfɛ]	-Seats in dining coaches and buffet compartments places are excluded.
3762	**confiture**	**jam**
	f	Jill fait de la confiture.
	[kɔ̃fityʁ]	-Jill is making jam.
3763	**manipuler**	**handle|manipulate**
	vb	Les munitions et les explosifs sont en soi plus dangereux à manipuler que les armes inertes.
	[manipyle]	-Ammunition and explosives are inherently more dangerous to handle than inert weapons.
3764	**vulnérable**	**vulnerable**
	adj	Petite île, Singapour est vulnérable aux effets des changements climatiques.
	[vylneʁabl]	-As a small island, Singapore is vulnerable to the effects of climate change.
3765	**tombeau**	**tomb**
	m	Il en était ainsi, sur le mont Sion, du Cénacle et du tombeau de David.
	[tɔ̃bo]	-This was the case of the Room of the Last Supper and the Tomb of David, on Mount Zion.
3766	**performance**	**performance**

	f [pɛʀfɔʀmɑ̃s]	Je fus ravi par la performance du groupe. -I was enchanted by the performance of the group.
3767	**appui** m [apɥi]	**support|rest** Il a l'appui d'un certain politicien. -He has the backing of a certain politician.
3768	**septième** num [sɛtjɛm]	**seventh** La Présidente prononce la clôture de la quarante-septième session de la Commission. -The Chairperson declared closed the forty-seventh session of the Commission.
3769	**tremblement** m [tʀɑ̃bləmɑ̃]	**trembling|tremor** Le tremblement de terre a tout détruit. -The earthquake smashed everything.
3770	**lécher** vb [leʃe]	**lick** La vie, c'est comme de lécher du miel sur un cactus. -Life is like licking honey off a cactus.
3771	**précision** f [pʀesizjɔ̃]	**precision|accuracy** Théodolites d'une précision égale ou supérieure à 15 secondes d'arc. -Theodolites with an accuracy of 15 arc seconds or greater accuracy.
3772	**thon** m [tɔ̃]	**tuna** J'ai mangé une salade de thon. -I ate a tuna salad.
3773	**péril** m [peʀil]	**peril|distress** Les conflits et le terrorisme mettent toutefois plus que jamais les enfants en péril. -Conflict and terrorism today presented an even greater danger to children, however.
3774	**sifflet** m [siflɛ]	**whistle** Pour les insomniaques, je suppose que le son du sifflet n'est pas un problème. -For insomniacs, I suppose the sound of the whistle would be no problem.
3775	**tricher** vb [tʀiʃe]	**cheat** Rien n'ennuie plus les gens que de voir son voisin ou son concurrent tricher. -There is nothing more annoying than to see a neighbour or competitor cheat.
3776	**instable** adj[ɛ̃stabl]	**unstable|unsteady** Jack a insisté qu'il n'avait pas bu, mais son élocution et sa démarche instable le trahissait. -Jack insisted he hadn't been drinking, but his slurred speech and unsteady gait gave him away.
3777	**conditionnel** adj [kɔ̃disjɔnɛl]	**conditional** Cliquez sur une des cellules auxquelles le formatage conditionnel a été assigné. -Click one of the cells that has been assigned conditional formatting.
3778	**substance** f [sypstɑ̃s]	**substance|material** Le sel est une substance utile. -Salt is a useful substance.
3779	**mâchoire** f [maʃwaʀ]	**jaw** Ces ombres apparurent en quelque sorte comme un dinosaure géant, au long cou et à la mâchoire très grosse, sans dents. -Those shadows appeared in a way like giant dinosaurs, with a long neck and a very big jaw without teeth.

3780	**jardinier**	**gardener**
	m	Quelqu'un a tiré sur le jardinier de l'ambassade avec un fusil à air comprimé.
	[ʒaʁdinje]	-A person shot at the gardener at the embassy with an air gun.
3781	**fureur**	**fury**
	f	Notre nation a subi sa fureur; nos soldats combattent et périssent dans ses batailles.
	[fyʁœʁ]	-Our nation has felt its fury; our soldiers have fought and died in its battles.
3782	**coureur**	**runner; racing**
	m; adj	Des prises importantes de calamars sont un signe avant-coureur de séisme.
	[kuʁœʁ]	-Large catches of squid are a sign of a coming earthquake.
3783	**tambour**	**drum**
	m	Le tambour est le seigneur de la musique.
	[tɑ̃buʁ]	-The drum is the lord of music.
3784	**dater**	**date**
	vb	Le certificat médical ne doit pas dater de plus de trois mois.
	[date]	-The certificate shall not date back more than three months.
3785	**protocole**	**protocol**
	m	Rôle des coordonnateurs pour le Protocole/la Convention et promotion du Protocole.
	[pʁɔtɔkɔl]	-The role of the Protocol's/Convention's Focal Points and the promotion of the Protocol
3786	**pieu**	**stake|pale**
	m	Placez la pointe du pieu exactement sur son coeur.
	[pjø]	-Now place the point of the stake directly over her heart.
3787	**soupçonner**	**suspect**
	vb	Il est donc infondé de soupçonner la Croatie d'être une nation "hostile à la minorité LGBT".
	[supsɔne]	-There is therefore no reason to suspect that Croatia is a nation hostile to the LGBT minority.
3788	**banquier**	**banker**
	m	Il s'agit indubitablement d'un banquier central exceptionnellement doué, capable et intelligent.
	[bɑ̃kje]	-He is clearly an exceptionally talented, able and intelligent central banker.
3789	**étendre**	**extend|expand**
	vb	La Division de la protection sociale visait aussi à les améliorer et les étendre.
	[etɑ̃dʁ]	-This was an attempt by the Social Welfare Division to improve and expand services.
3790	**ancrer**	**anchor**
	vb	Ancrer de façon permanente le principe de durabilité dans la législation européenne
	[ɑ̃kʁe]	-The sustainability principle to be given a permanent place in European legislation.
3791	**bander**	**get it up**
	vb	Je savais que JP pouvait pas bander.
	[bɑ̃de]	-I knew JP couldn't get it up.
3792	**frein**	**brake**
	m	As-tu déjà, dans ta voiture et après un long moment sans conduite, appuyé par inadvertance sur le frein et sur l'accélérateur ?
	[fʁɛ̃]	-Have you ever got in your car after a long absence and got the brake mixed up with the accelerator?

3793	**affecter**	**affect|assign**
	vb	Le code prévoit également que la travailleuse enceinte de six mois
	[afɛkte]	accomplis ne peut se voir affecter à un service de nuit.
		-It also provides that women who are over six months pregnant may not be included on night-shift rosters.

3793 **affecter** — **affect|assign**
vb [afɛkte]
Le code prévoit également que la travailleuse enceinte de six mois accomplis ne peut se voir affecter à un service de nuit.
-It also provides that women who are over six months pregnant may not be included on night-shift rosters.

3794 **turc** — **Turkish; Turkish**
adj; m [tyʁk]
Parlez-vous le turc ?
-Do you speak Turkish?

3795 **musulman** — **Muslim; Muslim**
adj; m [myzylmɑ̃]
Un enfant non musulman adopté par un musulman est considéré comme musulman.
-A non-Muslim child who is adopted by a Muslim shall be considered a Muslim.

3796 **brin** — **strand|sprig**
m [bʁɛ̃]
Tous les fils dans chaque brin sont fixés ensemble.
-All the wires in each strand are fixed together.

3797 **scanner** — **scanner**
m [skane]
Les experts en sécurité croient que la technologie d'Apple, pour scanner les empreintes digitales, détecte si un doigt est attaché à un être humain, de sorte que les phalanges sectionnées se révèlent incapables de déverrouiller un iPhone dérobé.
-Security experts believe Apple's fingerprint scanning technology senses whether a digit is attached to a living human, so severed phalanges should prove unsuccessful for unlocking a stolen iPhone.

3798 **momie** — **mummy**
f [mɔmi]
Par exemple, la momie qui arrive d'Égypte pour une exposition, où la classe-t-on ?
-For example, how do we classify a mummy that arrives here from Egypt for an exhibition?

3799 **blâme** — **blame|reprimand**
m [blam]
Je ne les blâme pas pour ceci.
-I don't blame them for this.

3800 **encourager** — **encourage**
vb[ɑ̃kuʁaʒe]
Les organismes de défense des droits de l'homme doivent encourager cette évolution. -Human rights organizations should encourage that development.

3801 **visiblement** — **visibly**
adv [viziblǝmɑ̃]
Ceci démontre en soi que le Conseil ignore visiblement les faits sur le terrain.
-That in itself demonstrates the Council's obvious ignorance of the facts on the ground.

3802 **parlement** — **parliament**
m [paʁlǝmɑ̃]
Le chef de l'opposition qualifie le parlement de« parlement à la Kalachnikov.
-There, the leader of the opposition calls the parliament a Kalashnikov parliament.

3803 **endurer** — **endure|undergo**
vb [ɑ̃dyʁe]
Les enfants continuent d'endurer les horreurs de la guerre.
-Children continue to suffer from the horrors of war.

3804 **pêcheur** — **fisherman**
m [pɛʃœʁ]
Il est absurde de penser que si un pêcheur dit quelque chose, cela doit être faux.
-It is a nonsense that if a fisherman says something, it must be wrong.

3805	**guérison** f [geʁizɔ̃]	**healing|cure** Ce patient est en bonne voie de guérison. -The patient is on a steady road to recovery.

3805 guérison f [geʁizɔ̃]
healing|cure
Ce patient est en bonne voie de guérison.
-The patient is on a steady road to recovery.

3806 syndrome m [sɛ̃dʁom]
syndrome
Il est étonnant de constater que les Iraniens, auxquels les Arabes ont imposé l'Islam en les battant militairement, sont devenus ses plus zélés adeptes au point d'opprimer ceux du Zoroastrisme, qui est pourtant la religion de leurs propres pères. Une sorte de syndrome de Stockholm à l'échelle nationale.
-It is astonishing to witness that the Iranians, onto whom the Arabs imposed Islam through military defeat, have become its most zealous followers to the point of oppressing those of Zoroastrianism, though it is the religion of their own fathers. A kind of Stockholm syndrome on the national scale.

3807 étrangler vb [etʁɑ̃gle]
strangle|choke
Nous avons vu le premier ministre étrangler un contribuable.
-We have seen the Prime Minister strangle a taxpayer.

3808 larguer vb [laʁge]
slip
Par "la totalité", on entend 80 % au moins de la longueur et/ou de la larguer du véhicule.
-"Entire" means at least 80 per cent of the length and/or width of a marked vehicle.

3809 malchance f [malʃɑ̃s]
bad luck|misfortune
Il attribue souvent ses échecs à la malchance.
-He often attributes his failures to bad luck.

3810 consacrer vb [kɔ̃sakʁe]
devote|spare
Ils ont donc moins de temps et d'énergie à consacrer pour les sports ou les arts.
-Consequently, they have less time and energy to volunteer for sports or the arts.

3811 nuire vb [nɥiʁ]
harm|damage
Est-ce là le fait d'une volonté délibérée de nuire, ou simplement d'une incompréhension ? -Is this the result of a deliberate desire to harm, or simply of misunderstanding?

3812 agressif adj [agʁesif]
aggressive
Il est entreprenant... agressif... expansif... jeune... audacieux... dépravé.
-He's enterprising...... aggressive...... outgoing...... young...... bold...... vicious.

3813 légiste m [leʒist]
jurist
Les constatations de l'expert légiste corroborent les allégations de mauvais traitements.
-The medical findings of the forensic expert corroborated the alleged beatings.

3814 pureté f [pyʁte]
purity
Je ne suis qu'un voyageur qui recherche la pureté de l'âme.
-I am just a traveller who seeks the purity of the soul.

3815 envahir vb [ɑ̃vaiʁ]
invade
On devrait les inviter à envahir notre village.
-You know, we should invite them down, to invade our village some time.

3816 épidémie f [epidemi]
epidemic
C'est une épidémie facile à contrôler.
-This is an easily controlled epidemic.

3817 insulte
insult

| | f | Il a presque insulté le porte-parole de l'opposition pour les affaires étrangères. |
| | [ɛ̃sylt] | -He was almost name calling with regard to the official opposition's foreign critic. |

3818 **chimie** — **chemistry**

f
[ʃimi]

Est-ce que tu étudies la chimie ?
 -Do you study chemistry?

3819 **falaise** — **cliff**

f
[falɛz]

Soyez prudent à proximité du bord de la falaise !
 -Be careful near the edge of the cliff.

3820 **braquage** — **defection**

m
[bʁakaʒ]

On est sur un braquage de station-service.
 -You know, we're working on this gas station robbery.

3821 **convention** — **convention|covenant**

f
[kɔ̃vɑ̃sjɔ̃]

Le Mexique est-il signataire de la convention de Genève ?
 -Is Mexico a signatory to the Geneva Convention?

3822 **lueur** — **glow|light**

f
[lɥœʁ]

Pas la moindre lueur vacillante ne vient gâter l'amusement.
 -Not the least glimmer inside to spoil the fun.

3823 **capture** — **capture|catch**

f
[kaptyʁ]

La récompense pour sa capture est substantielle.
 -The reward for his capture is a substantial sum.

3824 **hériter** — **inherit**

vb
[eʁite]

Étant elles-mêmes des biens, elles peuvent être léguées, mais ne peuvent pas hériter des biens.
 -Being possessions themselves, they stand to be inherited and cannot inherit property.

3825 **cherry** — **sherry**

f
[ʃeʁi]

Consultez votre fournisseur sur les conditions de vente de son American cherry.
 -Consult your supplier about how their sherry is being sold.

3826 **baser** — **base**

vb
[baze]

Il a aussi souligné qu'il fallait baser le budget sur la stratégie à moyen terme.
 -He also emphasized the need to base the budget on the medium term strategy.

3827 **beignet** — **fritter**

m
[bɛɲɛ]

Prends un beignet.
 -Have a donut.

3828 **diversion** — **diversion**

f
[divɛʁsjɔ̃]

Ces problèmes électriques sont une diversion.
 -Sir, these electrical problems were a diversion.

3829 **relâcher** — **release|relax**

vb
[ʁəlaʃe]

Une série de mesures à court terme peuvent être prises rapidement afin de relâcher la pression.
 -A number of short-term measures can be taken quickly to ease the situation.

3830 **convenable** — **suitable|appropriate**

adj
[kɔ̃vənabl]

Il peut être convenable d'utiliser d'autres formes de cibles, telles que celle représentée à la figure 14.

-It may be convenient to use other forms of target, such as that shown in figure 14.

3831	**dimension**	**dimension|size**
	f	Déterminez la dimension de ce sous-espace vectoriel.
	[dimãsjõ]	-Find the dimension of this subspace.
3832	**tare**	**stigma**
	f	Être un assisté social est devenu une tare.
	[taʁ]	-Being on welfare has become a stigma.
3833	**gigantesque**	**gigantic**
	adj	Faut-il à l'inverse plaider pour une gigantesque déstructuration des États ?
	[ʒigãtɛsk]	-Ought we then to advocate the deconstruction of States on a gigantic scale?
3834	**break**	**break**
	m	Ce sera votre dernier break donc reposez-vous.
	[bʁɛk]	-This will be your last break so rest up.
3835	**reflet**	**reflection**
	m	Jack a regardé son reflet dans le miroir.
	[ʁəflɛ]	-Jack looked at his reflection in the mirror.
3836	**chauffage**	**heating|heater**
	m	Il est interdit de chauffer les cales ou d'y faire fonctionner un appareil de chauffage.
	[ʃofaʒ]	-The heating of holds or the operation of a heating system in the holds is prohibited.
3837	**rappel**	**reminder|encore**
	m	La foule criait pour un rappel.
	[ʁapɛl]	-The crowd cried out for an encore.
3838	**fondé**	**based|founded**
	adj[fõde]	Kates, toute l'histoire du XXème siècle confirme le bien-fondé de cette position. -Twentieth-century history confirmed that that position was well founded.
3839	**caserne**	**barracks**
	f	La fumée sortait aussi d'une caserne voisine.
	[kazɛʁn]	-Smoke also came out of a nearby barrack.
3840	**écurie**	**stable**
	f	Une fois que le cheval s'est enfui, c'est trop tard pour fermer la porte de l'écurie.
	[ekyʁi]	-It's too late to shut the stable door after the horse has bolted.
3841	**utilisation**	**use**
	f	Je suis contre l'utilisation de la mort en tant que punition. Je suis aussi contre son utilisation en tant que récompense.
	[ytilizasjõ]	-I am against using death as a punishment. I am also against using it as a reward.
3842	**étroit**	**narrow|close**
	adj	Les autorités de santé sont engagées dans un dialogue étroit avec ces organisations.
	[etʁwa]	-The health authorities are engaged in close dialogue with these organizations.
3843	**toutou**	**doggie|lapdog**
	m	Oui, tu es un très bon toutou.
	[tutu]	-Yes, you're a very good doggy.
3844	**admirable**	**admirable**

	adj [admiʁabl]	Ils font un travail admirable dans des circonstances particulièrement difficiles. -They are doing admirable work in particularly difficult conditions.
3845	**lasser** vb [lase]	**weary|bore** Mais si tel n'est pas le cas, il ne faudra pas nous lasser. -But if that does not happen, we must never tire.
3846	**débris** mpl [debʁi]	**debris** Les micro-plastiques sont des particules microscopiques de débris de plastiques qui polluent les océans. -Microplastics are microscopic particles of plastic debris that pollute the oceans.
3847	**bourbon** m [buʁbɔ̃]	**bourbon** Deux doigts de votre meilleur bourbon. -Double shot of your best bourbon.
3848	**thèse** f [tɛz]	**thesis|theory** Avez-vous décidé de votre sujet de thèse ? -Have you decided the subject of your thesis?
3849	**diligence** f [diliʒɑ̃s]	**diligence** La réussite dans la vie réside dans la diligence et la vigilance. -Success in life lies in diligence and vigilance.
3850	**lin** m[lɛ̃]	**linen** C'est ennuyeux pour moi, Grand-mère, d'être assise à ne rien faire, heure après heure. Mes mains réclament du travail à faire. Va, en conséquence, m'acheter du lin, le meilleur et le plus fin qui puisse se trouver et au moins je pourrai filer ! -It is dull for me, grandmother, to sit idly hour by hour. My hands want work to do. Go, therefore, and buy me some flax, the best and finest to be found anywhere, and at least I can spin.
3851	**majeur** adj; m [maʒœʁ]	**major|middle finger; major** La main a cinq doigts: le pouce, l'index, le majeur, l'annulaire et l'auriculaire. -The hand has five fingers: the thumb, the index finger, the middle finger, the ring finger, and the pinky.
3852	**visible** adj [vizibl]	**visible** C'est aussi une expression visible, le plus visible puisqu'il est possible d'expliquer aux hommes. -It's also a visible expression, as much visible as it is possible to explain to men.
3853	**nécessiter** vb [nesesite]	**require** Cette mobilisation peut nécessiter l'achat urgent de matériels particuliers. -Mobilization may necessitate urgent procurement of specific equipment.
3854	**culte** m [kylt]	**worship** Une totale liberté de culte est garantie à tous. -Full religious freedom is assured to all people.
3855	**extraire** vb [ɛkstʁɛʁ]	**extract|draw** On peut utiliser des filtres pour extraire les particules solides de l'échantillon. -Filters may be used in order to extract the solid particles from the sample.
3856	**approuver** vb [apʁuve]	**approve|endorse** Il a demandé au CTI d'approuver la tenue de cette réunion les 30 et 31 mai 2002. -It requests the ITC to approve the holding of that meeting on 30 and 31 May 2002.

3857	**connexion**	**connection**
	f	Vous devez démontrer une connexion personnelle entre ces deux-là.
	[kɔnɛksjɔ̃]	-I'm going to need you to demonstrate a personal connection between these two.
3858	**raccourcir**	**shorten**
	vb	Voulons-nous raccourcir les délais que le Conseil a proposés pour cette directive ?
	[ʁakuʁsiʁ]	-Do we want to shorten the deadlines proposed by the Council for this directive?
3859	**protecteur**	**protective; protector**
	adj; m	Après tout, le Sénat est le protecteur des minorités et le protecteur des Canadiens.
	[pʁɔtɛktœʁ]	-After all, the Senate is the protector of minorities and the protector of Canadians.
3860	**procurer**	**obtain**
	vb[pʁɔkyʁe]	Il faudra du temps pour se procurer et distribuer des postes radio à la population timoraise. -It will take time to procure radio sets and distribute them to the Timorese population.
3861	**éprouver**	**experience|test**
	vb	Par ailleurs, les États parties peuvent éprouver des difficultés d'ordre technique.
	[epʁuve]	-Moreover, States parties could experience difficulties of a technical nature.
3862	**salir**	**soil|smear**
	vb	Il ne peut que salir toute cause, quel qu'en soit le mérite par ailleurs.
	[saliʁ]	-Its use could only defile any cause, however worthy.
3863	**divers**	**various|several**
	adj	L'entreprise fabrique des produits en papier divers.
	[divɛʁ]	-The company manufactures a variety of paper goods.
3864	**raciste**	**racist; racist**
	adj; m/f	Seul un raciste pourrait accorder du crédit à ces inepties.
	[ʁasist]	-Only a racist could give credence to such nonsense.
3865	**pâté**	**pâté**
	m	C'est du pâté de madame de la Tour.
	[pate]	-This is pâté from Madame de la Tour.
3866	**bouc**	**goat**
	m	Regarder les photos de tes amis Fesse-bouc est une perte de temps.
	[buk]	-Looking at your Facebook friends' photos is a waste of time.
3867	**racaille**	**riffraff**
	f	Borias, il faut inspirer de la terreur à cette racaille.
	[ʁakaj]	-I'm telling you, Borias - the only way to deal with these scum is through terror.
3868	**enseignement**	**education|teaching**
	m	L'enseignement des sciences humaines laisse fortement à désirer au Chili.
	[ãsɛɲmã]	-The teaching of humanities in Chile leaves much to be desired.
3869	**ambitieux**	**ambitious; careerist**
	adj; m/f	Bien qu'ambitieux pour une visite aussi brève, ces objectifs étaient importants.
	[ãbisjø]	-These are ambitious objectives for such a short visit, but they are important.
3870	**chancelier**	**chancellor**

m

[ʃɑ̃səlje]

Eloigne-la du chancelier jusqu'au couronnement.
-Keep her from the Chancellor until after the coronation.

3871 **alias**

adv

[aljas]

alias

Ndayambaje Aimable, alias Limbana (commandant de l'opération de Bwindi)
-Ndayambaje Aimable, alias Limbana (commanded the Bwindi operation).

3872 **psychologie**

f

[psikɔlɔʒi]

psychology

La psychologie se penche sur les émotions humaines.
-Psychology deals with human emotions.

3873 **discrétion**

f

[diskʁesjɔ̃]

discretion

J'espère que je peux compter sur votre discrétion.
-I hope I can count on your discretion.

3874 **dorer**

vb[dɔʁe]

brown

Ajouter les champignons et cuire jusqu'à ce qu'ils commencent à dorer. -Add the mushrooms and cook until they begin to brown.

3875 **cadet**

adj; m

[kadɛ]

cadet; cadet

Je suis son cadet de quatre ans.
-I am four years younger than him.

3876 **réalisation**

f

[ʁealizasjɔ̃]

realization|achievement

Pour beaucoup, c'était la réalisation d'un rêve.
-For many, it was a dream come true.

3877 **diagnostic**

m

[djagnɔstik]

diagnosis

C'est un diagnostic possible.
-It's a plausible diagnosis.

3878 **abîmer**

vb

[abime]

spoil|ruin

Ces débris peuvent abîmer encore davantage les écosystèmes vulnérables déjà dégradés.
-Debris can provoke further physical damage to already damaged vulnerable ecosystems.

3879 **intrusion**

f

[ɛ̃tʁyzjɔ̃]

intrusion

C'est une intrusion dans leur vie quotidienne et une entrave à leur moyen de subsistance.
-This is an intrusion into their daily lives, an intrusion into their economic lives.

3880 **aborder**

vb

[abɔʁde]

approach|tackle

Aussi pensait-il qu'il fallait aborder la question avec circonspection.
-For this reason, he felt that one has to approach this issue with caution.

3881 **vétérinaire**

adj; m/f

[veteʁinɛʁ]

veterinary; veterinary

Le vétérinaire officiel doit disposer des moyens légaux nécessaires pour faire respecter ces exigences.
-The official veterinarian must have the statutory means to enforce the requirements.

3882 **miséricorde**

f

[mizeʁikɔʁd]

mercy

De la sorte, la rédemption porte en soi la révélation de la miséricorde en sa plénitude.
-In this way, redemption involves the revelation of mercy in its fullness.

3883 **planche**

f

[plɑ̃ʃ]

board|plank

Prends la planche ou enlève ta culotte.
-You can either walk the plank or take your panties off.

3884 **savant**

learned; scholar

	adj; m	Il passe pour un savant dans notre communauté.
	[savɑ̃]	-He passes for a learned man in our community.
3885	**épave**	**wreck**
	f	L'épave est éparpillée sur une grande étendue.
	[epav]	-The wreckage is scattered over a large area.
3886	**vestiaire**	**cloakroom**
	m	Rendez-vous au vestiaire du sous-sol dans 10 minutes.
	[vɛstjɛʁ]	-Meet us downstairs in the locker room in 10 minutes.
3887	**mélodie**	**melody**
	f	Cette mélodie me semble vraiment familière.
	[melɔdi]	-There's something really familiar about that melody.
3888	**brume**	**mist**
	f[bʁym]	En regardant à travers la brume, j'ai entrevu mon futur. -In looking through the mist, I caught a glimpse of my future.
3889	**éthique**	**ethics; ethical**
	f; adj	Cette discussion est passionnante sur les plans éthique, politique et même
	[etik]	technique.
		-This discussion is fascinating on an ethical, political and even technical
		level.
3890	**surmonter**	**overcome|rise above**
	vb	Nous savons qu'il faudra surmonter de nombreux obstacles, ce qui ne sera
	[syʁmɔ̃te]	pas aisé.
		-We realize that many obstacles will have to be overcome, which will not
		be easy.
3891	**amer**	**bitter; bitter**
	adj; m	Ce café est trop amer.
	[amɛʁ]	-This coffee is too bitter.
3892	**signification**	**meaning|notification**
	f	On ignore la signification de tout ceci.
	[siɲifikasjɔ̃]	-We don't know the significance of this thing.
3893	**préférable**	**preferable**
	adj	Il serait également préférable de retenir un critère alternatif et non
	[pʁefeʁabl]	cumulatif.
		-It would also be preferable to take an alternative and not a cumulative
		approach.
3894	**affirmatif**	**affirmative**
	adj	Cette recommandation doit être formulée par un vote affirmatif de neuf
	[afiʁmatif]	membres de l'Organe.
		-Such recommendation shall be made by an affirmative vote of nine
		members of the Board.
3895	**anormal**	**abnormal**
	adj	Il n'y a rien d'anormal au fait que des députés rendent visite à cette détenue.
	[anɔʁmal]	-There is nothing unusual about parliamentarians visiting this prisoner.
3896	**soumettre**	**submit|refer**
	vb	Les administrateurs de projet et les consultants devront soumettre des
	[sumɛtʁ]	rapports sur l'action menée.
		-Project managers and consultants will be requested to submit progress
		reports.
3897	**chameau**	**camel**
	m	Le chameau défile tandis que les chiens aboient.
	[ʃamo]	-The camel marches while the dogs bark.

3898 **parachute** — **parachute**
m
[paʀaʃyt]
Le seul moyen de trouver asile ici sera d'arriver en Europe en parachute.
-The only way to get asylum here will be to jump out over Europe with a parachute.

3899 **interprète** — **interpreter**
m/f
[ɛ̃tɛʀpʀɛt]
Il est impératif que le titulaire de la présidence soit un interprète des droits de l'homme aux niveaux national et international, et qu'il soit perçu comme tel.
-It is imperative that the Chairperson be, and is perceived to be, an exponent of human rights at the domestic and international levels.

3900 **étiqueter** — **label|brand**
vb[etikte]
On peut alors se heurter à des obstacles lorsqu'il s'agit d'étiqueter ces produits. -In such cases, there can be obstacles to labelling manufactured products.

3901 **sermon** — **sermon**
m
[sɛʀmɔ̃]
Le pasteur délivra un sermon enflammé qui laissa les pécheurs parmi eux trembler dans leurs bottes.
-The pastor gave a fiery sermon that left the sinners among them shaking in their boots.

3902 **voyageur** — **traveler|passenger; traveling**
m; adj
[vwajaʒœʀ]
Le présent article ne s'applique pas au voyageur qui se trouve dans la localité où est située sa résidence.
-This section does not apply to a traveller in the traveller's home community.

3903 **doyen** — **dean|provost**
m
[dwajɛ̃]
Vice-rectrice pour les questions universitaires (Doyenne) de l'Université Boğaziçi depuis 2008
-Vice-Rector for Academic Affairs (Provost), Boğaziçi University, since 2008.

3904 **adapter** — **adapt|suit**
vb
[adapte]
La Cour de justice ou la Cour des comptes devront s'adapter à l'élargissement.
-The Court of Justice or the Court of Auditors will have to adapt to enlargement.

3905 **ignoble** — **despicable**
adj
[iɲɔbl]
Cela serait absolument ignoble aux yeux de nos concitoyens.
-That would be absolutely abhorrent in the eyes of our fellow citizens.

3906 **espionnage** — **espionage**
m
[ɛspjɔnaʒ]
C'est dans ce sens que la plupart des services opèrent l'espionnage industriel.
-To that extent most of the services engage in espionage in the economic domain.

3907 **location** — **hire**
f
[lɔkasjɔ̃]
Combien cela coûte-t-il en plus de laisser la voiture de location à un autre endroit ?
-How much more does it cost to return the rental car to another location?

3908 **rafraîchir** — **refresh**
vb
[ʀafʀeʃiʀ]
Monsieur le Président, je vais devoir rafraîchir la mémoire du premier ministre.
-Speaker, perhaps I will have to refresh the Prime Minister's memory.

3909 **habile** — **clever|skilful**

adj
[abil]

C'est là un pur sophisme et un moyen habile d'assimiler l'assaillant à la victime.
-This is mere sophistry; it is a crafty attempt to equate the assailant with the victim.

3910 **promouvoir** **promote|instigate**

vb
[pʁɔmuvwaʁ]

Ils ont mis en place une politique de communication afin de promouvoir leur nouveau concept.
-They implemented a communication policy so as to promote their new concept.

3911 **indépendant** **independent; independent**

adj; m[ɛ̃depɑ̃dɑ̃]

Il se compose notamment de membres issus des services nationaux et internationaux de statistique et des banques centrales, ainsi que d'universitaires et de personnalités indépendantes. -Members include officials from national and international statistical offices and central banks, as well as academics and unattached persons.

3912 **caverne** **cave**

f
[kavɛʁn]

Personne ne put trouver la caverne.
-No one could find the cave.

3913 **financer** **finance**

vb
[finɑ̃se]

Ils pourraient financer leurs entreprises commerciales beaucoup plus efficacement.
-They would be able to finance their business enterprises much more effectively.

3914 **rassurer** **reassure**

vb
[ʁasyʁe]

Le maintien de la présence de la MONUG à Zougdidi a contribué à rassurer les habitants.
-The continued presence of UNOMIG in Zugdidi helped to reassure the population.

3915 **lointain** **distant|far**

adj
[lwɛ̃tɛ̃]

Le désarmement général et complet demeure encore un objectif lointain.
-General and complete disarmament still remains a distant objective to be attained.

3916 **manifestement** **obviously**

adv
[manifɛstəmɑ̃]

Les estimations que ces entreprises ont réalisées sont manifestement surévaluées.
-The assessments these companies have carried out are clearly overvalued.

3917 **énigme** **enigma|puzzle**

f
[enigm]

La grande énigme de la réforme du Conseil de sécurité demeure sa composition.
-The big conundrum of Security Council reform remains composition.

3918 **box** **box**

m
[bɔks]

Elle a perdu un fer en dehors du box.
-She threw a shoe coming out of the box.

3919 **crevette** **shrimp**

f
[kʁəvɛt]

En 2002, la crevette est restée le principal produit de la pêche échangé en valeur.
-In 2002, shrimp continued to be the main fishery commodity traded in value terms.

3920 **occupation** **occupation|tenure**

f
[ɔkypasjõ]

Les discussions se poursuivent au sujet de l'occupation du bâtiment.
-Discussions are continuing in regard to the building's occupancy.

3921 **arrière** **rear|back; back**

adj; m
[aʁjɛʁ]

Application aux feux arrière pour véhicules automobiles.
-The invention is suitable for the rear lights of motor vehicles.

3922 scout — scout

m
[skut]

Le mouvement scout compte 2 000 enfants dont 300 enfants âgés entre 7 et 12 ans.
-As a result, opportunities for participating in the world scout movement increased.

3923 pétard — firecracker

m[petaʁ]

Le premier coup de feu a retenti comme un pétard. -The first shot sounded like a firecracker.

3924 atlantique — **Atlantic**

adj
[atlɑ̃tik]

Ce point est-il compris de la même manière des deux côtés de l'océan Atlantique ?
-Is the understanding of this point the same on both sides of the Atlantic Ocean?

3925 planifier — **plan|chart**

vb
[planifje]

J'ai pensé que ce serait utile aux membres de le savoir pour planifier la journée.
-I thought it would be useful for members to know this as they plan the day ahead.

3926 pagaille — **mess**

f
[pagaj]

Nettoyons cette pagaille.
-Let's clean up this mess.

3927 banquet — **banquet**

m
[bɑ̃kɛ]

Au banquet de l'humanité, il n'y a pas assez de place pour toutes les générations.
-At the banquet of humanity, there is not enough room for all of the generations.

3928 baguette — **baguette|stick**

f
[bagɛt]

Ma baguette est plus grande que la tienne.
-My baguette is bigger than yours.

3929 fraise — **strawberry**

f
[fʁɛz]

Sers-toi de la confiture de fraise.
-Help yourself to the strawberry jam.

3930 marbre — **marble; marble**

adj; m
[maʁbʁ]

Ses mains étaient froides comme le marbre.
-Her hands felt as cold as marble.

3931 catégorie — **category**

f
[kategɔʁi]

Elle joue dans la catégorie au-dessus de la tienne.
-She's out of your league.

3932 féroce — **fierce|savage**

adj
[feʁɔs]

La féroce déclaration de guerre du rapporteur s'applique-t-elle à ces produits aussi ?
-Does the rapporteur's ferocious war declaration apply here too?

3933 escadron — **squadron**

m
[ɛskadʁɔ̃]

La devise de l'escadron est: «Nous conquérons les hauteurs.»
-The motto of this squadron is "We Conquer in the Heights."

3934 dérouler — **unwind|roll**

vb
[deʁule]

S'il s'agit d'une ceinture à rétracteur, la sangle est déroulée sur toute sa longueur moins 300 mm + 3 mm.
-In the case of an assembly incorporating a retractor, the strap shall be unwound to full length less 300 + 3 mm.

3935	**chute**	**fall ǀ falling**
	f	Il y a une crise à cause d'une offre de lait trop abondante qui fait chuter les prix.
	[ʃyt]	-The crisis is caused by an over-abundant supply of milk, which is making prices drop sharply.
3936	**révélation**	**revelation**
	f[ʁevelasjɔ̃]	Il ne s'agit pas seulement de la récente révélation des évènements concernant SWIFT. -It is not only the recent disclosure of events in connection with SWIFT.
3937	**espionner**	**spy**
	vb	Nous débattons maintenant d'un texte législatif qui permettrait d'espionner ceux que la loi dit protéger.
	[ɛspjɔne]	-We are now debating a law that would make it possible to spy on those whom the law says are protected.
3938	**cartouche**	**cartridge**
	f	Tire ta cartouche.
	[kaʁtuʃ]	-Shoot your magazine empty.
3939	**bunker**	**bunker**
	m	Hissez le drapeau blanc, direction bunker.
	[bunkɛʁ]	-Time to wave the white flag and head for the bunker.
3940	**manuscrit**	**manuscript; manuscript**
	adj; m	Le manuscrit original, en français, est en cours d'impression.
	[manyskʁi]	-The original manuscript is in French and it is being printed.
3941	**appliquer**	**apply ǀ carry out**
	vb	Par conséquent, seulement environ 20 % des grandes banques peuvent l'appliquer.
	[aplike]	-Accordingly, only 20 or so largest banking organizations may implement Basel II.
3942	**cacahuète**	**peanut**
	f	Un vrai maître des baguettes sait ramasser une cacahuète.
	[kakaɥɛt]	-No, they say that the test of a true chopstick master is to pick up a peanut.
3943	**condamnation**	**conviction ǀ locking**
	f	J'obtiendrai une condamnation les yeux fermés.
	[kɔ̃danasjɔ̃]	-I'll get a conviction with my eyes closed.
3944	**empirer**	**worse**
	vb	Sinon, la situation dans cette partie de la République démocratique du Congo pourrait empirer.
	[ɑ̃piʁe]	-Otherwise, the situation in that part of the Democratic Republic of the Congo could get worse.
3945	**bousiller**	**botch**
	vb	Ils avaient tout le système nécessaire avant que les Européens arrivent et qu'ils viennent bousiller leurs systèmes.
	[buzije]	-They had everything they needed before the Europeans arrived and upset their systems.
3946	**conspiration**	**conspiracy ǀ plot**
	f	Pas plus qu'un tel traitement ne peut être justifié par des allégations de conspiration.
	[kɔ̃spiʁasjɔ̃]	-Nor can such treatment be justified by unsubstantiated allegations of conspiracy.
3947	**clope**	**butt**
	f	Johnny, va dehors fumer un clope.
	[klɔp]	-Johnny, step outside, have a smoke.

3948 **tentant** — **tempting**
adj
[tɑ̃tɑ̃]
Monsieur le Président, il serait en effet tentant d'entrer dans ce débat.
-Mr President, it would be indeed tempting to enter into this debate.

3949 **détecteur** — **detector | detecting**
m
[detɛktœʁ]
HC Détecteur à ionisation de flamme chauffé pour la mesure des hydrocarbures
-Heated flame ionisation detector (HFID) for the determination of the hydrocarbons.

3950 **orphelin** — **orphan; orphan**
adj; m
[ɔʁfəlɛ̃]
On dit habituellement que le succès a plusieurs pères, mais que l'échec est orphelin.
-It is said that 'success has many fathers, but failure is an orphan'.

3951 **opposition** — **opposition**
f
[ɔpozisjɔ̃]
L'opposition à l'embargo allait croissante.
-Opposition to the embargo was growing.

3952 **gestion** — **management**
f
[ʒɛstjɔ̃]
Un commerce prospère est affaire de prudence dans la gestion financière.
-A successful business is built on careful financial management.

3953 **ouf** — **crazy person; whew**
m/f; int
[uf]
Je vais entrer là comme un ouf.
-I'm gonna walk in there and be crazy.

3954 **orgasme** — **orgasm**
m
[ɔʁgasm]
Avec le tantra, on peut transformer une séance de sexe... en un orgasme géant.
-With tantra you can make an entire session of sex... feel like one giant orgasm.

3955 **griller** — **grill | toast**
vb
[gʁije]
Dites «tourisme» et ils partent tous se faire griller.
-Mention tourism and they leave their brains to broil on the beach.

3956 **tonne** — **tonne**
f
[tɔn]
Il y avait sur lui une tonne de pression.
-There was a ton of pressure on him.

3957 **informe** — **shapeless | unformed**
adj
[ɛ̃fɔʁm]
Quand je n'étais qu'une masse informe, tes yeux me voyaient ; et sur ton livre étaient tous inscrits les jours qui m'étaient destinés, avant qu'aucun d'eux existe.
-When I was woven together in the depths of the earth, your eyes saw my unformed body.. All the days ordained for me were written in your book before one of them came to be.

3958 **annuaire** — **directory | yearbook**
m
[anɥɛʁ]
J'aimerais travailler sur l'annuaire.
-I would like to work on the yearbook.

3959 **suède** — **suede; suede**
adj; f
[sɥɛd]
L'atelier a été ouvert par Mme Gun Lövblad (Suède) et M. Peringe Grennfelt (Suède).
-Gun Lövblad (Sweden) and Mr. Peringe Grennfelt (Sweden).

3960 **optimiste** — **optimistic; optimist**
adj; m/f
[ɔptimist]
J' ai tendance à être optimiste de nature, mais je suis un optimiste prudent.
-I tend to be an optimist by nature, but I am a cautious optimist.

3961 **audace** — **boldness; woodless**

f; adj | Ensuite, il faudrait amener une audace politique dans un Cotonou refondu.
[odas] | -Secondly, we should show political audacity in a reworked Cotonou Agreement.

3962 affamé | **starving|famished**
adj | Beaucoup de monde était affamé durant la guerre.
[afame] | -A lot of people starved during that war.

3963 anéantir | **annihilate|wreck**
vb | Le Plan pour anéantir la Nation Cubaine est en marche !
[aneãtiʁ] | -THE PLAN TO ANNIHILATE THE CUBAN NATION IS IN COURSE!

3964 propagande | **propaganda**
f | Tout le reste est propagande.
[pʁɔpagãd] | -All the rest is propaganda.

3965 immortel | **immortal; immortal**
adj; m | Aucun d'entre nous n'est immortel.
[imɔʁtɛl] | -No one of us is immortal.

3966 sottise | **folly|silliness**
f | Et Bruxelles découvre la sottise de sa politique d'étouffement de la production.
[sɔtiz] | -Brussels finally realised the folly of its policy to stifle production.

3967 saumon | **salmon**
m | Le saumon pond ses œufs en eau douce.
[somõ] | -Salmon lay their eggs in fresh water.

3968 carbone | **carbon; carbon**
adj; m | Le charbon est principalement constitué de carbone.
[kaʁbɔn] | -Coal consists mostly of carbon.

3969 paumer | **lose**
vb | Oui, et en argent massif, alors ne le paume pas !
[pome] | -Yeah, and it's also solid silver so don't lose it!

3970 maladroit | **awkward; blunderer**
adj; m | Il est maladroit dans ses mouvements.
[maladʁwa] | -He is awkward in his movements.

3971 acquérir | **acquire**
vb | D'acquérir de nouveaux savoirs permettant une amélioration des conditions de vie.
[akeʁiʁ] | -Acquisition of new skills providing opportunities to improve living conditions;

3972 violation | **violation|breach**
f | En parler à Arthur serait une violation du protocole.
[vjɔlasjõ] | -Any mention of it to Arthur would be a violation of protocol.

3973 revenant | **return|reverting; ghost**
adj; m | J'ai été pris sous une averse en revenant de l'école à la maison.
[ʁəvənã] | -I was caught in a shower on my way home from school.

3974 écarter | **exclude**
vb | De toute façon, l'écart est de 130 votes, ce qui est assez considérable.
[ekaʁte] | -In any case, there is a difference of 130 votes. It is not a small difference.

3975 définition | **definition**
f | La vraie définition de la science, c'est qu'elle est l'étude de la beauté du monde.
[definisjõ] | -The real definition of science is that it's the study of the beauty of the world.

3976 cuillère | **spoon**

f[kyijɛʁ]   Laisser refroidir et mélanger les aubergines à la ricotta, puis bien travailler l'appareil avec une cuillère. -Leave to cool, mix the aubergines with the ricotta and stir well with a spoon.

3977 menthe — **mint**
f
[mɑ̃t]
Antoine, ciselez la menthe fraîche.
-Antoine, can you chop the fresh mint?

3978 librement — **freely**
adv
[libʁəmɑ̃]
Depuis lors, tout Brésilien séropositif ou malade du sida y a librement accès.
-Since then, every Brazilian living with HIV or AIDS has had free access thereto.

3979 hostile — **hostile|opposed**
adj
[ɔstil]
Même les propos que nous échangeons sont de nature hostile.
-Even the words are antagonistic and protagonistic.

3980 interprétation — **interpretation**
f
[ɛ̃tɛʁpʁetasjɔ̃]
Une traduction comporte également toujours une part d'interprétation.
-A translation is always also an interpretation.

3981 biologique — **biological**
adj
[bjɔlɔʒik]
Il est essentiel de tirer parti de la diversité biologique dans les pays tropicaux.
-It was important to exploit the potential of biodiversity in tropical countries.

3982 introduire — **introduce|place**
vb
[ɛ̃tʁɔdɥiʁ]
Elle introduira également, dans nos relations extérieures, le postulat d'efficacité énergétique.
-It will also make energy efficiency a premise of our external relations.

3983 poignard — **dagger**
m
[pwaɲaʁ]
Le costume national de mon propre pays, l'Écosse, se porte avec un poignard dans la chaussette.
-The Scottish, my own country's national dress involves wearing a dagger in your sock.

3984 calendrier — **calendar**
m
[kalɑ̃dʁije]
Elle concerne le calendrier et l' amendement du groupe PPE-DE au calendrier.
-It concerns the calendar and the PPE-DE Group' s amendment to the calendar.

3985 retardé — **backward**
adj
[ʁətaʁde]
Cela avait retardé la comptabilisation du règlement des engagements correspondants.
-That delayed the recording of the liquidation of unliquidated obligations in the accounts.

3986 caviar — **caviar**
m
[kavjaʁ]
Prodi a noyé la question tchétchène dans la vodka et le caviar.
-At this summit, indeed, Mr Prodi drowned the Chechen question in vodka and caviar.

3987 banal — **banal**
adj
[banal]
L'un de ces points peut paraître banal: consultation, société civile et ressources.
-One of them is a point which might appear banal: consultation, civil society and resources.

3988 exagérer — **exaggerate**

	vb	
	[εgzaʒeʁe]	Par ailleurs, les répondants semblent exagérer leur niveau de scolarité.
		-Respondents also appear to exaggerate educational achievement.

3989 opérateur — **operator**

m
[ɔpeʁatœʁ]

Le capitaine du navire ordonna à l'opérateur radio d'envoyer un signal de détresse.
-The ship's captain ordered the radio operator to send a distress signal.

3990 initiative — **initiative|lead**

f
[inisjativ]

Ce sont les mêmes mots, Monsieur Désir, nouvelle initiative et initiative.
-The amendments relate to the same words, Mr Désir, 'new initiative' and 'initiative'.

3991 apocalypse — **apocalypse**

f
[apɔkalips]

La grippe aviaire est présentée comme un nouveau cavalier de l'Apocalypse.
-Avian influenza is being presented as a further horseman of the Apocalypse.

3992 dresser — **draw up|develop**

vb
[dʁese]

Une fois débarrassé de l' saurai dresser mes plans et harceler les gens.
-So I get rid of the advocate I can draw up my own plan and keep after the officials myself.

3993 intégrité — **integrity|honesty**

f
[ɛ̃tegʁite]

L'intégrité du programme gouvernemental soulève aussi des interrogations.
-The integrity of the government's program has to be questioned.

3994 contrarier — **upset|thwart**

vb
[kɔ̃tʁaʁje]

Des facteurs sociaux et politiques peuvent également contrarier la diversification.
-Social and political factors in CDDCs may also thwart diversification.

3995 foncé — **dark**

adj
[fɔ̃se]

La majorité ont déclaré appartenir à la catégorie brun clair ou foncé (43 %).
-The majority classified themselves as light or dark brown (43 per cent).

3996 vitrine — **showcase|window**

f
[vitʁin]

Ne touchez pas les objets en vitrine.
-Do not touch the exhibits in the showcase.

3997 sonder — **probe|sound**

vb
[sɔ̃de]

Par conséquent, les États membres et la Commission doivent sonder les possibilités qui existent.
-Consequently, the Member States and the Commission must sound out the opportunities that exist.

3998 vitre — **window**

f
[vitʁ]

Quelqu'un brisa la vitre.
-Someone broke the window.

3999 maréchal — **marshal**

m
[maʁeʃal]

Je te livre au maréchal fédéral.
-I'm turning you over to the Federal Marshal.

4000 hangar — **hangar**

m
[ãgaʁ]

Je vais ouvrir l'autre hangar.
-I'll open up the next hangar.

4001 éponger — **mop up|sponge**

vb[epɔ̃ʒe]

Nous devons également éponger les réserves d'armes se trouvant déjà dans ces régions. -We also have to mop up the reservoir of weapons already in those regions.

4002 bassin — **basin|pool**

	m	J'ai nagé deux longueurs de bassin.
	[basɛ̃]	-I swam two pool lengths.
4003	**branler**	**wobble|loose**
	vb	Il fait juste ces vidéos pour les regarder et se branler.
	[bʁɑ̃le]	-They're just tapes he makes so he can sit around and get off.
4004	**injustice**	**injustice|unfairness**
	f	Même votée à la majorité, une injustice reste une injustice.
	[ɛ̃ʒystis]	-Even when voted through by a majority, an injustice is still an injustice.
4005	**canot**	**canoe|dinghy**
	m	Il y avait une femme dans le canot.
	[kano]	-There was a woman in the canoe.
4006	**consoler**	**console**
	vb	Leur capacité de consoler les survivants et leurs familles se limite à des conversations téléphoniques.
	[kɔ̃sɔle]	-Their ability to console the survivors and their families is limited to the telephone.
4007	**caoutchouc**	**rubber**
	m	Mets tes bottes en caoutchouc, sinon tu auras les pieds mouillés !
	[kautʃu]	-Put the rubber boots on, or else you will get your feet wet!
4008	**crisser**	**screech**
	vb	Le seul bruit que j'ai entendu était celui de cris émanant de la cour.
	[kʁise]	-All I could hear was someone shouting down in the courtyard.
4009	**entrain**	**spirit|zest**
	m	Il est plein d'entrain.
	[ɑ̃tʁɛ̃]	-He is full of zest.
4010	**raisin**	**grape**
	m	Il refusait le concombre parce que l'autre singe avait la grappe de raisin.
	[ʁezɛ̃]	-He would not accept the cucumber because the other monkey had the grape.
4011	**provisoire**	**provisional**
	adj	Le Règlement intérieur provisoire est provisoire au point d'être inexistant.
	[pʁɔvizwaʁ]	-These provisional rules of procedure are provisional to the point of not being there.
4012	**file**	**queue|row**
	f	Changement de voie: action consistant à quitter la voie ou la file empruntée pour reprendre une trajectoire initiale.
	[fil]	-Lane change means moving out from the occupied lane while continuing to drive in the original direction.
4013	**vérification**	**verification|check**
	f	Ce certificat est délivré après vérification sur les lieus.
	[veʁifikasjɔ̃]	-Such certificate is issued upon verification in loco of the residence.
4014	**hallucination**	**hallucination**
	f	Techniquement, tu as une hallucination hypnopompique.
	[alysinasjɔ̃]	-Technically speaking, you're having a hypnopompic hallucination.
4015	**punch**	**punch**
	m[pɔ̃ʃ]	C'est certainement beaucoup de punch. -Well, that certainly is a lot of punch.
4016	**courtoisie**	**courtesy**
	f	Votre courtoisie est appréciée.
	[kuʁtwazi]	-Your courtesy is appreciated.
4017	**entente**	**agreement**

f
[ɑ̃tɑ̃t]

Toutefois, l'entente n'est qu'une entente de principe.
-However, the agreement itself is an agreement in principle.

4018 atout — **asset**

m
[atu]

C'est le moment pour toi de jouer ton atout.
-The time has come for you to play your trump card.

4019 ouragan — **hurricane**

m
[uʁagɑ̃]

Le territoire cubain vient d'être à nouveau touché par un autre ouragan, l'ouragan Paloma.
-The Cuban territory has just been hit by another hurricane, hurricane Paloma.

4020 cahier — **notebook**

m
[kaje]

Le cahier des charges est conforme aux normes de la Lloyd's de Londres.
-The specifications meet the standards of Lloyd's Register.

4021 kidnapper — **kidnap**

vb
[kidnape]

Elle ne permettra à personne de le kidnapper et de le faire sortir du royaume.
-It will not permit anyone to kidnap the child and spirit it out of the realm.

4022 contribution — **contribution|input**

f
[kɔ̃tʁibysjɔ̃]

Sur la contribution sur les transactions financières, nous connaissons les données.
-We are all familiar with the data relating to the tax on financial transactions.

4023 émeute — **riot**

f
[emøt]

Pas moins de dix personnes furent arrêtées comme étant impliquées dans l'émeute.
-Not less than 10 people were arrested for being involved in the riot.

4024 négociation — **negotiation**

f
[negɔsjasjɔ̃]

Un règlement peut intervenir par la négociation, et uniquement par la négociation.
-A settlement can be achieved through negotiation, and only through negotiation.

4025 bulle — **bubble|bull**

f
[byl]

Une nouvelle bulle remplace l'ancienne.
-A new bubble will replace the old one.

4026 extinction — **extinction**

f
[ɛkstɛ̃ksjɔ̃]

On dit que cette espèce d'oiseau est menacée d'extinction.
-That species of bird is said to be in danger of dying out.

4027 isolement — **isolation**

m
[izɔlmɑ̃]

Malheur à qui est seul, mes amis, et il faut croire que l'isolement a vite fait de détruire la raison.
-Woe to who be alone, my friends. It seems that social isolation quickly destroys one's reason.

4028 panama — **panama**

m[panama]

Nombre de navires de guerre étasuniens furent envoyés à Panama. -Several American warships were sent to Panama.

4029 manifestation — **event|manifestation**

f
[manifɛstasjɔ̃]

La manifestation à l'hôtel de ville commença à déborder.
-The demonstration at City Hall started getting out of hand.

4030 irresponsable — **irresponsible**

adj
[iʁɛspɔ̃sabl]

Si l'on est financièrement irresponsable, on est également socialement irresponsable.
-If we are fiscally irresponsible we are socially irresponsible.

4031 tequila — tequila

m
[təkila]

« Champagne », « Tequila » et « Roquefort » sont des exemples parfaits d'indications géographiques.
 -"Champagne", "Tequila" and "Rocquefort" are examples par excellence of geographical indications.

4032 urine — urine

f
[yʁin]

Les rainures doivent être perforées pour permettre le drainage de l'urine.
 -Grooves should be equipped with perforations to allow drainage of urine.

4033 hystérique — hysterical

adj
[isteʁik]

Ensuite, l'obsession hystérique du réchauffement planétaire provoqué par l'homme.
 -Second, a hysterical obsession with man-made global warming.

4034 impoli — impolite

adj
[ɛ̃pɔli]

Je sais que c'est impoli, mais je vous prie de me comprendre et de partager ce genre d'inconvénient avec moi.
 -I know that is impolite, but I would ask you to understand and bear with me.

4035 chœur — choir

m
[kœʁ]

Encore maintenant, elle participe tous les lundis à des exercices de chant en choeur et est membre d'une chorale.
 -To this day, every Monday she attends choir practice and sings in a choir.

4036 rôtir — roast

vb
[ʁotiʁ]

Je ne sais même pas faire bouillir de l'eau, alors faire rôtir une dinde...
 -I cannot even boil water, much less roast a turkey.

4037 immobile — motionless | immobile

adj
[imɔbil]

Non susceptible de dispersion - Fixé ou immobile sous la forme existante, par exemple, un métal solide.
 -Non-dispersible - Fixed and immobile in the existing form - for example, a solid metal.

4038 stopper — stop

vb
[stɔpe]

Pour stopper ce commerce, les nations du monde doivent se montrer fortes et déterminées.
 -To stop this trade, the nations of the world must be strong and determined.

4039 fourré — thicket; filled

m; adj
[fuʁe]

Je voudrais un manteau fourré en laine, s'il vous plait.
 -I'd like a coat with the wooly side in, please.

4040 discrètement — discreetly

adv
[diskʁɛtmã]

Il faut l'employer discrètement et efficacement si nous voulons qu'elle produise des résultats.
 -It has to be used discreetly and effectively if it is to bring results.

4041 judas — peephole | judas

m
[ʒyda]

Ce judas de Jake les mène droit à toi.
 -That Judas Jake, he's leading them right here to you.

4042 compagne — companion

f
[kɔ̃paɲ]

Mais le sénateur Robichaud et sa compagne semblaient nous ignorer complètement.
 -However, Senator Robichaud and his companion seemed to be ignoring us completely.

4043 vole — vole

f
[vɔl]

Si les enfants ont constamment faim, ils commenceront à mendier et même à voler.
 -If children are constantly hungry, they will begin to beg and even steal.

4044	**sentimental**	**sentimental**
	adj	Est-ce que je deviens sentimental ou quoi ?
	[sãtimãtal]	-Am I getting sentimental or what?
4045	**éclairage**	**lighting|illumination**
	m	Le mythe apporte un nouvel éclairage à cette ancienne civilisation.
	[eklɛʁaʒ]	-The myth offers insights into the ancient civilization.
4046	**centimètre**	**centimeter|tape**
	m	Cette valeur doit être exprimée en Newtons par centimètre de largeur de ruban.
	[sãtimɛtʁ]	-This value shall be expressed in Newtons per centimetre of width of the tape.
4047	**restaurant**	**restaurant|cafe**
	m	Dans ce pays, il est virtuellement impossible de restaurer les édifices chrétiens.
	[ʁɛstɔʁã]	-In that country, it is made virtually impossible to restore Christian buildings.
4048	**précédemment**	**previously**
	adv	Précédemment, ils apparaissaient dans les notes relatives aux états financiers.
	[pʁesedamã]	-Previously, these liabilities were disclosed in the notes to the financial statements.
4049	**punk**	**punk; punk**
	adj; m	Et toi, avec tes cheveux de punk, toujours ces remarques cruelles.
	[pɛ̃k]	-And you, with that little, punky hair... always with the cruel remarks.
4050	**triangle**	**triangle**
	m	S'il y a un triangle, les services d'intérêt général en sont le barycentre.
	[tʁijãgl]	-If there is a triangle, services of general interest are the barycentre of it.
4051	**bronzer**	**tan|brown**
	vb	In figure III the content of sulphate and nitrate on exposed bronze panels is shown.
	[bʁõze]	-La figure III indique la teneur en sulfate et en nitrate des feuilles de bronze exposées.
4052	**mécanisme**	**mechanism**
	m[mekanism]	J'ai ré-implémenté entièrement en C le programme htmlize du précédent article, incluant un mécanisme de greffons ainsi que les deux greffons d'exemples. -I've re-implemented the htmlize program from the previous article entirely in C, including a plugin mechanism and the same two sample plugins.
4053	**impérial**	**imperial**
	adj	Ce texte arrogant et impérial est inacceptable.
	[ɛ̃peʁjal]	-This text, which is of an arrogant and imperial nature, is not acceptable.
4054	**inoffensif**	**harmless**
	adj	Le but final est de stabiliser les concentrations dans l'atmosphère à un niveau inoffensif.
	[inɔfãsif]	-The ultimate goal is to stabilise concentrations in the atmosphere at harmless levels.
4055	**brebis**	**sheep**
	f	Une brebis galeuse infecte tout le troupeau.
	[bʁəbi]	-One black sheep ruins the whole herd.
4056	**émettre**	**emit|transmit**

	vb	émettre un signal optique et acoustique dans la timonerie.
	[emɛtʁ]	-It shall be possible to transmit the binary signal to the control facility using

4057 trac — **stage fright**
m
[tʁak]
Comme les footballeurs, j'ai le trac des grandes occasions.
-I get nerves, like footballers on big occasions.

4058 étang — **pond**
m
[etã]
L'étang fait 100 mètres de diamètre.
-The pond is 100 meters in diameter.

4059 divan — **couch**
m
[divã]
Poussons le divan devant la porte.
-We can push the couch in front of the door.

4060 lavage — **washing**
m
[lavaʒ]
The stomach should be emptied as soon as possible by careful gastric lavage, preferably within one hour of ingestion.
-Il convient de vider l'estomac dès que possible en procédant, avec précautions, à un lavage gastrique, de préférence dans l'heure suivant l'ingestion.

4061 sirop — **syrup**
m
[siʁo]
Concentré de tomates, vinaigre, sirop de maïs riche en fructose, fructose enrichi et sirop de maïs.
-Tomato concentrate, distilled vinegar, high-fructose corn syrup... high-fructose corn syrup and corn syrup.

4062 vieillir — **age**
vb
[vjejiʁ]
Tous les pays continueront de voir leur population vieillir rapidement.
-The population of all countries will continue to age substantially.

4063 embaucher — **hire|take on**
vb
[ãboʃe]
L'employeur avait refusé d'embaucher la femme concernée comme stagiaire.
-The employer rejected to employ the woman as a trainee.

4064 éclairer — **light|enlighten**
vb[ekleʁe]
Oui, ouvrons notre temps au Christ, pour qu'il puisse l'éclairer et l'orienter.
-Yes, let us open our time to Christ, that he may cast light upon it and give it direction.

4065 peso — **peso**
m
[peso]
Mort, je ne vaux pas un peso.
-Dead I am not worth one peso.

4066 alentour — **surrounding**
adj
[alãtuʁ]
D'ici là, celui-ci a l'obligation de rétablir l'ordre public dans les camps et alentour.
-By that date, they must restore law and order in and around the camps.

4067 hymne — **anthem|canticle**
m
[imn]
Le drapeau et l'hymne du FRETILIN, Patria Patria, ont été adoptés comme drapeau et hymne du pays.
-The FRETILIN flag and anthem, Patria Patria, were adopted as the national flag and anthem.

4068 strictement — **strictly**
adv
[stʁiktəmã]
Leurs effets juridiques sont strictement limités au cercle des contractants.
-Their legal effects are strictly limited to the circle of contracting parties.

4069 poisse — **rotten luck**
f
[pwas]
J'ai une telle poisse !
-I have such bad luck.

4070	**résurrection**	**resurrection**
	f	Et ils sont poursuivis par une malédiction ici-bas et au Jour de la
	[ʀezyʀɛksjɔ̃]	Résurrection.
		-And a curse was made to pursue them in this world, and on the Day of Resurrection.
4071	**amical**	**friendly**
	adj	De toute façon, je voulais poser un geste amical envers ces gens.
	[amikal]	-In any event I was being friendly and extending a friendly hand to those people.
4072	**détour**	**detour|bend**
	m	S'il en est ainsi, je pense qu'on pourrait vraiment se passer du détour par
	[detuʀ]	l'Union européenne.
		-That being the case, I for one would be only too happy to spare us the detour via the European Union.
4073	**envisager**	**consider**
	vb	L'inactivité n'est pas une option que cette Organisation devrait envisager.
	[ɑ̃vizaʒe]	-Inactivity is not an option that this Organization should contemplate.
4074	**radiation**	**radiation**
	f	Nous respirons toute cette radiation en permanence.
	[ʀadjasjɔ̃]	-We're breathing in all this radiation all the time.
4075	**africain**	**African**
	adj; m	Ou adopte un beau bébé africain.
	[afʀikɛ̃]	-Or you could try adopting an incredibly good-looking African baby.
4076	**maléfique**	**maleficent**
	adj	Le soleil bleu, Vécanoï, est attaqué par une force maléfique.
	[malefik]	-The blue sun, Vécanoï, is attacked by a maleficent force.
4077	**barre**	**bar**
	f	La danse à la barre est un art.
	[baʀ]	-Pole dancing is an art.
4078	**excitation**	**excitation|anticipation**
	f	Les enfants ne pouvaient contenir leur excitation.
	[ɛksitasjɔ̃]	-The children couldn't contain their excitement.
4079	**rétablir**	**restore|re-establish**
	vb	Pour autant que les conditions météorologiques restent meilleures, la
	[ʀetabliʀ]	croissance devrait se rétablir à son niveau antérieur en 2006.
		-If the improved weather conditions remain steady, growth in 2006 is expected to revert to its recent trend.
4080	**utilité**	**utility|value**
	f	En outre, leur utilité est entièrement dépendante de leur conception.
	[ytilite]	-Their usefulness also depends crucially on the way in which they are designed.
4081	**décéder**	**die**
	vb	Cette année, onze millions de personnes vont décéder de maladies curables.
	[desede]	-Eleven million people will die of preventable diseases this year.
4082	**vertige**	**vertigo|spell**
	m	Jill peut-être sujette au vertige.
	[vɛʀtiʒ]	-Jill may be feeling dizzy.
4083	**poteau**	**post|pole**
	m	Je suis rentré dans un poteau.
	[pɔto]	-I ran into a pole.
4084	**compteur**	**counter**

m
[kɔ̃tœʁ]
Laisse tourner le compteur.
 -Keep the meter running.

4085 **pédale**　　　　　　**pedal**
f
[pedal]
Le grand piano n'a aucune pédale.
 -The grand piano has no pedal at all.

4086 **émetteur**　　　　　　**transmitter**
m
[emetœʁ]
Ils veulent placer un émetteur là-devant.
 -They want to put a transmitter up on the lawn.

4087 **interviewer**　　　　　　**interview**
vb
[ɛ̃tɛʁvjuve]
J'ai eu la très grande chance, au cours des 20 dernières années, de pouvoir interviewer des aînés métis extraordinaires.
 -I had a marvellous opportunity over the last 20 years to interview some wonderful old Metis people.

4088 **via**　　　　　　**via**
prp
[vja]
La punition devrait être infligée via une sanction pénale et pas via la responsabilité civile.
 -Punishment should be meted out by criminal sanctions not civil liability.

4089 **annonce**　　　　　　**ad|announcement**
f
[anɔ̃s]
Le député de Skeena parlait d'une annonce, sujet qui, à mon avis, était pertinent.
 -The hon. member for Skeena was addressing an ad, which in my opinion was relevant.

4090 **obus**　　　　　　**shell; dense**
m; adj
[ɔby]
Munition encartouchée avec obus explosif et douille, équipée d'une fusée
 -Complete round with HE-shell and cartridge case, with fuze fitted.

4091 **immigration**　　　　　　**immigration**
f[imigʁasjɔ̃]
La destination de l'immigration, du moins de l'immigration intracommunautaire, évolue. -The destination of immigration, at least intra-European immigration, is changing.

4092 **antidote**　　　　　　**antidote**
m
[ɑ̃tidɔt]
Le meilleur antidote en est l'esprit d'indépendance au niveau des collectivités.
 -The best antidote to this is a spirit of independence at the community level.

4093 **hollandais**　　　　　　**Dutch; Dutch**
adj; mpl
[ɔlɑ̃dɛ]
Le premier européen à apercevoir le Samoa était un hollandais, Jacob Roggeveen.
 -The first European to sight Samoa was a Dutchman, Jacob Roggeveen.

4094 **maternel**　　　　　　**maternal**
adj
[matɛʁnɛl]
Source : Étude sur l'allaitement maternel au Luxembourg, Direction de la santé & Ass.
 -Source: Study on maternal breast-feeding in Luxembourg, health directorate and Ass.

4095 **prédire**　　　　　　**predict|prophesy**
vb
[pʁediʁ]
Toutefois, pour le moment, nous ne pouvons prédire avec confiance si notre souhait sera exaucé.
 -However, at the moment we cannot confidently predict whether our wish will be fulfilled.

4096 **corbeau**　　　　　　**raven**
m
[kɔʁbo]
À la famille des corbeaux appartiennent le corbeau proprement dit, la corneille et la pie.
 -To the crow family belong the raven, the rook and the magpie.

4097	**ruser**	**use cunning**
	vb	Il va falloir ruser, menacer !
	[ʁyze]	-Then you'll have to trick her, threaten her.

4098	**avancée**	**progress**
	f	Quand je suis arrivé, la fête était déjà bien avancée.
	[avãse]	-The party was well along when I came.

4099	**sourcil**	**eyebrow**
	m	Si on lève un sourcil, ça peut signifier "J'ai envie d'avoir des relations sexuelles avec toi" mais aussi "Je trouve que ce que tu viens de dire est complètement idiot."
	[suʁsil]	-If you raise an eyebrow, it can mean "I want to have sex with you", but also "I find that what you just said is completely idiotic."

4100	**hétéro-**	**hetero-**
	pfx	Je suis Jay, et lui, c'est mon compagnon hétéro, Bob La Sourdine.
	[eteʁo-]	-I´m Jay, and this is my hetero life mate, Silent Bob.

4101	**légendaire**	**legendary**
	adj	Sa compassion pour la souffrance et les malheurs des autres était légendaire.
	[leʒãdɛʁ]	-His compassion for the suffering and misfortunes of others was legendary.

4102	**karma**	**karma**
	m	Je vends juste le concept d'amélioration du karma.
	[kaʁma]	-I'm selling only the concept of karmic realignment.

| 4103 | **naïf** | **naive; babe** |
| | adj; m[naif] | Arrête d'être si naïf. -Stop being so naive. |

4104	**humilier**	**humiliate**
	vb	Il ne fait pas de doute que cette mesure a été prise pour l'humilier et pour l'intimider.
	[ymilje]	-There is no doubt this measure was taken to humiliate her and to frighten her.

4105	**cérébral**	**cerebral**
	adj	Le taux de la mortalité due à l'accident vasculaire cérébral a baissé sensiblement pour les deux sexes.
	[seʁebʁal]	-The mortality rates for stroke have decreased markedly for both sexes.

4106	**supplémentaire**	**additional**
	adj	S'il faut une journée supplémentaire, allouons une journée supplémentaire.
	[syplemãtɛʁ]	-If that needs an additional day, we should allocate an additional day.

4107	**squelette**	**skeleton**
	f	Cet enfant qui s'accrochait à la vie n'était pratiquement plus qu'un squelette.
	[skəlɛt]	-The child was basically just the skeleton of someone who was barely clinging to life.

4108	**huer**	**boo|hoot**
	vb	Je défendrai mes convictions et je serai à la tribune pour les huer si nécessaire, particulièrement les députés bloquistes.
	[ɥe]	-I will stand up for what I believe in and I will boo them from the gallery, if necessary, especially the Bloc members.

4109	**heurter**	**hit|offend**
	vb	Le meilleur moyen de présenter la situation aux citoyens européens est de leur dire: «c'est vrai, nous avons heurté un obstacle sur la route, mais ce n'est pas la fin du projet européen».
	[œʁte]	-The best way for us to present this to the people of Europe is to say that yes, we have hit a bump on the road, but this is not the end of the European project.

4110	**gymnase**	**gymnasium**
	m	Il y a beaucoup d'étudiants dans le gymnase.
	[ʒimnaz]	-There are a lot of students in the gym.
4111	**cabaret**	**cabaret**
	m	Cet homme est un artiste de cabaret renommé.
	[kabaʁɛ]	-That man is a famous cabaret performer.
4112	**oubli**	**oversight|oblivion**
	m	Ces travailleurs ont déjà payé le prix de notre oubli.
	[ubli]	-These workers have already paid the price for our forgetfulness.
4113	**préméditation**	**premeditation**
	f	Je veux dire, ça prouve la préméditation.
	[pʁemeditasjɔ̃]	-I mean, that shows premeditation.
4114	**architecture**	**architecture**
	f	L'architecture décrite dans cet article est une architecture de référence de haut niveau.
	[aʁʃitɛktyʁ]	-The architecture explained in this paper is a high-level reference architecture.
4115	**librairie**	**bookstore**
	f[libʁeʁi]	Il lui était notamment reproché d'avoir à domicile une librairie indépendante. -He is accused in particular of possessing an independent bookshop at his home.
4116	**déguisement**	**disguise**
	m	La dissimulation ou le déguisement de produits du crime [art. 6 1) a) ii)];
	[degizmɑ̃]	-Concealment or disguise of the proceeds of crime (article 6.1 (a) (ii));
4117	**coût**	**cost**
	m	Le coût systémique et le coût institutionnel sont également cruciaux.
	[ku]	-Equally critical is the systemic cost and institutional cost.
4118	**semestre**	**half**
	m	Programmes d'initiation: ceux-ci durent un semestre, à plein temps.
	[səmɛstʁ]	-Initiation programmes: these are run on a half-year, full-time basis.
4119	**capsuler**	**cap**
	vb	De préférence, un système de refroidissement est intégré avec la machine à capsuler.
	[kapsyle]	-Preferably a cooling system is integrated with the capping machine.
4120	**braquer**	**shine|point**
	vb	Je n'étais pas fait pour braquer les banques.
	[bʁake]	-I wasn't made to rob banks.
4121	**corne**	**horn**
	f	6600km en ligne droite vers la corne de l'Afrique.
	[kɔʁn]	-4,125 miles in a straight line to the Horn of Africa.
4122	**gratter**	**scratch|strum**
	vb	Il a l'habitude de se gratter la tête.
	[gʁate]	-He has the habit of scratching his head.
4123	**humiliation**	**humiliation**
	f	Néanmoins, l'enfant prodigue est prêt à affronter cette humiliation et cette honte.
	[ymiljasjɔ̃]	-Nevertheless, the prodigal son is ready to undergo that humiliation and shame.
4124	**piège**	**trap|snare**
	m	Le 30 septembre, une femme kosovare serbe a été tuée à Klokot par un engin piégé placé sur la route.
	[pjɛʒ]	

-On 30 September, a Kosovar Serb woman in Klokot was killed by a booby-trap on the road.

4125	**réacteur**	**reactor**
	m	Ciel rouge du matin, la terre va pas bien; ciel rouge du soir, le réacteur repart.
	[ʁeaktœʁ]	-Red sky in morning; global warming. Red sky at night, reactor's alight.
4126	**chiot**	**puppy**
	m	Jack dit qu'il veut un chiot pour Noël.
	[ʃjo]	-Jack says he wants a puppy for Christmas.
4127	**reproduire**	**reproduce**
	vb	Ces institutions peuvent créer, refléter et reproduire les déséquilibres de pouvoir.
	[ʁəpʁɔdɥiʁ]	-Such institutions can create, reflect and reproduce imbalances of power.
4128	**fonctionnaire**	**official|officer**
	m/f[fɔ̃ksjɔnɛʁ]	Le Médiateur doit être un fonctionnaire indépendant, non partisan et impartial. -The Ombudsman must be an independent, non-partisan and impartial public servant.
4129	**impeccable**	**impeccable|spotless**
	adj	Comme d'habitude, l'information du sénateur Forrestall est impeccable quant aux nombres.
	[ɛ̃pekabl]	-As usual, Senator Forrestall's information is impeccable with respect to numbers.
4130	**entrailles**	**womb; insides**
	f; fpl	L'humour peut être disséqué comme une grenouille, mais la chose meurt dans l'opération et les entrailles rebutent quiconque à l'exception du pur esprit scientifique.
	[ɑ̃tʁaj]	-Humor can be dissected, as a frog can, but the thing dies in the process and the innards are discouraging to any but the pure scientific mind.
4131	**chaton**	**kitten**
	m	Tu veux voir mon chaton ?
	[ʃatɔ̃]	-Do you want to see my kitten?
4132	**psychologue**	**psychologist**
	m/f	Je suis une très bonne psychologue.
	[psikɔlɔg]	-Well, I'm a very good psychologist.
4133	**cueillir**	**pick|collect**
	vb	De plus, lorsque je suis allé cueillir l'objet, j'ai trouvé une facture de Douanes Canada.
	[kœjiʁ]	-On top of all that, when I went to pick it up, there was a bill from Canada Customs.
4134	**seuil**	**threshold|sill**
	m	46 millions d'Américains vivaient sous le seuil de pauvreté en 2010.
	[sœj]	-46 million Americans lived under the poverty line in 2010.
4135	**mécanicien**	**mechanic**
	m	Le mécanicien a réparé ma voiture sans me charger un sou.
	[mekanisjɛ̃]	-The mechanic fixed my car without charging me a dime.
4136	**noyau**	**core|kernel**
	m	Vous êtes tous les deux le noyau de l'équipe.
	[nwajo]	-You two are the nucleus of the team.
4137	**gentilhomme**	**gentleman**
	m	Vous resterez à tout jamais gravé dans ma mémoire comme un officier et un gentilhomme.
	[ʒɑ̃tijɔm]	-You will remain in my mind always as an officer and a gentleman.

4138	**malais** adj; m [malɛ]	**Malay; Malay** Le malais est la langue nationale, tandis que l'anglais est celle de l'administration. -Malay is the national language while English is the language of administration.
4139	**oie** f [wa]	**goose** Tu engraisserais comme une oie polonaise. -You'd become as fat as a Polish goose.
4140	**overdose** f [ɔvɛʁdoz]	**overdose** Par ailleurs, cette directive n'élimine pas le risque d'une overdose. -Nor will the risk of overdose disappear with this directive.
4141	**impasse** f [ɛ̃pas]	**impasse|deadlock** Nous nous dirigeons vers une impasse. -We're heading down a dead end.
4142	**boche** adj; m/f [bɔʃ]	**German; Jerry (derogative)** Un gros boche se cassait la gueule dans le brouillard. -This fat jerry came stumbling through the fog.
4143	**fraiser** vb [fʁeze]	**mill** L'invention concerne des structures d'ébauches à fraiser de prothèses dentaires. -The present invention relates generally to mill blank constructions.
4144	**roc** m [ʁɔk]	**rock** Tapisser le secteur où la pompe se déverse avec du roc propre pour prévenir l'érosion. -Line the area where intake discharges with clean rock to prevent erosion.
4145	**gouvernant** adj [guvɛʁnɑ̃]	**governing** Le gouvernement du temps de l'apartheid prétendait gouverner au nom du christianisme. -The previous apartheid government purported to rule in the name of Christianity.
4146	**brandy** m [bʁɑ̃di]	**brandy** Les coffres sont bons pour le brandy et les bijoux de grand-mère. -The house safe is for brandy and grandmother's pearls.
4147	**tarif** m [taʁif]	**rate** Les heures supplémentaires sont rémunérées à un tarif supérieur au tarif normal. -Compensation for such overtime shall be at a rate higher than the normal rate.
4148	**topo** m [tɔpo]	**sketch** Les gars, voilà le topo. -Guys, here's the outlay.
4149	**odieux** adj [ɔdjø]	**odious|heinous** Le meurtre qui a été commis était un acte absolument condamnable et odieux. -The murder that occurred there was a profoundly condemnable, abhorrent act.
4150	**adjudant** m [adʒydɑ̃]	**adjutant** L'adjudant a accompli sa mission. -The adjutant has successfully completed his task.
4151	**prairie**	**meadow**

f

[pʁɛʁi]

La technique de l'enfouissement n'est pas applicable aux prairies permanentes.
-Incorporation is not applicable on permanent grassland.

4152 livreur — **delivery man**

m

[livʁœʁ]

Tu l'as éjecté, comme le gentil livreur de pizzas.
-You were dismissive like you dismissed the nice pizza guy.

4153 puzzle — **puzzle**

m

[pœzœl]

Vient ensuite la grande pièce manquante du puzzle: l' accès à la justice.
-Then there is the big missing part of the jigsaw: access to justice.

4154 yard — **yard**

m[jaʁd]

Eventually, he broke out of the jungle into the yard of a house. -Finalement, il a déboulé de la jungle dans la cour d'une maison.

4155 lézard — **lizard**

m

[lezaʁ]

Elle a un lézard tatoué sur la cuisse.
-She has a tattoo of a lizard on her thigh.

4156 nocturne — **nocturnal**

adj

[nɔktyʁn]

Il règne vraiment une atmosphère historique dans cette session nocturne du Parlement.
-A really historic atmosphere prevails in this late-night session of Parliament.

4157 égratignure — **scratch**

f

[egʁatiɲyʁ]

C'est quoi cette égratignure sur ton visage?
-What's this scratch on your face?

4158 sexualité — **sexuality**

f

[sɛksɥalite]

Elle ignore tout de la sexualité.
-She knows nothing about sexuality.

4159 omelette — **omelette**

f

[ɔmlɛt]

On ne peut pas faire d'omelette sans casser des oeufs.
-One might even say a few eggs have to be broken if you are to make an omelette.

4160 timbrer — **stamp**

vb

[tɛ̃bʁe]

N'oublie pas, s'il te plait, de timbrer les lettres que je t'ai données à poster.
-Please don't forget to put stamps on the letters that I gave you to mail.

4161 mauviette — **wimp; weakling**

adj; f

[movjɛt]

Vous êtes une mauviette.
-You are a moron.

4162 klaxon — **horn|klaxon**

m

[klaksɔn]

L'usage du klaxon est à éviter de nuit. De nuit, préférez les appels de phares.
-Using the horn at night should be avoided. At night, flash the headlights instead.

4163 gardon — **roach**

m

[gaʁdɔ̃]

Pouvez prendre un gardon ramper dans le sable.
-You can pick up a roach crawling through the sand.

4164 infirme — **infirm**

adj

[ɛ̃fiʁm]

je ne suis pas infirme !
-I'm not an invalid!

4165 grotesque — **grotesque; grotesque**

adj; m

[gʁɔtɛsk]

Nous devons réduire la différence grotesque entre les qualités de vie des personnes.

-We must reduce the grotesque disparity between the qualities of life of peoples.

| 4166 | **juridique** | **legal** |

adj
[ʒyʁidik]

Le Gouvernement a décidé de combler le vide juridique qui existe dans ce domaine.
-The Government has undertaken to address the lack of legislation on trafficking.

| 4167 | **glorieux** | **glorious** |

adj[glɔʁjø]

Dans le quatrième mystère glorieux est envisagé] 'Assomption de Marie au ciel. -In the Fourth Glorious Mystery is contemplated] 'Assumption of Mary into heaven.

| 4168 | **précaution** | **precaution** |

f
[pʁekosjɔ̃]

Traçabilité, responsabilité, précaution sont des principes essentiels.
-Traceability, liability, responsibility, precaution; they are all essential principles.

| 4169 | **distinguer** | **distinguish** |

vb
[distɛ̃ge]

Il était clair qu'il fallait distinguer les incertitudes aléatoires des incertitudes systématiques.
-The need to distinguish random uncertainties from systematic ones was noted.

| 4170 | **remué** | **stirred** |

adj
[ʁəmɥe]

Est-ce que tu as bien remué ?
-Have you stirred it well?

| 4171 | **gonfler** | **inflate|rise** |

vb
[gɔ̃fle]

Cette attaque risquerait de gonfler les rangs des mécontents dans le monde musulman.
-Such an attack could swell the ranks of the discontented in the Muslim world.

| 4172 | **pellicule** | **film** |

f
[pelikyl]

Il n'y a aucune pellicule dans cet appareil photo.
-There isn't any film in this camera.

| 4173 | **spectaculaire** | **spectacular** |

adj
[spɛktakylɛʁ]

Tout d'abord a lieu une première lecture spectaculaire au Parlement européen.
-First of all, there is a dramatic first reading in the European Parliament.

| 4174 | **détacher** | **detach|loose** |

vb
[detaʃe]

Les derniers fragments devraient se détacher à une altitude comprise entre 50 et 40 km.
-The final fragment formation altitude is likely to be between 50 and 40 km.

| 4175 | **pourcentage** | **percentage** |

m
[puʁsɑ̃taʒ]

Quel pourcentage des gens parlent trois langues ?
-What percentage of people speak three languages?

| 4176 | **coude** | **elbow|bend** |

m
[kud]

Tu casses et puis coude gauche.
-Good. Now break it and then the left elbow.

| 4177 | **ceinturer** | **engirdle** |

vb
[sɛ̃tyʁe]

Mais nous disons parallèlement : le fait d'inciter de jeunes gens à se ceinturer d'explosifs afin de tuer d'autres personnes constitue un crime !
-At the same time, though, we declare it to be criminal to talk young people into strapping self-detonating devices to themselves in order to kill both themselves and others as well.

4178	**réjouir**	**rejoice**
	vb[ʁeʒwiʁ]	Il s'agit dès lors vraiment d'une situation dans laquelle tout un chacun peut se réjouir de ce qui se produit, car dans les faits, nous en bénéficierons tous. -The situation is therefore really one in which everyone can be pleased and elated about what is happening, because we shall, in actual fact, all benefit from it.
4179	**agresser**	**attack|mug**
	vb [agʁese]	Les États dotés des forces armées les plus puissantes devront s'engager à ne pas agresser les plus petits. -States with more powerful armed forces should state their intention not to attack smaller countries.
4180	**ragot**	**dirty; gossip**
	adj; m [ʁago]	Je viens juste d'entendre le meilleur ragot à propos de Nicholas Deering. -So, I just heard the best dirt on Nicholas Deering.
4181	**inattendu**	**unexpected**
	adj [inatɑ̃dy]	Ce rapport est devenu de manière inattendue très important pour le citoyen. -This report has unexpectedly become very important for the man in the street.
4182	**acheteur**	**buyer|shopper**
	m [aʃtœʁ]	J'ai trouvé un acheteur pour votre maison. -I found a buyer for your house.
4183	**sultan**	**sultan**
	m [syltɑ̃]	J'avouerais être le sultan turc. -I'd confess I was the Turkish sultan.
4184	**embrasse**	**embrace|kiss**
	f [ɑ̃bʁas]	Est-ce qu'il embrasse bien? -Is he a good kisser?
4185	**soixante**	**sixty**
	num [swasɑ̃t]	Il s'est également réuni pendant les soixante-sixième et soixante-septième sessions. -The working group also met during the sixty-sixth and sixty-seventh sessions.
4186	**écrouler**	**collapse**
	vb [ekʁule]	Comme nous l'avons vu, de tels soutiens et de tels piliers sont très fragiles et peuvent s'écrouler soudainement. -As we have seen, such props and such pillars are very fragile and can suddenly collapse.
4187	**exploiter**	**exploit|operate**
	vb [ɛksplwate]	Édouard Mwangachuchu, sénateur national, a obtenu l'autorisation d'exploiter la mine en 2001. -Edouard Mwangachuchu, a national senator, obtained a licence to exploit the mine in 2001.
4188	**toux**	**cough**
	f [tu]	Notamment de forts maux de tête, des crises de toux persistantes et des infections urinaires. -Among them were severe headaches, persistent coughing and urinary tract infections.
4189	**intégrer**	**integrate|include**
	vb[ɛ̃tegʁe]	Le Gouvernement azerbaïdjanais cherche à intégrer temporairement les personnes déplacées. -The Azerbaijani Government was trying to integrate displaced persons temporarily.
4190	**gène**	**gene**

m
[ʒɛn]

En thérapie génique, un vecteur est employé pour transporter le gène sain dans les cellules cibles.
-In gene therapy, a vector is used to transport the healthy gene to the target cells.

4191 **enfreindre**

vb
[ɑ̃fʁɛ̃dʁ]

violate|infringe

Sami était assez ennuyé d'avoir à enfreindre les règles.
-Sami was pretty annoyed for having to break the rules.

4192 **ruelle**

f
[ʁɥɛl]

alley

Ils se sont rendus dans une ruelle proche de là pour avoir une relation sexuelle.
-They proceeded into a nearby alley to have sex.

4193 **évaluation**

f
[evalɥasjɔ̃]

evaluation

Le rapport livre une évaluation mesurée de l'état actuel de l'enseignement scientifique aux USA.
-The report gives a sober assessment of the current state of science education in the US.

4194 **masculin**

adj; m
[maskylɛ̃]

male; masculine

Un étudiant américain masculin sur cinq a déclaré boire plus de 10 verres d'alcool lors d'une journée.
-One male American student out of five said that he drank more than 10 drinks a day.

4195 **rédacteur**

m
[ʁedaktœʁ]

editor

Ne veux-tu pas être rédacteur ?
-You don't want to be an editor?

4196 **matelot**

m
[matlo]

sailor

Un matelot et le cuisinier ont disparu.
-Another sailor and our cook have disappeared without a trace.

4197 **duo**

m
[dɥo]

duo

Batofar présente le duo allemande Motorcitysoul.
-Batofar's house party plays host to German production duo Motorcitysoul.

4198 **trappe**

f; adj
[tʁap]

hatch|trap; cobwebby

Avoir un emploi n'est plus un gage de non-pauvreté, ce peut être une trappe à pauvreté.
-Merely having a job, far from being a guarantee of being free of poverty, may prove to be a poverty trap.

4199 **inspecter**

vb
[ɛ̃spɛkte]

inspect|examine

S'il est possible d'inspecter les produits, examinez-en soigneusement l'étiquetage et la qualité.
-If products are available for inspection, examine carefully the labelling and quality.

4200 **camping**

m
[kɑ̃piŋ]

camping|campsite

Pour ce qui est du camping, le Service a trois terrains de camping aménagés.
-As to camping, the Service runs three nature camping sites on the island.

4201 **détourner**

vb[detuʁne]

divert|deflect

Il vous est facile d'essayer de détourner le débat, mais il ne doit pas être détourné. -It is easy for you to try and divert this debate, but it must not be diverted.

4202 **vital**

adj
[vital]

vital

Mais, dans le contexte de la motion à l'étude, il est important que les députés se rendent compte que l'exportation n'est qu'une des facettes de la gestion de cette ressource vitale.

-But in the context of the motion under debate it is important that members realize that export is but one facet of how we manage this life giving resource.

| 4203 | **distributeur** | **distributor** |

m
[distʁibytœʁ]

Ce distributeur automatique a été cassé par une bande de voyous la nuit dernière.
-This vending machine was destroyed by hoodlums last night.

| 4204 | **melon** | **melon** |

m
[məlɔ̃]

Voici un melon pour votre table.
-Here is a melon for your table.

| 4205 | **clicher** | **stereotype** |

vb
[kliʃe]

La moitié du temps, je suis un cliché dont on rit !
-Half the time, I'm a stereotype they make fun of.

| 4206 | **maestro** | **maestro** |

m
[maɛstʁo]

Maestro Neil Chotem, nous saluons votre mémoire et nous vous disons un immense merci.
-Maestro Neil Chotem, we honour your memory and extend to you our heartfelt thanks.

| 4207 | **crotter** | **poop|drop** |

vb
[kʁɔte]

Quand le poulet a arrêté de crotter... j'ai eu un numéro outre-mer prenant les paris 24 heures sur 24.
-When the chicken drop stopped, I got the number of a place overseas that takes bets 24 hours a day.

| 4208 | **chargeur** | **charger** |

m
[ʃaʁʒœʁ]

Dans le cadre du 1.4.1, le chargeur a notamment les obligations suivantes :
-In the context of 1.4.1, the loader has the following obligations in particular:

| 4209 | **peinture** | **painting|paint** |

f
[pɛ̃tyʁ]

De même, la peinture rouge lancée sur le bâtiment a laissé des taches sur la façade.
-Likewise, the red paint thrown to the building remained on the façade.

| 4210 | **projection** | **projection|screening** |

f
[pʁɔʒɛksjɔ̃]

Vas-tu assister à la projection d'un film ?
-Are you going to a movie?

| 4211 | **découper** | **carve|clip** |

vb
[dekupe]

Silence ou je vous épluche avant de vous découper.
-Silence or I will peel you before I slice you.

| 4212 | **parleur** | **talker** |

m
[paʁlœʁ]

Sommes-nous sur haut-parleur ?
-Are we on speakerphone?

| 4213 | **gratis** | **free; free** |

adv; adj
[gʁatis]

J'ai eu les poires gratis.
-I got the pears for nothing.

| 4214 | **carreau** | **tile** |

m
[kaʁo]

Vous avez choisi évidemment ce carreau pour une raison.
-You obviously chose this tile for a reason.

| 4215 | **caillou** | **pebble** |

m
[kaju]

Il lança un caillou sur le gros chien.
-He threw a stone at the big dog.

| 4216 | **imiter** | **imitate|mimic** |

	vb	
	[imite]	Tout cela pour satisfaire la croisade coercitive des réformistes et pour imiter la façon de faire de nos voisins du Sud.
		-And it is doing this to keep the Reform Party happy and ape our neighbours to the south.

4217 **stage** — **course**

m

[staʒ]

Mon maître de stage m'a laissé prendre un jour de congé.
-My placement supervisor allowed me to take a day off.

4218 **alléluia** — **alleluia**

int

[alelyja]

Seulement que tu as amené ton bateau sur la rive, alléluia.
-Only that you rode your boat ashore, hallelujah.

4219 **Ding!** — **Ding-Dong!**

int

[diŋ!]

Cette année, marke[ding] sera le 06 septembre à Wels, et le 09 septembre à Vienne.
-The brand [ding] held this year on 6 September in catfish (Wels) and 9 September in Vienna.

4220 **faculté** — **faculty|ability**

f

[fakylte]

Elle fit clairement comprendre qu'elle voulait aller à la faculté.
-She made it plain that she wanted to go to college.

4221 **gorgée** — **mouthful|gulp**

f

[gɔʁʒe]

Il avala la bière en une seule gorgée.
-He drank the beer in one gulp.

4222 **redoutable** — **formidable|dreadful**

adj

[ʁədutabl]

La question est de savoir ce que nous faisons face à cette redoutable paralysie de l'ensemble du fonctionnement de l'Union.
-The issue facing us is what to do about this dangerous paralysis of our general functioning.

4223 **peignoir** — **robe**

m

[pɛɲwaʁ]

Un connard en peignoir qui déverse ses toilettes dans mon égout.
-An asshole, in a bathrobe, emptying a chemical toilet into my sewer.

4224 **plaider** — **plead**

vb

[plede]

À cet égard, je voudrais faire une parenthèse pour plaider en faveur du Tribunal spécial pour la Sierra Leone.
-In this regard, let me digress and make a plea for the Special Court for Sierra Leone.

4225 **vanter** — **boast**

vb

[vãte]

Non, honorables sénateurs, notre premier ministre n'a pas de raison de se vanter.
-No, honourable senators, our Prime Minister has nothing about which to boast.

4226 **aiguille** — **needle**

f

[eɡɥij]

Mes mains tremblaient trop pour enfiler l'aiguille.
-My hands were shaking too much to thread the needle.

4227 **monastère** — **monastery**

m[mɔnastɛʁ]

Cela a été suivi de deux tentatives d'incendie criminel contre les vestiges du monastère. -This was followed by two arson attempts against the remnants of the monastery.

4228 **recul** — **recoil|retreat**

m

[ʁəkyl]

Le secteur immobilier est en sérieux recul et les gens qui y travaillent disent que le pire est à venir.
-The real estate industry is in a serious slump, and industry people say the worst is yet to come.

4229 **mémé** — **granny|nanny**

	f	Je donnerai une chemise à mémé pour Noël.
	[meme]	-I'll give grandma a shirt for Christmas.
4230	**lecteur**	**reader|pickup**
	m	Les définitions suivantes visent à fournir des orientations au lecteur.
	[lɛktœʁ]	-The following terms are intended to provide orientation to the reader of the Notes.
4231	**fraternité**	**fraternity**
	f	Leur universalité suppose la fraternité universelle du genre humain.
	[fʁatɛʁnite]	-Their universality presumes the universal brotherhood of humankind.
4232	**blaireau**	**badger**
	m	J'aime imaginer Jésus en blaireau espiègle.
	[blɛʁo]	-I like to picture Jesus like a mischievous badger.
4233	**caleçon**	**pants|underpants**
	m	Le caleçon, je vois le tableau.
	[kalsɔ̃]	-Underwear - I got the picture.
4234	**gala**	**gala**
	m	Yuri Ariel Gala López Counsellor Mrs. Yaima González de Gala
	[gala]	-Yuri Ariel Gala López Conseiller Mme Yaima González de Gala
4235	**flux**	**flow|flux**
	m	Nul flux sans reflux.
	[fly]	-No flow without reflow.
4236	**vocation**	**vocation|call**
	f	En tant que députés, cette responsabilité est plutôt notre vocation.
	[vɔkasjɔ̃]	-Rather, as parliamentarians, that responsibility is our calling.
4237	**bombardier**	**bomber**
	m	On est censé retaper le bombardier.
	[bɔ̃baʁdje]	-We got to get back to fixing up the bomber, all right.
4238	**raid**	**raid**
	m	L'inspecteur planifie un raid au night-club.
	[ʁɛd]	-The Inspector was just organising a raid on the nightclub.
4239	**lamentable**	**lamentable**
	adj	Ainsi, il serait lamentable de réduire les aides accordées aux pays de la cohésion.
	[lamɑ̃tabl]	-So it would be deplorable if aid to the cohesion countries were reduced.
4240	**short**	**shorts**
	m	Je parie sur le short jaune.
	[ʃɔʁt]	-I got the guy in the yellow trunks.
4241	**déception**	**disappointment**
	f[desɛpsjɔ̃]	Il comprenait ma déception et la déception des consommateurs: -He said that he understood my disappointment and the disappointment of the consumers.
4242	**contexte**	**context**
	m	Cette phrase prise hors contexte ne présente pas beaucoup d'intérêt.
	[kɔ̃tɛkst]	-This sentence isn't very interesting out of context.
4243	**dispositif**	**device**
	m	Nous mettrons en œuvre un dispositif de coopération Nord Sud repensé.
	[dispozitif]	-We will implement a reconsidered North-South cooperation mechanism.
4244	**plier**	**bend**
	vb	Nous sommes prêts à nous plier à la volonté de la communauté internationale.
	[plije]	-We are prepared to bend to the will of the international community.

4245 régner — **reign|take over**
vb
[ʁeɲe]
Sortez des ténèbres et reconnaissez qu'on ne peut plus régner comme jadis en maintenant les gens au secret!
 -Come out into the open and acknowledge that it is no longer possible to govern with old-fashioned secrecy.

4246 universitaire — **university; postgraduate student**
adj; m/f
[yniveʁsitɛʁ]
Département de zoologie, Université de Kelaniya, Sri Lanka, année universitaire 2002.
 -Department of Zoology, University of Kelaniya, Sri Lanka, 2002 academic year.

4247 massif — **massive; massif**
adj; m
[masif]
Quel chien massif !
 -What a big dog!

4248 drague — **dredge**
f
[dʁag]
Sept ans de courbettes pour acheter ma drague.
 -Seven years of crawling, that's what the dredge outside cost me.

4249 soupirer — **sigh**
vb
[supiʁe]
Et pourtant, chaque année, cette Assemblée se contente de hausser les épaules, de soupirer et de regarder ailleurs.
 -Yet every year this House just shrugs its shoulders, sighs and looks the other way.

4250 neutre — **neutral|neuter**
adj
[nøtʁ]
Le choix des indicateurs entrant dans la composition de l'indice ne peut toutefois pas être neutre.
 -However, the choice of indicators used to build the index cannot be value-neutral.

4251 bilan — **balance sheet**
m
[bilɑ̃]
Le bilan des pays communistes est globalement positif.
 -The assessment of communist countries is positive overall.

4252 fortement — **strongly**
adv
[fɔʁtəmɑ̃]
Le marché du travail est fortement différencié horizontalement et verticalement.
 -The labour market in Slovenia is strongly segregated horizontally and vertically.

4253 smoking — **tuxedo**
m
[smɔkiŋ]
Il te faut porter un smoking.
 -You need to wear a tuxedo.

4254 imprévisible — **unpredictable**
adj
[ɛ̃pʁevizibl]
Au début, il y avait une apparence anodine et totalement imprévisible.
 -In the beginning, there was a seemingly trivial and entirely unforeseeable.

4255 saloon — **saloon**
m
[salɔ̃]
Retrouvez-moi au saloon quand vous serez habillée.
 -Come find me in the saloon when you're decent.

4256 coque — **hull**
f
[kɔk]
Il est urgent de remplacer les pétroliers à simple coque par des pétroliers à double coque.
 -Single-hull tankers must be replaced by double-hull ones as a matter of urgency.

4257 répandre — **spill|scatter**
vb
[ʁepɑ̃dʁ]
Toute personne a le droit de former, d'exprimer et de répandre librement son opinion.

-Every person has the right freely to form, express and disseminate his opinion.

4258	**effondrer**	**collapse**
	vb	Réduire le budget européen revient, en fait, à laisser l'Europe s'effondrer.
	[efɔ̃dʁe]	-Reducing the European budget is in fact tantamount to letting Europe collapse.

4259	**mouchard**	**sneak|informer**
	m	Tu devais mettre ce mouchard sur Larry.
	[muʃaʁ]	-You were supposed to plant that bug on Larry.

4260	**distribuer**	**distribute|deliver**
	vb	On ne devrait pas proposer de distribuer de l'argent quand ce n'est pas légal.
	[distʁibɥe]	-It should not be proposed that money be given away when it is not legal to do so.

4261	**postal**	**postal**
	adj	Malheureusement, le secteur postal constitue une exception de taille.
	[pɔstal]	-Unfortunately, the postal services are a major exception to the rule.

4262	**clore**	**rule off**
	vb	Nous allons donc clore l' heure des questions en le remerciant de sa présence.
	[klɔʁ]	-We will therefore conclude questions to the Council and thank him for being here.

4263	**identique**	**identical**
	adj	Il s' agit d' une résolution identique émanant du même Conseil de sécurité.
	[idɑ̃tik]	-It is an identical resolution by an identical council, the Security Council.

4264	**apprêter**	**ready**
	vb	L'Irlande s'apprête à quitter le Conseil de sécurité avec la fierté de s'être acquittée de son mandat.
	[apʁete]	-Ireland finishes our Security Council with a strong sense of pride at having served.

4265	**scie**	**saw**
	f	Je n'ai jamais utilisé de scie à métaux avant. Tu pourrais me montrer ?
	[si]	-I've never used a hacksaw before. Could you show me how?

4266	**fossé**	**ditch|moat**
	m	Dan creusait un fossé le long de la route.
	[fose]	-Dan was digging a ditch along the road.

4267	**remuer**	**stir|move**
	vb	C'est notre priorité essentielle et nous devons remuer ciel et terre pour y parvenir.
	[ʁəmɥe]	-It is our top priority and we must move heaven and earth to make it happen.

4268	**ingrat**	**ungrateful**
	adj	Plus acéré qu'une dent de serpent est un fils ingrat.
	[ɛ̃gʁa]	-Sharper than the serpent's tooth is an ungrateful child.

4269	**corrompre**	**corrupt|taint**
	vb	Doit-on s'étonner que les agriculteurs se plaignent de ce que tout le processus est corrompu ?
	[kɔʁɔ̃pʁ]	-Is it any wonder why farmers are complaining that this whole process is corrupt?

4270	**vivement**	**deeply**
	adv	Bien sûr, je déplore vivement ces pertes d'emplois ainsi que la méthode utilisée par la société.
	[vivmɑ̃]	

-Of course I keenly deplore these lost jobs, and the methods employed by the company.

4271	**couillon**	**sod**
	m	Plus genre un couillon pompeux, si tu me demandes.
	[kujɔ̃]	-More like a pompous schmuck, you ask me.

4272	**agitation**	**agitation|restlessness**
	f	Cette phrase a vraiment causé de l'agitation, dis donc.
	[aʒitasjɔ̃]	-Boy, that sentence sure caused a kerfuffle.

4273	**tenon**	**tenon**
	m	L'invention concerne également un tenon dentaire facile à enlever.
	[tənɔ̃]	-Also, an easily removable dental post is disclosed.

4274	**choquer**	**shock|hit**
	vb	Schengen présente justement les caractéristiques totalitaires qui devraient choquer tout démocrate.
	[ʃɔke]	-Schengen has the kind of totalitarian features which would shock any democrat.

4275	**combine**	**combination**
	f	Ce poème combine prose et poésie.
	[kɔ̃bin]	-This poem combines prose with poetry.

4276	**notion**	**notion**
	f	La notion même de droits implique l'idée de devoirs ou d'obligations.
	[nosjɔ̃]	-The very notion of rights implies the notion of duties or obligations.

4277	**collaboration**	**collaboration**
	f	Elles seront examinées en collaboration avec les organisations compétentes.
	[kɔlabɔʁasjɔ̃]	-These will be investigated in collaboration with the relevant organizations.

4278	**habituellement**	**usually**
	adv	Ces répondants pratiquent habituellement dans la région de la capitale, Halifax.
	[abitɥɛlmɑ̃]	-Those respondents usually practise in the region of the capital city, Halifax.

4279	**dominer**	**dominate|control**
	vb[dɔmine]	Les conflits et l'instabilité en Afrique continuent de dominer l'activité du Conseil. -Conflict and instability in Africa continue to dominate the work of the Council.

4280	**perturber**	**disrupt**
	vb	E. vise à perturber lourdement ou à endommager gravement un système électronique.
	[pɛʁtyʁbe]	-(E) is intended seriously to interfere with or seriously to disrupt an electronic system.

4281	**mariner**	**marinate**
	vb	On retrouve, entre autres mets traditionnels, l'anguille marinée, le boudin noir et la choucroute à la viande de porc.
	[maʁine]	-Among the traditional dishes are marinated eel, blood sausage and sauerkraut stew with pork.

4282	**purement**	**purely**
	adv	Pour Cuba, l'importance de tels droits est loin d'être purement formelle.
	[pyʁmɑ̃]	-Cuba believes that the importance of those rights is not merely a formality.

4283	**gerber**	**throw up**
	vb	Tu me fais gerber, Lou.
	[ʒɛʁbe]	-Ah, you make me sick, Lou.

4284	**compétence**	**competence|skill**
	f	Ce travail dépasse ma compétence.
	[kɔ̃petɑ̃s]	-This job is beyond my ability.
4285	**blouson**	**blouse|jacket**
	m	Ce blouson sent le fauve à faire vomir.
	[bluzɔ̃]	-This jacket, it stinks of B.O. It's enough to make a person sick.
4286	**antécédent**	**antecedent**
	adj	Antécédents: Juzgado de Primera Instancia núm.1 de Cambados, 7 mai 2007
	[ɑ̃tesedɑ̃]	-Antecedents: Judgement of the Cambados Court of First Instance No. 1, 7 May 2007
4287	**voisinage**	**neighborhood|neighbors**
	m	La plupart des accidents ont lieu dans le voisinage.
	[vwazinaʒ]	-Most accidents happen in the neighborhood.
4288	**proximité**	**proximity|vicinity**
	f	À proximité de l'équateur, le climat est chaud et humide tout au long de l'année.
	[pʁɔksimite]	-Near the equator, the weather is hot and humid year-round.
4289	**intact**	**intact|unspoiled**
	adj	La centrale ressemble comme le seul intact.
	[ɛ̃takt]	-The power plant looks like the only one intact.
4290	**partisan**	**partisan|adherent; partisan**
	adj; m	Il n'a pas le droit d'afficher du matériel partisan dans son bureau de député.
	[paʁtizɑ̃]	-They are not allowed to display partisan material in their offices.
4291	**envoi**	**sending|dispatch**
	m	L'envoi de ces lettres ne prendra pas beaucoup de temps.
	[ɑ̃vwa]	-The sending of these letters won't take long.
4292	**spectre**	**spectrum|ghost**
	m[spɛktʁ]	Il faut pousser les radiodiffuseurs à utiliser le spectre efficacement. -There is a need to push broadcasters to use spectrum efficiently.
4293	**abuser**	**abuse|impose**
	vb	Je vous demanderais de ne pas abuser du règlement pour prendre la parole.
	[abyze]	-I would ask you not to abuse the Rules of Procedure in order to take the floor.
4294	**comédien**	**actor**
	m	Comédien dans son adolescence, il est devenu à 21 ans un pionnier de la radio francophone.
	[kɔmedjɛ̃]	-A teenage actor, he became a pioneer of French-language radio at the age of 21.
4295	**passage**	**passage|passing**
	m	Le passage des marchandises à la frontière est actuellement difficile.
	[pasaʒ]	-The passage of goods between our two borders is currently under strain.
4296	**sexuellement**	**sexually**
	adv	J'ai oublié de te dire que le sandwich est sexuellement libéré.
	[sɛksɥɛlmɑ̃]	-I forgot to tell you the sandwich is sexually liberated.
4297	**monstrueux**	**monstrous**
	adj	Le but de cet acte monstrueux était d'exterminer la population de la ville.
	[mɔ̃stʁyø]	-The purpose of this monstrous act was to destroy the town's entire population.
4298	**crapule**	**scoundrel**

	f	
	[kʁapyl]	Rudabaugh est un ignorant et une crapule.
		-Dave Rudabaugh is an ignorant scoundrel.
4299	**gain**	**gain|benefit**
	m	Votre perte est devenue notre gain.
	[gɛ̃]	-Well, your loss has been our gain.
4300	**idole**	**idol|goddess**
	f	Elle est à la recherche de l'idole d'immunité.
	[idɔl]	-She's off looking for the immunity idol.
4301	**grandiose**	**grandiose**
	adj	Quand nous sommes partis, nous ignorions cet accueil grandiose.
	[gʁɑ̃djoz]	-When we first started out... we got no idea you give us this grand reception.
4302	**prétentieux**	**pretentious|snooty**
	adj	Jack était loin d'être prétentieux.
	[pʁetɑ̃sjø]	-Jack certainly was not a pretentious person.
4303	**exploitation**	**exploitation**
	f	Exploitation économique, notamment travail des enfants et exploitation sexuelle.
	[ɛksplwatasjõ]	-Economic exploitation, including child labour and sexual exploitation.
4304	**gaspiller**	**waste|throw away**
	vb	Pour terminer, nos ressources humaines sont trop précieuses pour être gaspillées.
	[gaspije]	-In conclusion, our human resources are too valuable to squander.
4305	**carotte**	**carrot; carroty**
	f; adj	Le lapin mange la carotte.
	[kaʁɔt]	-The rabbit is eating the carrot.
4306	**crabe**	**crab**
	m[kʁab]	Vous ne pouvez pas forcer un crabe à marcher droit. -You cannot make a crab walk straight.
4307	**repère**	**landmark**
	m	Ce programme d'action demeure une année repère quant à l'évolution du processus de désarmement.
	[ʁəpɛʁ]	-This action programme remains a performance benchmark for the disarmament process.
4308	**compartiment**	**compartment**
	m	Je découvris le compartiment secret tout à fait par accident.
	[kõpaʁtimɑ̃]	-I found the secret compartment quite by accident.
4309	**dialogue**	**dialogue**
	m	Le dialogue diplomatique aida à mettre fin au conflit.
	[djalɔg]	-Diplomatic dialogue helped put an end to the conflict.
4310	**festin**	**feast**
	m	Le festin devait durer toute la nuit.
	[fɛstɛ̃]	-The feast was to last all night.
4311	**chronique**	**chronic; chronicle**
	adj; f	Ma conjonctivite est chronique.
	[kʁɔnik]	-My conjunctivitis is chronic.
4312	**grue**	**crane**
	f	Apprends-moi à faire une grue en origami. J'ai oublié comment plier le papier.
	[gʁy]	-Teach me how to fold a paper crane. I forgot how to fold it.
4313	**régulier**	**regular; regular**

adj; m
[ʁegylje]

Pour faciliter une gestion réactive, le mécanisme régulier va devoir opérer en cycles successifs.
-In order to support adaptive management, the regular process will need to go through a succession of cycles.

4314 cargo

m
[kaʁgo]

cargo

Receipts will continue to be necessary for following up the cargo (tracing).
-Afin de suivre la cargaison (traçage), des récépissés resteront nécessaires.

4315 pratiquer

vb
[pʁatike]

practice|use

Nul ne peut être contraint à pratiquer ou à s'abstenir de pratiquer un acte religieux.
-No one shall be forced to practice or restrain from practicing a religious exercise.

4316 frotter

vb
[fʁɔte]

rub|scrub

L'Asie doit se frotter les mains en voyant comment l'Europe, son premier rival, bat de l'aile.
-Asia should rub its hands as it sees how Europe, its main competitor, is flagging.

4317 fourchette

f
[fuʁʃɛt]

fork

Retire la fourchette de la prise électrique.
-Take the fork out of the electric socket.

4318 exclure

vb
[ɛksklyʁ]

exclude

Nous ne pouvons pas nous permettre d'exclure certaines ONG des financements.
-We cannot allow ourselves to exclude some NGOs from the financing.

4319 naviguer

vb[navige]

navigate

Durant ses loisirs, il aimait naviguer sur les eaux de la côte du Pacifique et il était commodore du West Vancouver Yacht Club. -In recreation he enjoyed the waters of the Pacific coast as commodore of the West Vancouver Yacht Club.

4320 roupie

f
[ʁupi]

rupee

Ce que tu te fais est de la roupie de sansonnet, comparé au salaire de la patronne.
-What you make is small potatoes compared to the boss's salary.

4321 efficacité

f
[efikasite]

efficiency

Charles Moore a créé le Forth dans une tentative pour accroître la productivité du programmeur sans sacrifier l'efficacité de la machine.
-Charles Moore created Forth in an attempt to increase programmer productivity without sacrificing machine efficiency.

4322 consul

m
[kɔ̃syl]

consul

1961-1964 Vice-Consul général de la République arabe unie au Nigéria (Kaduna)
-1961-64: Vice-Consul General of the United Arab Republic in Nigeria (Kaduna).

4323 cynique

adj; m
[sinik]

cynical; cynic

Je ne suis pas cynique à ce point-là.
-I'm not that cynical.

4324 municipal

adj
[mynisipal]

municipal

D'abord conseiller municipal, il est devenu maire de la ville de St. Boniface.
-He was first an alderman and went on to become Mayor of the Town of St. Boniface.

4325 velours

velvet

	m	Cette étoffe a le toucher du velours.
	[vəluʁ]	-This cloth feels like velvet.
4326	**pourriture**	**decay|rot**
	f	Je peux juste enlever la pourriture externe.
	[puʁityʁ]	-Best I can do is remove the outside rot.
4327	**parasite**	**parasite; parasitic**
	m; adj	Le cerveau pourrait être considéré comme un type de parasite de
	[paʁazit]	l'organisme, un pensionnaire qui réside dans le corps.
		-The brain may be regarded as a kind of parasite of the organism, a pensioner, as it were, who dwells with the body.
4328	**élan**	**elan|elk**
	m	Est-ce un élan ?
	[elã]	-Is it an elk?
4329	**philosophe**	**philosopher**
	m/f	Continuer comme avant, voilà la catastrophe, disait le philosophe Walter
	[filɔzɔf]	Benjamin.
		-To carry on as before is disastrous, said the philosopher, Walter Benjamin.
4330	**dortoir**	**dormitory**
	m	Mon collège comporte un dortoir.
	[dɔʁtwaʁ]	-My college has a dormitory.
4331	**récent**	**recent**
	adj[ʁesã]	Tous ces instruments sont relativement récents et sont, en outre, de nature assez originale. -All these instruments are of a relatively recent date and are, moreover, of quite an original nature.
4332	**ado**	**teenager**
	m	Le programme «Ado et jeune parent» (Teen and Young Parent Program)
	[ado]	est un programme bénévole destiné aux jeunes parents.
		-The Teen and Young Parent program is a voluntary program targeted at young parents.
4333	**distorsion**	**distortion**
	f	Nous avons la distorsion énergétique en visuel.
	[distɔʁsjõ]	-We're within visual range of the energy distortion, Captain.
4334	**dévorer**	**devour|eat up**
	vb	Une autre menace du même ordre risque de dévorer nos enfants, l'atout le
	[devɔʁe]	plus précieux de toute nation.
		-Another similar menace is threatening to devour our children, the most valuable asset of any nation.
4335	**représentant**	**representative|agent**
	m	Ils l'ont élu comme leur représentant.
	[ʁəpʁezãtã]	-They chose him as their representative.
4336	**bouclé**	**curly**
	adj	En cas d'accident, toute personne qui n'a pas bouclé sa ceinture risque
	[bukle]	d'être projetée dans le bus et de blesser ses voisins.
		-Anyone who, in a bus accident, does not have their seat belt fastened, with the result that they are thrown around the bus, will also injure their fellow passengers.
4337	**délibérément**	**deliberately|willfully**
	adv	Les Conventions de Genève sont délibérément méconnues.
	[delibeʁemã]	-The Geneva Conventions are being wilfully ignored.
4338	**torpille**	**torpedo**

	f	Un navire transportant 1300 hommes avait percuté une torpille.
	[tɔʀpij]	-A transport carrying 1,300 men had been split by a torpedo.
4339	**bled**	**boondocks**
	m	Comme c'est votre bled, peut-être pouvez-vous nous dire où trouver une bonne pizzeria.
	[blɛd]	-Since this is your neck of the woods, maybe you can tell us where to find a good pizza joint.
4340	**compositeur**	**composer; compositive**
	m; adj	Outre ses activités professionnelles, il est musicien et compositeur de jazz.
	[kɔ̃pozitœʀ]	-In addition to his professional activities, he is a jazz musician and composer.
4341	**uni**	**united|plain**
	adj	Quatrièmement, garder le Canada uni et indivisible.
	[yni]	-Fourth is the aim to keep Canada as one, united and indivisible.
4342	**taxe**	**tax**
	f	Il s'agit seulement d'une estimation car certaines entreprises ne versent pas ou ne peuvent pas verser de taxes.
	[taks]	-This is only an estimate because some companies do not or cannot afford to pay the taxes.
4343	**frérot**	**little brother**
	m[fʀeʀo]	Prends un nouveau départ, frérot. -Make a fresh start, little brother.
4344	**bâbord**	**port**
	m	Arrêt des moteurs bâbord et tribord.
	[babɔʀ]	-Port and starboard motors, all stop.
4345	**homard**	**lobster**
	m	Celui qui ne voit rien d'étrange n'a jamais regardé un homard en face.
	[ɔmaʀ]	-He who does not see anything strange has never looked a lobster in the eyes.
4346	**puer**	**stink|smell**
	vb	Ils brûlaient leurs empreintes, ça puait grave!
	[pɥe]	-They were burning their fingertips, the stink was unbelievable.
4347	**noblesse**	**nobility**
	f	Le pays était gouverné par une famille de la noblesse française.
	[nɔblɛs]	-The country was governed by a French noble family.
4348	**industriel**	**industrial; industrialist**
	adj; m	Je vous ai déjà dit que je ne suis ni planteur, ni industriel, ni commerçant.
	[ɛ̃dystʀijɛl]	-I have already told you that I am not a planter, or an industrialist, or a trader.
4349	**contrôleur**	**controller|supervisor**
	m	Jack est contrôleur aérien.
	[kɔ̃tʀolœʀ]	-Jack is an air traffic controller.
4350	**critiquer**	**criticize**
	vb	Si l'opposition officielle veut critiquer le gouvernement, qu'elle le fasse.
	[kʀitike]	-If the official opposition wants to criticize the federal government that is fine.
4351	**fléau**	**scourge|plague**
	m	Les campagnols du jardin sont un fléau.
	[fleo]	-The voles in the garden are a scourge.
4352	**convoquer**	**convene|call**
	vb	Si le mineur est pubère, le juge doit éventuellement le convoquer pour l'entendre.
	[kɔ̃vɔke]	

-If a minor has reached puberty the judge may summon him for a personal hearing.

4353	**politesse**	**politeness**
	f	J'admire la culture et la politesse des Allemands.
	[pɔlitɛs]	-I admire the culture and the politeness of the Germans.

4354	**sélection**	**selection|team**
	f	Ayant pour but une sélection juste, le sujet d'examen sera le même pour vous tous scientifiques du monde: écrivez un article scientifique en anglais !
	[selɛksjɔ̃]	-Aiming at a fair selection, the test's subject will be the same for all of you scientists of the world: write a scientific publication in English!

4355	**Hollande**	**Holland**
	f	Quand viendras-tu en Hollande ?
	[ɔlɑ̃d]	-When are you coming to the Netherlands?

4356	**accouchement**	**delivery|childbirth**
	m	L'accouchement a été très difficile.
	[akuʃmɑ̃]	-The delivery was very difficult.

4357	**cerise**	**cherry; cherry**
	adj; f[səʁiz]	Vous pouvez décorer ce cocktail avec une cerise ou de l'ananas. -You can decorate the cocktail with a cherry or a pineapple.

4358	**réservation**	**booking|reservation**
	f	Impossible. J'ai confirmé ma réservation hier.
	[ʁezɛʁvasjɔ̃]	-That's impossible, I confirmed my reservation last night.

4359	**famine**	**famine**
	f	La famine n'est pas un phénomène naturel, ce n'est pas un phénomène inévitable.
	[famin]	-Famine is not a natural occurrence and is not inevitable.

4360	**navigation**	**navigation**
	f	Navigation, very short term ahead is the operational navigation process.
	[navigasjɔ̃]	-La navigation à très courte échéance est le processus opérationnel de navigation.

4361	**perroquet**	**parrot**
	m	Je veux un perroquet.
	[peʁɔkɛ]	-I want a parrot.

4362	**coquin**	**rascal; naughty**
	m; adj	Non, Bunty, je suis le coquin.
	[kɔkɛ̃]	-No, Bunty, I am the rascal.

4363	**centime**	**centime**
	m	Ces ails chinois, officiels et clandestins, partent de Chine à dix centimes le kilo.
	[sɑ̃tim]	-Both the official and illegal Chinese garlic leaves China at 10 centimes per kilo.

4364	**pendaison**	**hanging|hang**
	f	La pendaison serait trop clémente pour vous.
	[pɑ̃dɛzɔ̃]	-Well, hanging is too good for the likes of you.

4365	**vexer**	**vex|upset**
	vb	Quoi que fassent les libéraux, ils ne veulent pas vexer les pollueurs.
	[vɛkse]	-Whatever the Liberals do they do not want to upset the polluter.

4366	**obligatoire**	**compulsory|binding**
	adj	Une obligation internationale souscrite unilatéralement a force obligatoire.
	[ɔbligatwaʁ]	-An international obligation that was assumed unilaterally was binding.

4367	**capter**	capture|receive
	vb	Dans l'idéal, les mesures du capital humain devraient capter ces trois dimensions.
	[kapte]	-Ideally, measures of human capital should capture these three dimensions.
4368	**furax**	hopping mad
	adj	Avec des champignons, elle serait pas si furax.
	[fyʁaks]	-Maybe if she put it about more, she wouldn't be angry.
4369	**portière**	door
	f	Un voleur professionnel peut crocheter une portière de voiture en un rien de temps.
	[pɔʁtjɛʁ]	-A professional thief can jimmy a car door in no time.
4370	**gramme**	gram|ounce
	m	Un gramme d'uranium radioactif peut donc nuire pendant des millions d'années.
	[gʁam]	-One gram of radioactive uranium can cause damage for millions of years.
4371	**étalon**	standard|stallion
	m[etalɔ̃]	C'est l'étalon or. -It's the gold standard.
4372	**rouleau**	roller|roll
	m	Le dynamomètre doit avoir un seul rouleau d'un diamètre d'au moins 0,400 m.
	[ʁulo]	-The dynamometer shall have a single roll with a diameter of at least 0.400 m.
4373	**peine**	penalty|sentence
	f	Ces délinquants reçoivent une peine atténuée.
	[pɛn]	-These offenders will be punished with a mitigated penalty.
4374	**exil**	exile
	m	Après avoir vérifié si la personne fait déjà l'objet de condamnations pénales à l'exil, au confinement à domicile ou à la détention, le Comité décide du traitement à appliquer.
	[ɛgzil]	-The committee decides on treatment and checks whether the person has other pending legal sentences for banishment, house arrest or jail.
4375	**canadien**	Canadian
	adj	Le titulaire du poste n'aura pas besoin d'être Canadien français ou Canadien anglais.
	[kanadjɛ̃]	-The new appointee need not be either a French Canadian or an English Canadian.
4376	**traquer**	track|track down
	vb	Solana veut désarmer l'Irak et traquer les dictateurs du monde.
	[tʁake]	-Mr Solana wants to disarm Iraq and hunt down the dictators of the world.
4377	**initial**	initial
	adj	Rapport initial et deuxième rapport périodique (CEDAW) et rapport initial (CRC).
	[inisjal]	-Initial and second periodic reports (CEDAW) and initial report (CRC)
4378	**taudis**	slum
	m	Le film est une peinture déchirante de la vie dans un taudis urbain.
	[todi]	-The movie is a harrowing depiction of life in an urban slum.
4379	**circuler**	circulate
	vb	Aujourd'hui, nous pouvons dire qu'il n'y a plus d'armes dans ces régions et qu'on peut circuler de façon sécurisée.
	[siʁkyle]	-We can now say that there are no more weapons in those areas and that we can move about safely.
4380	**sirène**	siren

f
[siʁɛn]

À Sdérot, la sirène d'alarme a retenti plus de 14 fois.
-In Sderot, the Red Alert siren was sounded more than 14 times.

4381 **levier** **lever**

m
[ləvje]

L'intensification de nos actions dans ces domaines pourra nous servir de levier pour améliorer nos résultats.
-The intensification of our activity in these areas will help us as a level to improve our results.

4382 **intermédiaire** **intermediate; intermediate**

adj; m
[ɛ̃tɛʁmedjɛʁ]

Du DDT est fabriqué sur place pour être utilisé comme intermédiaire dans la fabrication du dicofol.
-DDT is produced as a site-limited intermediate in the production of dicofol.

4383 **armement** **armament**

m[aʁməmã]

La société de Jakovic fabrique des systèmes d'armement pour l'armée. -Jakovic's company makes weapon systems for the military.

4384 **collecte** **collection**

f
[kɔlɛkt]

Cette ville excelle dans la collecte sélective.
-This town excels in waste separation.

4385 **ringard** **tacky; has-been**

adj; m
[ʁɛ̃gaʁ]

Mon père est un peu ringard.
-My father is a bit old-fashioned.

4386 **deuxièmement** **secondly**

num
[døzjɛmmã]

Deuxièmement, nous ne travaillons pas uniquement sur le principe de la majorité.
-Secondly, we are not operating exclusively on the principle of majority rule.

4387 **robinet** **tap|faucet**

m
[ʁɔbinɛ]

Le robinet fuit, il faut un nouveau joint.
-The tap's dripping and needs a new washer.

4388 **réparation** **repair|satisfaction**

f
[ʁepaʁasjõ]

Ma montre a besoin d'une réparation.
-My clock needs to be fixed.

4389 **boulevard** **boulevard|parade**

m
[bulvaʁ]

Je roulais tranquillement sur le boulevard.
-I'm riding on the boulevard, minding my own business.

4390 **dispute** **dispute|argument**

f
[dispyt]

Le «Somaliland» et le «Puntland» continuaient toutefois de se disputer les régions de Sool et de Sanaag.
-The regions of Sool and Sanaag, however, remained "contested areas" between "Somaliland" and "Puntland".

4391 **invincible** **invincible**

adj
[ɛ̃vɛ̃sibl]

Le secret invincible de Dieu est la croix de Jésus Christ, qui effraie chaque démon en enfer.
-God's invincible secret is the cross of Christ, which frightens every demon in hell.

4392 **vagabond** **vagabond; vagabond**

adj; m
[vagabõ]

Je suis un vagabond qui n'a rien à perdre.
-I'm a drifter with nothing to lose.

4393 **agiter** **shake|wave**

vb
[aʒite]

Monsieur le Président, personne n'a à agiter ou à ameuter le groupe d'électeurs le plus influent au pays.

-Speaker, nobody has to agitate or stir up the most powerful voting constituency in the country.

4394	**gazon**	**grass|lawn**
	m	Alors que l'automobiliste n'a qu'une vue approximative des pelouses fleuries, le cycliste urbain perçoit les couleurs et les différents parfums des fleurs, l'odeur du gazon fraîchement coupé, le bruissement des feuilles de marronnier, ou le soleil scintillant à travers le vert chatoyant des arbres au printemps.
	[gazɔ̃]	-While the car driver obtains an approximate view of a blooming meadow the city cyclist notices the different colors and scents of the blossoms, the smell of freshly mown grass, the swoosh of leaves of a chestnut tree, the sunlight twinkling through trees shimmering green in springtime.
4395	**bravoure**	**bravery**
	f	Sa bravoure pour sauver l'enfant de la noyade est au-delà des éloges.
	[bʁavuʁ]	-His bravery to save the child from drowning is above praise.
4396	**animer**	**animate|conduct**
	vb	Voyons si ça marche et donnons-nous une chance d'animer nos débats.
	[anime]	-Give us the chance to enliven our debates.
4397	**fugitif**	**fugitive; fugitive**
	adj; m	La haute cour a décidé de juger le chef de guerre fugitif par contumace.
	[fyʒitif]	-The high court decided to try the fugitive warlord in abstentia.
4398	**souverain**	**sovereign; sovereign**
	adj; m	Le Tsar était le souverain de la Russie.
	[suvʁɛ̃]	-The czar was the ruler of Russia.
4399	**embarras**	**embarrassment**
	m	Il remarqua son embarras.
	[ãbaʁa]	-He noticed her embarrassment.
4400	**offensif**	**aggressive**
	adj	Il a déclaré qu'il était du côté du défensif, et Mme Reding du côté de l'offensif.
	[ɔfãsif]	-He said that he is responsible for defensive measures whereas Mrs Reding is responsible for proactive measures.
4401	**brusquement**	**suddenly|sharply**
	adv	Il établit que le lisier transformé en biogaz devient brusquement un déchet.
	[bʁyskəmã]	-It lays down that slurry processed into biogas suddenly becomes a waste product.
4402	**irrésistible**	**irresistible**
	adj	La logique du compromis nous semble irrésistible.
	[iʁezistibl]	-The logic for compromise seems to us to be a compelling one.
4403	**doublure**	**lining|understudy**
	f	Vos bijoux étaient cousus dans la doublure.
	[dublyʁ]	-Jewelry of yours was sewn into the lining along with cash.
4404	**bicyclette**	**bicycle**
	f	En outre, une bicyclette a été fournie à chaque enfant pour qu'il soit plus mobile.
	[bisiklɛt]	-In addition, a bicycle has also been provided to each child to improve their mobility.
4405	**biologie**	**biology**
	f	Ce n'est pas mon objectif d'enquêter sur l'impact de la théorie d'Emmet sur la biologie.
	[bjɔlɔʒi]	-It is not my purpose to investigate the impact of Emmet's theory on biology.

4406	**enquête**	**survey|investigation**
	f	Il devrait enquêter sur ces crimes et poursuivre et sanctionner tous les auteurs.
	[ãkɛt]	-It should investigate such crimes and prosecute and punish all the perpetrators.
4407	**pleinement**	**fully**
	adv	Nous devons examiner pleinement cette question.
	[plɛnmã]	-Let us have a full review of this issue.
4408	**criant**	**crying**
	adj[kʁijã]	Nous avons commencé à crier, appelant Achraf, pour lui demander de sortir au plus vite. -We began to scream, shouting to Ashraf to get out as soon as possible.
4409	**détachement**	**detachment**
	m	Un détachement de légionnaires français va peut-être arriver.
	[detaʃmã]	-There's also a word that the detachment of French regime may be sent here.
4410	**ferry**	**ferry**
	m	En 2006, un ferry s'est mis à assurer la liaison entre Saint-George et Hamilton pour les voyageurs.
	[feʁi]	-In 2006, a ferry boat began to provide commuter service from St. George's to Hamilton.
4411	**canaille**	**vulgar**
	f	C'est cette canaille qui nous persécutait.
	[kanaj]	-This is the scoundrel who used to harass us.
4412	**paralyser**	**paralyze|cripple**
	vb	À elles seules, ces répercussions suffisent à paralyser l'économie de la Colombie-Britannique.
	[paʁalize]	-These impacts alone are big enough to cripple the British Columbia economy.
4413	**débuter**	**start|enter**
	vb	J'ai hâte d'entendre les commentaires de mes collègues dans ce débat qui va débuter.
	[debyte]	-I look forward to the comments from colleagues in the debate which now follows.
4414	**satisfait**	**satisfied|pleased**
	adj	J' ai été très satisfait de voir que le Conseil a accepté nos propositions.
	[satisfɛ]	-I was very gratified to see that the Council agreed with our proposals.
4415	**terminal**	**terminal; terminal**
	adj; m	On améliore ainsi les capacités de communications supportées par le terminal.
	[tɛʁminal]	-As a result, the communications capability supported by the terminal is improved.
4416	**fasciste**	**fascist; fascist**
	m/f; adj	Un footballeur s'est même présenté sur le terrain en exécutant le salut fasciste.
	[faʃist]	-A footballer even came on to the pitch exalting fascist symbols.
4417	**déprimant**	**depressing**
	adj	L'absence de travail sérieux constitue un autre aspect déprimant des camps de réfugiés.
	[depʁimã]	-The absence of meaningful work was another depressing aspect of the refugee camps.
4418	**secte**	**sect|connection**

f
[sɛkt]

L'instruction religieuse par telle ou telle secte ou confession est facultative.
-Religious education by any sect or denomination in Pakistan is optional.

4419 équipier — **team member**

m
[ekipje]

Avec l'arme et les résultats du labo... peu importe ce que j'aurais pu leur raconter sur la mort de ton équipier.
-If you have a gun and forensics...... wouldn't matter what I said about you killing your partner.

4420 poster — **post|poster**

vb[pɔste]

Or, j'ai moi-même fait l'essai de poster une plainte via votre site hier. - However, I myself made a trial attempt to post a complaint on your website yesterday.

4421 biche — **doe**

f
[biʃ]

Bonjour ma biche !
-Hello honey.

4422 gibier — **game|prey**

m
[ʒibje]

Le gibier est levé » est l'expression laconique de Holmes, signifiant qu'il faut entrer en action.
-The game's afoot" is Holmes's laconic call to action.

4423 re- — **re-**

pfx
[ʁə-]

i) Restructuration des Résolutions d'ensemble.
-(i) Restructuring of Consolidated Resolutions.

4424 pou — **louse**

m
[pu]

L'inspecteur s'accroche comme un pou.
-The inspector clings like a louse.

4425 interdiction — **prohibition**

f
[ɛ̃tɛʁdiksjɔ̃]

Interdiction de fumer.
-No smoking.

4426 pôle — **pole**

m
[pol]

Évidemment, le pôle Nord n'est pas le pôle Sud et l'Arctique n'est pas l'Antarctique.
-Obviously, there is a difference between the North Pole and the South Pole, the Arctic and the Antarctic.

4427 agenda — **diary**

m
[aʒɛ̃da]

Franchement, votre agenda est plus souple que le mien.
-To be honest, your diary is much more flexible than the President's.

4428 donneur — **giver|dealer**

m
[dɔnœʁ]

Jack est un donneur de leçons.
-Jack is a preacher.

4429 décorer — **decorate**

vb
[dekɔʁe]

Les enfants occupent des chambres à un, deux ou trois lits, qu'ils peuvent aménager et décorer eux-mêmes.
-Children have single, double or three-person rooms which they can arrange and decorate themselves.

4430 érection — **erection|stand**

f
[eʁɛksjɔ̃]

Une érection matinale : est-ce qu'elle durera jusqu'à ce que j'aille pisser ?
-A morning erection: Will it last only until I take a leak?

4431 colombe — **dove**

f
[kɔlɔ̃b]

Une colombe est un symbole de paix.
-A dove is a symbol of peace.

4432 insoler — **expose**

	vb [ɛ̃sɔle]	Pour obtenir ceux-ci, on peut insoler une couche de résine positive, à travers la plaque destinée à porter ces éléments et préalablement munie de couches opaques sur les parties correspondant à ces éléments. -In order to obtain them, a positive resin layer may be isolated, through the plate intended to carry these elements and previously provided with opaque layers on the portions corresponding to said elements.
4433	**terrifier** vb[teʁifje]	**terrify** Ces mesures visent à terrifier et à humilier. -These measures are meant to terrify and humiliate people.
4434	**baver** vb [bave]	**drool|run** Nous avons vu des réformistes baver d'envie devant le récent budget libéral. -We saw Reformers drooling over the Liberal's recent budget.
4435	**plombier** m [plɔ̃bje]	**plumber** As-tu appelé le plombier ? -Did you call the plumber?
4436	**gale** f [gal]	**scabies** Ammoniac, huile de sassafras, et du zinc contre la gale. -Ammonia, oil of sassafras, and zinc for scabies.
4437	**embrouillé** adj [ɑ̃bʁuje]	**confused|muddled** Le sujet devient chaque jour plus embrouillé. -The subject is becoming more muddled every day.
4438	**lumineux** adj [lyminø]	**luminous** Le flux lumineux normal est indiqué sur la feuille de données présentée. -The objective luminous flux is indicated on the submitted data sheet.
4439	**comète** f [kɔmɛt]	**comet** C'est ainsi qu'il découvrit la comète. -That's how he discovered the comet.
4440	**cannabis** m [kanabis]	**cannabis** Il s'agit essentiellement des produits du cannabis (haschisch/marijuana) (38 %), ecstasy (17 %), stimulants (14 %), LSD (11 %) et cocaïne (9 %). -This concerned primarily cannabis products (hashish/marijuana) (38%), ecstasy (17%), stimulants (14%), LSD (11%), and cocaine (9%).
4441	**pincer** vb [pɛ̃se]	**pinch|pluck** Certaines se faisaient pincer et étaient arrêtées par les agents de sécurité. -Occasionally they were caught and arrested by security agents.
4442	**défoncé** adj [defɔ̃se]	**stoned** As-tu déjà été défoncé au boulot? -Have you ever been high at work?
4443	**masse** f [mas]	**mass|body** Veuillez me notifier par courriel tout bogue détecté ou fonctions manquantes que vous voulez voir incluses dans les futures versions du calculateur d'indice de masse corporelle. -Please notify me by e-mail about any bugs found or missing functions that you want to be included in future versions of the BMI calculator.
4444	**prospérité** f [pʁɔspeʁite]	**prosperity** Notre prospérité dépend de la prospérité de nos voisins et de l'Afrique. -Our prosperity depends on the prosperity of our neighbours and of Africa.
4445	**décoration** f [dekɔʁasjɔ̃]	**decoration** Qui se charge de votre décoration ? -Who does your decorating?

4446	**impuissant**	**powerless**
	adj	Ces arrêts rendent le mouvement syndical impuissant.
	[ɛ̃pɥisɑ̃]	-The trade union movement is rendered powerless by these rulings.
4447	**ketchup**	**ketchup**
	m[kɛtʃy]	Marc, veux-tu du ketchup ? -Marc, do you want the ketchup?
4448	**crêpe**	**crepe|pancake**
	f	Aussi plate que tu fasses une crêpe, elle a toujours deux côtés.
	[kʁɛp]	-No matter how flat you make a pancake, it always has two sides.
4449	**permanent**	**permanent; permanent**
	adj; m	Le greffier est toutefois un employé permanent de la Chambre des communes et, à ce titre, il observe une stricte neutralité.
	[pɛʁmanɑ̃]	-The clerk, however, is a permanent employee of the House of Commons and as such is strictly non-partisan.
4450	**télécommande**	**remote control**
	f	Télécommande et télécommande automatisée des installations de propulsion.
	[telekɔmɑ̃d]	-Remote control and automated remote control of propulsion installation.
4451	**rivage**	**shore**
	m	J'ai vu le rivage au loin.
	[ʁivaʒ]	-I saw land in the distance.
4452	**fracturer**	**fracture**
	vb	Il nous incombe de contribuer à le renforcer, à l'affaiblir ou à le fracturer.
	[fʁaktyʁe]	-It is up to us to either help strengthen it or help to weaken and fracture it.
4453	**ragoût**	**stew**
	m	Allez-vous manger le reste de votre ragoût ?
	[ʁagu]	-Are you going to eat the rest of your stew?
4454	**sorcellerie**	**witchcraft|sorcery**
	f	Le Code pénal devrait être modifié pour abolir l'incrimination de la sorcellerie.
	[sɔʁsɛlʁi]	-The Penal Code should be amended to abolish the criminalization of witchcraft.
4455	**sentier**	**path|trail**
	m	C'est une question d'emphase: le sentier entre l'enfer et le paradis est étroit.
	[sɑ̃tje]	-It is a question of emphases: the path between heaven and hell is a narrow one.
4456	**expulser**	**expel|deport**
	vb	On a même menacé d'expulser la famille de quiconque est impliqué dans ces attaques.
	[ɛkspylse]	-There is even a threat to deport the families of anyone involved in such attacks.
4457	**proviseur**	**principal|headmaster**
	m	Il vient de devenir proviseur.
	[pʁɔvizœʁ]	-He has just become headmaster.
4458	**argument**	**argument**
	m	C'est plutôt un argument économique, voire un argument de protection de l'environnement.
	[aʁgymɑ̃]	-Now that is more of an economic argument or an environmental protection argument.
4459	**mystique**	**mystical; mystic**
	adj; m/f	Toute cette histoire de transsubstantiation mystique.
	[mistik]	-You have that whole mystical transubstantiation bit going.

4460 dégonfler — deflate
vb[degɔ̃fle]
Cette taxe appliquée à la seule Europe permettrait de dégonfler la bulle financière. -Implementing this tax solely in Europe would help deflate the bubble.

4461 protester — protest
vb
[pʁɔtɛste]
Je suis généralement gentil avec vous, mais je dois protester. -I am usually kind to your good self but I have to protest.

4462 vanité — vanity|pride
f
[vanite]
Sa vanité ne connaît pas de frontières. -Her vanity knows no bounds.

4463 tic — tic
m
[tik]
Ils ont une sorte de tic neveux. -They have a sort of a nervous tic.

4464 aliment — food
m
[alimã]
Le juge avait qualifié l'information d'«aliment de tous les jours de la pensée». -The learned judge described information as "the staple food of thought".

4465 étonnant — surprising|astonishing
adj
[etɔnã]
Il est étonnant que la Commission ait pu l'accepter sous la forme actuelle. -It is amazing that the Commission has seen fit to accept it in its current form.

4466 caresser — caress|stroke
vb
[kaʁese]
Nous caressons l'espoir que nos partenaires au sein de cette organisation paneuropéenne tireront les enseignements qui s'imposent. -We cherish the hope that the necessary lessons will be learnt by our partners of this pan-European organization.

4467 détroit — strait
m
[detʁwa]
Le bateau passe par le Détroit de Gibraltar. -This boat sails through the Strait of Gibraltar.

4468 exploit — feat
m
[ɛksplwa]
C'est donc là un premier exploit dont il faut féliciter le rapporteur. -This is the first achievement on which the rapporteur is to be congratulated.

4469 natal — native
adj
[natal]
Une personne très réputée dans son Yorkshire natal. -A person of great reputation in his native county of Yorkshire.

4470 impitoyable — ruthless|merciless
adj
[ɛ̃pitwajabl]
Pour les voyageurs, la concurrence venue de l'usage de la voiture particulière sera impitoyable. -In the passenger transport sector, competition from private cars would be merciless.

4471 sensationnel — sensational
adj
[sãsasjɔnɛl]
Je voudrais que ce résultat sensationnel figure dans le compte rendu d'aujourd'hui. -I ask that this sensational achievement be recorded in today's minutes.

4472 retarder — delay|postpone
vb
[ʁətaʁde]
Il est potentiellement dangereux de retarder ce processus pour le plaisir de le retarder. -Delaying the process for delay's sake is a potentially dangerous exercise.

4473 inventaire — inventory
m[ɛ̃vãtɛʁ]
L'inventaire est plein. -The inventory is full.

4474	**porto**	**port**
	m	Tu as toujours le meilleur porto.
	[pɔʁto]	-You always have the best port wine.
4475	**pharaon**	**Pharaoh**
	m	Il règnera jusqu'au prochain pharaon.
	[faʁaɔ̃]	-Till next Pharaoh is in place, he's in charge.
4476	**télescoper**	**telescope**
	vb	Au pire, nous voulons éviter le risque que les objectifs des fonds structurels et le souci de l'Union européenne de protéger ses habitats naturels ne se télescopent.
	[telɛskɔpe]	-At its worst, we want to avoid the possibility that the aims of the structural funds and the European Union's concern to protect its natural habitats may collide.
4477	**immortalité**	**immortality**
	f	Si seulement tu voulais lui donner l'immortalité.
	[imɔʁtalite]	-If only it be your intention to give her immortality.
4478	**poêler**	**fry**
	vb	Détailler 4 tranches bien épaisses de morilles des pins, bien les laver puis poêler comme un steak avec la gousse d'ail.
	[pwale]	-Cut 4 very thick slices of cauliflower mushrooms, wash well, then pan-fry like a steak with the clove of garlic.
4479	**quereller**	**quarrel**
	vb	Monsieur le Président, je pense qu'ils veulent faire une querelle avec un rien.
	[kəʁele]	-Speaker, I think he wants to quarrel over nothing.
4480	**graver**	**engrave|carve**
	vb	La décision de la Russie a de graves implications humanitaires et politiques.
	[gʁave]	-Russia's decision has grave humanitarian and political implications.
4481	**bourgeois**	**bourgeois; bourgeois**
	adj; m	Son libéralisme serait donc ultimement bourgeois ou même aristocratique.
	[buʁʒwa]	-His liberalism was therefore in the last analysis bourgeois or even aristocratic.
4482	**divertir**	**entertain**
	vb	M. Barker pourra te divertir pendant mon absence.
	[divɛʁtiʁ]	-Mr. Barker will be able to amuse you while I'm gone.
4483	**inacceptable**	**unacceptable**
	adj	Ce qui est inacceptable; comme poser des mines est également inacceptable.
	[inaksɛptabl]	-That is an unacceptable relationship — as mine laying is unacceptable anyway.
4484	**itinéraire**	**route; itinerary**
	m; adj	Des démonstrations d'artisans ponctuent cet itinéraire autour du patrimoine rural normand.
	[itineʁɛʁ]	-The craftsmanship displays mark this itinerary on the Norman rural heritage.
4485	**carnage**	**carnage**
	m	Le carnage se poursuit sans arrêt.
	[kaʁnaʒ]	-The carnage goes on and on without stopping.
4486	**provenir**	**result**
	vb	Mention est faite d'avantages, mais sans préciser d'où ils pourraient provenir.
	[pʁɔvəniʁ]	

-Benefits are mentioned without this report making it clear where they could come from.

4487	**citation**	**quote	summons**
	f	Le passage suivant est une citation d'une célèbre fable.
	[sitasjɔ̃]	-The following passage is a quotation from a well-known fable.
4488	**potion**	**potion**
	f	Princesse, ne buvez pas la potion.
	[posjɔ̃]	-Princess, don't drink the potion.
4489	**annuel**	**annual**
	adj	Un examen annuel du programme aura lieu dans le cadre de chaque examen annuel du PNUAD.
	[anɥɛl]	-Annual reviews of the programme will be part of the annual reviews of UNDAF.
4490	**limiter**	**limit	restrict**
	vb	Nous voulons limiter la souffrance.
	[limite]	-We wish to limit the suffering caused.
4491	**zombi**	**zombie**
	m	Elle regarde par la fenêtre comme un zombi statufié.
	[zombi]	-She's just staring out the front window like a zombie mannequin robot statue.
4492	**astronaute**	**astronaut**
	m/f	Aussi ai-je posé ma candidature pour être le premier astronaute de l'Union européenne.
	[astʁɔnot]	-I therefore put my name forward to become the first European Union astronaut.
4493	**bombardement**	**bombardment	bombing**
	m	Techniquement, c'était un bombardement.
	[bɔ̃baʁdəmɑ̃]	-Well, technically, that was a bombing.
4494	**saliver**	**salivate**
	vb	Ils m'ont donné un nouveau médicament, ça me fait saliver.
	[salive]	-They have me on some new medication it makes me salivate.
4495	**caresse**	**caress**
	f	Mon chat ronronne de plaisir lorsque je le caresse.
	[kaʁɛs]	-My cat purrs with pleasure when I pet it.
4496	**messie**	**messiah**
	m	Puis savons que ce mot est donnée par les prophètes de la révélation du Messie.
	[mesi]	-Then know that this word is given by the prophets to the revelation of the Messiah.
4497	**ressemblance**	**resemblance	likeness**
	f	Il crée l'homme à son image et ressemblance, comme homme et femme.
	[ʁəsɑ̃blɑ̃s]	-He fashions mankind, male and female, in his own image and likeness.
4498	**double**	**double	twin; double**
	adj; m	Je suis garé en double-file. Peux-tu te dépêcher ?
	[dubl]	-I'm double-parked. Could you hurry it up?
4499	**pin**	**pine**
	m[pɛ̃]	Il y avait une pile de pommes de pin au pied de l'arbre. -There was a pile of pinecones under the tree.
4500	**baronne**	**baroness**
	f	C'est pourquoi la contribution de la baronne Nicholson of Winterbourne est cruciale.
	[baʁɔn]	

-In this light, the contribution by Baroness Nicholson of Winterbourne is crucial.

4501	**téter**	**suck**
	vb	Jacob tétait une bouteille, mais je suppose que cela n'a pas suffi à calmer la nervosité qu'il ressentait d'être dans cette enceinte.
	[tete]	-Jacob was sucking on a bottle, but I guess even the bottle could not sooth his jangled nerves caused by being in this place.
4502	**surfer**	**go surfing**
	vb	Mettre un bikini et apprendre comment surfer.
	[syʁfe]	-Put on a bikini and learn how to surf.
4503	**allusion**	**allusion|reference**
	f	Dans votre déposition initiale, Helen, vous faites allusion à la fiancée de Danny.
	[alyzjɔ̃]	-In your original interview, Helen, you mention Danny's fiancee.
4504	**volcan**	**volcano**
	m	Le Mont Aso est un volcan actif.
	[vɔlkã]	-Mt. Aso is an active volcano.
4505	**fonder**	**base|set up**
	vb	Notre tâche est de fonder cette crédibilité sur l'efficacité et la transparence.
	[fɔ̃de]	-Our task is to build credibility based on effectiveness and transparency.
4506	**barbare**	**barbaric; barbarian**
	adj; m	Il y a dix-huit ans, un régime barbare totalitaire a pris fin dans ces pays.
	[baʁbaʁ]	-Eighteen years ago a barbarian totalitarian regime came to an end in these countries.
4507	**ému**	**affected**
	adj	J'ai été profondément ému par les condoléances exprimées par mon homologue pakistanais.
	[emy]	-I was deeply moved by the condolences expressed by my Pakistani counterpart.
4508	**pécheur**	**sinner**
	m	Tout saint a un passé et tout pécheur a un avenir.
	[peʃœʁ]	-Every saint has a past and every sinner has a future.
4509	**dentaire**	**dental**
	adj	La chirurgie dentaire est couverte, à condition qu'elle ne soit pas entraînée par la carie dentaire.
	[dãtɛʁ]	-Dental surgery is covered provided that it is not necessitated by tooth decay.
4510	**verrouiller**	**lock on**
	vb	Nous avons également eu la possibilité de verrouiller les réformes dans le système commercial multilatéral.
	[veʁuje]	-We had the possibility here to also lock the reforms into the multilateral trading system.
4511	**assommer**	**knock|stun**
	vb	Je ne vais pas vous assommer de détails; nous sommes finalement arrivés à bon port.
	[asɔme]	-I will not bore you with the details, but we finally arrived here.
4512	**humidité**	**moisture|humidity**
	f	Comment supportez-vous cette humidité ?
	[ymidite]	-How do you stand this humidity?
4513	**admiration**	**admiration**
	f	Il pleura d'admiration pour sa performance.
	[admiʁasjɔ̃]	-He cried in admiration of her performance.

4514 coudre — **sew|sew on**

vb

[kudʁ]

Dieu coudre parmi ce peuple sans numéro de miracles.

-God sew among this people unnumbered miracles.

4515 calculer — **calculate|time**

vb

[kalkyle]

L'étape suivante de la MIP consiste à calculer les stocks de capital productif.

-A next step in the PIM is the compilation of so-called productive capital stocks.

4516 clin — **wink**

m

[klɛ̃]

Une nouvelle décennie est passée en un clin d'œil.

-Another ten years went by in the wink of an eye.

4517 provenance — **origin**

f

[pʁɔvənãs]

Nous entendîmes une détonation en provenance d'à côté.

-We heard gunshots from next door.

4518 centrer — **center**

vb

[sãtʁe]

Permet de centrer horizontalement le contenu des cellules.

-Choose this option to center the contents of the selected cell horizontally.

4519 pneumonie — **pneumonia**

f

[pnømɔni]

Une opération sur sa gorge lui a permis de guérir de la pneumonie, mais elle l'a laissé sans voix.

-An operation on his throat helped him recover from the pneumonia, but it left him without his voice.

4520 réduction — **reduction|discount**

f

[ʁedyksjɔ̃]

La langue n'est que la cartographie des pensées humaines, des sentiments et des souvenirs. Comme toutes les cartes, elle est une réduction au cent millième de ce qu'elle tente de représenter.

-Language is just a map of human thoughts, feelings and memories. And like all maps, language is a hundred thousand times the thumbnail image of what it is trying to convey.

4521 rébellion — **rebellion|rebel**

f

[ʁebeljɔ̃]

Il s'agit d'une forme de rébellion.

-It's a form of rebellion.

4522 audacieux — **bold**

adj

[odasjø]

Elle devrait être appuyée par un programme industriel audacieux et imaginatif.

-That should be supported by a bold and imaginative industrial programme.

4523 interpréter — **interpret**

vb

[ɛ̃tɛʁpʁete]

C' est pourquoi il est toujours difficile d' interpréter toute différence.

-Therefore it is always difficult to interpret any differences.

4524 harceler — **harass|nag**

vb[aʁsəle]

Je ne vois vraiment pas comment on pourrait me harceler quand j'achète un bien ou un service. -I really do not see how I could be harassed when buying a commodity or service.

4525 regagner — **regain**

vb

[ʁəgaɲe]

Les victimes innocentes de ce conflit veulent simplement regagner leurs foyers.

-The innocent victims of this conflict want only to return to their homes.

4526 réplique — **replica|reply**

f

[ʁeplik]

C'est ma réplique !

-That's MY line!

4527	**flou**	**vague; blurring; fuzzily**
	adj; m; adv	Le problème est le suivant: c'est qu'ensuite notre règlement est beaucoup plus flou.
	[flu]	-The problem is as follows: after that the Rules of Procedure are much vaguer.
4528	**dénommer**	**name**
	vb	Il est proposé de dénommer le groupe «Groupe consultatif du marché immobilier».
	[denɔme]	-It is proposed to assign the name Real Estate Market Advisory Group and the acronym REM.
4529	**dériver**	**derive|drift**
	vb	However, it can be derived from other sources as well.
	[deʁive]	-Néanmoins, on peut tout aussi bien le dériver d'autres sources.
4530	**polo**	**polo**
	m	J'aime autant ne pas être le joueur de polo.
	[pɔlo]	-I'd really rather not be the polo player.
4531	**souffrant**	**suffering|ill**
	adj	Notre monde interdépendant est souffrant.
	[sufʁɑ̃]	-Our highly interdependent world is ailing.
4532	**contourner**	**get around**
	vb	Tout le reste, qui tend à contourner plus sournoisement les États, a été conservé.
	[kɔ̃tuʁne]	-The rest, which bypasses the Member States more insidiously, has been retained.
4533	**anomalie**	**anomaly**
	f	Surement une anomalie due au virus.
	[anɔmali]	-I'm sure it was just an anomaly brought on by the virus.
4534	**correspondance**	**correspondence**
	f	Correspondance avec le Secrétaire général, relative au conflit du Moyen-Orient.
	[kɔʁɛspɔ̃dɑ̃s]	-Correspondence with the Secretary-General concerning the Middle East conflict
4535	**étinceler**	**sparkle|flash**
	vb	Kaylie, montre que tu peux étinceler !
	[etɛ̃sle]	-Kaylie, let's see you shine.
4536	**clientèle**	**customers|clientele**
	f	Ce magasin ne distribuera plus de sacs en plastique pour sa clientèle.
	[klijɑ̃tɛl]	-This store will no longer give plastic bags to its customers.
4537	**bancaire**	**banking**
	adj[bɑ̃kɛʁ]	Le système bancaire algérien ne privilégie pas ce mode de paiement et de transfert. -The Algerian banking system does not favour this method of payment and transfer.
4538	**favorite**	**favored**
	adj	Select a favorite in this area.
	[favɔʁit]	-Sélectionnez un favori dans cette section.
4539	**dauphin**	**dolphin**
	m	Le dauphin est un mammifère.
	[dofɛ̃]	-A dolphin is a mammal.
4540	**infecter**	**infect**
	vb	Quand on travaille avec des pays de cet acabit, il est facile de se laisser infecter.
	[ɛ̃fɛkte]	

-If you have to work with countries of this sort, then what they do is infect you.

4541	**évier**	**sink**
	m	Elle a mis les assiettes sales dans l'évier.
	[evje]	-She put the dirty dishes in the sink.

4542	**émissaire**	**emissary**
	m	Pourquoi suis-je le seul dont ils se plaignent ? Ils veulent juste faire de moi
	[emisɛʁ]	un exemple et m'utilisent comme bouc émissaire.
		-Why am I the only one they complain of? They're just making an example out of me and using me as a scapegoat.

4543	**emprunt**	**borrowing**
	m	Combien d'échéances seront-elles nécessaires pour liquider cet emprunt ?
	[ɑ̃pʁɛ̃]	-How many payments will it take to pay off this loan?

4544	**poivre**	**pepper**
	m	Tu as mis trop de poivre.
	[pwavʁ]	-You put in too much pepper.

4545	**karaté**	**karate**
	m	Je veux apprendre le karaté.
	[kaʁate]	-I want to learn karate.

4546	**scorpion**	**scorpion**
	m	Les douze signes du Zodiac sont : le bélier, le taureau, les gémeaux, le
	[skɔʁpjɔ̃]	cancer, le lion, la vierge, la balance, le scorpion, le sagittaire, le capricorne, le verseau et les poissons.
		-The twelve signs of the Zodiac are: Aries, Taurus, Gemini, Cancer, Leo, Virgo, Libra, Scorpio, Sagittarius, Capricorn, Aquarius and Pisces.

4547	**buisson**	**bush**
	m	Ta passion a enflammé mon buisson.
	[bɥisɔ̃]	-Your thoughtfulness has given me the burning bush.

4548	**tricheur**	**cheater**
	m	C'est un tricheur et un menteur.
	[tʁiʃœʁ]	-He's a cheat and a liar.

4549	**paroisse**	**parish**
	f	Membre du Conseil de la paroisse de St. Benedict, La Romain; ministre
	[paʁwas]	laïc à la paroisse La Romain
		-Member, Parish Council, St. Benedict's Parish, La Romain; lay minister, La Romain Parish.

4550	**locataire**	**tenant|lodger**
	m/f[lɔkatɛʁ]	Simultanément, un nouveau locataire avait également acquitté une partie du loyer impayé. -At the same time, a new tenant settled part of the outstanding rent as well.

4551	**reconstruire**	**rebuild|reconstruct**
	vb	L'obligation du Gouvernement de reconstruire s'étend également aux sites
	[ʁəkɔ̃stʁɥiʁ]	religieux.
		-The Government's obligation to reconstruct extends also to religious sites.

4552	**manie**	**mania**
	f	Je ne comprendrai jamais cette manie du noir.
	[mani]	-I'll never understand this mania for black.

4553	**revers**	**reverse|back**
	m	Malgré tous ses revers, il reste optimiste.
	[ʁəvɛʁ]	-Despite all his setbacks, he remains an optimist.

4554	**transformation**	**transformation**

		f [tʁɑ̃sfɔʁmasjɔ̃]	Votre corps vit une magnifique transformation. -Your body is going through a beautiful transformation.
4555	**séminaire**	m [seminɛʁ]	**seminar** Si tu ne veux pas assister aux classes du séminaire sur "Combattre la corruption en entreprise", alors tu peux juste payer 200 hryvni et recevoir le certificat. -If you don't want to attend classes in the seminar on the topic "Fighting Corruption Inside the Enterprise", you can just pay 200 hryven' and receive the certificate.
4556	**plâtre**	m [platʁ]	**plaster** Il est resté pour les votes jusqu'au jeudi matin, après quoi il a dû être plâtré. -He stayed on to vote on Thursday morning and then his foot was put in plaster.
4557	**écossais**	adj; m: mpl [ekɔsɛ]	**Scottish; Scottish; Scots** Un autre groupe fait actuellement campagne en faveur de l'écossais d'Ulster. -In addition, other individuals now campaign on behalf of the Ulster Scots language.
4558	**béguin**	m [begɛ̃]	**crush** Elle a eu le béguin pour lui. -She had a crush on him.
4559	**comparaison**	f [kɔ̃paʁɛzɔ̃]	**comparison** En comparaison de Tokyo, Londres n'est pas très grande. -In comparison with Tokyo, London is small.
4560	**compliquer**	vb [kɔ̃plike]	**complicate** Au contraire, cela ne fera que politiser et compliquer davantage la question. -On the contrary, it will only further politicize and complicate the issue.
4561	**pet**	m [pɛ]	**fart** C'est comme lâcher un énorme pet et quitter la pièce. -You know, it's like cutting a huge fart and then walking out of the room.
4562	**déborder**	vb[debɔʁde]	**overflow|spill** Le rapport déborde d' hypocrisie en ce qui concerne les droits de l' homme. -The report is brimming with hypocrisy as far as human rights are concerned.
4563	**yuan**	m [jɥɑ̃]	**yuan** Comment fais-tu des affaires avec 300 yuan ? -How do you do business with 300 yuan?
4564	**implorer**	vb [ɛ̃plɔʁe]	**implore|plead** Nous devrions plutôt lui demander pardon et l'implorer. -We must implore his forgiveness.
4565	**cataloguer**	vb [katalɔge]	**catalog|label** Nous devons cataloguer chaque objet du coffre. -We have to catalogue every item in that vault.
4566	**activer**	vb [aktive]	**activate** C'est quelque chose que nous devrons maintenant activer. -This is something that we will now have to expedite.
4567	**pépé**	m [pepe]	**grandpa** J'ai dormi avec pépé, au parc. -Slept with Gramps in the park.
4568	**légion**		**legion**

f
[leʒjɔ̃]

Mon nom est Légion, car nous sommes nombreux.
-My name is Legion; for we are many.

4569 concurrent

competitor|contestant; concurrent

m; adj
[kɔ̃kyʁɑ̃]

Le concurrent lâcha la bonne réponse juste avant que le temps ne soit écoulé.
-The contestant blurted out the right answer just before the time ran out.

4570 socialiste

socialist; socialist

adj; m
[sɔsjalist]

D'aucuns ont critiqué le trop grand nombre de commissaires d'obédience socialiste.
-No one criticised the excessive number of Commissioners with Socialist allegiances.

4571 foulard

scarf|foulard

m
[fulaʁ]

Mon amie m'a donné un foulard de soie.
-My friend gave me a silk scarf.

4572 cricket

cricket

m
[kʁikɛt]

Je n'y connais rien en cricket.
-I don't know anything about cricket.

4573 constant

constant

adj
[kɔ̃stɑ̃]

Je souhaite remercier la population de Munster pour leur soutien constant au fil des ans.
-I want to thank the people of Munster for their consistent support over the years.

4574 sensibilité

sensibility

f
[sɑ̃sibilite]

J'ignore comment dessiner pas plus que je n'ai la sensibilité d'un artiste.
-I don't know how to draw, nor do I have the sensibility of an artist.

4575 bavard

talkative; chatterbox

adj; m
[bavaʁ]

Un bavard vend toujours la mèche et met en péril les intérêts des autres.
-A talkative person is always letting the cat out of the bag and jeopardizing the interests of others.

4576 abandon

abandonment|surrender

m[abɑ̃dɔ̃]

La maison est laissée à l'abandon. -The house has been left to go to ruin.

4577 microbe

microbe

m
[mikʁɔb]

« Microbe's genome reveals insight into ocean ecology », The Institute for Genomic Research, communiqué de presse daté du 15 décembre 2004.
-"Microbe's genome reveals insight into ocean ecology", The Institute for Genomic Research, press release dated 15 December 2004. 36 Rogers: K.

4578 doucher

douche|shower

vb
[duʃe]

Pendant que les blancs se faisaient dire de se doucher, les enfants dénés jouaient dans la poussière radioactive.
-While whites were told to shower, the Dene children played with radioactive dust.

4579 statistique

statistical; statistics

adj; f
[statistik]

Source: Bureau national de la statistique, Annuaire statistique national, 2001.
-Source: National Bureau of Statistics, China National Statistics Yearbook, 2001.

4580 immonde

unclean

adj
[imɔ̃d]

Une coalition contre ce crime immonde s'est constituée et s'est rangée fraternellement aux côtés du peuple américain.
-A coalition against that vile crime stood side by side with the people of the United States.

4581 errer

wander

	vb	Mère, vas-tu errer à jamais en fantôme rancunier ?
	[eʁe]	-Mother... will you wander as a vengeful ghost forever?
4582	**regrettable**	**regrettable|unfortunate**
	adj	Elle est particulièrement regrettable et fâcheuse pour les personnes touchées.
	[ʁəgʁetabl]	-It is particularly unfortunate and regrettable for people who are hit by it.
4583	**satané**	**devilish**
	adj	Les ayant appelés près de lui, il leur disait en paraboles: « Comment Satan peut-il expulser Satan ?
	[satane]	-And he called them to him, and said to them in parables, 'How can Satan cast out Satan?
4584	**choral**	**choral; choral**
	adj; m	Gagnant au Festival choral de Montréal 2001!
	[kɔʁal]	-Montreal Choral Festival 2001 - another win!
4585	**refroidir**	**cool**
	vb	De l'eau peut être utilisée pour refroidir et protéger les matières exposées.
	[ʁəfʁwadiʁ]	-Water can be used to cool and protect exposed material.
4586	**lècher**	**lick**
	vb	Jill lèche un cornet de crème glacée.
	[leʃe]	-Jill is licking an ice cream cone.
4587	**carotter**	**diddle**
	vb	Il est toujours en train de penser comment il peut me carotter.
	[kaʁote]	-He's always thinking how he can wangle something out of me.
4588	**cosmos**	**cosmos**
	m	Contempler la naissance du cosmos avec son télescope.
	[kɔsmos]	-Peering through his telescope at the birth of the cosmos.
4589	**embauche**	**hiring**
	f[ãboʃ]	Promouvoir l'embauche des personnes handicapées sur le marché du travail ordinaire. -To promote hiring of persons with disabilities in the regular labour market.
4590	**infâme**	**infamous|vile**
	adj	Ma délégation aimerait centrer quelques instants l'attention sur l'effet que cet acte infâme a eu au plan national, au plan régional et au plan international.
	[ɛ̃fam]	-My delegation would like to focus for a few moments on the impact that this dastardly act has had nationally, regionally and internationally.
4591	**plantation**	**planting**
	f	Il faut continuer à suivre la situation dans cette plantation.
	[plɑ̃tasjɔ̃]	-The situation on this plantation must continue to be monitored.
4592	**transaction**	**transaction|deal**
	f	Transaction to transaction calculations, for example, have not yet been addressed.
	[tʁɑ̃zaksjɔ̃]	-La question des calculs transaction par transaction, par exemple, ne s'est pas encore posée.
4593	**noces**	**nuptials**
	fpl	Après les noces, Grace accompagne Peter à Montréal, où ils vivent jusqu'en 1881.
	[nɔs]	-Grace accompanied Peter back to Montreal after their nuptials where they lived until 1881.
4594	**sardine**	**sardine**

f
   C'était ça ou une sardine.

[saʁdin]
   -It was either that or a sardine.

4595 cordon   **cordon**

m
   Elle refuse de donner le sang du cordon.

[kɔʁdɔ̃]
   -She's refusing to release the cord blood.

4596 journalisme   **journalism**

m
   En Amérique, le Président gouverne pendant quatre ans, et le Journalisme

[ʒuʁnalism]
   gouverne pour toujours.
   -In America the President reigns for four years, and Journalism governs
   forever and ever.

4597 rechanger   **change again**

vb
   Alors faites-le rechanger d'avis.

[ʁəʃɑ̃ʒe]
   -Then change it back.

4598 détermination   **determination|fixing**

f
   J'admire votre persévérance et votre détermination.

[detɛʁminasjɔ̃]
   -I admire your perseverance and determination.

4599 arroser   **water**

vb
   Il est recommandé de continuer à arroser la piste tout au long l'essai.

[aʁoze]
   -It is recommended that track-side wetting be continuously applied
   throughout testing.

4600 nourrice   **nurse**

f
   J'ai acheté une nourrice pour lui hier.

[nuʁis]
   -I purchased a wet nurse for him yesterday.

4601 croyance   **belief**

f
   La science est la croyance en l'ignorance des experts.

[kʁwajɑ̃s]
   -Science is the belief in the ignorance of experts.

4602 talentueux   **talented**

adj
   Il est nécessaire d'assurer de bonnes conditions aux individus talentueux en

[talɑ̃tɥø]
   Europe.
   -It is necessary to secure good conditions for talented people in Europe.

4603 athlète   **athlete**

m/f
   Si un athlète professionnel tombe malade, il bénéficie d'un traitement

[atlɛt]
   préférentiel.
   -If a professional athlete falls ill he or she is given preferential treatment.

4604 faciliter   **facilitate|aid**

vb
   Gestion – La conception du schéma XSD du CEFACT-ONU doit faciliter

[fasilite]
   la gestion.
   -Maintenance - The design of UN/CEFACT XSD Schema must facilitate
   maintenance.

4605 applaudir   **applaud|cheer**

vb
   Je peux donc vous applaudir pour votre engagement, mais je ne peux pas

[aplodiʁ]
   vous applaudir pour votre tolérance.
   -So I can applaud your commitment but I cannot applaud your tolerance.

4606 nausée   **nausea**

f
   Je me suis mise à avoir la nausée.

[noze]
   -I got nauseous.

4607 crédible   **credible**

adj
   Le solliciteur général de notre pays n'est tout simplement pas crédible.

[kʁedibl]
   -The solicitor general of our country is simply not believable.

4608 motivation   **motivation**

	f	La motivation est la clé du succès.
	[mɔtivasjɔ̃]	-Motivation is the key to success.
4609	**gémissement**	**groan|whine**
	m	Je m'en irai dans un éclat, pas un gémissement.
	[ʒemismɑ̃]	-I'm going out with a bang, not a whimper.
4610	**mutation**	**mutation**
	f	On doit envoyer Fenway pour la mutation.
	[mytasjɔ̃]	-We've got to send Fenway for the mutation.
4611	**cocher**	**check; coachman**
	vb; m	Veuillez cocher les fichiers à compacter.
	[kɔʃe]	-Please check the files you want to compress.
4612	**capot**	**hood**
	m	La voiture avait deux larges bandes peintes sur le capot et le coffre.
	[kapo]	-The car had two broad stripes painted on the hood and the trunk.
4613	**mûr**	**mature|grown**
	adj	L'édification de ce mur s'inscrit dans un plan plus général qui saute aux yeux.
	[myʁ]	-The construction of this wall falls within a larger scheme that is plain to see.
4614	**exigence**	**requirement**
	f	Les équipes d'évaluation multidisciplinaires répondent bien à cette exigence.
	[ɛgziʒɑ̃s]	-And multidisciplinary assessment teams make a good match with this requirement.
4615	**accessoire**	**accessory|incidental; accessory**
	adj; m[akseswaʁ]	La sûreté est un élément accessoire et dépendant de l'obligation qu'elle garantit. -Security rights are accessory to and dependent upon the obligation they secure.
4616	**bide**	**belly**
	m	Un gros bide est un risque professionnel pour les employés de bureau.
	[bid]	-A pot belly is an occupational hazard for office workers.
4617	**ouvrager**	**tool**
	vb	C'est le sort que réservent les États-Unis au peuple iraquien; et c'est l'ouvrage auquel ils s'attèlent.
	[uvʁaʒe]	-That is what the United States wants for the Iraqi people; and that is what it is working for.
4618	**moduler**	**modulate**
	vb	Il se peut qu'il ait à moduler cette démarche en fonction des données fournies.
	[mɔdyle]	-The Panel may need to vary this approach according to the data provided.
4619	**mitrailleuse**	**machine gun**
	f	Son petit coeur battait comme une mitrailleuse...
	[mitʁajøz]	-Its tiny heart was pattering like a machine gun...
4620	**jument**	**mare**
	f	Nous accueillons des jeunes et chacun d'eux s'occupera d'une jument poulinière qui doit mettre bas dans six à huit semaines.
	[ʒymɑ̃]	-We take youths and we team them up with a brood mare 6 to 8 weeks prior to the mare's foaling.
4621	**flot**	**stream|flood**
	m	Tout au contraire, la situation s'est détériorée, et le flot de réfugiés s'est accru.
	[flo]	

-On the contrary, the situation has deteriorated and the flow of refugees increased.

4622	**flatter**	**flatter|gratify**
	vb	On peut imaginer qu' il est facile, aisé de flatter une opinion publique.
	[flate]	-You may imagine that it is easy to pander to public opinion.
4623	**catch**	**wrestling**
	m	How can we be given that opportunity if it is a Catch-22?
	[katʃ]	-Comment pouvons-nous saisir cette occasion, si nous sommes dans une impasse ?
4624	**loto**	**lotto**
	m	Au plus, un résident de Richmond gagnera le loto.
	[lɔto]	-At most, one Richmonder will win the lottery.
4625	**esthétique**	**aesthetic; aesthetics**
	adj; f	Qu'est ce qui peut satisfaire ton sens de l'esthétique ?
	[ɛstetik]	-What is it that satisfies your aesthetic sense?
4626	**communisme**	**Communism**
	m	Un fantôme hante l'Europe - le fantôme du communisme.
	[kɔmynism]	-A spectre is haunting Europe — the spectre of communism.
4627	**classer**	**classify|rank**
	vb	Comment faudrait-il classer les protestations de la classe moyenne dans les pays arabes ?
	[klase]	-How should we classify the middle-class protests in the Arab countries?
4628	**hostie**	**host**
	f	Tu vas recevoir la sainte hostie!
	[ɔsti]	-Open his mouth for the Sacred Host!
4629	**enrager**	**annoy|enrage**
	vb	Ma thése fait enrager don Antonio.
	[ãʁaʒe]	-My thesis will enrage don Antonio.
4630	**exquis**	**exquisite|delicious**
	adj	Vu les circonstances, j'espérais pouvoir goûter à ces gaufres exquises, mais ce sera pour la prochaine fois.
	[ɛkski]	-In the circumstances I had expected to be able to sample these extremely delicious waffles, but that might be for another occasion.
4631	**rogner**	**crop|trim**
	vb	Glissez n'importe laquelle des huit poignées de rognage pour rogner l'image.
	[ʁɔɲe]	-Drag any of the eight cropping handles to crop the picture.
4632	**scandaleux**	**scandalous|outrageous**
	adj	Gollnisch a pris publiquement position en soutien à un communiqué scandaleux.
	[skãdalø]	-Mr Gollnisch publicly took a stand in support of an outrageous press release.
4633	**camper**	**camp|plant**
	vb	L'officier responsable a ordonné aux soldats de retourner camper dans une colline à Xalcuatla.
	[kãpe]	-The officer-in-charge ordered the soldiers to return to camp on a hillside at Xalcuatla.
4634	**stupéfier**	**amaze|astound**
	vb	» C'est de l'hypocrisie et c'est vraiment stupéfiant à voir.
	[stypefje]	-It is hypocrisy and it is truly amazing to watch.
4635	**antique**	**antique|ancient; antique**

adj; m | Un trésor enfoui fut trouvé à l'intérieur de l'antique tombe.
[ɑ̃tik] | -A buried treasure was found inside the ancient tomb.

4636 divertissement — **entertainment**

m
[divɛʁtismɑ̃]

Le divertissement sur sa planète consistait à faire des mathématiques multidimensionnelles de haut niveau.
-Entertainment on his planet meant doing multidimensional higher mathematics.

4637 infidèle — **unfaithful**

adj
[ɛ̃fidɛl]

Tuer un infidèle n'est pas un meurtre c'est la route vers le paradis.
-To kill an infidel is not murder, it is the path to heaven.

4638 console — **console**

f
[kɔ̃sɔl]

Ne posez aucun objet sur la console.
-Do not put any objects on the console.

4639 enfiler — **put on**

vb
[ɑ̃file]

Laissez-moi vous aider à enfiler votre manteau.
-Let me help you put on your coat.

4640 consommation — **consumption**

f
[kɔ̃sɔmasjɔ̃]

La consommation d'alcool est plus élevée en Europe de l'Est qu'en Europe de l'Ouest.
-Alcohol consumption is higher in Eastern Europe than in Western Europe.

4641 confondre — **confound|mix**

vb[kɔ̃fɔ̃dʁ]

N'essaye pas de me confondre. -Don't you try to confuse me.

4642 déprimé — **depressed**

adj
[depʁime]

J'étais déprimé de voir que l'opposition officielle n'était pas au pouvoir.
-I was depressed to see that the official opposition is not the government of the day.

4643 délivrer — **issue|deliver**

vb
[delivʁe]

Le service technique doit délivrer un certificat relatif aux matériaux.
-The technical service shall issue a certificate for the materials.

4644 dictionnaire — **dictionary**

m
[diksjɔnɛʁ]

Je vérifie les mots dans mon dictionnaire.
-I looked up the words in my dictionary.

4645 composition — **composition**

f
[kɔ̃pozisjɔ̃]

Levez la main si vous avez fini la composition.
-Raise your hand if you have finished the composition.

4646 spot — **spot|blip**

m
[spɔt]

Je ne pense pas pouvoir me souvenir de ce spot.
-And I don't really think I'd remember this spot.

4647 éclaircir — **clear|lighten**

vb
[eklɛʁsiʁ]

Au cours des cinq dernières années, le Groupe de travail a pu éclaircir 2 791 cas.
-Over the past five years, the Working Group has been able to clarify 2,791 cases.

4648 obsèques — **obsequies; funeral**

adj; f; fpl
[ɔpsɛk]

Les salariées ont droit à 15 jours de congé rémunéré en cas d'obsèques si leur mari ne peut pas obtenir ce congé, et si elles doivent elles-mêmes s'acquitter de cette tâche.
-Women employees get 15 days obsequies paid leave if her husband cannot get such leave and also if his wife has to perform such obsequies.

4649 intellectuel — **intellectual; intellectual**

adj; m [ɛ̃telɛktɥɛl]	Le docteur Patterson, une psychologue, a testé le quotient intellectuel de Koko. -Dr. Patterson, a psychologist, has tested Koko's IQ.

4650 liquider   **liquidate | wind up**

vb
[likide]

Dans les cas extrêmes, des producteurs ont été forcés de tout liquider.
-In extreme cases producers have been forced to sell out.

4651 escalade   **climbing | escalation**

f
[ɛskalad]

Jack a commencé l'escalade.
-Jack started climbing.

4652 contagieux   **contagious; communicable**

adj
[kɔ̃taʒjø]

Pouvons -nous déterminer si un animal vacciné est encore contagieux?
-Can we examine whether a vaccinated animal is still infectious?

4653 reproduction   **reproduction**

f
[ʁəpʁɔdyksjɔ̃]

Le poulpe ne sort de sa tanière que pour chercher de la nourriture ou à des fins de reproduction.
-The octopus only exits its lair to look for food or for reproductive purposes.

4654 trimestre   **quarter**

m[tʁimɛstʁ]

Le document final devrait être publié à la fin du premier trimestre ou au deuxième trimestre de 2007. -Publication of the final document is expected in late first quarter or second quarter 2007.

4655 pente   **slope | incline; heavy**

f; adj
[pɑ̃t]

Le pays est sur la mauvaise pente.
-The country is headed on the wrong track.

4656 anesthésier   **anesthetize; anesthetic**

vb; m
[anɛstezje]

Il a fui au bar pour s'anesthésier.
-He fled to the bar to anesthetize himself.

4657 comptabilité   **accounting | accounts**

f
[kɔ̃tabilite]

Jack a adopté notre méthode de comptabilité.
-Jack adopted our method of bookkeeping.

4658 bêta   **beta**

m
[beta]

Les calculs utilisent l'algorithme de fonction bêta normalisé.
-The computations use the normalized, incomplete beta function algorithm.

4659 nécessairement   **necessarily**

adv
[nesesɛʁmɑ̃]

Cela implique que la libéralisation doit nécessairement être asymétrique.
-That means that liberalisation must, of necessity, be asymmetrical.

4660 dérangement   **disturbance | inconvenience**

m
[deʁɑ̃ʒmɑ̃]

Nous présentons nos excuses pour le dérangement.
-We apologise for the inconvenience.

4661 désigner   **designate | nominate**

vb
[deziɲe]

La troisième option permet de désigner la clé publique d'une Partie contractante.
-The third choice is suitable to reference the public key of a Contracting Party .

4662 cobra   **cobra**

m
[kɔbʁa]

Que faire si vous avez été mordu par un cobra ?
-What should you do if you are bitten by a cobra?

4663 milice   **militia**

f
[milis]

Servir la milice est un honneur.
-To help the militia, it's an honor.

4664 tracteur   **tractor; towing**

	m; adj	Lorsque les poulets sont plats comme des crêpes, c'est que le tracteur devait être plus rapide qu'eux.
	[tʁaktœʁ]	-When the chickens are flat as pancakes, then again the tractor must have been faster than them.

4665 **manège** — **carousel\|treadmill**
m
[manɛʒ]
Les autres battraient pas un manège.
-The rest of the pack couldn't beat a merry-go-round.

4666 **apprenti** — **apprentice\|novice**
m
[apʁɑ̃ti]
L' homme continue à jouer à l' apprenti sorcier, à jongler avec la sécurité alimentaire.
-Humans are continuing to play the sorcerer' s apprentice, juggling with food safety.

4667 **cambrioleur** — **burglar**
m
[kɑ̃bʁijɔlœʁ]
Avez-vous entendu dire qu'un cambrioleur a forcé la maison du voisin ?
-Did you hear that a burglar broke into the neighbor's house?

4668 **boulette** — **pellet**
f
[bulɛt]
Ladite boulette comporte un matériau porteur qui fournit une source concentrée de protéines et d'autres éléments nutritifs essentiels.
-The pellet includes a carrier material that provides a concentrated source of protein and other essential nutrients.

4669 **puanteur** — **stench**
f
[pɥɑ̃tœʁ]
Il s'en dégage en permanence une puanteur épouvantable.
-The bucket causes a constant stench.

4670 **vaccin** — **vaccine**
m
[vaksɛ̃]
Accord portant création du Centre International du Vaccin.
-Agreement on the establishment of the International Vaccine Institute.

4671 **siffler** — **whistle\|hiss**
vb
[sifle]
À lui qui a été arbitre, je dirais, très sportivement, que j'avais bien fait à ce moment-là de le siffler.
-I would say to him, very sportingly, as he was once a referee, that I was right to blow the whistle on him then.

4672 **sordide** — **sordid\|wretched**
adj
[sɔʁdid]
C'est tout simplement sordide.
-That is nothing short of sleazy.

4673 **évoluer** — **evolve\|change**
vb
[evɔlɥe]
Le Groupe de la cession des actifs serait appelé à évoluer avec la Mission.
-The organization of the Unit would evolve gradually with the Mission's maturity.

4674 **instituteur** — **teacher**
m
[ɛ̃stitytœʁ]
Il sera un bon instituteur.
-He will be a good teacher.

4675 **baptême** — **baptism**
m
[batɛm]
Pour lui parler du baptême d'Aida qui aura lieu dimanche.
-To talk to him about Aida's baptism, which is this Sunday.

4676 **compatriote** — **compatriot**
m/f
[kɔ̃patʁijɔt]
Naismith serait certainement fier de son compatriote, comme nous le sommes tous d'ailleurs.
-Naismith would be proud of his fellow countryman, as are we all.

4677 **piaule** — **room\|pad**
f
[pjol]
Un scotch tassé, une piaule et le réveil.
-A fifth of scotch, a room and a wake-up call.

4678	**soûler**	**get drunk**
	vb	Je ne peux plus me soûler.
	[sule]	-I can't get drunk anymore.
4679	**défenseur**	**defender**
	m	Le défenseur pria le juge de prendre en considération l'âge de l'accusé.
	[defɑ̃sœʁ]	-The lawyer asked the judge to make allowance for the age of the accused.
4680	**miner**	**undermine**
	vb	Le chômage mine la confiance des citoyens européens.
	[mine]	-Unemployment is sapping the confidence of Europe's citizens.
4681	**caïd**	**boss**
	m	Le caïd nous honore de sa présence.
	[kaid]	-The boss honors us with his presence.
4682	**boucherie**	**butchery**
	f[buʃʁi]	Je suis déjà allée à la boucherie ce matin. -I already went to the butcher's shop this morning.
4683	**brocher**	**stitch**
	vb	En outre, dans le cas d'un livret, par exemple un passeport, qui utilise un fil
	[bʁɔʃe]	à brocher pour fixer les pages ensemble, de l'encre provenant de l'image imprimée s'infiltre dans le fil.
		-In addition, in the case of a booklet, for example a passport, that uses a stitching thread to secure the pages together, ink from the printed image bleeds into the thread.
4684	**sanguin**	**blood**
	adj	Passer un test sanguin ou autre.
	[sɑ̃gɛ̃]	-I can take a test, blood, whatever.
4685	**won**	**won**
	m	Au total, 360 milliards de won ont ainsi été octroyés entre 2001 et la fin
	[wɔ̃]	2004.
		-A total of 360 billion won was provided from 2001 to the end of 2004.
4686	**effectuer**	**perform|make**
	vb	Je crois que le moment sera venu d' approfondir et d' effectuer ce type de
	[efɛktɥe]	comparaisons.
		-I believe that that will be the time to carry out this type of comparison in more depth.
4687	**coquille**	**shell|typo**
	f	Ce doit être une coquille.
	[kɔkij]	-That has to be a misprint.
4688	**chaleureux**	**warm|cordial**
	adj	Mais nous adressons à nouveaux nos remerciements chaleureux pour la
	[ʃalœʁø]	qualité de ce rapport.
		-But once again, our heartiest congratulations on the quality of this report.
4689	**susceptible**	**susceptible**
	adj	This seems to be an adequate interpretation also susceptible to application
	[sysɛptibl]	in the ERW-context.
		-Cela semble être une interprétation appropriée, également susceptible de s'appliquer aux restes explosifs de guerre.
4690	**aspirer**	**aspire|aspirate**
	vb	Aucune société ne peut aspirer à progresser sans des mères et des enfants
	[aspiʁe]	en santé.
		-No society can hope to progress without healthy mothers and children.
4691	**infarctus**	**infarct**

m

[ɛ̃faʁktys]

Il souffrait de troubles cardiaques depuis son premier infarctus en 1984.
-His coronary problems dated back to his first heart attack in 1984.

4692 civiliser — **civilize**

vb

[sivilize]

Civiliser signifie soumettre au raisonnement, mettre en application la rationalité de la pensée, de la religion ou de la loi.
-To civilize means to subject to reason, to apply the rationality of thought, religion or law.

4693 enthousiaste — **enthusiastic; enthusiast**

adj; m

[ɑ̃tuzjast]

Howard était un agriculteur de renom ainsi qu'un enthousiaste amateur de hockey.
-Howard was a pre-eminent farmer and a hockey enthusiast.

4694 particule — **part|particle**

f[paʁtikyl]

C'est très inquiétant, car une seule particule peut être fatale pour certains groupes à risques. -This is extremely worrying, because one particle is already enough to be fatal amongst certain risk categories.

4695 reprise — **recovery**

f

[ʁəpʁiz]

La reprise devrait être favorisée par plusieurs évolutions positives.
-Several positive trends are likely to have a beneficial effect on recovery.

4696 hormone — **hormone**

f

[ɔʁmɔn]

Eventuellement, la mélatonine et l'hormone androgène peuvent être combinées à une progestérone.
-Optionally, the melatonin and androgenic hormone can be further combined with a progesterone.

4697 contrebande — **smuggling**

f

[kɔ̃tʁəbɑ̃d]

Effectivement, la contrebande de tabac a diminué.
-In terms of decreasing the smuggling of tobacco, that issue was addressed because it decreased.

4698 coffre — **safe|trunk**

m

[kɔfʁ]

Jack garde toujours des câbles de démarrage dans le coffre de sa voiture.
-Jack always keeps a set of jumper cables in the trunk of his car.

4699 acceptable — **acceptable|fair**

adj

[aksɛptabl]

Il semble que l'agression contre leur pays soit devenue acceptable pour la communauté internationale.
-It appears that aggression against their country has become palatable to the international community.

4700 joker — **joker**

m

[ʒɔke]

Il dispose d'un joker.
-He has the Joker.

4701 effondrement — **collapse|crash**

m

[efɔ̃dʁəmɑ̃]

Les enquêteurs ont découvert que l'entreprise a continué à commercer tout en étant insolvable, durant les mois précédant son effondrement.
-Investigators found that the company had continued to trade while insolvent in the months leading up to its collapse.

4702 avortement — **abortion**

m

[avɔʁtəmɑ̃]

La foule protestait contre l'avortement.
-The throng protested against abortion.

4703 martyr — **martyr; martyred**

m; adj

[maʁtiʁ]

« Le testament du martyr Walid Al-Shehri », diffusé à travers les forums de l'Internet.
-"The will of martyr Walid Al-Shehri", circulated through forums on the Internet.

4704 installation — **installation|plant**

f
[ɛ̃stalasjɔ̃]

En ce qui concerne la nouvelle installation au Brésil, nous n'avons pas encore pris de décision.
-Regarding the new facility in Brazil we have not made a decision yet.

4705 résumer — summarize|resume

vb
[ʁezyme]

Il sera désigné un rapporteur qui sera chargé de suivre et de résumer les débats.
-A rapporteur will be nominated to follow and summarize the discussion.

4706 hausser — raise|increase

vb
[ose]

Trichet ne devrait pas hausser les taux d'intérêt.
-We are not saying that Mr Trichet should not raise interest rates.

4707 chalet — chalet

m
[ʃalɛ]

Dans ce cas, Son Altesse m'a chargé... de vous inviter à dîner ce soir, à 8h, à son chalet.
-In that case, Her Highness has instructed me... to invite you for dinner this evening, 8: 00 at her chalet.

4708 pansement — dressing

m
[pɑ̃smɑ̃]

Il vit un pansement sur son genou gauche.
-He saw a small Band-Aid on her left knee.

4709 gifler — slap

vb
[ʒifle]

C'est une gifle lancée à chaque électeur et une gifle pour la crédibilité de l'Europe.
-This is a slap in the face for every voter and a slap in the face for Europe's credibility.

4710 ronger — gnaw

vb
[ʁɔ̃ʒe]

L'OIT en est seulement revenue avec un os à ronger: elle peut travailler à la question.
-The ILO was packed off home with a pat on the back and permission to deal with this issue.

4711 adolescent — teenager; adolescent

m; adj
[adɔlesɑ̃]

C'est un jeune adolescent impressionnable.
-He's a young, impressionable teenager.

4712 frisson — thrill|shivers

m
[fʁisɔ̃]

Un frisson parcourut ma colonne vertébrale.
-A shiver ran down my spine.

4713 commando — commando

m
[kɔmɑdo]

Un commando est venu ramasser toutes nos affaires.
-And a commando came in... and removed all our belongings right away.

4714 principalement — mainly|mostly

adv
[pʁɛ̃sipalmɑ̃]

Il sera totalement isolé... dans le principal edifiicio, au centre de la place.
-He's going to be isolated...... in the main edificio in the center of the plaza.

4715 juridiction — jurisdiction

f
[ʒyʁidiksjɔ̃]

Ça ne fait pas partie de ma juridiction.
-That's not in my bailiwick.

4716 insensible — insensitive

adj
[ɛ̃sɑ̃sibl]

La proposition d' aujourd' hui est insensible dans les circonstances actuelles.
-Of course the proposal you have made today is insensitive given the circumstances.

4717 baptiste — baptist

m
[batist]

En août 2000, Vitali Tereshin, missionnaire baptiste, aurait été arrêté et expulsé du pays.

-Vitaly Tereshin, a Baptist missionary, was reportedly arrested and deported in August 2000.

4718	**carnaval**	**carnival**
	m	
	[kaʁnaval]	Certains volontaires boycottent le carnaval si les Atrians viennent.
		-Some of my volunteers are boycotting the carnival if the Atrians attend.
4719	**écouler**	**sell**
	vb[ekule]	Nous avons assisté au cours de l'année écoulée à un mouvement extraordinaire dans le sens d'une responsabilité collective. -Over the last year there has been an extraordinary shift towards a collective responsibility.
4720	**crucial**	**crucial|critical**
	adj	
	[kʁysjal]	Les procédures spéciales jouent un rôle crucial dans les activités du Conseil.
		-The special procedures played a pivotal role in the activities of the Council.
4721	**pion**	**pawn|piece**
	m	
	[pjɔ̃]	L'Afrique n'est pas et ne sera jamais un simple pion sur l'échiquier du monde.
		-Africa is not and will never be a mere pawn on the chessboard of the world.
4722	**spécimen**	**specimen**
	m	
	[spesimɛn]	Ce merveilleux spécimen et moi comptons passer la journée seuls.
		-This perfect specimen and I were planning to spend the day alone together.
4723	**participation**	**participation|contribution**
	f	
	[paʁtisipasjɔ̃]	Participation aux décisions, participation aussi aux résultats.
		-Participation in decision making and also participation in the results.
4724	**poney**	**pony**
	m	
	[pɔnɛ]	Sophie avait un poney à elle, que lui avait donné son papa.
		-Sophie had her own pony. It had been given to her by her father.
4725	**endommager**	**damage**
	vb	
	[ɑ̃dɔmaʒe]	Remplacer «et éventuellement d'endommager gravement» par «ou d'endommager gravement».
		-Replace "and possibly serious damage" by "or serious damage".
4726	**cola**	**cola**
	m	
	[kɔla]	Le coca cola me picota la langue.
		-The cola made my tongue tingle.
4727	**renaître**	**come back to life**
	vb	
	[ʁənɛtʁ]	Elle pourrait éventuellement renaître sous une autre forme.
		-It might be revived, possibly in another form.
4728	**disco**	**disco; disco**
	adj; m	
	[disko]	Programas para desfragmentar el disco duro.
		-Programs to defragment your hard disk.
4729	**trafiquer**	**traffic**
	vb	
	[tʁafike]	On a demandé à deux reprises à Dussault de trafiquer les chiffres pour que le ministre fasse meilleure figure.
		-Dussault was asked twice to fudge the numbers to make the minister look better.
4730	**soigneusement**	**carefully**
	adv	
	[swaɲøzmɑ̃]	Elles sont soigneusement réparties au sein des différents États.
		-They are neatly shared out among the various states.

4731	**anarchie**	**anarchy**
	f	Je n'y vois aucune anarchie.
	[anaʁʃi]	-I fail to see any anarchy there.

4732	**ramper**	**crawl | trail**
	vb[ʁɑ̃pe]	On va passer par derrière... et ramper sous le grillage au fond de leur propriété. -We'll go around back... and crawl under the fence at the rear of the lot.

4733	**vibration**	**vibration | pulse**
	f	Je ressens une très forte vibration psychique...
	[vibʁasjɔ̃]	-I'm getting a very, very strong psychic vibration...

4734	**fermement**	**firmly**
	adv	Nous sommes fermement attachés à la conservation et à la gestion saines des océans.
	[fɛʁməmɑ̃]	-We are firmly committed to the proper conservation and management of the oceans.

4735	**garnison**	**garrison**
	f	La garnison anglaise va venir brûler nos maisons.
	[gaʁnizɔ̃]	-We'll have no homes left when the English garrison burns us out.

4736	**tronc**	**trunk | stem**
	m	L'invention porte sur un système pour un tronc d'arbre décoratif à verrouillage mutuel.
	[tʁɔ̃]	-System for a decorative interlocking tree trunk is provided.

4737	**informateur**	**informant**
	m	Un informateur nous a tuyautés sur les frères Tatupo.
	[ɛ̃fɔʁmatœʁ]	-We only got tipped off to the Tatupo brothers from an informant.

4738	**aurore**	**dawn**
	f	Cela veut dire «peuple de l'aurore» ou «peuple qui est le plus à l'est».
	[ɔʁɔʁ]	-It means ``people of the dawn" or ``those the furthest east".

4739	**hypnose**	**hypnosis**
	f	L'hypnose fait des miracles en Europe.
	[ipnoz]	-They're doing some amazing things with hypnosis now in Europe.

4740	**set**	**set**
	m	Je possède enfin un set complet !
	[sɛt]	-I've finally got the whole set!

4741	**perdant**	**losing; loser**
	adj; m	Vous n'êtes pas un perdant.
	[pɛʁdɑ̃]	-You're not a loser.

4742	**hébreu**	**Hebrew; Hebrew**
	adj; m	Parfois, l'avis est rédigé en hébreu uniquement, sans traduction arabe.
	[ebʁø]	-Sometimes the order is written in Hebrew only, with no Arabic translation.

4743	**indigène**	**native; native**
	adj; m/f	À l'heure actuelle, on recense 17 peuples autochtones ou indigènes et noirs ou afro-équatoriens.
	[ɛ̃diʒɛn]	-At present the existence of 17 aboriginal or indigenous and black or Afro-Ecuadorian peoples is recognized.

4744	**suicidaire**	**suicidal**
	adj	Persévérer dans cette voie est suicidaire et conduira l'Europe à l'éclatement.
	[sɥisidɛʁ]	-Pursuing this path is suicidal and will lead to the fragmentation of Europe.

4745	**remontant**	**pick-me-up; tonic**

	adj; m	Mais avant, il nous faut un petit remontant.
	[ʁəmɔ̃tɑ̃]	-But first you need a little pick-me-up.
4746	**engueuler**	**shout**
	vb[ɑ̃gœle]	J'essaierai de les engueuler plus souvent. -I try to yell at them as often as I can.
4747	**brèche**	**breach|gap**
	f	Nous ouvrons une brèche dangereuse dans notre défense contre la peine de
	[bʁɛʃ]	mort. -We are opening up an enormous breach in our defences against the death penalty.
4748	**façade**	**façade|front**
	f	Cette affaire de teinturerie est une façade pour la maffia.
	[fasad]	-That dry-cleaning business is a front for the mob.
4749	**ace**	**ace**
	m	C'est mon ace contre votre reine.
	[ɛs]	-This is my ace against your queen.
4750	**remporter**	**win|take**
	vb	Ce n'est qu'à ce moment-là que nous pourrons remporter la lutte contre la
	[ʁɑ̃pɔʁte]	pandémie. -Only then can we win the fight against the pandemic.
4751	**programmer**	**program**
	vb	On pourrait les programmer avec les réponses.
	[pʁɔgʁame]	-I mean, we could program them with the answers.
4752	**radin**	**tightwad; mean**
	m; adj	Il est très radin avec son argent.
	[ʁadɛ̃]	-He is very stingy with his money.
4753	**immatriculation**	**registration**
	f	Dan a photographié la plaque d'immatriculation.
	[imatʁikylasjɔ̃]	-Dan took a picture of the license plate.
4754	**artificiel**	**artificial**
	adj	L'agriculture européenne dans son ensemble paierait finalement le prix d'un
	[aʁtifisjɛl]	démembrement artificiel et forcé des exploitations. -European agriculture as a whole would then ultimately pay the price of an artificial and forced break-up of farms.
4755	**subtil**	**subtle**
	adj	L'un des moyens est de se prêter au jeu subtil, ou peu subtil, des
	[syptil]	responsabilités. -One way is to indulge in a subtle, or not so subtle, blame game.
4756	**rigueur**	**rigor**
	f	Dans tous les cas la règle s'applique dans toute sa rigueur.
	[ʁigœʁ]	-That rule holds good in all it's rigor.
4757	**portier**	**porter|doorkeeper**
	m	N'êtes-vous pas le portier ?
	[pɔʁtje]	-Aren't you the doorman?
4758	**évaluer**	**assess|rate**
	vb	Les pays touchés par les mines doivent évaluer leurs propres besoins et
	[evalɥe]	définir leurs propres priorités. -Mine-affected countries must assess their own needs and define their own priorities.
4759	**vautour**	**vulture**

| | m | Je ne travaillerais jamais pour le vautour. |
| | [votuʁ] | -I wouldn't be working for the vulture. |

4760 **raisonner** — **reason**
vb[ʁɛzɔne]
Je voudrais que l'on commence aussi à raisonner un peu sur ce sujet. -I would appreciate it if we began to reason a little on this point.

4761 **épingle** — **pin**
f
[epɛ̃gl]
Le camion a fait un virage à droite en épingle. -The truck made a sharp turn to the right.

4762 **volet** — **flap**
m
[vɔlɛ]
Les deux types de ventilateur sont équipés de volets d'aération qui s'ouvrent et se ferment automatiquement. -Both systems are equipped with air flaps, which open and close automatically.

4763 **nounours** — **teddy bear**
m
[nunuʁ]
Je viens de trouver 118000 $ dans le nounours d'Ellie. -I just found $118,000 in Ellie's teddy bear.

4764 **inoubliable** — **unforgettable**
adj
[inublijabl]
Ernest Hemingway créa un monument littéraire inoubliable en souvenir de cette génération. -Ernest Hemingway created an unforgettable literary monument to that generation.

4765 **talon** — **heel**
m
[talɔ̃]
J'ai mal au talon. -I have a sore heel.

4766 **porche** — **porch**
m
[pɔʁʃ]
Être sous le porche des Radley suffisait. -Just standing on the Radley porch was enough.

4767 **métaphore** — **metaphor**
f
[metafɔʁ]
Dans une métaphore violente, il dit au Prince que l'on doit frapper la Fortune. -In a typically violent metaphor, he tells the Prince that Fortune must be beaten.

4768 **intensité** — **intensity|severity**
f
[ɛ̃tɑ̃site]
Il se fatigue vite d'une chose, indépendamment de l'intensité avec laquelle il l'aimait pour commencer. -He soon grows tired of a thing regardless of how much he liked it to begin with.

4769 **ironique** — **ironic|quizzical**
adj
[iʁɔnik]
Il est ironique que cette session aborde sept situations nationales spécifiques. -It is ironic that this session will address seven individual country situations.

4770 **golfe** — **gulf**
m
[gɔlf]
Un site de paris en ligne laisse les usagers parier sur quelles espèces animales s'éteindront à cause de la fuite de pétrole dans le Golfe du Mexique. -Gambling site lets users bet on which species will go extinct because of the oil spill in the Gulf of Mexico.

4771 **préjuger** — **prejudge**
vb
[pʁeʒyʒe]
Nous ne voudrions pas préjuger de l' issue de la conférence intergouvernementale.

-We would not wish to prejudge the outcome of the Intergovernmental Conference.

4772	**silhouette** f[silwɛt]	**outline** Nous percevons une silhouette en limite du champ radar. -Sir, we're picking up a silhouette at the edge of scanner range.
4773	**kidnapping** m [kidnapiŋ]	**kidnapping** Jack a été impliqué dans le kidnapping de la fille de Jill. -Jack took part in the kidnapping of Jill's daughter.
4774	**volant** m; adj [vɔlɑ̃]	**steering wheel; flying** Quelqu'un a coupé la corde de mon cerf-volant. -Someone has cut my kite string.
4775	**refrain** m [ʁəfʁɛ̃]	**refrain** Tu connais le refrain. -You know the drill.
4776	**oignon** m [ɔɲɔ̃]	**onion** Il me faut seulement un oignon pour cette recette. -I only need one onion for this recipe.
4777	**ciment** m [simɑ̃]	**cement** Les produits manufacturés incluent textiles et vêtements, ciment et plastique. -Manufacturing sectors include textiles and garment production, cement and plastics.
4778	**découvert** adj; m [dekuvɛʁ]	**discovered; overdraft** Le gouvernement a réussi à supprimer un déficit-découvert de 42 milliards de dollars. -The government has been successful in eliminating a $42 billion deficit-overdraft.
4779	**renforcer** vb [ʁɑ̃fɔʁse]	**strengthen|reinforce** Il a souligné qu'il fallait renforcer la capacité des FARDC à cet égard. -It stressed that there was a need to reinforce the capacity of FARDC in that regard.
4780	**emprisonné** adj; m [ɑ̃pʁizɔne]	**jailed; detainee** Le leader du syndicat étudiant, Honnjo Mawudzuro, a été emprisonné. -The leader of the students ' union, Hounjo Mawudzuro, has been imprisoned.
4781	**suspension** f [syspɑ̃sjɔ̃]	**suspension|stay** Mes facultés mentales restaient en suspension tandis que j'obéissais aux ordres des supérieurs. C'est typique de tout le monde dans l'armée. -My mental faculties remained in suspended animation while I obeyed the orders of the higher-ups. This is typical with everyone in the military.
4782	**saisi** adj [sezi]	**grasped** La mission a noté que le Conseil était activement saisi du dossier de la Somalie. -The mission noted that the Council was actively seized of the Somalia dossier.
4783	**renaissance** f [ʁənɛsɑ̃s]	**renaissance|reawakening** L'annihilation donne naissance à ma renaissance. -Annihilation gives birth to my rebirth.
4784	**enseignant** m [ɑ̃sɛɲɑ̃]	**schoolteacher** Chaque chef d'établissement désigne un enseignant qui aide le conseil des élèves dans sa tâche. -Each head teacher shall appoint one teacher to assist the pupils' council.

4785	**prometteur**	**promising**
	adj[pʁɔmetœʁ]	Il existe en outre un programme prometteur de détection de mines par des chiens. -In addition, there is a promising mine detection programme using dogs.
4786	**hameçon**	**hook**
	m [amsɔ̃]	Il a tout avalé : l'hameçon, la canne et le plomb. -He fell for it hook, line, and sinker.
4787	**clochard**	**tramp; down-at-heel**
	m; adj [klɔʃaʁ]	Le voyageur du temps consacra son attention au déjeuner et montra un appétit de clochard. -The Time Traveller devoted his attention to his dinner, and displayed the appetite of a tramp.
4788	**proverbe**	**proverb|saying**
	m [pʁɔvɛʁb]	Est-ce que tu as un proverbe similaire en français ? -Do you have a similar proverb in French?
4789	**diplôme**	**diploma**
	m [diplom]	Félicitations pour votre diplôme ! -Congratulations on your diploma.
4790	**trouillard**	**yellow belly; yellow-livered**
	adj; m [tʁujaʁ]	Naj, je suis un trouillard. -Naj, I'm a coward.
4791	**inférieur**	**lower; inferior**
	adj; m [ɛ̃feʁjœʁ]	La phénolphtaléine vire au fuchsia en présence d'une base dont le pH est supérieur ou égal à 10 et reste incolore en présence d'une solution dont le pH est inférieur ou égale à 8,2. -Phenolphthalein will turn fuchsia in the presence of a base with a pH of or above 10.0 and will remain colorless in the presence of a solution with a pH of or below 8.2.
4792	**adultère**	**adultery; adulterous**
	m; adj [adyltɛʁ]	Il est prévu également réparation pour adultère, qui est un délit pénal. -There is also provision for damages for adultery, which is a criminal offence.
4793	**étrangement**	**strangely**
	adv [etʁɑ̃ʒmɑ̃]	L'attitude de la Commission dans ce domaine est étrangement contradictoire. -The Commission's attitude in this field is strangely contradictory.
4794	**mare**	**pond**
	f [maʁ]	Ces évènements, comme si l'on avait jeté un pavé dans la mare, ont provoqué une onde de choc. -Those events were rather like throwing a large stone into a pond, creating ripples.
4795	**bruyant**	**noisy**
	adj [bʁɥijɑ̃]	Je dois dire que j'ai pu suivre le débat, mais je reconnais que c'est bruyant. -I must say that I was able to hear the debate but I am aware there is some noise in the House.
4796	**moelle**	**marrow**
	f [mwal]	Une rafale glaciale m'a glacé jusqu'à la moelle des os. -An icy blast of wind cut me to the bonemarrow.
4797	**durement**	**harshly**
	adv[dyʁmɑ̃]	Si nous continuons à temporiser, nous serons jugés durement - et nous l'aurons bien mérité - pour avoir sans scrupule compromis grandement leur patrimoine et leur avenir. -If we continue to delay action, we will be judged

harshly, and deservedly so, for having callously placed their inheritance and future in great jeopardy.

4798	**offense**	**offense|insult**
	f	Cela t'offense-t-il ?
	[ɔfɑ̃s]	-Does it offend you?
4799	**médium**	**medium**
	m	Elle est médium.
	[medjɔm]	-She is a psychic.
4800	**taverne**	**tavern**
	f	On apprend beaucoup dans une taverne.
	[tavɛʀn]	-You learn a great deal about life in a tavern.
4801	**rajouter**	**add**
	vb	S'il y a quelque chose à rajouter à la fin du vote, je vous le ferai savoir.
	[ʀaʒute]	-If there is anything to add at the end of the vote, I will bring it to you.
4802	**réconforter**	**comfort**
	vb	En fait, il nous appartient de réconforter et de guérir les communautés déchirées par ces crimes.
	[ʀekɔ̃fɔʀte]	-Indeed, it is our responsibility to comfort and heal the communities savaged by these crimes.
4803	**convaincant**	**convincing**
	adj	Elle présente également une approche équilibrée et transmet un message convaincant.
	[kɔ̃vɛ̃kɑ̃]	-It also includes a balanced approach and a convincing message.
4804	**ivresse**	**drunkenness**
	f	Notre police municipale conduit une nouvelle campagne ciblant la conduite en état d'ivresse.
	[ivʀɛs]	-Our city police have a new campaign targeting drunken driving.
4805	**crocodile**	**crocodile**
	m	Un crocodile mangea un chien.
	[kʀɔkɔdil]	-A crocodile ate a dog.
4806	**radical**	**radical; radical**
	adj; m	Ce qui est radical aujourd'hui sera cliché demain, peut-être.
	[ʀadikal]	-What's radical today may be cliché tomorrow.
4807	**marathon**	**marathon**
	m	Pour conclure, le marathon de l'élargissement approche de la ligne d'arrivée.
	[maʀatɔ̃]	-In conclusion, the enlargement marathon is nearing the finish line.
4808	**sérum**	**serum**
	m	Que 58,5 % des professionnels administraient le sérum selon les normes.
	[seʀɔm]	-Serum is administered according to the rules by 58.5% of the personnel.
4809	**adoption**	**adoption|passage**
	f	L'adoption (politique et législation, l'adoption dans le pays ou à l'étranger).
	[adɔpsjɔ̃]	-Adoption (policy and legislation; domestic and intercountry adoption).
4810	**vingtaine**	**around twenty**
	num [vɛ̃tɛn]	La Suède a aussi conclu des conventions de sécurité sociale avec une vingtaine de pays. -Sweden also has conventions on social security with about twenty countries.
4811	**cactus**	**cactus**
	m	Et du livre illustré Mimi: Fleur de cactus, accompagné d'une carte de confiance.
	[kaktys]	

-And the illustrated book Mimi: cactus flower, accompanied by a confidential card.

4812	**abondance** f [abɔ̃dɑ̃s]	**abundance** Lorsque de tels règlements s'appliquent, il y a une abondance d'informations. -When such regulations apply, an abundance of information will be available.
4813	**considération** f [kɔ̃sideʁasjɔ̃]	**consideration|account** L'importance des activités recommandées devrait être la considération principale. -The importance of the activities recommended should be the primary consideration;
4814	**carrefour** m [kaʁfuʁ]	**crossroads** L'accident a eu lieu à un carrefour. -The accident took place at a crossroads.
4815	**confrérie** f [kɔ̃fʁeʁi]	**brotherhood** On appartient à la même confrérie. -We, too, are members of the Sengh Brotherhood.
4816	**égarer** vb [egaʁe]	**mislead|stray** Si le système n'est pas fiable, le chaos actuel risque de perdurer et d'autres dossiers pourraient être égarés. -If the system was unreliable, the current intolerable situation involving misplaced files was sure to continue.
4817	**républicain** adj; m [ʁepyblikɛ̃]	**republican; republican** Source : Annuaires statistiques de l'Office républicain de la statistique -Source: Statistical Yearbooks of the Republican Statistical Office.
4818	**dinosaure** m [dinozoʁ]	**dinosaur** D'aucuns disent également que l'organisation de marché du sucre est un dinosaure. -Some people also say that the common organisation of the market in sugar is a dinosaur.
4819	**occident** m [ɔksidɑ̃]	**West** L'Occident considère l'Éthiopie presque comme une alliée, et quand je dis l'Occident, j'entends également l'Amérique. -The West views Ethiopia almost as an ally, and by the West I also mean America.
4820	**dédier** vb [dedje]	**dedicate** Madame la Présidente, je veux dédier mon discours à la ministre du Patrimoine. -Madam Speaker, I wish to dedicate my speech to the Minister of Canadian Heritage.
4821	**humiliant** adj[ymiljɑ̃]	**humiliating** C'est un châtiment cruel et humiliant auquel peut être condamné un innocent. -It is cruel and demeaning, and a punishment to which an innocent person can be sentenced.
4822	**hygiène** f [iʒjɛn]	**hygiene** La priorité est donnée à l'hygiène du milieu et à l'hygiène personnelle des enfants. -Emphasis is placed on the environment and on the personal hygiene of children.
4823	**essuyer**	**wipe|dry**

| | vb
[esɥije] | Deux euros par citoyen ne suffiront pas pour essuyer les larmes en cas de pertes aussi énormes.
-Two euros per citizen will not suffice to wipe away the tears when such enormous losses are incurred. |

4824 asiatique — Asian
adj
[azjatik]
Une statue de bronze représentant un homme du sud-est asiatique jouant d'un instrument de musique.
-One bronze statuette of a South-East Asian man playing a musical instrument.

4825 arène — arena
f
[aʁɛn]
Économise tes cris pour l'arène.
-You can save your screams for the arena.

4826 mendier — beg; sponge
vb; m
[mɑ̃dje]
Si les enfants ont constamment faim, ils commenceront à mendier et même à voler.
-If children are constantly hungry, they will begin to beg and even steal.

4827 pousse — shoot
f
[pus]
Il faut pousser les radiodiffuseurs à utiliser le spectre efficacement.
-There is a need to push broadcasters to use spectrum efficiently.

4828 fabrication — manufacturing|production
f
[fabʁikasjɔ̃]
La fabrication d'histoire ravive l'intérêt pour la narration.
-Storytelling rekindles the interest in narrative.

4829 impulsion — pulse|impetus
f
[ɛ̃pylsjɔ̃]
Je pense pouvoir atteindre la branche si vous me donnez une impulsion.
-I think I can reach the branch if you'll give me a boost.

4830 ficeler — tie up
vb
[fisle]
Le sénateur Nolin: L'autre option est de rapidement ficeler le projet de loi dans l'état où il est, en acceptant le message de l'autre endroit.
-Senator Nolin: The other option is to quickly tie up the loose ends of the bill as it stands, by accepting the message from the other place.

4831 toxique — toxic
adj
[tɔksik]
Si la substance est toxique, elle est toxique et il faut un plan de prévention de la pollution.
-If it is toxic, it is toxic and it requires a pollution prevention plan.

4832 pi — pi
m
[pi]
Je peux citer 20 chiffres de pi.
-I can recite pi up to 20 digits.

4833 adrénaline — adrenaline
f
[adʁenalin]
Les accros à l'adrénaline aiment prendre des risques extrêmes.
-Adrenaline junkies love taking extreme risks.

4834 résider — reside|live
vb
[ʁezide]
Les tribus "énumérées" résident dans tous les États sauf l'Haryana, le Penjab, le Chandigarh, Delhi et Pondichéry.
-STs inhabit all the States except Haryana, Punjab, Chandigarh, Delhi and Pondicherry.

4835 revendre — sell
vb
[ʁəvɑ̃dʁ]
Il lui a été impossible de revendre les marchandises, qui ont été mises au rebut en 1992.
-It was unable to resell the goods and scrapped them in 1992.

4836 bougre — guy
m
[bugʁ]
Il est encore vert, le vieux bougre.
-This old guy is still sprightly.

4837	**abominable**	**abominable**
	adj	Une autre pratique particulièrement abominable est celle des mutilations génitales féminines.
	[abɔminabl]	-Another particularly abhorrent practice was that of female genital mutilation.

4838	**préciser**	**specify|point out**
	vb	Extraordinary and exceptional help should be considered in these precise cases.
	[pʁesize]	-Une aide extraordinaire et exceptionnelle doit être envisagée dans ces cas précis.

4839	**succession**	**succession|inheritance**
	f	Le Code civil établit une distinction entre la succession légale et la succession testamentaire.
	[syksesjõ]	-The Civil Code distinguishes between statutory succession and testamentary succession.

4840	**morsure**	**bite**
	f	La morsure de cette araignée provoque une douleur intense.
	[mɔʁsyʁ]	-The bite of this spider causes intense pain.

4841	**créatif**	**creative**
	adj	Ce programme d'apprentissage créatif s'est développé à une vitesse extraordinaire.
	[kʁeatif]	-The creative learning programme has expanded with incredible rapidity.

4842	**occidental**	**western; western**
	adj; m	Rien de nouveau sur le front occidental.
	[ɔksidãtal]	-Nothing new on the Western Front.

4843	**hectare**	**hectare**
	m	Ces fonds s'avéreront pourtant capitaux si nous voulons arrêter de perdre nos forêts hectare après hectare.
	[ɛktaʁ]	-These funds will prove vital if the loss of hectare after hectare of forest is not to continue.

4844	**pudding**	**pudding**
	m	Je ne peux m'empêcher de manger du pudding.
	[pydiŋ]	-I cannot resist eating pudding.

4845	**caramel**	**caramel**
	m	J'apprécie une bonne coupe glacée au caramel chaud, après l'église, le dimanche.
	[kaʁamɛl]	-I enjoy a good hot-fudge sundae after church on Sundays.

| 4846 | **asthme** | **asthma** |
| | m[asm] | Je souffre d'asthme. -I suffer from asthma. |

4847	**réciproque**	**reciprocal|mutual**
	adj	Troisièmement, l'harmonisation et la reconnaissance réciproque sont intrinsèquement liées.
	[ʁesipʁɔk]	-Thirdly, harmonisation and mutual recognition are intrinsically linked.

4848	**vaguement**	**vaguely**
	adv	Il l'a vaguement abordée, mais il n'a pas parlé de cette équipe en particulier.
	[vagmã]	-He has outlined something of this, but not perhaps talked about that precise team.

4849	**tata**	**auntie**
	f	Viens voir ta méchante tata Lucy.
	[tata]	-You want to see your mean Aunt Lucy.

| 4850 | **intendant** | **steward** |

	m	Donnez-la à l'intendant, sauvez Shimazo.
	[ɛ̃tɑ̃dɑ̃]	-Take it to the intendant, and save Shimazo's life.

4851 scénariste — **scriptwriter**

m/f
[senaʁist]

La première session de formation pour scénaristes lancée dans le cadre des activités Euro-Méditerranée a eu lieu à Beyrouth au mois de mai 2002.
-The first training session for scriptwriters launched within the framework of Euro-Mediterranean activities was held in Beirut in May 2002.

4852 sincérité — **sincerity|honesty**

f
[sɛ̃seʁite]

Le député parle avec sincérité, mais cette sincérité est quelque peu affaiblie.
-The hon. member with some sincerity is trying to make his points but that sincerity is somewhat diluted.

4853 souriant — **smiling**

adj
[suʁjɑ̃]

Pour tirer un souriant portrait à 16, ou à 17, si le Président du Parlement est toléré?
-To have a smiling portrait of 16 or 17, including the President of the European Parliament?

4854 couture — **sewing**

f
[kutyʁ]

Les filles ne pouvaient attendre pour nous montrer leur beau travail de couture.
-The girls couldn't wait to show off their fine needle work to us.

4855 joint — **joint; joint**

adj; m
[ʒwɛ̃]

Heureux celui qui joint la santé à l'intelligence.
-Health and intellect are the two blessings of life.

4856 puant — **stinking**

adj
[pɥɑ̃]

Un putréfié, impopulaire, puant, et irresponsable putois.
-A rotten, unpopular, smelly, freeloading skunk.

4857 forgeron — **black-smith**

m
[fɔʁʒəʁɔ̃]

La situation ici rappelle l'atelier d'un forgeron dont les réserves de charbon diminueraient.
-The situation of the CD resembles a furnace of a blacksmith with dwindling coal.

4858 hurlant — **howling**

adj[yʁlɑ̃]

Les honorables sénateurs peuvent-ils s'imaginer ce que ce doit être que de mettre 56 chaussons à 14 chiens hurlant et impatients de courir ? -Can honourable senators just imagine putting 56 booties on 14 howling dogs that only want to run?

4859 courbe — **curve|bending**

f
[kuʁb]

La route courbe légèrement en direction du lac.
-The road curves gently toward the lake.

4860 brouhaha — **hubbub**

m
[bʁuaa]

La beauté résiste au brouhaha de l'absurde.
-Beauty is resistant to the hubbub of the absurd.

4861 junkie — **junkie**

f
[ʒɛ̃ki]

Écrit en 1797 par un junkie appelé Coleridge.
-It was written in 1797 by a junkie called Coleridge.

4862 escadrille — **squadron**

f
[ɛskadʁij]

Le commandement de l'escadrille sera ravi d'apprendre que le système est opérationnel.
-I'm sure Squadron Command will be pleased that the device is operational.

4863 trousser — **truss**

	vb [tʁuse]	Il est percé de 20 trous de 0,5 mm de diamètre (4 séries de 5 trous) sur la périphérie. -It is pierced by 20 holes 0.5 mm in diameter (four sets of five holes) on the circumference.
4864	**investisseur** m; adj [ɛ̃vɛstisœʁ]	**investor; investing** Vous êtes un investisseur rusé, pasteur. -You sound like quite a shrewd investor, Pastor.
4865	**fumeur** adj; m [fymœʁ]	**smoking; smoker** Peut-être vaut -il mieux être fumeur à la campagne que non-fumeur à la ville. -Perhaps it is better to be a smoker in the countryside than a non-smoker in the town.
4866	**immunité** f [imynite]	**immunity** Les parlementaires méritent l'immunité et un salaire afin de garantir leur indépendance. -Members of parliament deserve immunity and a paid salary to guarantee their independence.
4867	**handicap** m [ɑ̃dikap]	**handicap** Je ne considère pas ma myopie comme un handicap. -I don't consider my myopia as an handicap.
4868	**gamme** f [gam]	**range** Ce magasin vend des sacs-à-main haut de gamme mais tout le monde sait que ce sont juste de vulgaires contrefaçons fabriquées en Chine. -That store sells top of the line purses but everyone knows they're really just cheap knock-offs made in China.
4869	**étui** m [etɥi]	**case** Dans leur étui... ils sembleront vrais. -When it's in its holster... it should look like the real thing.
4870	**dévouement** m [devumɑ̃]	**devotion** J'admire ton dévouement. -I admire your dedication.
4871	**répit** m [ʁepi]	**respite|reprieve** J'ai besoin d'un répit. -I need a breather.
4872	**tirage** m [tiʁaʒ]	**drawing|print** Après l'événement de tirage de la mise, les numéros gagnants sont publiés. -After the lottery pool drawing event, the winning numbers are posted.
4873	**déplacement** m [deplasmɑ̃]	**shifting|displacement** Faites votre déplacement. -Make your move.
4874	**morse** m [mɔʁs]	**morse** Non, c'est pas du morse. -No, that's not morse.
4875	**cultiver** vb [kyltive]	**cultivate|grow** Il offre la possibilité de promouvoir et de cultiver le modèle européen du sport. -It opens up the opportunity to promote and cultivate the European model of sport.
4876	**firme**	**firm**

f
[fiʁm]
Toutes les femmes à votre ancienne firme voulaient coucher avec vous.
-I'm sure all the women at your old firm wanted to sleep with you, but here's the deal.

4877 **cheville** | **ankle**
f
[ʃəvij]
Je ne vais pas jouer parce que je me suis tordu la cheville.
-I won't play because I've twisted my ankle.

4878 **tuteur** | **guardian**
m
[tytœʁ]
Leur ancien tuteur qui commit une erreur de jugement.
-Count Olaf is their old guardian, who made an error in judgment.

4879 **humilité** | **humility**
f
[ymilite]
Cela exige deux qualités apparemment contradictoires: humilité et intransigeance.
-Two apparently opposing characteristics are needed for this: humility and tenacity.

4880 **primitif** | **primitive; primitive**
adj; m
[pʁimitif]
À cette époque, un peuple primitif vivait là.
-At that time a primitive people lived there.

4881 **plouc** | **slob|bumpkin**
m
[pluk]
Tu me prends pour un plouc.
-I know you think I'm a hick.

4882 **animation** | **animation|liveliness**
f
[animasjɔ̃]
Shinichiro Watanabe a envisagé de réaliser un dessin animé sur Christophe Colomb, mais il est arrivé à la conclusion que même un film d'animation ne serait pas assez expressif pour rendre la magnificence des exploits de Colomb.
-Shinichirō Watanabe once considered making an anime about Christopher Columbus, but came to the conclusion that not even anime was expressive enough to properly portray the surreal greatness of Columbus's exploits.

4883 **grecque** | **Greek**
adj
[gʁɛk]
Son nom est d'origine grecque.
-Her name is of Greek origin.

4884 **gomme** | **gum**
f
[gɔm]
Les calculettes de poche coûtent autant qu'une paire de chaussettes et sont aussi essentielles qu'un crayon et une gomme pour les écoliers britanniques.
-Pocket calculators are as cheap to buy as a pair of socks, and as essential to thousands of British school children as a pencil and eraser.

4885 **trentaine** | **about thirty**
num
[tʁɑ̃tɛn]
Cette base renferme une trentaine de variables tirées des recensements de population de 1981 et de 1991.
-This database contains about thirty variables from the 1981 and 1991 population censuses.

4886 **tousser** | **cough**
vb
[tuse]
Personne ne doit tousser, éternuer, pleurer, ni même chuchoter.
-Nobody coughs, nobody sneezes, nobody cries, nobody even whispers.

4887 **hongrois** | **Hungarian**
adj
[ɔ̃gʁwa]
Cela sonnerait le glas de la diffusion en hongrois, en ruthénien et en ukrainien.
-This would mean an end to broadcasting in Hungarian, Ruthenian and Ukrainian.

4888 **escroquerie** | **fraud|swindle**

f
[ɛskʁɔkʁi]

Il ne m'est jamais venu à l'esprit que toute l'affaire pouvait être une escroquerie.
-It never occurred to me that the whole thing might be a scam.

4889 **psychotique**
adj; m/f
[psikɔtik]

psychotic; psychotic
D'un côté j'étais convaincu que Dobel était fou à lier et psychotique.
-On the one hand, I was convinced Dobel was a raving, psychotic lunatic.

4890 **mercure**
m
[mɛʁkyʁ]

mercury
Le mercure est-il véritablement un métal ?
-Is mercury really a metal?

4891 **coréen**
adj; m
[kɔʁeɛ̃]

Korean; Korean
J'étudie le coréen.
-I study Korean.

4892 **vieillesse**
f
[vjɛjɛs]

old age | old
Les scientifiques commencent lentement à assembler les mécanismes de la vieillesse.
-Scientists are slowly piecing together the mechanism of aging.

4893 **labyrinthe**
m
[labiʁɛ̃t]

labyrinth
Il eut beau essayer, il ne put pas s'extirper du labyrinthe.
-No matter how hard he tried, he could not get out of the maze.

4894 **driver**
m
[dʁive]

driver
Vu comme tu tapes, prends un fer au lieu d'un driver.
-I'm thinking, the way you're hitting, you might want to use an iron instead of a driver.

4895 **roulette**
f
[ʁulɛt]

roulette | wheel
La roulette est un jeu de hasard.
-Roulette is a game of chance.

4896 **redevable**
adj; vb[ʁədəvabl]

beholden; put under stress
Je lui suis personnellement redevable de l'amitié qu'il m'a toujours témoignée. -I am personally beholden to him for the friendship he has always shown me.

4897 **mentalement**
adv
[mɑ̃talmɑ̃]

mentally
On sait aujourd'hui que la malnutrition peut retarder le développement mental et physique.
-We now know that malnutrition can retard mental and physical development.

4898 **moralité**
f
[mɔʁalite]

morality
La moralité n'est jamais que l'attitude que nous adoptons face aux gens que nous détestons.
-Morality is simply the attitude we adopt toward people we dislike.

4899 **loisir**
m
[lwaziʁ]

leisure
Zurich soutient votre condition physique et votre bien-être grâce à différentes offres de loisir.
-Zurich promotes your personal fitness and well-being with a number of great free-time offers.

4900 **contraindre**
vb
[kɔ̃tʁɛ̃dʁ]

compel | force
Aucun gouvernement démocratique ne peut contraindre ses successeurs par l'irrévocable.
-No democratic government can bind its successor with the irrevocable.

4901 **héroïque**
adj
[eʁɔik]

heroic
Lubbers et son équipe font un travail héroïque pour faire face à ce problème.

-Lubbers and his people are making a truly heroic effort to deal with this problem.

4902	**fouine**	**weasel**
	f	J'ai toujours su que tu étais une fouine.
	[fwin]	-I always knew you were a weasel.
4903	**chercheur**	**researcher|seeker; inquiring**
	m; adj	Ce chercheur ne révèle pas la source de son financement.
	[ʃɛʁʃœʁ]	-This researcher does not disclose the source of his funding.
4904	**médiocre**	**poor|mediocre; second-rater**
	adj; m/f	Il est préférable de ne rien faire que de faire quelque chose de médiocre.
	[medjɔkʁ]	-It's better to do nothing than to do something poorly.
4905	**électeur**	**elector**
	m	Êtes-vous un électeur inscrit ?
	[elɛktœʁ]	-Are you a registered voter?
4906	**employeur**	**employer**
	m	Bien que j'eusse presque instinctivement conçu du ressentiment du fait que
	[ɑ̃plwajœʁ]	mon employeur m'avait placé en observation, après mon erreur, je surmontai bientôt mon animosité à son égard et, au lieu de nourrir une rancune, je me résolus à prendre toute l'affaire pour une nécessaire expérience d'apprentissage.
		-Although I almost instinctively felt some resentment that my employer had placed me on probation after my mistake, I soon overcame my feelings of animus towards her and, instead of harbouring a grudge, resolved to treat the entire affair as a necessary learning experience.
4907	**sofa**	**sofa**
	m[sɔfa]	Elle était allongée sur un sofa, les yeux clos. -She lay on a sofa with her eyes closed.
4908	**totalité**	**totality|integrity**
	f	La totalité du département informatique a été délocalisée.
	[tɔtalite]	-The entire IT department has been bangalored.
4909	**violoncelle**	**cello**
	m	J'ai entendu que c'est Jack qui t'a appris à jouer du violoncelle.
	[vjɔlɔ̃sɛl]	-I hear Jack was the one who taught you how to play the cello.
4910	**planning**	**schedule**
	m	On est en retard sur le planning.
	[planiŋ]	-We're behind on schedule.
4911	**ferment**	**ferment**
	m	Un élément essentiel du ferment idéologique a été introduit.
	[fɛʁmɑ̃]	-A vital element of ideological ferment has been introduced.
4912	**follement**	**madly**
	adv	Il est follement épris de moi.
	[fɔlmɑ̃]	-He's crazy about me.
4913	**situer**	**locate|situate**
	vb	Il est recommandé de ne pas situer les garages dans des courbes horizontales, si possible (RP).
	[situe]	-It is recommended not to locate lay-bys in horizontal curves, if possible (RP).
4914	**actionnaire**	**shareholder**
	m/f	L'État actionnaire entend agir ainsi en investisseur avisé.
	[aksjɔnɛʁ]	-The State shareholder thus intends to act like a prudent investor.
4915	**réduit**	**reduced**

| | | adj
[ʁedɥi] | Ils ont réduit plutôt qu'amélioré la sécurité régionale de ces nations elles-mêmes.
-They diminished rather than improved regional security for those nations themselves. |

4916 sécuriser — **reassure**

vb
[sekyʁize]

On a pu sécuriser deux autres sections.
-We've managed to secure two more sections of the ship.

4917 gâté — **spoiled|tainted**

adj
[gate]

J'ai déjà été gâté, mais jamais aussi élégamment.
-I've been spoiled before, but never so beautifully.

4918 danois — **Danish; Danish**

adj; m
[danwa]

Le premier ministre danois a déjà offert un siège aux critiques de l'Union danois.
-The Danish Prime Minister has already offered the Danish critics of the EU a place.

4919 chialer — **blubber**

vb
[ʃjale]

Nous ne sommes pas dans l'opposition uniquement pour le plaisir de critiquer ou de chialer.
-We are not in the opposition for the sole purpose of criticizing and complaining.

4920 vocabulaire — **vocabulary**

m
[vɔkabylɛʁ]

Les étudiants devraient se servir du vocabulaire appris.
-The students should make use of the vocabulary learned.

4921 dessein — **design|plan**

m[desɛ̃]

Pourquoi quiconque ferait-il cela à dessein ? -Why would anyone do that on purpose?

4922 collision — **collision|clash**

f
[kɔlizjɔ̃]

Sa voiture est entrée en collision avec un train.
-His car collided with a train.

4923 seringue — **syringe**

f
[səʁɛ̃g]

Lucy, branchez l'adaptateur sur la seringue.
-All right, Lucy. Hook up the adapter to the syringe.

4924 combustible — **fuel; combustible**

m; adj
[kɔ̃bystibl]

Il n'y avait pas assez de combustible.
-There was not enough fuel.

4925 constater — **note**

vb
[kɔ̃state]

Constater la fermeture des soupapes et des ouvertures d'inspection.
-Take note of the closure of valves and inspection openings.

4926 attentif — **attentive|careful**

adj
[atɑ̃tif]

Au contraire, le WP.24 les encourage et sera attentif à leurs résultats.
-On the contrary, WP.24 must encourage them and be attentive to results.

4927 arsenal — **arsenal|navy yard**

m
[aʁsənal]

Votre arsenal est très impressionnant, Capitaine.
-It's a very impressive arsenal you have here, Captain.

4928 élégance — **elegance**

f
[elegɑ̃s]

L'élégance, en toutes circonstances.
-Elegance at all times.

4929 outrager — **outrage|insult**

vb
[utʁaʒe]

Une telle démarche est un outrage direct à l'intégrité des dirigeants politiques africains.
-This was a direct affront to the integrity of African political leadership.

4930	**fonctionnement**	**operation|running**
	m	Tout est en parfait état de fonctionnement.
	[fɔ̃ksjɔnmɑ̃]	-Everything is in perfect working order.
4931	**yoga**	**yoga**
	m	Il s'agit des formes Ayurveda, Siddha, Unani, du yoga et de la naturopathie.
	[jɔga]	-These systems are Ayurveda, Siddha, Unani, Yoga and naturopathy.
4932	**cygne**	**swan**
	m	Ce cygne est noir.
	[siɲ]	-This swan is black.
4933	**successeur**	**successor**
	m	Par la suite, il fut le secrétaire du successeur de Dorion, Télesphore Fournier.
	[syksesœʁ]	-He subsequently served as secretary to Dorion's successor, Télesphore Fournier.
4934	**meeting**	**meeting**
	m	J'assisterai au prochain meeting.
	[mitiŋ]	-I'll attend the next meeting.
4935	**ampleur**	**extent|magnitude**
	f[ɑ̃plœʁ]	L'astronomie est peut-être la science dont les découvertes doivent le moins au hasard, dans laquelle l'entendement humain apparaît dans toute son ampleur et par laquelle l'homme peut le mieux apprendre combien il est petit. -Astronomy is perhaps the science whose discoveries owe least to chance, in which human understanding appears in its whole magnitude, and through which man can best learn how small he is.
4936	**prospérer**	**prosper|floor**
	vb	Nous, peuples, ne pourrons prospérer, voire survivre à moins que ce fossé ne soit comblé.
	[pʁɔspeʁe]	-We the peoples cannot flourish or even survive unless this gap is narrowed.
4937	**tolérer**	**tolerate|bear**
	vb	L'Europe de l'intégration ne peut tolérer le nationalisme.
	[tɔleʁe]	-This integrated Europe must not accept nationalism.
4938	**poulette**	**pullet**
	f	La viande d'un poulet correctement élevé sera bien meilleure dans l'assiette.
	[pulɛt]	-Properly reared chicken will be a better piece of meat when it goes on the plate.
4939	**ridiculiser**	**ridicule**
	vb	Il est temps que les chats cessent de se faire ridiculiser par les souris.
	[ʁidikylize]	-It is time now for the cats to stop suffering the ridicule of the mice.
4940	**guet**	**watch**
	m	Sean faisait le guet pour protéger Jimmy.
	[gɛ]	-Jimmy left Sean outside as a lookout to keep him out of harms' way.
4941	**subitement**	**suddenly**
	adv	Ce sont des années de certitude qui ont semblé subitement remises en cause.
	[sybitmɑ̃]	-Years of certainty suddenly all seemed to be called into question.
4942	**étoffer**	**enrich**
	vb	À présent, l'Assemblée générale doit rapidement en étoffer les modalités et la structure.
	[etɔfe]	-Now the General Assembly must move swiftly to flesh out the modalities and the structure.

4943	**excentrique**	**eccentric; eccentric**
	adj; m/f	Le sénateur Stollery est excentrique, mais un adorable excentrique.
	[ɛksɑ̃tʁik]	-He is eccentric, but a likeable eccentric.
4944	**ballade**	**ballad**
	f	Ça ferait une superbe ballade tragique.
	[balad]	-That is the stuff of a wonderful, tragic ballad.
4945	**cube**	**cube**
	m	C'est un carré, pas un cube.
	[kyb]	-It's a square, not a cube.
4946	**préférence**	**preference**
	f	Servir de préférence frais.
	[pʁefeʁɑ̃s]	-Best served chilled.
4947	**suspense**	**suspension**
	m[syspɑ̃s]	Les députés de l'opposition et l'ensemble des Canadiens vivent un certain suspense. -Members of the opposition and all Canadians are waiting with some degree of suspense.
4948	**acompte**	**down payment|installment**
	m	Plus que suffisant comme acompte pour 2 appartements.
	[akɔ̃t]	-More than enough for a down payment on a couple of condos.
4949	**impératrice**	**empress**
	f	L'impératrice a les mêmes craintes.
	[ɛ̃peʁatʁis]	-Our Empress has those same fears, Baroness.
4950	**obscène**	**obscene**
	adj	Allons regarder cette obscène pile de cadeaux.
	[ɔpsɛn]	-Let's go check out that obscene pile of gifts.
4951	**colocataire**	**room-mate**
	m/f	Vous êtes ses colocataires ?
	[kɔlɔkatɛʁ]	-Are you her flatmates, like?
4952	**restau**	**restaurant**
	m	Pile au vieux restau.
	[ʁɛsto]	-Right to the restaurant.
4953	**lièvre**	**hare; hare's**
	m; adj	Il est difficile d'attraper un lièvre à la main.
	[ljɛvʁ]	-It is not easy to catch a hare with your bare hands.
4954	**à bout**	**overwrought**
	adj	Nous avons besoin d' une coopération renforcée pour venir à bout de la drogue.
	[a bu]	-We have many social problems, but we are completely determined to overcome them.
4955	**érotique**	**erotic**
	adj	Linda était une danseuse érotique populaire à Londres.
	[eʁɔtik]	-Linda was a popular exotic dancer in London.
4956	**repaire**	**den**
	m	Allons traîner dans notre repaire.
	[ʁəpɛʁ]	-Let's hang out at our hangout.
4957	**inventeur**	**inventor**
	m	Benjamin Franklin était un homme d'État américain et un inventeur.
	[ɛ̃vɑ̃tœʁ]	-B. Franklin was an American statesman and inventor.
4958	**splendeur**	**splendor**

f
[splãdœʁ]

Donc, nous, dans notre intérêt à profiter de cette splendeur de la foi évangélique.
-So we, in our interest to take advantage of this splendor of evangelical faith.

4959 approbation   **approval | endorsement**
f
[apʁɔbasjõ]

Il m'a donné son approbation.
-He gave me his stamp of approval.

4960 tranquillité   **peace | quiet**
f
[tʁãkilite]

Les Maldives sont un pays connu pour sa tranquillité et son accueil chaleureux.
-The Maldives is a country renowned for its tranquillity and warm welcomes.

4961 séparément   **separately | apart**
adv[sepaʁemã]

Cette réparation peut prendre la forme de la restitution, de l'indemnisation ou de la satisfaction, séparément ou conjointement. -This reparation may take the form of restitution, compensation or satisfaction, either singly or in combination.

4962 infraction   **offense | infringement**
f
[ɛ̃fʁaksjõ]

Elle a voté pour Mr Nishioka en infraction avec les consignes du parti.
-She voted for Mr Nishioka, infringing on the party's guidelines.

4963 chandelle   **candle**
f
[ʃãdɛl]

Bonne chance dans la nuit sans chandelle, Freddy.
-Good luck finding your way in the dark without a candle, Freddie.

4964 européen   **European**
adj
[øʁɔpeɛ̃]

Elle a un Premier ministre pro-européen et un président remarquable tout aussi pro-européen.
-It has a pro-European prime minister and an outstanding pro-European president.

4965 testicule   **testicle**
m
[tɛstikyl]

Un lapin avec un seul testicule.
-Maybe a bunny with one testicle.

4966 marionnette   **marionette**
f
[maʁjɔnɛt]

Un de ces artistes est le fabricant de marionnettes Alex Sztasko, dont les marionnettes, qui semblent vivantes, reflètent bien la nature bien particulière de cette région.
-One of those artists is marionette maker Alex Sztasko whose lifelike puppets reflect the character of this region.

4967 définir   **define**
vb
[definiʁ]

Le « Guide » devra définir les spécifications en termes d'objectifs.
-The "Guide" will need to define specifications in terms of survey objectives.

4968 élu   **elected; elect**
adj; m
[ely]

Nous l'avons élu maire.
-We elected him mayor.

4969 flatteur   **flattering; flatterer**
adj; m
[flatœʁ]

Apprenez que tout flatteur vit aux dépens de celui qui l'écoute.
-Know that every flatterer lives at the expense of those who like to listen to him.

4970 forge   **forge**
f
[fɔʁʒ]

Nous devons faire de ce défi l'occasion de forger une entente religieuse.
-We must make this challenge an opportunity to forge religious understanding.

4971	**ferrer**	**shoe**
	vb	Je ne sais pas non plus ferrer un cheval.
	[feʁe]	-I don't know how to shoe a horse either.
4972	**vipère**	**viper**
	f	Il a une langue de vipère.
	[vipɛʁ]	-He has a sharp tongue.
4973	**négliger**	**neglect | overlook**
	vb	Rien ne serait plus regrettable que de négliger ce socle indispensable.
	[negliʒe]	-To disregard this indispensable foundation would be an unpardonable mistake.
4974	**informé**	**informed**
	adj[ɛ̃fɔʁme]	Si vous ne lisez pas le journal, vous n'êtes pas informé. Si vous le lisez, vous êtes désinformé. -If you don't read the newspaper, you're uninformed. If you read the newspaper, you're mis-informed.
4975	**snob**	**snob; snobbish**
	m/f; adj	Il est un peu snob.
	[snɔb]	-He's a bit of a snob.
4976	**débat**	**debate | argument**
	m	Ils eurent un débat sur le mariage homosexuel.
	[deba]	-They had a debate on same-sex marriage.
4977	**balise**	**buoy | beacon**
	f	La balise vous connectera au pont.
	[baliz]	-The beacon will connect you to the Bridge.
4978	**perception**	**perception**
	f	Les aveugles ont souvent une perception auditive accrue.
	[pɛʁsɛpsjɔ̃]	-A blind person's hearing is often very acute.
4979	**virginité**	**virginity**
	f	Dans de nombreux pays, la virginité constitue un élément primordial pour la poursuite d'un viol.
	[viʁʒinite]	-In many countries virginity is a primordial element in the prosecution of rape.
4980	**secrètement**	**secretly**
	adv	Les électeurs votent dans une salle spéciale où le principe du scrutin secret est garanti.
	[səkʁɛtmɑ̃]	-The voter votes in the special room in which the voting secrecy is ensured.
4981	**compréhensible**	**understandable**
	adj	Il est compréhensible que la Commission ne puisse pas ignorer ce défaut d'action.
	[kɔ̃pʁeɑ̃sibl]	-It is understandable that the Commission could not ignore this failure to act.
4982	**labeur**	**labor | toil**
	m	Ils représentent un labeur énorme, des sacrifices et la tristesse de l'éloignement de la famille et de la communauté.
	[labœʁ]	-They represent enormous toil, sacrifice and the sorrow of separation from family and community.
4983	**romancer**	**romanticize**
	vb	I almost lost this war because of your little romance.
	[ʁɔmɑ̃se]	-J'ai presque perdu cette guerre à cause de ton idylle.
4984	**planer**	**plane**

	vb	Un oiseau peut planer dans les airs sans bouger ses ailes.
	[plane]	-A bird can glide through the air without moving its wings.
4985	**souterrain**	**underground**
	adj	Parmi les morts se trouvent plusieurs petits vendeurs des rues qui, ayant
	[sutɛʁɛ̃]	voulu s'abriter dans un passage souterrain, ont péri noyés ou emportés par
		la crue soudaine.
		-The dead included a large number of street vendors, who, having run to
		street underpasses for protection, drowned in flash flooding or were swept
		away.
4986	**définitif**	**final**
	adj[definitif]	Cet élan doit être poursuivi pour permettre le règlement définitif de cette
		question. -That work must continue for the definitive settlement of this
		question.
4987	**brûlure**	**burn**
	f	La porte de derrière présente aussi des marques de brûlure.
	[bʁylyʁ]	-Don't know if it was forced, but we've got the same burn marks on the
		back door.
4988	**apprentissage**	**learning**
	m	L'apprentissage traditionnel a cédé la place à l'apprentissage électronique et
	[apʁɑ̃tisaʒ]	en ligne.
		-Traditional learning has been replaced with e-learning and online
		learning.
4989	**maximal**	**terminal**
	adj	«Couple maximal», la valeur maximale du couple net mesurée à pleine
	[maksimal]	charge.
		-"Maximum torque" means the maximum value of the net torque measured
		at full engine load.
4990	**rodeo**	**rodeo**
	m	Monsieur le Président, la semaine prochaine les finales canadiennes de
	[ʁɔdəo]	rodéo auront lieu à Edmonton, en Alberta.
		-Speaker, next week marks the Canadian Finals Rodeo Week in Edmonton,
		Alberta.
4991	**abbé**	**abbot**
	m	Et l'abbé décida de les faire rôtir.
	[abe]	-Where the abbot decided to roast them.
4992	**relier**	**connect**
	vb	Il faudrait plus d'un pont pour relier Palerme à Berlin, Madame la
	[ʁəlje]	Commissaire.
		-To link Palermo with Berlin, more than a bridge would be needed,
		Commissioner.
4993	**croc**	**fang**
	m	Tu pourrais casser un croc dessus.
	[kʁo]	-You could chip a fang on it.
4994	**grossir**	**swell|magnify**
	vb	À Dartmouth, il y a de milliers de gens qui risquent de grossir les rangs des
	[gʁosiʁ]	sans-abri.
		-In Dartmouth there are thousands of people who I would say are the
		homeless in waiting.
4995	**violeur**	**rapist**
	m	Le violeur ne montra aucun signe de remords, au cours du procès.
	[vjɔlœʁ]	-The rapist showed no signs of remorse during his trial.
4996	**nickel**	**nickel**

m
[nikɛl]

La première couche comporte un alliage comportant du nickel et du tungstène.
-The first layer comprises an alloy comprising nickel and tungsten.

4997 infiltrer — **infiltrate**

vb
[ɛ̃filtʀe]

« Le DG2 peut diffamer ou sanctionner qui il veut, infiltrer ses agents partout ».
-It can "slander or sanction anyone, infiltrate its agents anywhere".

4998 relance — **revival**

f[ʀəlɑ̃s]

Nous devons travailler avec la Commission afin de relancer l'industrie du tourisme. -We need to work with the Commission to boost the tourism industry.

4999 pénitencier — **penitentiary**

m
[penitɑ̃sje]

On peut vous envoyer au pénitencier.
-And you can be sent to the penitentiary.

5000 prototype — **prototype**

m
[pʀɔtɔtip]

Ce n'est pas là un prototype idéaliste : il peut s'appliquer au monde réel.
-That was not an idealistic prototype but could be applied to the real world.

5001 superviseur — **supervisor**

m
[sypɛʀvizœʀ]

Quant à mon superviseur, il est très incohérent, du coup le travail n'est jamais fait.
-When it comes to my supervisor, he's very inconsistent, so we never get any work done.

5002 préparé — **prepared**

adj
[pʀepaʀe]

Le Gouvernement a déjà préparé deux plans quinquennaux pour traiter la pandémie.
-The Government has already prepared two five-year plans to address the pandemic.

5003 manœuvrer — **maneuver|manipulate**

vb
[manœvʀe]

Barroso doit manœuvrer avec art entre ces propositions.
-Mr Barroso has to manoeuvre artfully between these propositions.

5004 faisable — **feasible|doable**

adj
[fəzabl]

Le sénateur LeBreton : Honorables sénateurs, nous tentons de faire ce qui est faisable.
-Senator LeBreton: Honourable senators, we are trying to achieve the doable.

5005 ampoule — **bulb|ampoule**

f
[ɑ̃pul]

Combien de gens cela prend-il de changer une ampoule ?
-How many people does it take to change a lightbulb?

5006 numérique — **digital|numerical**

adj
[nymeʀik]

L'hébreu servait de système numérique.
-Ancient Jews used Hebrew as their numerical system.

5007 consentement — **consent**

m
[kɔ̃sɑ̃tmɑ̃]

J'ai débattu avec lui jusqu'à obtenir son consentement.
-I argued him into consent.

5008 orientation — **orientation|guidance**

f
[ɔʀjɑ̃tasjɔ̃]

Vous avez vraiment un bon sens de l'orientation.
-You have a really good sense of direction.

5009 connecter — **log on**

vb
[kɔnɛkte]

Activez le menu contextuel des objets sélectionnés et choisissez la commande Connecter.
-Open the context menu for the selected object and select the Connect command.

5010	**pilotage**	**control; piloting**
	m; f	Pilotage intégral de DAW dans une surface de contrôle grand format extensible.
	[pilɔtaʒ]	-Get powerful DAW control in an expandable large-format control surface.
5011	**tracé**	**route|course; tracing**
	m; adj	Tu ne peux pas analyser les données efficacement avant d'avoir tracé un graphique.
	[tʁase]	-You cannot analyse the data efficiently unless you draw a plot.
5012	**aquarium**	**aquarium**
	m	Voulez-vous aller à l'aquarium ?
	[akwaʁjɔm]	-Do you want to go to the aquarium?
5013	**concession**	**concession|dealership**
	f	Yasugoro veut la concession du gué depuis longtemps.
	[kɔ̃sesjɔ̃]	-Yasugoro has been eyeing the concession at the ford for a long time.
5014	**rédaction**	**writing|redaction**
	f	Le point D) (Remorques) a été adopté avec la rédaction proposée par le secrétariat.
	[ʁedaksjɔ̃]	-Section (D) (Trailers) was adopted with the wording proposed by the secretariat.
5015	**diplomatique**	**diplomatic**
	adj	N'y aurait-il aucune possibilité de protection diplomatique pour cette société ?
	[diplɔmatik]	-Would there be no possibility of diplomatic protection for such corporations?
5016	**ravin**	**ravine**
	m	Alors qu'ils skiaient, ils eurent un accident: ils tombèrent dans un profond ravin.
	[ʁavɛ̃]	-Whilst they were out skiing they had an accident: they fell down a deep ravine.
5017	**venin**	**venom**
	m	Voici, en substance, le venin qu'il vient de cracher.
	[vənɛ̃]	-This is the type of poison which he spouts here.
5018	**immoral**	**immoral**
	adj	Ce qui est vraiment immoral, et mérite ce qualificatif, c'est l'occupation.
	[imɔʁal]	-The truly immoral thing, which needs to be characterized as such, is occupation.
5019	**merveilleusement**	**wonderfully**
	adv	Même merveilleusement peinte, en effet, cette pipe ne permettra jamais de fumer.
	[mɛʁvɛjøzmɑ̃]	-Magnificently painted it may be, but this pipe can never be smoked.
5020	**boulangerie**	**bakery**
	f	Tu peux aller chercher du pain à la boulangerie, deux petites et une grosse, s'il te plait ? Et s'ils n'en ont plus, tu peux prendre quatre ficelles à la place.
	[bulɑ̃ʒʁi]	-Could you please go buy bread at the baker's, two small ones and a large one please? And if they ran out, you can buy four thin baguettes instead.
5021	**maquette**	**model**
	f	Réaliser une maquette d'avion est intéressant.
	[makɛt]	-Making a model plane is interesting.
5022	**greffer**	**graft|engraft**
	vb	Un malade à greffer sur quatre mourra avant de recevoir la greffe salvatrice.
	[gʁefe]	-One in four people awaiting a donor will die before they get a transplant.

5023 **écharpe**
f
[eʃaʁp]

scarf

Cette écharpe est à Jacqueline.
-This scarf is Jacqueline's.

5024 **sonore**
f; adj
[sɔnɔʁ]

sound; acoustic

Le film doublé est ennuyeux à regarder parce que la bande sonore est décalée de l'image.
-The dubbed movie is annoying to watch because the audio is out of sync with the video.

5025 **doctorat**
m
[dɔktɔʁa]

doctorate|phD

Votre thèse de doctorat doit être écrite en anglais.
-Your PhD thesis has to be written in English.

Adjectives

Rank	French-PoS	Translation
2507	**disponible**-*adj; adv*	available; on call
2510	**pacifique**-*adj*	peaceful| pacific
2512	**mystérieux**-*adj*	mysterious
2514	**historique**-*adj*	historical
2516	**missile**-*adj; m*	missile; missile
2519	**légitime**-*adj*	legitimate
2520	**cuit**-*adj*	cooked| baked
2534	**assistant**-*adj; m*	assistant; assistant
2537	**honorable**-*adj*	honorable
2538	**minimum**-*adj; m*	minimum; minimum
2539	**absent**-*adj; m*	absent; absentee
2546	**confortable**-*adj*	comfortable
2555	**clef**-*f; adj*	key; pivotal
2564	**survivant**-*m; adj*	survivor; surviving
2567	**conscient**-*adj*	aware| conscious
2577	**marchand**-*m; adj*	dealer| seller; mercantile
2579	**protégé**-*adj*	protected
2589	**poli**-*adj*	polished| polite
2590	**pénible**-*adj*	painful| hard
2616	**probable**-*adj*	likely
2621	**irlandais**-*adj; m|mpl*	Irish; Irish
2623	**amateur**-*adj; m*	amateur; amateur
2626	**gênant**-*adj*	embarrassing
2631	**muet**-*adj; m*	silent; mute
2642	**cachette**-*f; adj*	hiding place| cache; hideaway
2643	**cavalier**-*m; adj*	rider; cavalier
2649	**lent**-*adj*	slow
2652	**acide**-*adj; m*	acid| sour; acid
2654	**sèche**-*f; adj*	fag; dry
2655	**rebelle**-*m/f; adj*	rebel; rebellious
2659	**brut**-*adj; m*	gross; crude
2660	**intime**-*adj*	intimate
2664	**douloureux**-*adj*	painful
2666	**brillant**-*adj; m*	brilliant| bright; gloss
2674	**comique**-*adj; m/f*	comic; comic
2676	**silencieux**-*adj; m*	silent; silencer
2678	**renversé**-*adj*	reversed
2680	**pâle**-*adj*	pale
2689	**comptable**-*adj; m/f*	accounting; accountant
2691	**international**-*adj; m*	international; international
2697	**jumeau**-*adj; m*	twin; twin
2701	**grec**-*adj; m*	Greek; Greek
2702	**interne**-*adj; m/f*	internal; intern
2703	**potentiel**-*adj; m*	potential; potential
2721	**fée**-*f; adj*	fairy; pixy
2725	**vulgaire**-*adj*	vulgar
2735	**Maya**-*m; adj*	Maya; Maya
2750	**soûl**-*adj*	drunk
2754	**local**-*adj*	local
2759	**extrême**-*adj; m*	extreme; extreme
2761	**ultime**-*adj*	ultimate
2762	**vainqueur**-*m; adj*	winner| conqueror; winning
2779	**fédéral**-*adj*	federal
2791	**insensé**-*adj; m*	senseless; madman
2799	**citron**-*adj; m*	lemon; lemon
2801	**ivrogne**-*m/f; adj*	drunkard; drunken
2806	**osé**-*adj*	bold| racy
2807	**automatique**-*adj*	automatic
2813	**fauché**-*adj*	broke| hard
2816	**maigre**-*adj*	lean| meager; lean
2818	**positif**-*adj; m*	positive; positive
2819	**candidat**-*m; adj*	candidate; elect
2827	**paysan**-*adj; m*	peasant; peasant
2838	**domestique**-*adj; m/f*	domestic; domestic
2839	**cinquième**-*adj*	fifth
2855	**désespéré**-*adj*	desperate| hopeless
2860	**pop**-*adj; m*	pop; pop
2861	**fumé**-*adj*	smoked
2862	**discret**-*adj*	discreet
2867	**actuel**-*adj*	current
2873	**mouillé**-*adj*	wet
2876	**latin**-*adj*	Latin
2880	**explosif**-*adj; m*	explosive; explosive
2888	**divorcé**-*adj; m*	divorced; divorcee
2889	**louche**-*f; adj*	ladle; shady
2891	**soviétique**-*adj*	Soviet
2892	**tactique**-*adj; f*	tactical; tactics
2893	**humble**-*adj*	humble
2894	**artistique**-*adj*	artistic
2897	**saoul**-*adj*	drunk
2900	**trouble**-*m; adj*	disorder| trouble; dim
2902	**copine**-*f; adj*	girlfriend; pally
2907	**quelconque**-*adj; prn*	any; some or other
2915	**intense**-*adj*	intense

2916	**grossier**-*adj*	coarse| rude
2918	**chrétien**-*adj; m*	Christian; Christian
2933	**vaste**-*adj*	vast| wide
2937	**confus**-*adj*	confused
2938	**inverse**-*adj; m*	reverse; reverse
2942	**sympathique**-*adj*	sympathetic
2952	**aîné**-*adj; m*	eldest; senior
2953	**pathétique**-*adj; m*	pathetic; pathos
2955	**laid**-*adj*	ugly
2966	**exceptionnel**-*adj*	exceptional
2973	**mexicain**-*adj*	Mexican
2975	**homicide**-*m; adj*	homicide; homicidal
2979	**religieux**-*adj; m*	religious; religious
2983	**économique**-*adj*	economic| thrifty
2984	**femelle**-*adj; f*	female; female
2990	**typique**-*adj*	typical
2991	**rempli**-*adj; m*	filled| full; tuck
2992	**grillé**-*adj*	grilled
2993	**taupe**-*f; adj*	mole; taupe
2996	**relevé**-*m; adj*	statement; raised
2997	**solaire**-*adj*	solar
2999	**âgé**-*adj*	old
3000	**aérien**-*adj*	air| aerial
3004	**polonais**-*adj; m|mpl*	Polish; Polish
3010	**terrestre**-*adj*	terrestrial| earthly
3011	**jumelle**-*adj; f*	twin; twin
3013	**travailleur**-*m; adj*	worker| employee; industrious
3016	**épouvantable**-*adj*	terrible| appalling
3017	**sublime**-*adj*	sublime
3019	**atroce**-*adj*	atrocious
3024	**inscrit**-*m/f; adj*	registered voter/student; enrolled
3028	**dramatique**-*adj*	dramatic
3037	**loyal**-*adj*	loyal| fair
3049	**pressé**-*adj*	pressed
3054	**yankee**-*adj*	Yankee
3057	**désagréable**-*adj*	unpleasant
3063	**mis**-*adj*	placed
3066	**authentique**-*adj*	authentic| genuine
3073	**inévitable**-*adj*	inevitable
3075	**immobilier**-*adj*	immovable
3079	**anonyme**-*adj*	anonymous
3083	**drogué**-*adj; m*	drugged; junkie
3096	**standard**-*adj; m*	standard; standard
3099	**insupportable**-*adj*	unbearable| insupportable
3108	**judiciaire**-*adj; m/f*	judicial; judiciary
3112	**valable**-*adj*	valid
3123	**chauve**-*adj*	bald
3124	**futé**-*adj*	smart
3132	**familier**-*adj; m*	familiar; familiar
3139	**stable**-*adj*	stable| steady
3141	**marron**-*adj; m*	brown; brown
3143	**nain**-*adj; m*	dwarf; dwarf
3154	**précédent**-*adj; m*	previous; precedent
3168	**sensé**-*adj*	sensible
3172	**atomique**-*adj*	atomic
3176	**mou**-*adj; m*	soft; slack
3178	**formé**-*adj*	formed| trained
3187	**familial**-*adj*	family
3188	**romain**-*adj*	Roman
3199	**mineur**-*adj; m*	minor; minor
3206	**mat**-*adj; m; abr*	matt; mate; morning
3217	**humide**-*adj*	wet| damp
3218	**diabolique**-*adj*	diabolical| devilish
3223	**insigne**-*m; adj*	badge| insignia; signal
3226	**sinistre**-*adj; m*	sinister| grim; fire
3227	**inconscient**-*adj; m*	unconscious; unconscious
3229	**réaliste**-*adj; m/f*	realistic; realist
3239	**creux**-*adj; m*	hollow| sunken; hollow
3249	**respectable**-*adj*	respectable
3251	**rituel**-*adj; m*	ritual; ritual
3255	**confidentiel**-*adj*	confidential
3257	**touchant**-*adj*	touching
3264	**musical**-*adj*	musical
3266	**paisible**-*adj*	peaceful| quiet
3279	**visuel**-*adj*	visual
3284	**féminin**-*adj*	female| feminine
3287	**génétique**-*adj; f*	genetic; genetics
3288	**psychiatrique**-*adj*	psychiatric
3289	**décédé**-*adj; m*	deceased; defunct
3291	**continent**-*adj; m*	continent; continent
3297	**informatique**-*f; adj*	data processing; paperless
3301	**séduisant**-*adj*	attractive| seductive
3302	**brun**-*adj; m*	brown; brown
3303	**mécanique**-*adj; f*	mechanical; mechanics
3311	**croisé**-*adj; m*	cross; crusader
3312	**détenu**-*adj; m*	detained; inmate

3315	**exemplaire**-*m; adj*	copy; exemplary
3316	**merdique**-*adj*	crappy| shitty
3321	**extra-terrestre**-*adj; m/f*	alien; alien
3324	**inhabituel**-*adj*	unusual
3325	**ras**-*adj*	all clear| short
3327	**porteur**-*m; adj*	carrier| holder; supporting
3331	**actif**-*adj; m*	active| working; assets
3334	**portail**-*adj; m*	portal; portal
3337	**mental**-*adj*	mental
3339	**semblable**-*adj; m*	similar; fellow creature
3344	**cellulaire**-*adj*	cellular
3349	**alcoolique**-*adj; m/f*	alcoholic; alcoholic
3351	**chauffé**-*adj*	heated
3366	**quotidien**-*adj; m*	daily; daily
3377	**sobre**-*adj*	sober
3379	**imaginaire**-*adj*	imaginary
3381	**honteux**-*adj*	shameful| ashamed
3390	**élégant**-*adj; m*	elegant; dandy
3398	**martial**-*adj*	martial
3408	**électronique**-*adj; f*	electronic; electronics
3415	**croyant**-*m; adj*	believer; god-fearing
3417	**indispensable**-*adj*	essential
3431	**temporaire**-*adj*	temporary
3446	**pitoyable**-*adj*	pitiful
3450	**fiable**-*adj*	reliable
3452	**véhicule**-*m; adj*	vehicle; vehicular
3453	**financier**-*adj; m*	financial; financier
3461	**infini**-*adj; m*	infinite; infinity
3469	**scolaire**-*adj*	school
3471	**bloqué**-*adj*	blocked
3475	**révolutionnaire**-*adj; m/f*	revolutionary; revolutionary
3481	**morveux**-*adj; m*	snotty; snot
3482	**croyable**-*adj*	believable
3487	**conséquent**-*adj*	consequent
3505	**défunt**-*adj; m*	late; deceased person
3509	**commode**-*adj; f*	convenient| handy; chest of drawers
3514	**épais**-*adj*	thick| heavy
3516	**automobile**-*adj; f*	automotive; automobile
3521	**nouille**-*f; adj*	noodle| dope; dumb
3524	**obscur**-*adj*	obscure| dim
3526	**psychologique**-*adj*	psychological
3529	**intrus**-*m; adj*	intruder; intruding
3531	**immédiat**-*adj*	immediate
3543	**allergique**-*adj*	allergic
3544	**spatial**-*adj*	spatial
3551	**primaire**-*adj*	primary; primary
3555	**câlin**-*adj; m*	hugging; hug
3556	**céleste**-*adj*	celestial| unworldly
3562	**veinard**-*adj*	lucky
3565	**brutal**-*adj; m*	brutal; brute
3592	**téléphonique**-*adj*	telephone
3595	**dément**-*adj*	demented| insane
3598	**chimique**-*adj*	chemical
3605	**générateur**-*m; adj*	generator; generating
3609	**fondu**-*adj*	molten
3616	**sévère**-*adj*	severe| strict
3620	**embarrassant**-*adj*	embarrassing
3628	**indigne**-*adj*	unworthy
3631	**violet**-*adj; m*	purple; purple
3638	**têtu**-*adj*	stubborn| headstrong
3646	**excès**-*adj; m; mpl*	excess; excess; debauchery
3667	**paresseux**-*adj; m*	lazy; sloth
3671	**bouffon**-*m; adj*	buffoon; fool
3681	**terrifiant**-*adj*	terrifying
3685	**coupure**-*f; adj*	cut; clipping
3689	**comptant**-*adj*	spot| cash
3690	**promis**-*adj*	promised
3698	**combattant**-*m; adj*	fighter; fighting
3709	**loué**-*adj*	rented| leased
3716	**gaze**-*adj; f*	gauze; gauze
3726	**arrogant**-*adj*	arrogant
3736	**minuscule**-*adj; f*	tiny| lowercase; minuscule
3737	**suédois**-*adj; m*	Swedish; Swedish
3742	**crépuscule**-*adj; m*	dusk; dusk
3750	**vicieux**-*adj; m*	vicious; lecher
3751	**habituel**-*adj*	usual| regular
3754	**cardinal**-*adj; m*	cardinal; cardinal
3764	**vulnérable**-*adj*	vulnerable
3776	**instable**-*adj*	unstable| unsteady
3777	**conditionnel**-*adj*	conditional
3782	**coureur**-*m; adj*	runner; racing
3794	**turc**-*adj; m*	Turkish; Turkish
3795	**musulman**-*adj; m*	Muslim; Muslim
3812	**agressif**-*adj*	aggressive
3830	**convenable**-*adj*	suitable| appropriate
3833	**gigantesque**-*adj*	gigantic
3838	**fondé**-*adj*	based| founded

3842	**étroit**-*adj*	narrow	close
3844	**admirable**-*adj*	admirable
3851	**majeur**-*adj; m*	major	middle finger; major
3852	**visible**-*adj*	visible
3859	**protecteur**-*adj; m*	protective; protector
3863	**divers**-*adj*	various	several
3864	**raciste**-*adj; m/f*	racist; racist
3869	**ambitieux**-*adj; m/f*	ambitious; careerist
3875	**cadet**-*adj; m*	cadet; cadet
3881	**vétérinaire**-*adj; m/f*	veterinary; veterinary
3884	**savant**-*adj; m*	learned; scholar
3889	**éthique**-*f; adj*	ethics; ethical
3891	**amer**-*adj; m*	bitter; bitter
3893	**préférable**-*adj*	preferable
3894	**affirmatif**-*adj*	affirmative
3895	**anormal**-*adj*	abnormal
3902	**voyageur**-*m; adj*	traveler	passenger; traveling
3905	**ignoble**-*adj*	despicable
3909	**habile**-*adj*	clever	skilful
3911	**indépendant**-*adj; m*	independent; independent
3915	**lointain**-*adj*	distant	far
3921	**arrière**-*adj; m*	rear	back; back
3924	**atlantique**-*adj*	Atlantic
3930	**marbre**-*adj; m*	marble; marble
3932	**féroce**-*adj*	fierce	savage
3940	**manuscrit**-*adj; m*	manuscript; manuscript
3948	**tentant**-*adj*	tempting
3950	**orphelin**-*adj; m*	orphan; orphan
3957	**informe**-*adj*	shapeless	unformed
3959	**suède**-*adj; f*	suede; suede
3960	**optimiste**-*adj; m/f*	optimistic; optimist
3961	**audace**-*f; adj*	boldness; woodless
3962	**affamé**-*adj*	starving	famished
3965	**immortel**-*adj; m*	immortal; immortal
3968	**carbone**-*adj; m*	carbon; carbon
3970	**maladroit**-*adj; m*	awkward; blunderer
3973	**revenant**-*adj; m*	return	reverting; ghost
3979	**hostile**-*adj*	hostile	opposed
3981	**biologique**-*adj*	biological
3985	**retardé**-*adj*	backward
3987	**banal**-*adj*	banal
3995	**foncé**-*adj*	dark
4011	**provisoire**-*adj*	provisional
4030	**irresponsable**-*adj*	irresponsible
4033	**hystérique**-*adj*	hysterical
4034	**impoli**-*adj*	impolite
4037	**immobile**-*adj*	motionless	immobile
4039	**fourré**-*m; adj*	thicket; filled
4044	**sentimental**-*adj*	sentimental
4049	**punk**-*adj; m*	punk; punk
4053	**impérial**-*adj*	imperial
4054	**inoffensif**-*adj*	harmless
4066	**alentour**-*adj*	surrounding
4071	**amical**-*adj*	friendly
4075	**africain**-*adj; m*	African
4076	**maléfique**-*adj*	maleficient
4090	**obus**-*m; adj*	shell; dense
4093	**hollandais**-*adj; mpl*	Dutch; Dutch
4094	**maternel**-*adj*	maternal
4101	**légendaire**-*adj*	legendary
4103	**naïf**-*adj; m*	naive; babe
4105	**cérébral**-*adj*	cerebral
4106	**supplémentaire**-*adj*	additional
4129	**impeccable**-*adj*	impeccable	spotless
4138	**malais**-*adj; m*	Malay; Malay
4142	**boche**-*adj; m/f*	German; Jerry (derogative)
4145	**gouvernant**-*adj*	governing
4149	**odieux**-*adj*	odious	heinous
4156	**nocturne**-*adj*	nocturnal
4161	**mauviette**-*adj; f*	wimp; weakling
4164	**infirme**-*adj*	infirm
4165	**grotesque**-*adj; m*	grotesque; grotesque
4166	**juridique**-*adj*	legal
4167	**glorieux**-*adj*	glorious
4170	**remué**-*adj*	stirred
4173	**spectaculaire**-*adj*	spectacular
4180	**ragot**-*adj; m*	dirty; gossip
4181	**inattendu**-*adj*	unexpected
4194	**masculin**-*adj; m*	male; masculine
4198	**trappe**-*f; adj*	hatch	trap; cobwebby
4202	**vital**-*adj*	vital
4213	**gratis**-*adv; adj*	free; free
4222	**redoutable**-*adj*	formidable	dreadful
4239	**lamentable**-*adj*	lamentable
4246	**universitaire**-*adj; m/f*	university; postgraduate student
4247	**massif**-*adj; m*	massive; massif

4250	**neutre**-*adj*	neutral| neuter
4254	**imprévisible**-*adj*	unpredictable
4261	**postal**-*adj*	postal
4263	**identique**-*adj*	identical
4268	**ingrat**-*adj*	ungrateful
4286	**antécédent**-*adj*	antecedent
4289	**intact**-*adj*	intact| unspoiled
4290	**partisan**-*adj; m*	partisan| adherent; partisan
4297	**monstrueux**-*adj*	monstrous
4301	**grandiose**-*adj*	grandiose
4302	**prétentieux**-*adj*	pretentious| snooty
4305	**carotte**-*f; adj*	carrot; carroty
4311	**chronique**-*adj; f*	chronic; chronicle
4313	**régulier**-*adj; m*	regular; regular
4323	**cynique**-*adj; m*	cynical; cynic
4324	**municipal**-*adj*	municipal
4327	**parasite**-*m; adj*	parasite; parasitic
4331	**récent**-*adj*	recent
4336	**bouclé**-*adj*	curly
4340	**compositeur**-*m; adj*	composer; compositive
4341	**uni**-*adj*	united| plain
4348	**industriel**-*adj; m*	industrial; industrialist
4357	**cerise**-*adj; f*	cherry; cherry
4362	**coquin**-*m; adj*	rascal; naughty
4366	**obligatoire**-*adj*	compulsory| binding
4368	**furax**-*adj*	hopping mad
4375	**canadien**-*adj*	Canadian
4377	**initial**-*adj*	initial
4382	**intermédiaire**-*adj; m*	intermediate; intermediate
4385	**ringard**-*adj; m*	tacky; has-been
4391	**invincible**-*adj*	invincible
4392	**vagabond**-*adj; m*	vagabond; vagabond
4397	**fugitif**-*adj; m*	fugitive; fugitive
4398	**souverain**-*adj; m*	sovereign; sovereign
4400	**offensif**-*adj*	aggressive
4402	**irrésistible**-*adj*	irresistible
4408	**criant**-*adj*	crying
4414	**satisfait**-*adj*	satisfied| pleased
4415	**terminal**-*adj; m*	terminal; terminal
4416	**fasciste**-*m/f; adj*	fascist; fascist
4417	**déprimant**-*adj*	depressing
4437	**embrouillé**-*adj*	confused| muddled
4438	**lumineux**-*adj*	luminous
4442	**défoncé**-*adj*	stoned

4446	**impuissant**-*adj*	powerless
4449	**permanent**-*adj; m*	permanent; permanent
4459	**mystique**-*adj; m/f*	mystical; mystic
4465	**étonnant**-*adj*	surprising| astonishing
4469	**natal**-*adj*	native
4470	**impitoyable**-*adj*	ruthless| merciless
4471	**sensationnel**-*adj*	sensational
4481	**bourgeois**-*adj; m*	bourgeois; bourgeois
4483	**inacceptable**-*adj*	unacceptable
4484	**itinéraire**-*m; adj*	route; itinerary
4489	**annuel**-*adj*	annual
4498	**double**-*adj; m*	double| twin; double
4506	**barbare**-*adj; m*	barbaric; barbarian
4507	**ému**-*adj*	affected
4509	**dentaire**-*adj*	dental
4522	**audacieux**-*adj*	bold
4527	**flou**-*adj; m; adv*	vague; blurring; fuzzily
4531	**souffrant**-*adj*	suffering| ill
4537	**bancaire**-*adj*	banking
4538	**favorite**-*adj*	favored
4557	**écossais**-*adj; m: mpl*	Scottish; Scottish; Scots
4569	**concurrent**-*m; adj*	competitor| contestant; concurrent
4570	**socialiste**-*adj; m*	socialist; socialist
4573	**constant**-*adj*	constant
4575	**bavard**-*adj; m*	talkative; chatterbox
4579	**statistique**-*adj; f*	statistical; statistics
4580	**immonde**-*adj*	unclean
4582	**regrettable**-*adj*	regrettable| unfortunate
4583	**satané**-*adj*	devilish
4584	**choral**-*adj; m*	choral; choral
4590	**infâme**-*adj*	infamous| vile
4602	**talentueux**-*adj*	talented
4607	**crédible**-*adj*	credible
4613	**mûr**-*adj*	mature| grown
4615	**accessoire**-*adj; m*	accessory| incidental; accessory
4625	**esthétique**-*adj; f*	aesthetic; aesthetics
4630	**exquis**-*adj*	exquisite| delicious
4632	**scandaleux**-*adj*	scandalous| outrageous
4635	**antique**-*adj; m*	antique| ancient; antique
4637	**infidèle**-*adj*	unfaithful
4642	**déprimé**-*adj*	depressed

4648	**obsèques**-*adj; f; fpl*	obsequies; funeral
4649	**intellectuel**-*adj; m*	intellectual; intellectual
4652	**contagieux**-*adj*	contagious; communicable
4655	**pente**-*f; adj*	slope| incline; heavy
4664	**tracteur**-*m; adj*	tractor; towing
4672	**sordide**-*adj*	sordid| wretched
4684	**sanguin**-*adj*	blood
4688	**chaleureux**-*adj*	warm| cordial
4689	**susceptible**-*adj*	susceptible
4693	**enthousiaste**-*adj; m*	enthusiastic; enthusiast
4699	**acceptable**-*adj*	acceptable| fair
4703	**martyr**-*m; adj*	martyr; martyred
4711	**adolescent**-*m; adj*	teenager; adolescent
4716	**insensible**-*adj*	insensitive
4720	**crucial**-*adj*	crucial| critical
4728	**disco**-*adj; m*	disco; disco
4741	**perdant**-*adj; m*	losing; loser
4742	**hébreu**-*adj; m*	Hebrew; Hebrew
4743	**indigène**-*adj; m/f*	native; native
4744	**suicidaire**-*adj*	suicidal
4745	**remontant**-*adj; m*	pick-me-up; tonic
4752	**radin**-*m; adj*	tightwad; mean
4754	**artificiel**-*adj*	artificial
4755	**subtil**-*adj*	subtle
4764	**inoubliable**-*adj*	unforgettable
4769	**ironique**-*adj*	ironic| quizzical
4774	**volant**-*m; adj*	steering wheel; flying
4778	**découvert**-*adj; m*	discovered; overdraft
4780	**emprisonné**-*adj; m*	jailed; detainee
4782	**saisi**-*adj*	grasped
4785	**prometteur**-*adj*	promising
4787	**clochard**-*m; adj*	tramp; down-at-heel
4790	**trouillard**-*adj; m*	yellow belly; yellow-livered
4791	**inférieur**-*adj; m*	lower; inferior
4792	**adultère**-*m; adj*	adultery; adulterous
4795	**bruyant**-*adj*	noisy
4803	**convaincant**-*adj*	convincing
4806	**radical**-*adj; m*	radical; radical
4817	**républicain**-*adj; m*	republican; republican
4821	**humiliant**-*adj*	humiliating
4824	**asiatique**-*adj*	Asian
4831	**toxique**-*adj*	toxic
4837	**abominable**-*adj*	abominable
4841	**créatif**-*adj*	creative
4842	**occidental**-*adj; m*	western; western
4847	**réciproque**-*adj*	reciprocal| mutual
4853	**souriant**-*adj*	smiling
4855	**joint**-*adj; m*	joint; joint
4856	**puant**-*adj*	stinking
4858	**hurlant**-*adj*	howling
4864	**investisseur**-*m; adj*	investor; investing
4865	**fumeur**-*adj; m*	smoking; smoker
4880	**primitif**-*adj; m*	primitive; primitive
4883	**grecque**-*adj*	Greek
4887	**hongrois**-*adj*	Hungarian
4889	**psychotique**-*adj; m/f*	psychotic; psychotic
4891	**coréen**-*adj; m*	Korean; Korean
4896	**redevable**-*adj; vb*	beholden; put under stress
4901	**héroïque**-*adj*	heroic
4903	**chercheur**-*m; adj*	researcher| seeker; inquiring
4904	**médiocre**-*adj; m/f*	poor| mediocre; second-rater
4915	**réduit**-*adj*	reduced
4917	**gâté**-*adj*	spoiled| tainted
4918	**danois**-*adj; m*	Danish; Danish
4924	**combustible**-*m; adj*	fuel; combustible
4926	**attentif**-*adj*	attentive| careful
4943	**excentrique**-*adj; m/f*	eccentric; eccentric
4950	**obscène**-*adj*	obscene
4953	**lièvre**-*m; adj*	hare; hare's
4954	**à bout**-*adj*	overwrought
4955	**érotique**-*adj*	erotic
4964	**européen**-*adj*	European
4968	**élu**-*adj; m*	elected; elect
4969	**flatteur**-*adj; m*	flattering; flatterer
4974	**informé**-*adj*	informed
4975	**snob**-*m/f; adj*	snob; snobbish
4981	**compréhensible**-*adj*	understandable
4985	**souterrain**-*adj*	underground
4986	**définitif**-*adj*	final
4989	**maximal**-*adj*	terminal
5002	**préparé**-*adj*	prepared
5004	**faisable**-*adj*	feasible| doable
5006	**numérique**-*adj*	digital| numerical
5011	**tracé**-*m; adj*	route| course; tracing

5015	**diplomatique**-*adj*	diplomatic
5018	**immoral**-*adj*	immoral
5024	**sonore**-*f; adj*	sound; acoustic

Adverbs

Rank	French-PoS	Translation
2507	**disponible**-*adj; adv*	available; on call
2536	**effectivement**-*adv*	effectively
2540	**vachement**-*adv*	really
2576	**gentiment**-*adv*	kindly| gently
2578	**aussitôt**-*adv*	immediately
2588	**constamment**-*adv*	constantly
2607	**infiniment**-*adv*	infinitely
2700	**tranquillement**-*adv*	quietly
2771	**différemment**-*adv*	differently
2844	**drôlement**-*adv*	funnily
2872	**contrairement**-*adv*	counter
2910	**spécialement**-*adv*	specially| notably
2913	**dernièrement**-*adv*	recently| at last
3014	**éternellement**-*adv*	eternally
3031	**soudainement**-*adv*	suddenly
3051	**définitivement**-*adv*	definitively
3085	**quasiment**-*adv*	almost
3107	**néanmoins**-*con; adv*	however; withal
3126	**bizarrement**-*adv*	oddly| peculiarly
3173	**voire**-*adv*	indeed
3230	**physiquement**-*adv*	physically
3360	**généralement**-*adv*	generally| usually
3361	**gratuitement**-*adv*	free of charge
3363	**sacrément**-*adv*	mighty
3364	**littéralement**-*adv*	literally
3389	**techniquement**-*adv*	technically
3397	**légèrement**-*adv*	slightly| lightly
3414	**toutefois**-*con; adv*	however; nevertheless
3419	**gravement**-*adv*	seriously| gravely
3427	**régulièrement**-*adv*	regularly
3581	**calmement**-*adv*	calmly
3599	**premièrement**-*adv*	firstly
3697	**légalement**-*adv*	legally
3704	**largement**-*adv*	widely
3801	**visiblement**-*adv*	visibly
3871	**alias**-*adv*	alias
3916	**manifestement**-*adv*	obviously
3978	**librement**-*adv*	freely
4040	**discrètement**-*adv*	discreetly
4048	**précédemment**-*adv*	previously
4068	**strictement**-*adv*	strictly
4213	**gratis**-*adv; adj*	free; free
4252	**fortement**-*adv*	strongly
4270	**vivement**-*adv*	deeply
4278	**habituellement**-*adv*	usually
4282	**purement**-*adv*	purely
4296	**sexuellement**-*adv*	sexually
4337	**délibérément**-*adv*	deliberately| willfully
4401	**brusquement**-*adv*	suddenly| sharply
4407	**pleinement**-*adv*	fully
4527	**flou**-*adj; m; adv*	vague; blurring; fuzzily
4659	**nécessairement**-*adv*	necessarily
4714	**principalement**-*adv*	mainly| mostly
4730	**soigneusement**-*adv*	carefully
4734	**fermement**-*adv*	firmly
4793	**étrangement**-*adv*	strangely
4797	**durement**-*adv*	harshly
4848	**vaguement**-*adv*	vaguely
4897	**mentalement**-*adv*	mentally
4912	**follement**-*adv*	madly
4941	**subitement**-*adv*	suddenly
4961	**séparément**-*adv*	separately| apart
4980	**secrètement**-*adv*	secretly
5019	**merveilleusement**-*adv*	wonderfully

Conjunctions

Rank	French-*PoS*	Translation
3107	**néanmoins**-*con; adv*	however; withal
3414	**toutefois**-*con; adv*	however; nevertheless

Prepositions

Rank	French-PoS	Translation
2995	**outre**-*prp; f*	besides; skin
3688	**excepté**-*prp*	except
4088	**via**-*prp*	via

Pronouns

Rank	French-PoS	Translation	
2907	**quelconque**-*adj; prn*	any; some or other	adj; prn

Numerals

Rank	French-*PoS*	Translation	
3092	**quarante**-*num*	forty	num
3276	**treize**-*num*	thirteen	num
3412	**seize**-*num*	sixteen	num
3445	**sixième**-*num*	sixth	num
3580	**quatorze**-*num*	fourteen	num
3768	**septième**-*num*	seventh	num
4185	**soixante**-*num*	sixty	num
4386	**deuxièmement**-*num*	secondly	num
4810	**vingtaine**-*num*	around twenty	num
4885	**trentaine**-*num*	about thirty	num

Nouns

Rank	French-PoS	Translation
2502	touche-*f*	key
2503	profil-*m*	profile
2504	budget-*m*	budget
2505	panneau-*m*	panel| sign
2506	lame-*f*	blade
2508	illusion-*f*	illusion
2509	caravane-*f*	caravan| trailer
2511	scotch-*m*	Scotch tape| whisky
2515	régiment-*m*	regiment
2516	missile-*adj; m*	missile; missile
2517	boucher-*m; vb*	butcher; plug
2521	pilote-*m*	pilot
2526	héroïne-*f*	heroin
2527	bruit-*m*	noise| sound
2528	tendance-*f*	trend| movement
2529	serviteur-*m*	servant
2532	répétition-*f*	repetition| rehearsal
2533	punition-*f*	punishment
2534	assistant-*adj; m*	assistant; assistant
2535	apparence-*f*	appearance
2538	minimum-*adj; m*	minimum; minimum
2539	absent-*adj; m*	absent; absentee
2542	possession-*f*	possession
2543	chanteur-*m*	singer
2544	colonne-*f*	column
2547	héritage-*m*	heritage| legacy
2549	troupeau-*m*	herd| flock
2550	vaisselle-*f*	dishes
2551	photographe-*m/f*	photographer
2552	ambassade-*f*	embassy
2553	engin-*m*	machine| engine
2554	âne-*m*	donkey
2555	clef-*f; adj*	key; pivotal
2556	villa-*f*	villa
2557	réussite-*f*	success
2558	muscle-*m*	muscle
2559	selle-*f*	saddle
2561	noyer-*m; vb*	walnut; drown
2562	nage-*m*	swim
2563	psychiatre-*m/f*	psychiatrist
2564	survivant-*m; adj*	survivor; surviving
2565	profession-*f*	profession
2566	déesse-*f*	goddess
2569	allure-*f*	look| pace
2570	thérapie-*f*	therapy
2571	expédition-*f*	shipment| expedition
2573	ambiance-*f*	ambience| environment
2574	festival-*m*	festival| celebration
2575	thème-*m*	theme
2577	marchand-*m; adj*	dealer| seller; mercantile
2580	pan-*m; int*	panel; bang!
2584	défaut-*m*	fault| failing
2587	taureau-*m*	bull
2591	Brésil-*m*	Brazil
2592	coke-*m*	coke
2594	cognac-*m*	cognac
2595	spécialiste-*m/f*	specialist
2598	routine-*f*	routine
2600	soda-*m*	soda
2601	douzaine-*f*	dozen
2603	majorité-*f*	majority
2604	instrument-*m*	instrument| implement
2605	angoisse-*f*	anguish
2606	serveur-*m*	waiter
2608	dinde-*f*	turkey
2609	canal-*m*	channel| canal
2610	janvier-*m*	January
2611	coma-*m*	coma
2613	batte-*f*	bat
2614	formule-*f*	formula| form
2615	jules-*m*	stud
2617	manager-*m*	manager
2619	vertu-*f*	virtue
2621	irlandais-*adj; m|mpl*	Irish; Irish
2622	équilibre-*m*	balance
2623	amateur-*adj; m*	amateur; amateur
2624	désordre-*m*	disorder
2625	marchandise-*f*	commodity
2627	galerie-*f*	gallery
2628	navette-*f*	shuttle
2629	résidence-*f*	residence
2630	ressource-*f*	resource
2631	muet-*adj; m*	silent; mute
2632	tissu-*m*	fabric| tissue
2633	foudre-*f*	lightning
2634	engagement-*m*	commitment| engagement

2635	**moustache**-*f*	mustache| whiskers		2694	**papillon**-*m*	butterfly
2636	**filet**-*m*	net| fillet		2695	**intimité**-*f*	privacy
2637	**parrain**-*m*	sponsor		2696	**jalousie**-*f*	jealousy
2638	**nièce**-*f*	niece		2697	**jumeau**-*adj; m*	twin; twin
2639	**exposition**-*f*	exposure| exhibition		2698	**individu**-*m*	individual
2640	**coiffure**-*f*	hairdressing| coiffure		2699	**démocratie**-*f*	democracy
2641	**baignoire**-*f*	bath		2701	**grec**-*adj; m*	Greek; Greek
2642	**cachette**-*f; adj*	hiding place| cache; hideaway		2702	**interne**-*adj; m/f*	internal; intern
2643	**cavalier**-*m; adj*	rider; cavalier		2703	**potentiel**-*adj; m*	potential; potential
2644	**intervention**-*f*	intervention| speech		2704	**agneau**-*m*	lamb
2645	**peintre**-*m*	painter		2705	**danseur**-*m*	dancer
2647	**capacité**-*f*	capacity| ability		2707	**sauvetage**-*m*	rescue| salvage
2648	**violon**-*m*	violin		2708	**hommage**-*m*	tribute
2650	**visite**-*f*	visit		2709	**steak**-*m*	steak
2651	**montage**-*m*	mounting		2711	**stress**-*m*	stress
2652	**acide**-*adj; m*	acid| sour; acid		2713	**duel**-*m*	duel
2653	**correction**-*f*	correction| patch		2714	**rideau**-*m*	curtain
2654	**sèche**-*f; adj*	fag; dry		2715	**berger**-*m*	shepherd
2655	**rebelle**-*m/f; adj*	rebel; rebellious		2716	**poursuite**-*f*	pursuit| prosecution
2656	**verdict**-*m*	verdict		2717	**carnet**-*m*	book
2657	**bénédiction**-*f*	blessing		2718	**légume**-*m*	vegetable
2659	**brut**-*adj; m*	gross; crude		2721	**fée**-*f; adj*	fairy; pixy
2662	**marteau**-*m*	hammer		2723	**grotte**-*f*	cave
2663	**conducteur**-*m*	driver| conductor		2726	**jet**-*m*	jet| stream
2665	**héritier**-*m*	heir| heirdom		2727	**tournoi**-*m*	tournament
2666	**brillant**-*adj; m*	brilliant| bright; gloss		2728	**développement**-*m*	development
2667	**mafia**-*f*	mafia		2729	**évasion**-*f*	evasion
2670	**quantité**-*f*	amount| number		2731	**poumon**-*m*	lung
2672	**fermeture**-*f*	closing| closure		2732	**rocher**-*m; vb*	rock; spit
2673	**tatouage**-*m*	tattoo		2734	**priorité**-*f*	priority| preference
2674	**comique**-*adj; m/f*	comic; comic		2735	**Maya**-*m; adj*	Maya; Maya
2675	**compassion**-*f*	compassion		2737	**assassinat**-*m*	assassination
2676	**silencieux**-*adj; m*	silent; silencer		2738	**structure**-*f*	structure
2679	**pneu**-*m*	tire		2739	**innocence**-*f*	innocence
2682	**grange**-*f*	barn		2740	**aspect**-*m*	aspect| appearance
2683	**atterrissage**-*m*	landing		2741	**faiblesse**-*f*	weakness
2685	**galaxie**-*f*	galaxy		2742	**mont**-*m*	mount
2686	**messe**-*f*	mass		2743	**deuil**-*m*	mourning
2687	**stratégie**-*f*	strategy		2744	**euro**-*m*	euro
2688	**flash**-*m*	flash| flashlight		2745	**hôte**-*m*	host
2689	**comptable**-*adj; m/f*	accounting; accountant		2746	**bandit**-*m*	bandit| gangster
2690	**descente**-*f*	descent		2747	**étage**-*m*	floor| stage
2691	**international**-*adj; m*	international; international		2748	**insecte**-*m*	insect
				2749	**complice**-*m/f*	accomplice
				2751	**archives**-*fpl*	archives
2692	**plafond**-*m*	ceiling| plafond		2752	**malentendu**-*m*	misunderstanding

2753	**drame**-*m*	drama		2820	**février**-*m*	February
2755	**robe**-*f*	dress| gown		2821	**coiffeur**-*m*	hairdresser| barber
2756	**veine**-*f*	vein| luck		2822	**chômage**-*m*	unemployment
2757	**col**-*m*	collar| pass		2823	**gin**-*m*	gin
2759	**extrême**-*adj; m*	extreme; extreme		2825	**balai**-*m*	broom
2760	**bougie**-*f*	candle| spark plug		2826	**plomb**-*m*	lead| plumb
2762	**vainqueur**-*m; adj*	winner| conqueror; winning		2827	**paysan**-*adj; m*	peasant; peasant
				2828	**sénat**-*m*	senate
2763	**concierge**-*m/f*	concierge		2832	**jazz**-*m*	jazz
2764	**dépôt**-*m*	deposit| filing		2833	**recette**-*f*	recipe
2766	**facture**-*f*	invoice| statement		2835	**char**-*m*	tank
2768	**marais**-*m*	marsh		2836	**altitude**-*f*	altitude| height
2769	**grain**-*m*	grain		2837	**coq**-*m*	rooster
2770	**bip**-*m*	beep| beeper		2838	**domestique**-*adj; m/f*	domestic; domestic
2772	**libération**-*f*	release| releasing				
2774	**délit**-*m*	offense| misdemeanor		2840	**coton**-*m*	cotton
2775	**noce**-*f*	nuptials		2843	**décor**-*m*	decor
2776	**renard**-*m*	fox		2845	**élection**-*f*	election
2777	**orient**-*m*	east		2847	**refuge**-*m*	refuge| shelter
2778	**ring**-*m*	ring		2849	**mannequin**-*m*	model| dummy
2780	**biscuit**-*m*	biscuit		2850	**danse**-*f*	dance
2781	**cache**-*m*	cover		2851	**disposition**-*f*	provision| disposal
2782	**barrage**-*m*	dam		2853	**reporter**-*m; vb*	reporter; postpone
2783	**profondeur**-*f*	depth| hollowness		2854	**maîtrise**-*f*	control| proficiency
2784	**moine**-*m*	monk		2857	**musicien**-*m*	musician
2785	**longueur**-*f*	length		2858	**express**-*m*	express
2786	**philosophie**-*f*	philosophy		2859	**radar**-*m*	radar
2787	**compromis**-*m*	compromise		2860	**pop**-*adj; m*	pop; pop
2788	**alpha**-*m*	alpha		2863	**entrepôt**-*m*	warehouse| store
2789	**évolution**-*f*	evolution		2865	**tube**-*m*	tube| hit
2790	**invention**-*f*	invention		2866	**fermier**-*m*	farmer
2791	**insensé**-*adj; m*	senseless; madman		2868	**haricot**-*m*	bean
2792	**banc**-*m*	bench| bank		2869	**proie**-*f*	prey| decoy
2793	**tiroir**-*m*	drawer		2871	**sueur**-*f*	sweat| sweating
2798	**championnat**-*m*	championship		2874	**fiction**-*f*	fiction
2799	**citron**-*adj; m*	lemon; lemon		2875	**complot**-*m*	conspiracy
2800	**désespoir**-*m*	despair		2877	**perle**-*f*	pearl| jewel
2801	**ivrogne**-*m/f; adj*	drunkard; drunken		2878	**organe**-*m*	organ
2802	**montre**-*f*	watch		2880	**explosif**-*adj; m*	explosive; explosive
2803	**visiteur**-*m*	visitor		2881	**tronche**-*f*	face
2809	**conclusion**-*f*	conclusion		2887	**encre**-*f*	ink
2811	**facteur**-*m*	factor| mailman		2888	**divorcé**-*adj; m*	divorced; divorcee
2814	**grille**-*f*	grid| gate		2889	**louche**-*f; adj*	ladle; shady
2815	**concept**-*m*	concept		2892	**tactique**-*adj; f*	tactical; tactics
2818	**positif**-*adj; m*	positive; positive		2895	**camionnette**-*f*	van
2819	**candidat**-*m; adj*	candidate; elect		2896	**interrogatoire**-*m*	examination| questioning

2898	**regret**-*m*	regret	2967	**démonstration**-*f*	demonstration| proof
2900	**trouble**-*m; adj*	disorder| trouble; dim	2968	**cloche**-*f*	bell
2901	**roue**-*f*	wheel	2971	**touriste**-*m/f*	tourist
2902	**copine**-*f; adj*	girlfriend; pally	2972	**ressort**-*m*	spring| resilience
2904	**élite**-*f*	elite	2974	**phénomène**-*m*	phenomenon
2905	**périmètre**-*m*	perimeter	2975	**homicide**-*m; adj*	homicide; homicidal
2906	**escroc**-*m*	crook	2976	**amende**-*f*	fine| penalty
2909	**bataillon**-*m*	battalion	2977	**cocktail**-*m*	cocktail
2912	**bec**-*m*	beak| spout	2978	**option**-*f*	option
2914	**cavalerie**-*f*	cavalry	2979	**religieux**-*adj; m*	religious; religious
2918	**chrétien**-*adj; m*	Christian; Christian	2980	**triomphe**-*m*	triumph
2920	**fouet**-*m*	whip	2981	**convoi**-*m*	convoy
2922	**culot**-*m*	base| nerve	2984	**femelle**-*adj; f*	female; female
2924	**bazar**-*m*	bazaar	2985	**chirurgie**-*f*	surgery
2925	**grenade**-*f*	grenade	2987	**crack**-*m*	crack| wiz
2926	**cristal**-*m*	crystal	2988	**domicile**-*m*	home| residence
2928	**relais**-*m*	relay	2989	**pull**-*m*	sweater
2930	**ligue**-*f*	league	2991	**rempli**-*adj; m*	filled| full; tuck
2931	**square**-*m*	square	2993	**taupe**-*f; adj*	mole; taupe
2932	**compliment**-*m*	compliment	2995	**outre**-*prp; f*	besides; skin
2934	**intuition**-*f*	intuition	2996	**relevé**-*m; adj*	statement; raised
2936	**minou**-*m*	kitty	3001	**ver**-*m*	worm
2938	**inverse**-*adj; m*	reverse; reverse	3003	**chantier**-*m*	site| yard
2939	**corruption**-*f*	corruption	3004	**polonais**-*adj; m|mpl*	Polish; Polish
2940	**cicatrice**-*f*	scar			
2941	**édition**-*f*	edition	3005	**barrière**-*f*	barrier| fence
2943	**mouchoir**-*m*	handkerchief	3006	**fiançailles**-*fpl*	engagement
2944	**rasoir**-*m*	razor	3007	**institut**-*m*	institute
2945	**vieillard**-*m*	old man	3008	**autobus**-*m*	bus
2946	**confession**-*f*	confession	3011	**jumelle**-*adj; f*	twin; twin
2947	**arrangement**-*m*	arrangement| understanding	3012	**vomi**-*m*	vomit
			3013	**travailleur**-*m; adj*	worker| employee; industrious
2949	**fréquence**-*f*	frequency	3018	**lard**-*m*	bacon
2950	**bouclier**-*m*	shield	3020	**gage**-*m*	pledge
2951	**fardeau**-*m*	burden| charge	3021	**canne**-*f*	cane
2952	**aîné**-*adj; m*	eldest; senior	3022	**agression**-*f*	aggression
2953	**pathétique**-*adj; m*	pathetic; pathos	3023	**concentration**-*f*	concentration| focus
2954	**affiche**-*f*	poster| public notice	3024	**inscrit**-*m/f; adj*	registered voter/student; enrolled
2957	**maïs**-*m*	corn			
2959	**colis**-*m*	package	3025	**séparation**-*f*	separation
2960	**surnom**-*m*	nickname	3026	**crayon**-*m*	pencil
2961	**froc**-*m*	frock| pants	3027	**oreiller**-*m*	pillow
2962	**brosse**-*f*	brush	3029	**allumette**-*f*	match
2963	**difficulté**-*f*	difficulty	3032	**paysage**-*m*	landscape
2964	**addition**-*f*	addition| sum	3033	**patate**-*f*	potato (chip)
2965	**jupe**-*f*	skirt	3034	**fouille**-*f*	search

3036	chantage-*m*	blackmail	3117	maillot-*m*	shirt
3038	laser-*m*	laser	3119	province-*f*	province
3039	indépendance-*f*	independence	3120	refus-*m*	refusal| rejection
3040	académie-*f*	academy	3121	souhait-*m*	wish
3041	récolte-*f*	harvest| crop	3122	cape-*f*	mantle
3042	aigle-*m/f*	eagle	3125	bracelet-*m*	bracelet| strap
3043	piqûre-*f*	sting| puncture	3127	duchesse-*f*	duchess
3046	trajet-*m*	path	3130	arc-*m*	arc| longbow
3047	fusillade-*f*	shooting	3131	massage-*m*	massage
3050	toubib-*m*	doctor| medic	3132	familier-*adj; m*	familiar; familiar
3053	brique-*f*	brick	3133	réservoir-*m*	tank
3055	Bouddha-*m*	Buddha	3135	cachet-*m*	stamp| cachet
3059	réserve-*f*	reserve| reservation	3136	bouquin-*m*	book
3060	artifice-*m*	artifice| trick	3137	égard-*m*	respect
3062	grandeur-*f*	size| magnitude	3141	marron-*adj; m*	brown; brown
3064	fondation-*f*	foundation	3142	clou-*m*	nail
3065	barman-*m*	bartender	3143	nain-*adj; m*	dwarf; dwarf
3067	vase-*m; f*	vase; mud	3144	marijuana-*f*	marijuana
3068	matelas-*m*	mattress	3145	appât-*m*	bait
3072	ruine-*f*	ruin| doom	3146	fourmi-*f*	ant
3074	gâchis-*m*	mess	3147	attentat-*m*	attempt| attack| bombing
3076	pic-*m*	peak| woodpecker	3148	colonie-*f*	colony
3077	faillite-*f*	bankruptcy	3149	gentillesse-*f*	kindness
3078	couvent-*m*	convent	3150	reportage-*m*	report
3080	éditeur-*m*	editor	3153	constitution-*f*	constitution| incorporation
3081	privilège-*m*	privilege	3154	précédent-*adj; m*	previous; precedent
3082	sauveur-*m*	savior	3155	badge-*m*	badge
3083	drogué-*adj; m*	drugged; junkie	3156	boxeur-*m*	boxer
3086	jambon-*m*	ham	3157	flipper-*m; vb*	pinball; freak out
3090	rupture-*f*	break| rupture	3160	farce-*f*	farce| joke
3092	quarante-*num*	forty	3161	armure-*f*	armor
3093	pyjama-*m*	pajamas	3162	marée-*f*	tide
3096	standard-*adj; m*	standard; standard	3163	autographe-*m*	autograph
3097	entreprise-*f*	business	3164	delta-*m*	delta
3098	tango-*m*	tango	3165	commentaire-*m*	comment| commentary
3100	paille-*f*	straw	3166	campus-*m*	campus
3101	tomate-*f*	tomato	3167	grenier-*m*	attic| granary
3102	glace-*f*	ice| mirror	3169	délai-*m*	period| delay
3104	mairie-*f*	town hall	3170	billard-*m*	billiards
3106	gym-*f*	gym	3171	grenouille-*f*	frog
3108	judiciaire-*adj; m/f*	judicial; judiciary	3174	horizon-*m*	horizon
3110	richesse-*f*	wealth| richness	3176	mou-*adj; m*	soft; slack
3111	nettoyage-*m*	cleaning| scrub	3177	conviction-*f*	conviction| belief
3113	augmentation-*f*	increase| rise	3182	hockey-*m*	hockey
3115	certificat-*m*	certificate| degree			
3116	valet-*m*	valet			

3183	**pharmacie**-*f*	pharmacy| dispensary	3244	**poignet**-*m*	wrist
3185	**flingue**-*m*	gun| shooter	3245	**vice**-*m*	vice
3186	**épicerie**-*f*	grocery	3246	**assistance**-*f*	assistance| audience
3189	**saké**-*m*	sake	3251	**rituel**-*adj; m*	ritual; ritual
3190	**observation**-*f*	observation| comment	3252	**quarantaine**-*f*	quarantine| about forty
3191	**briquet**-*m*	lighter	3253	**caca**-*m*	poo
3192	**description**-*f*	description| depiction	3254	**créateur**-*m*	creator
3194	**bulletin**-*m*	newsletter	3256	**symptôme**-*m*	symptom
3197	**téléphone**-*m*	phone	3258	**éclat**-*m*	eclat| brightness
3198	**applaudissement**-*m*	cheering	3259	**évacuation**-*f*	evacuation| draining
3199	**mineur**-*adj; m*	minor; minor	3260	**rime**-*f*	rhyme
3200	**office**-*m*	office| pantry	3261	**slip**-*m*	briefs| panties
3201	**barbecue**-*m*	barbecue	3263	**score**-*m*	score
3202	**balcon**-*m*	balcony	3265	**code**-*m*	code
3203	**licence**-*f*	license	3268	**obstacle**-*m*	obstacle
3205	**mallette**-*f*	briefcase	3269	**soulier**-*m*	shoe
3206	**mat**-*adj; m; abr*	matt; mate; morning	3270	**apparition**-*f*	appearance
3207	**comptoir**-*m*	counter	3271	**confusion**-*f*	confusion
3208	**arbitre**-*m*	referee	3272	**ruse**-*f*	cunning| ruse
3209	**bœuf**-*m*	beef	3273	**wagon**-*m*	car| wagon
3211	**aspirine**-*f*	aspirin	3274	**infection**-*f*	infection
3212	**bacon**-*m*	bacon	3276	**treize**-*num*	thirteen
3213	**suggestion**-*f*	suggestion	3277	**ego**-*m*	ego
3214	**mule**-*f*	mule	3278	**inspection**-*f*	inspection
3215	**rabbin**-*m*	rabbi	3280	**stock**-*m*	stock
3216	**district**-*m*	district	3282	**plaie**-*f*	wound
3219	**rançon**-*f*	ransom	3283	**gonzesse**-*f*	chick
3220	**sperme**-*m*	sperm	3286	**rampe**-*f*	ramp| rail
3221	**député**-*m*	member| deputy	3287	**génétique**-*adj; f*	genetic; genetics
3223	**insigne**-*m; adj*	badge| insignia; signal	3289	**décédé**-*adj; m*	deceased; defunct
3225	**seau**-*m*	bucket	3290	**pressentiment**-*m*	feeling
3226	**sinistre**-*adj; m*	sinister| grim; fire	3291	**continent**-*adj; m*	continent; continent
3227	**inconscient**-*adj; m*	unconscious; unconscious	3292	**bout**-*m*	end| toe
3229	**réaliste**-*adj; m/f*	realistic; realist	3293	**menton**-*m*	chin
3231	**chapelle**-*f*	chapel	3294	**récit**-*m*	story| recital
3232	**marge**-*f*	margin	3295	**tsar**-*m*	tsar
3233	**fontaine**-*f*	fountain| spring	3296	**dépense**-*f*	expenditure| expense
3235	**plume**-*f*	feather	3297	**informatique**-*f; adj*	data processing; paperless
3237	**pourboire**-*m*	tip| fee	3299	**serrure**-*f*	lock
3239	**creux**-*adj; m*	hollow| sunken; hollow	3300	**chèvre**-*f*	goat
3240	**perruque**-*f*	wig	3302	**brun**-*adj; m*	brown; brown
3241	**supermarché**-*m*	supermarket	3303	**mécanique**-*adj; f*	mechanical; mechanics
3242	**harmonie**-*f*	harmony	3304	**ciseau**-*m*	chisel
3243	**décollage**-*m*	take-off	3305	**coutume**-*f*	custom| practice
			3308	**prudence**-*f*	caution| prudence

3309	**provision**-*f*	provision	3376	**échantillon**-*m*	sample
3310	**ballet**-*m*	ballet	3378	**investissement**-*m*	investment
3311	**croisé**-*adj; m*	cross; crusader	3380	**identification**-*f*	identification
3312	**détenu**-*adj; m*	detained; inmate	3382	**tank**-*m*	tank
3313	**enthousiasme**-*m*	enthusiasm	3383	**pacte**-*m*	pact| agreement
3314	**parade**-*f*	parade	3384	**écho**-*m*	echo
3315	**exemplaire**-*m; adj*	copy; exemplary	3385	**cuisinier**-*m*	cook
3318	**aire**-*f*	area	3386	**fosse**-*f*	pit| grave
3319	**marquis**-*m*	marquis	3387	**rhum**-*m*	rum
3320	**enlèvement**-*m*	removal| abduction	3390	**élégant**-*adj; m*	elegant; dandy
3321	**extra-terrestre**-*adj; m/f*	alien; alien	3391	**borne**-*f*	terminal
3322	**racine**-*f*	root	3392	**coopération**-*f*	cooperation
3327	**porteur**-*m; adj*	carrier| holder; supporting	3393	**cambriolage**-*m*	burglary
3328	**béton**-*m*	concrete	3394	**arche**-*f*	ark
3329	**butin**-*m*	booty| loot	3395	**statut**-*m*	status
3330	**saucisse**-*f*	sausage	3400	**détente**-*f*	relaxation
3331	**actif**-*adj; m*	active| working; assets	3401	**obligation**-*f*	obligation| bond
3332	**mousse**-*f*	foam| moss	3402	**climat**-*m*	climate
3333	**fusion**-*f*	fusion	3403	**pois**-*m*	pea
3334	**portail**-*adj; m*	portal; portal	3405	**faucon**-*m*	falcon
3336	**psychopathe**-*m/f*	psychopath	3408	**électronique**-*adj; f*	electronic; electronics
3339	**semblable**-*adj; m*	similar; fellow creature	3409	**vagin**-*m*	vagina
3340	**virage**-*m*	turn| shift	3410	**rive**-*f*	bank| shore
3341	**casquette**-*f*	cap	3411	**script**-*m*	script
3343	**farine**-*f*	flour	3412	**seize**-*num*	sixteen
3345	**vermine**-*f*	vermin	3413	**capote**-*f*	hood
3347	**zone**-*f*	area	3415	**croyant**-*m; adj*	believer; god-fearing
3348	**déchet**-*m*	wretch	3421	**politicien**-*m*	politician
3349	**alcoolique**-*adj; m/f*	alcoholic; alcoholic	3423	**fidélité**-*f*	loyalty| fidelity
3352	**honnêteté**-*f*	honesty	3424	**pauvret**-*m/f*	poor looking
3353	**canyon**-*m*	canyon	3425	**soulever**-*vb; m*	raise; bench press
3354	**soupçon**-*m*	suspicion| soupcon	3426	**flûte**-*f*	flute
3355	**torche**-*f*	torch	3428	**fourrure**-*f*	fur
3356	**égalité**-*f*	equality	3429	**aveu**-*m*	confession
3358	**détention**-*f*	detention| possession	3430	**bac**-*m*	tray
3359	**bouquet**-*m*	bouquet| bunch	3432	**graine**-*f*	seed
3362	**orphelinat**-*m*	orphanage	3433	**rail**-*m*	rail
3365	**mèche**-*f*	wick	3434	**confort**-*m*	comfort
3366	**quotidien**-*adj; m*	daily; daily	3435	**lessive**-*f*	laundry| lye
3367	**prophète**-*m*	prophet	3436	**gâchette**-*f*	trigger
3370	**orgueil**-*m*	pride	3439	**champignon**-*m*	mushroom
3372	**fichier**-*m*	catalog| file	3440	**écoute**-*f*	listening
3374	**architecte**-*m*	architect	3442	**gilet**-*m*	vest
3375	**tailleur**-*m*	tailor	3443	**établissement**-*m*	establishment
			3444	**volume**-*m*	volume| tonnage
			3445	**sixième**-*num*	sixth

3447	**manoir**-*m*	manor
3451	**villageois**-*m*	villager
3452	**véhicule**-*m; adj*	vehicle; vehicular
3453	**financier**-*adj; m*	financial; financier
3454	**jeep**-*f*	jeep
3455	**connasse**-*f*	motherfucker
3457	**châtiment**-*m*	punishment
3458	**martini**-*m*	martini
3459	**cire**-*f*	wax
3460	**distribution**-*f*	distribution| delivery
3461	**infini**-*adj; m*	infinite; infinity
3462	**moulin**-*m*	mill
3463	**banlieue**-*f*	suburbs
3464	**salutation**-*f*	greeting
3465	**réflexion**-*f*	reflection| thinking
3466	**graisse**-*f*	fat
3468	**vaurien**-*m*	rascal| scoundrel
3472	**table**-*f*	table| calculator
3473	**gangster**-*m*	gangster
3475	**révolutionnaire**-*adj; m/f*	revolutionary; revolutionary
3478	**clôture**-*f; vb*	closing| fence; conclude
3480	**représentation**-*f*	representation| performance
3481	**morveux**-*adj; m*	snotty; snot
3483	**millionnaire**-*m/f*	millionaire
3484	**herbe**-*f*	grass| herb
3485	**tumeur**-*f*	tumor| growth
3486	**œuvre**-*f*	work
3489	**faîte**-*m*	ridge| top
3490	**yacht**-*m*	yacht
3491	**ruban**-*m*	ribbon
3492	**démission**-*f*	resignation
3493	**malle**-*f*	trunk
3494	**bowling**-*m*	bowling
3495	**cruauté**-*f*	cruelty
3496	**sanctuaire**-*m*	sanctuary
3497	**stand**-*m*	stall
3498	**orteil**-*m*	toe
3499	**bourreau**-*m*	executioner
3500	**cafard**-*m*	cockroach
3502	**sherry**-*m*	sherry
3503	**infirmerie**-*f*	infirmary
3504	**fédération**-*f*	federation
3505	**défunt**-*adj; m*	late; deceased person
3506	**crapaud**-*m*	toad
3507	**autel**-*m*	altar
3508	**purée**-*f*	puree
3509	**commode**-*adj; f*	convenient| handy; chest of drawers
3510	**infanterie**-*f*	infantry
3511	**grade**-*m*	grade
3512	**recours**-*m*	recourse| remedy
3516	**automobile**-*adj; f*	automotive; automobile
3517	**trajectoire**-*f*	path
3518	**ciné**-*m*	pics
3519	**tribord**-*m*	starboard
3520	**cuisse**-*f*	thigh
3521	**nouille**-*f; adj*	noodle| dope; dumb
3522	**rassemblement**-*m*	gathering| rally
3525	**cale**-*f*	hold| wedge
3527	**parapluie**-*f*	umbrella
3529	**intrus**-*m; adj*	intruder; intruding
3530	**pavillon**-*m*	flag
3532	**surf**-*m*	surf
3536	**achat**-*m*	purchase
3537	**barreau**-*m*	bar
3539	**shopping**-*m*	shopping
3541	**tapette**-*f*	pansy
3542	**loterie**-*f*	lottery
3545	**générosité**-*f*	generosity
3547	**confirmation**-*f*	confirmation| swearing
3549	**phare**-*m*	lighthouse| headlight
3550	**iris**-*m*	iris
3555	**câlin**-*adj; m*	hugging; hug
3557	**enchère**-*f*	bid| raise
3558	**impatience**-*f*	impatience
3559	**sonnerie**-*f*	ring| bell
3560	**nounou**-*f*	nanny
3561	**baise**-*f*	fuck| sex
3563	**préfet**-*m*	prefect
3564	**forteresse**-*f*	fortress
3565	**brutal**-*adj; m*	brutal; brute
3567	**fourgon**-*m*	van
3570	**dirigeant**-*m*	leader
3571	**frappe**-*f*	strike| striking
3572	**sentence**-*f*	sentence
3573	**certitude**-*f*	certainty
3574	**ail**-*m*	garlic
3575	**ski**-*m*	ski
3577	**abeille**-*f*	bee

3580	**quatorze**-*num*	fourteen
3582	**veau**-*m*	calf| veal
3583	**tâche**-*f*	task
3584	**attraction**-*f*	attraction| pull
3587	**palace**-*m*	palace
3588	**nœud**-*m*	node| knot
3589	**trophée**-*m*	trophy
3590	**compréhension**-*f*	comprehension
3591	**intrigue**-*f*	plot
3593	**berceau**-*m*	cradle| bed
3596	**satisfaction**-*f*	satisfaction
3600	**préparation**-*f*	preparation
3601	**servante**-*f*	servant| maid
3602	**rancune**-*f*	grudge| rancor
3604	**logement**-*m*	housing| accommodation
3605	**générateur**-*m; adj*	generator; generating
3606	**paiement**-*m*	payment| payoff
3610	**solde**-*m*	balance
3611	**grossesse**-*f*	pregnancy
3612	**ghetto**-*m*	ghetto
3614	**banane**-*f*	banana
3615	**embuscade**-*f*	ambush| fall
3619	**trousse**-*f*	kit
3621	**institution**-*f*	institution
3622	**chargement**-*m*	loading| charge
3624	**croissance**-*f*	growth| growing
3627	**alimentation**-*f*	supply| food
3630	**flanc**-*m*	flank
3631	**violet**-*adj; m*	purple; purple
3632	**nuque**-*f*	neck
3633	**bouchon**-*m*	plug| cork
3634	**tigre**-*m*	tiger
3635	**croisière**-*f*	cruise
3636	**horaire**-*m*	schedule
3637	**reproche**-*m*	reproach| rebuke
3639	**pelouse**-*f*	lawn
3640	**commencement**-*m*	beginning| start
3642	**calcul**-*m*	calculation| calculus
3643	**répondeur**-*m*	answering machine
3644	**emplacement**-*m*	location| site
3646	**excès**-*adj; m; mpl*	excess; excess; debauchery
3647	**cocaïne**-*f*	cocaine
3649	**sonnette**-*f*	doorbell| buzzer
3650	**ignorance**-*f*	ignorance
3651	**scoop**-*m*	scoop

3653	**dot**-*f*	dowry
3658	**aviation**-*f*	aviation| air force
3659	**relâche**-*f*	respite
3660	**tentation**-*f*	temptation
3661	**imposteur**-*m*	impostor
3663	**embarquement**-*m*	boarding| shipping
3665	**cerf**-*m*	deer| stag
3667	**paresseux**-*adj; m*	lazy; sloth
3669	**bridge**-*m*	bridge
3671	**bouffon**-*m; adj*	buffoon; fool
3672	**tendresse**-*f*	tenderness| kindness
3673	**barque**-*f*	bark| small boat
3674	**peloton**-*m*	pack
3675	**cycle**-*m*	cycle
3676	**égout**-*m*	sewer| drain
3677	**hanche**-*f*	hip
3679	**sympathie**-*f*	sympathy
3682	**alternative**-*f*	alternative
3684	**ironie**-*f*	irony
3685	**coupure**-*f; adj*	cut; clipping
3686	**céréale**-*f*	cereal| fruit
3687	**pâte**-*f*	paste
3691	**ruisseau**-*m*	stream| creek
3692	**baratin**-*m*	spiel| flannel
3693	**hamburger**-*m*	hamburger
3694	**évêque**-*m*	bishop
3695	**bénéfice**-*m*	profit| income
3698	**combattant**-*m; adj*	fighter; fighting
3699	**clochette**-*f*	bell
3701	**miette**-*f*	crumb
3702	**olive**-*f*	olive
3703	**dizaine**-*f*	about ten| decade
3705	**bonnet**-*m*	cap
3706	**dépit**-*m*	spite
3707	**hypothèse**-*f*	hypothesis
3710	**hémorragie**-*f*	hemorrhage
3711	**milord**-*m*	milord
3712	**boom**-*m*	boom
3713	**abus**-*m*	abuse
3714	**soulagement**-*m*	relief| solace
3715	**célébrité**-*f*	celebrity| stardom
3716	**gaze**-*adj; f*	gauze; gauze
3717	**injection**-*f*	injection
3719	**présidence**-*f*	presidency
3720	**spectateur**-*m*	spectator| onlooker
3721	**soupir**-*m*	sigh

3722	**néant**-*m*	nothingness	
3723	**hospitalité**-*f*	hospitality	
3725	**écureuil**-*m*	squirrel	
3727	**organisme**-*m*	organization	
3729	**gorille**-*m*	gorilla	
3730	**morphine**-*f*	morphine	
3731	**andouille**-*f*	dummy	
3733	**batteur**-*m*	drummer| batter	
3734	**réconfort**-*m*	comfort| reassurance	
3735	**disciple**-*m*	disciple	
3736	**minuscule**-*adj; f*	tiny| lowercase; minuscule	
3737	**suédois**-*adj; m*	Swedish; Swedish	
3738	**présentation**-*f*	presentation	
3739	**trompette**-*f*	trumpet| trumpeter	
3741	**baleine**-*f*	whale	
3742	**crépuscule**-*adj; m*	dusk; dusk	
3743	**trêve**-*f*	truce	
3744	**inscription**-*f*	registration| entry	
3746	**conception**-*f*	design| designing	
3747	**western**-*m*	western	
3748	**poussin**-*m*	chick	
3749	**peigne**-*m*	comb	
3750	**vicieux**-*adj; m*	vicious; lecher	
3753	**révolte**-*f*	revolt| mutiny	
3754	**cardinal**-*adj; m*	cardinal; cardinal	
3755	**sapin**-*m*	pine	
3756	**rein**-*m*	kidney	
3759	**limonade**-*f*	lemonade	
3760	**prophétie**-*f*	prophecy	
3761	**buffet**-*m*	buffet| dresser	
3762	**confiture**-*f*	jam	
3765	**tombeau**-*m*	tomb	
3766	**performance**-*f*	performance	
3767	**appui**-*m*	support| rest	
3768	**septième**-*num*	seventh	
3769	**tremblement**-*m*	trembling| tremor	
3771	**précision**-*f*	precision| accuracy	
3772	**thon**-*m*	tuna	
3773	**péril**-*m*	peril| distress	
3774	**sifflet**-*m*	whistle	
3778	**substance**-*f*	substance| material	
3779	**mâchoire**-*f*	jaw	
3780	**jardinier**-*m*	gardener	
3781	**fureur**-*f*	fury	
3782	**coureur**-*m; adj*	runner; racing	
3783	**tambour**-*m*	drum	
3785	**protocole**-*m*	protocol	
3786	**pieu**-*m*	stake| pale	
3788	**banquier**-*m*	banker	
3792	**frein**-*m*	brake	
3794	**turc**-*adj; m*	Turkish; Turkish	
3795	**musulman**-*adj; m*	Muslim; Muslim	
3796	**brin**-*m*	strand| sprig	
3797	**scanner**-*m*	scanner	
3798	**momie**-*f*	mummy	
3799	**blâme**-*m*	blame| reprimand	
3802	**parlement**-*m*	parliament	
3804	**pêcheur**-*m*	fisherman	
3805	**guérison**-*f*	healing| cure	
3806	**syndrome**-*m*	syndrome	
3809	**malchance**-*f*	bad luck| misfortune	
3813	**légiste**-*m*	jurist	
3814	**pureté**-*f*	purity	
3816	**épidémie**-*f*	epidemic	
3817	**insulte**-*f*	insult	
3818	**chimie**-*f*	chemistry	
3819	**falaise**-*f*	cliff	
3820	**braquage**-*m*	defection	
3821	**convention**-*f*	convention| covenant	
3822	**lueur**-*f*	glow| light	
3823	**capture**-*f*	capture| catch	
3825	**cherry**-*f*	sherry	
3827	**beignet**-*m*	fritter	
3828	**diversion**-*f*	diversion	
3831	**dimension**-*f*	dimension| size	
3832	**tare**-*f*	stigma	
3834	**break**-*m*	break	
3835	**reflet**-*m*	reflection	
3836	**chauffage**-*m*	heating| heater	
3837	**rappel**-*m*	reminder| encore	
3839	**caserne**-*f*	barracks	
3840	**écurie**-*f*	stable	
3841	**utilisation**-*f*	use	
3843	**toutou**-*m*	doggie| lapdog	
3846	**débris**-*mpl*	debris	
3847	**bourbon**-*m*	bourbon	
3848	**thèse**-*f*	thesis| theory	
3849	**diligence**-*f*	diligence	
3850	**lin**-*m*	linen	
3851	**majeur**-*adj; m*	major| middle finger; major	

3854	**culte**-*m*	worship
3857	**connexion**-*f*	connection
3859	**protecteur**-*adj; m*	protective; protector
3864	**raciste**-*adj; m/f*	racist; racist
3865	**pâté**-*m*	pâté
3866	**bouc**-*m*	goat
3867	**racaille**-*f*	riffraff
3868	**enseignement**-*m*	education| teaching
3869	**ambitieux**-*adj; m/f*	ambitious; careerist
3870	**chancelier**-*m*	chancellor
3872	**psychologie**-*f*	psychology
3873	**discrétion**-*f*	discretion
3875	**cadet**-*adj; m*	cadet; cadet
3876	**réalisation**-*f*	realization| achievement
3877	**diagnostic**-*m*	diagnosis
3879	**intrusion**-*f*	intrusion
3881	**vétérinaire**-*adj; m/f*	veterinary; veterinary
3882	**miséricorde**-*f*	mercy
3883	**planche**-*f*	board| plank
3884	**savant**-*adj; m*	learned; scholar
3885	**épave**-*f*	wreck
3886	**vestiaire**-*m*	cloakroom
3887	**mélodie**-*f*	melody
3888	**brume**-*f*	mist
3889	**éthique**-*f; adj*	ethics; ethical
3891	**amer**-*adj; m*	bitter; bitter
3892	**signification**-*f*	meaning| notification
3897	**chameau**-*m*	camel
3898	**parachute**-*m*	parachute
3899	**interprète**-*m/f*	interpreter
3901	**sermon**-*m*	sermon
3902	**voyageur**-*m; adj*	traveler| passenger; traveling
3903	**doyen**-*m*	dean| provost
3906	**espionnage**-*m*	espionage
3907	**location**-*f*	hire
3911	**indépendant**-*adj; m*	independent; independent
3912	**caverne**-*f*	cave
3917	**énigme**-*f*	enigma| puzzle
3918	**box**-*m*	box
3919	**crevette**-*f*	shrimp
3920	**occupation**-*f*	occupation| tenure
3921	**arrière**-*adj; m*	rear| back; back
3922	**scout**-*m*	scout
3923	**pétard**-*m*	firecracker
3926	**pagaille**-*f*	mess
3927	**banquet**-*m*	banquet
3928	**baguette**-*f*	baguette| stick
3929	**fraise**-*f*	strawberry
3930	**marbre**-*adj; m*	marble; marble
3931	**catégorie**-*f*	category
3933	**escadron**-*m*	squadron
3935	**chute**-*f*	fall| falling
3936	**révélation**-*f*	revelation
3938	**cartouche**-*f*	cartridge
3939	**bunker**-*m*	bunker
3940	**manuscrit**-*adj; m*	manuscript; manuscript
3942	**cacahuète**-*f*	peanut
3943	**condamnation**-*f*	conviction| locking
3946	**conspiration**-*f*	conspiracy| plot
3947	**clope**-*f*	butt
3949	**détecteur**-*m*	detector| detecting
3950	**orphelin**-*adj; m*	orphan; orphan
3951	**opposition**-*f*	opposition
3952	**gestion**-*f*	management
3953	**ouf**-*m/f; int*	crazy person; whew
3954	**orgasme**-*m*	orgasm
3956	**tonne**-*f*	tonne
3958	**annuaire**-*m*	directory| yearbook
3959	**suède**-*adj; f*	suede; suede
3960	**optimiste**-*adj; m/f*	optimistic; optimist
3961	**audace**-*f; adj*	boldness; woodless
3964	**propagande**-*f*	propaganda
3965	**immortel**-*adj; m*	immortal; immortal
3966	**sottise**-*f*	folly| silliness
3967	**saumon**-*m*	salmon
3968	**carbone**-*adj; m*	carbon; carbon
3970	**maladroit**-*adj; m*	awkward; blunderer
3972	**violation**-*f*	violation| breach
3973	**revenant**-*adj; m*	return| reverting; ghost
3975	**définition**-*f*	definition
3976	**cuillère**-*f*	spoon
3977	**menthe**-*f*	mint
3980	**interprétation**-*f*	interpretation
3983	**poignard**-*m*	dagger
3984	**calendrier**-*m*	calendar
3986	**caviar**-*m*	caviar
3989	**opérateur**-*m*	operator
3990	**initiative**-*f*	initiative| lead

3991	**apocalypse**-*f*	apocalypse	4060	**lavage**-*m*	washing
3993	**intégrité**-*f*	integrity| honesty	4061	**sirop**-*m*	syrup
3996	**vitrine**-*f*	showcase| window	4065	**peso**-*m*	peso
3998	**vitre**-*f*	window	4067	**hymne**-*m*	anthem| canticle
3999	**maréchal**-*m*	marshal	4069	**poisse**-*f*	rotten luck
4000	**hangar**-*m*	hangar	4070	**résurrection**-*f*	resurrection
4002	**bassin**-*m*	basin| pool	4072	**détour**-*m*	detour| bend
4004	**injustice**-*f*	injustice| unfairness	4074	**radiation**-*f*	radiation
4005	**canot**-*m*	canoe| dinghy	4075	**africain**-*adj; m*	African
4007	**caoutchouc**-*m*	rubber	4077	**barre**-*f*	bar
4009	**entrain**-*m*	spirit| zest	4078	**excitation**-*f*	excitation| anticipation
4010	**raisin**-*m*	grape	4080	**utilité**-*f*	utility| value
4012	**file**-*f*	queue| row	4082	**vertige**-*m*	vertigo| spell
4013	**vérification**-*f*	verification| check	4083	**poteau**-*m*	post| pole
4014	**hallucination**-*f*	hallucination	4084	**compteur**-*m*	counter
4015	**punch**-*m*	punch	4085	**pédale**-*f*	pedal
4016	**courtoisie**-*f*	courtesy	4086	**émetteur**-*m*	transmitter
4017	**entente**-*f*	agreement	4089	**annonce**-*f*	ad| announcement
4018	**atout**-*m*	asset	4090	**obus**-*m; adj*	shell; dense
4019	**ouragan**-*m*	hurricane	4091	**immigration**-*f*	immigration
4020	**cahier**-*m*	notebook	4092	**antidote**-*m*	antidote
4022	**contribution**-*f*	contribution| input	4093	**hollandais**-*adj; mpl*	Dutch; Dutch
4023	**émeute**-*f*	riot	4096	**corbeau**-*m*	raven
4024	**négociation**-*f*	negotiation	4098	**avancée**-*f*	progress
4025	**bulle**-*f*	bubble| bull	4099	**sourcil**-*m*	eyebrow
4026	**extinction**-*f*	extinction	4102	**karma**-*m*	karma
4027	**isolement**-*m*	isolation	4103	**naïf**-*adj; m*	naive; babe
4028	**panama**-*m*	panama	4107	**squelette**-*f*	skeleton
4029	**manifestation**-*f*	event| manifestation	4110	**gymnase**-*m*	gymnasium
4031	**tequila**-*m*	tequila	4111	**cabaret**-*m*	cabaret
4032	**urine**-*f*	urine	4112	**oubli**-*m*	oversight| oblivion
4035	**chœur**-*m*	choir	4113	**préméditation**-*f*	premeditation
4039	**fourré**-*m; adj*	thicket; filled	4114	**architecture**-*f*	architecture
4041	**judas**-*m*	peephole| judas	4115	**librairie**-*f*	bookstore
4042	**compagne**-*f*	companion	4116	**déguisement**-*m*	disguise
4043	**vole**-*f*	vole	4117	**coût**-*m*	cost
4045	**éclairage**-*m*	lighting| illumination	4118	**semestre**-*m*	half
4046	**centimètre**-*m*	centimeter| tape	4121	**corne**-*f*	horn
4047	**restaurant**-*m*	restaurant| cafe	4123	**humiliation**-*f*	humiliation
4049	**punk**-*adj; m*	punk; punk	4124	**piège**-*m*	trap| snare
4050	**triangle**-*m*	triangle	4125	**réacteur**-*m*	reactor
4052	**mécanisme**-*m*	mechanism	4126	**chiot**-*m*	puppy
4055	**brebis**-*f*	sheep	4128	**fonctionnaire**-*m/f*	official| officer
4057	**trac**-*m*	stage fright	4130	**entrailles**-*f; fpl*	womb; insides
4058	**étang**-*m*	pond	4131	**chaton**-*m*	kitten
4059	**divan**-*m*	couch	4132	**psychologue**-*m/f*	psychologist

4134	**seuil**-*m*	threshold| sill	4203	**distributeur**-*m*	distributor
4135	**mécanicien**-*m*	mechanic	4204	**melon**-*m*	melon
4136	**noyau**-*m*	core| kernel	4206	**maestro**-*m*	maestro
4137	**gentilhomme**-*m*	gentleman	4208	**chargeur**-*m*	charger
4138	**malais**-*adj; m*	Malay; Malay	4209	**peinture**-*f*	painting| paint
4139	**oie**-*f*	goose	4210	**projection**-*f*	projection| screening
4140	**overdose**-*f*	overdose	4212	**parleur**-*m*	talker
4141	**impasse**-*f*	impasse| deadlock	4214	**carreau**-*m*	tile
4142	**boche**-*adj; m/f*	German; Jerry (derogative)	4215	**caillou**-*m*	pebble
4144	**roc**-*m*	rock	4217	**stage**-*m*	course
4146	**brandy**-*m*	brandy	4220	**faculté**-*f*	faculty| ability
4147	**tarif**-*m*	rate	4221	**gorgée**-*f*	mouthful| gulp
4148	**topo**-*m*	sketch	4223	**peignoir**-*m*	robe
4150	**adjudant**-*m*	adjutant	4226	**aiguille**-*f*	needle
4151	**prairie**-*f*	meadow	4227	**monastère**-*m*	monastery
4152	**livreur**-*m*	delivery man	4228	**recul**-*m*	recoil| retreat
4153	**puzzle**-*m*	puzzle	4229	**mémé**-*f*	granny| nanny
4154	**yard**-*m*	yard	4230	**lecteur**-*m*	reader| pickup
4155	**lézard**-*m*	lizard	4231	**fraternité**-*f*	fraternity
4157	**égratignure**-*f*	scratch	4232	**blaireau**-*m*	badger
4158	**sexualité**-*f*	sexuality	4233	**caleçon**-*m*	pants| underpants
4159	**omelette**-*f*	omelette	4234	**gala**-*m*	gala
4161	**mauviette**-*adj; f*	wimp; weakling	4235	**flux**-*m*	flow| flux
4162	**klaxon**-*m*	horn| klaxon	4236	**vocation**-*f*	vocation| call
4163	**gardon**-*m*	roach	4237	**bombardier**-*m*	bomber
4165	**grotesque**-*adj; m*	grotesque; grotesque	4238	**raid**-*m*	raid
4168	**précaution**-*f*	precaution	4240	**short**-*m*	shorts
4172	**pellicule**-*f*	film	4241	**déception**-*f*	disappointment
4175	**pourcentage**-*m*	percentage	4242	**contexte**-*m*	context
4176	**coude**-*m*	elbow| bend	4243	**dispositif**-*m*	device
4180	**ragot**-*adj; m*	dirty; gossip	4246	**universitaire**-*adj; m/f*	university; postgraduate student
4182	**acheteur**-*m*	buyer| shopper	4247	**massif**-*adj; m*	massive; massif
4183	**sultan**-*m*	sultan	4248	**drague**-*f*	dredge
4184	**embrasse**-*f*	embrace| kiss	4251	**bilan**-*m*	balance sheet
4185	**soixante**-*num*	sixty	4253	**smoking**-*m*	tuxedo
4188	**toux**-*f*	cough	4255	**saloon**-*m*	saloon
4190	**gène**-*m*	gene	4256	**coque**-*f*	hull
4192	**ruelle**-*f*	alley	4259	**mouchard**-*m*	sneak| informer
4193	**évaluation**-*f*	evaluation	4265	**scie**-*f*	saw
4194	**masculin**-*adj; m*	male; masculine	4266	**fossé**-*m*	ditch| moat
4195	**rédacteur**-*m*	editor	4271	**couillon**-*m*	sod
4196	**matelot**-*m*	sailor	4272	**agitation**-*f*	agitation| restlessness
4197	**duo**-*m*	duo	4273	**tenon**-*m*	tenon
4198	**trappe**-*f; adj*	hatch| trap; cobwebby	4275	**combine**-*f*	combination
4200	**camping**-*m*	camping| campsite	4276	**notion**-*f*	notion

4277	collaboration-*f*	collaboration
4284	compétence-*f*	competence| skill
4285	blouson-*m*	blouse| jacket
4287	voisinage-*m*	neighborhood| neighbors
4288	proximité-*f*	proximity| vicinity
4290	partisan-*adj; m*	partisan| adherent; partisan
4291	envoi-*m*	sending| dispatch
4292	spectre-*m*	spectrum| ghost
4294	comédien-*m*	actor
4295	passage-*m*	passage| passing
4298	crapule-*f*	scoundrel
4299	gain-*m*	gain| benefit
4300	idole-*f*	idol| goddess
4303	exploitation-*f*	exploitation
4305	carotte-*f; adj*	carrot; carroty
4306	crabe-*m*	crab
4307	repère-*m*	landmark
4308	compartiment-*m*	compartment
4309	dialogue-*m*	dialogue
4310	festin-*m*	feast
4311	chronique-*adj; f*	chronic; chronicle
4312	grue-*f*	crane
4313	régulier-*adj; m*	regular; regular
4314	cargo-*m*	cargo
4317	fourchette-*f*	fork
4320	roupie-*f*	rupee
4321	efficacité-*f*	efficiency
4322	consul-*m*	consul
4323	cynique-*adj; m*	cynical; cynic
4325	velours-*m*	velvet
4326	pourriture-*f*	decay| rot
4327	parasite-*m; adj*	parasite; parasitic
4328	élan-*m*	elan| elk
4329	philosophe-*m/f*	philosopher
4330	dortoir-*m*	dormitory
4332	ado-*m*	teenager
4333	distorsion-*f*	distortion
4335	représentant-*m*	representative| agent
4338	torpille-*f*	torpedo
4339	bled-*m*	boondocks
4340	compositeur-*m; adj*	composer; compositive
4342	taxe-*f*	tax
4343	frérot-*m*	little brother
4344	bâbord-*m*	port

4345	homard-*m*	lobster
4347	noblesse-*f*	nobility
4348	industriel-*adj; m*	industrial; industrialist
4349	contrôleur-*m*	controller| supervisor
4351	fléau-*m*	scourge| plague
4353	politesse-*f*	politeness
4354	sélection-*f*	selection| team
4355	Hollande-*f*	Holland
4356	accouchement-*m*	delivery| childbirth
4357	cerise-*adj; f*	cherry; cherry
4358	réservation-*f*	booking| reservation
4359	famine-*f*	famine
4360	navigation-*f*	navigation
4361	perroquet-*m*	parrot
4362	coquin-*m; adj*	rascal; naughty
4363	centime-*m*	centime
4364	pendaison-*f*	hanging| hang
4369	portière-*f*	door
4370	gramme-*m*	gram| ounce
4371	étalon-*m*	standard| stallion
4372	rouleau-*m*	roller| roll
4373	peine-*f*	penalty| sentence
4374	exil-*m*	exile
4378	taudis-*m*	slum
4380	sirène-*f*	siren
4381	levier-*m*	lever
4382	intermédiaire-*adj; m*	intermediate; intermediate
4383	armement-*m*	armament
4384	collecte-*f*	collection
4385	ringard-*adj; m*	tacky; has-been
4386	deuxièmement-*num*	secondly
4387	robinet-*m*	tap| faucet
4388	réparation-*f*	repair| satisfaction
4389	boulevard-*m*	boulevard| parade
4390	dispute-*f*	dispute| argument
4392	vagabond-*adj; m*	vagabond; vagabond
4394	gazon-*m*	grass| lawn
4395	bravoure-*f*	bravery
4397	fugitif-*adj; m*	fugitive; fugitive
4398	souverain-*adj; m*	sovereign; sovereign
4399	embarras-*m*	embarrassment
4403	doublure-*f*	lining| understudy
4404	bicyclette-*f*	bicycle
4405	biologie-*f*	biology

4406	**enquête**-*f*	survey| investigation	
4409	**détachement**-*m*	detachment	
4410	**ferry**-*m*	ferry	
4411	**canaille**-*f*	vulgar	
4415	**terminal**-*adj; m*	terminal; terminal	
4416	**fasciste**-*m/f; adj*	fascist; fascist	
4418	**secte**-*f*	sect| connection	
4419	**équipier**-*m*	team member	
4421	**biche**-*f*	doe	
4422	**gibier**-*m*	game| prey	
4424	**pou**-*m*	louse	
4425	**interdiction**-*f*	prohibition	
4426	**pôle**-*m*	pole	
4427	**agenda**-*m*	diary	
4428	**donneur**-*m*	giver| dealer	
4430	**érection**-*f*	erection| stand	
4431	**colombe**-*f*	dove	
4435	**plombier**-*m*	plumber	
4436	**gale**-*f*	scabies	
4439	**comète**-*f*	comet	
4440	**cannabis**-*m*	cannabis	
4443	**masse**-*f*	mass| body	
4444	**prospérité**-*f*	prosperity	
4445	**décoration**-*f*	decoration	
4447	**ketchup**-*m*	ketchup	
4448	**crêpe**-*f*	crepe| pancake	
4449	**permanent**-*adj; m*	permanent; permanent	
4450	**télécommande**-*f*	remote control	
4451	**rivage**-*m*	shore	
4453	**ragoût**-*m*	stew	
4454	**sorcellerie**-*f*	witchcraft| sorcery	
4455	**sentier**-*m*	path| trail	
4457	**proviseur**-*m*	principal| headmaster	
4458	**argument**-*m*	argument	
4459	**mystique**-*adj; m/f*	mystical; mystic	
4462	**vanité**-*f*	vanity| pride	
4463	**tic**-*m*	tic	
4464	**aliment**-*m*	food	
4467	**détroit**-*m*	strait	
4468	**exploit**-*m*	feat	
4473	**inventaire**-*m*	inventory	
4474	**porto**-*m*	port	
4475	**pharaon**-*m*	Pharaoh	
4477	**immortalité**-*f*	immortality	
4481	**bourgeois**-*adj; m*	bourgeois; bourgeois	
4484	**itinéraire**-*m; adj*	route; itinerary	

4485	**carnage**-*m*	carnage
4487	**citation**-*f*	quote| summons
4488	**potion**-*f*	potion
4491	**zombi**-*m*	zombie
4492	**astronaute**-*m/f*	astronaut
4493	**bombardement**-*m*	bombardment| bombing
4495	**caresse**-*f*	caress
4496	**messie**-*m*	messiah
4497	**ressemblance**-*f*	resemblance| likeness
4498	**double**-*adj; m*	double| twin; double
4499	**pin**-*m*	pine
4500	**baronne**-*f*	baroness
4503	**allusion**-*f*	allusion| reference
4504	**volcan**-*m*	volcano
4506	**barbare**-*adj; m*	barbaric; barbarian
4508	**pécheur**-*m*	sinner
4512	**humidité**-*f*	moisture| humidity
4513	**admiration**-*f*	admiration
4516	**clin**-*m*	wink
4517	**provenance**-*f*	origin
4519	**pneumonie**-*f*	pneumonia
4520	**réduction**-*f*	reduction| discount
4521	**rébellion**-*f*	rebellion| rebel
4526	**réplique**-*f*	replica| reply
4527	**flou**-*adj; m; adv*	vague; blurring; fuzzily
4530	**polo**-*m*	polo
4533	**anomalie**-*f*	anomaly
4534	**correspondance**-*f*	correspondence
4536	**clientèle**-*f*	customers| clientele
4539	**dauphin**-*m*	dolphin
4541	**évier**-*m*	sink
4542	**émissaire**-*m*	emissary
4543	**emprunt**-*m*	borrowing
4544	**poivre**-*m*	pepper
4545	**karaté**-*m*	karate
4546	**scorpion**-*m*	scorpion
4547	**buisson**-*m*	bush
4548	**tricheur**-*m*	cheater
4549	**paroisse**-*f*	parish
4550	**locataire**-*m/f*	tenant| lodger
4552	**manie**-*f*	mania
4553	**revers**-*m*	reverse| back
4554	**transformation**-*f*	transformation
4555	**séminaire**-*m*	seminar
4556	**plâtre**-*m*	plaster

4557	écossais-*adj; m: mpl*	Scottish; Scottish; Scots	
4558	béguin-*m*	crush	
4559	comparaison-*f*	comparison	
4561	pet-*m*	fart	
4563	yuan-*m*	yuan	
4567	pépé-*m*	grandpa	
4568	légion-*f*	legion	
4569	concurrent-*m; adj*	competitor| contestant; concurrent	
4570	socialiste-*adj; m*	socialist; socialist	
4571	foulard-*m*	scarf| foulard	
4572	cricket-*m*	cricket	
4574	sensibilité-*f*	sensibility	
4575	bavard-*adj; m*	talkative; chatterbox	
4576	abandon-*m*	abandonment| surrender	
4577	microbe-*m*	microbe	
4579	statistique-*adj; f*	statistical; statistics	
4584	choral-*adj; m*	choral; choral	
4588	cosmos-*m*	cosmos	
4589	embauche-*f*	hiring	
4591	plantation-*f*	planting	
4592	transaction-*f*	transaction| deal	
4593	noces-*fpl*	nuptials	
4594	sardine-*f*	sardine	
4595	cordon-*m*	cordon	
4596	journalisme-*m*	journalism	
4598	détermination-*f*	determination| fixing	
4600	nourrice-*f*	nurse	
4601	croyance-*f*	belief	
4603	athlète-*m/f*	athlete	
4606	nausée-*f*	nausea	
4608	motivation-*f*	motivation	
4609	gémissement-*m*	groan| whine	
4610	mutation-*f*	mutation	
4611	cocher-*vb; m*	check; coachman	
4612	capot-*m*	hood	
4614	exigence-*f*	requirement	
4615	accessoire-*adj; m*	accessory| incidental; accessory	
4616	bide-*m*	belly	
4619	mitrailleuse-*f*	machine gun	
4620	jument-*f*	mare	
4621	flot-*m*	stream| flood	
4623	catch-*m*	wrestling	
4624	loto-*m*	lotto	
4625	esthétique-*adj; f*	aesthetic; aesthetics	
4626	communisme-*m*	Communism	
4628	hostie-*f*	host	
4635	antique-*adj; m*	antique| ancient; antique	
4636	divertissement-*m*	entertainment	
4638	console-*f*	console	
4640	consommation-*f*	consumption	
4644	dictionnaire-*m*	dictionary	
4645	composition-*f*	composition	
4646	spot-*m*	spot| blip	
4648	obsèques-*adj; f; fpl*	obsequies; funeral	
4649	intellectuel-*adj; m*	intellectual; intellectual	
4651	escalade-*f*	climbing| escalation	
4653	reproduction-*f*	reproduction	
4654	trimestre-*m*	quarter	
4655	pente-*f; adj*	slope| incline; heavy	
4656	anesthésier-*vb; m*	anesthetize; anesthetic	
4657	comptabilité-*f*	accounting| accounts	
4658	bêta-*m*	beta	
4660	dérangement-*m*	disturbance| inconvenience	
4662	cobra-*m*	cobra	
4663	milice-*f*	militia	
4664	tracteur-*m; adj*	tractor; towing	
4665	manège-*m*	carousel| treadmill	
4666	apprenti-*m*	apprentice| novice	
4667	cambrioleur-*m*	burglar	
4668	boulette-*f*	pellet	
4669	puanteur-*f*	stench	
4670	vaccin-*m*	vaccine	
4674	instituteur-*m*	teacher	
4675	baptême-*m*	baptism	
4676	compatriote-*m/f*	compatriot	
4677	piaule-*f*	room| pad	
4679	défenseur-*m*	defender	
4681	caïd-*m*	boss	
4682	boucherie-*f*	butchery	
4685	won-*m*	won	
4687	coquille-*f*	shell| typo	
4691	infarctus-*m*	infarct	
4693	enthousiaste-*adj; m*	enthusiastic; enthusiast	
4694	particule-*f*	part| particle	
4695	reprise-*f*	recovery	
4696	hormone-*f*	hormone	

4697	**contrebande**-*f*	smuggling
4698	**coffre**-*m*	safe| trunk
4700	**joker**-*m*	joker
4701	**effondrement**-*m*	collapse| crash
4702	**avortement**-*m*	abortion
4703	**martyr**-*m; adj*	martyr; martyred
4704	**installation**-*f*	installation| plant
4707	**chalet**-*m*	chalet
4708	**pansement**-*m*	dressing
4711	**adolescent**-*m; adj*	teenager; adolescent
4712	**frisson**-*m*	thrill| shivers
4713	**commando**-*m*	commando
4715	**juridiction**-*f*	jurisdiction
4717	**baptiste**-*m*	baptist
4718	**carnaval**-*m*	carnival
4721	**pion**-*m*	pawn| piece
4722	**spécimen**-*m*	specimen
4723	**participation**-*f*	participation| contribution
4724	**poney**-*m*	pony
4726	**cola**-*m*	cola
4728	**disco**-*adj; m*	disco; disco
4731	**anarchie**-*f*	anarchy
4733	**vibration**-*f*	vibration| pulse
4735	**garnison**-*f*	garrison
4736	**tronc**-*m*	trunk| stem
4737	**informateur**-*m*	informant
4738	**aurore**-*f*	dawn
4739	**hypnose**-*f*	hypnosis
4740	**set**-*m*	set
4741	**perdant**-*adj; m*	losing; loser
4742	**hébreu**-*adj; m*	Hebrew; Hebrew
4743	**indigène**-*adj; m/f*	native; native
4745	**remontant**-*adj; m*	pick-me-up; tonic
4747	**brèche**-*f*	breach| gap
4748	**façade**-*f*	façade| front
4749	**ace**-*m*	ace
4752	**radin**-*m; adj*	tightwad; mean
4753	**immatriculation**-*f*	registration
4756	**rigueur**-*f*	rigor
4757	**portier**-*m*	porter| doorkeeper
4759	**vautour**-*m*	vulture
4761	**épingle**-*f*	pin
4762	**volet**-*m*	flap
4763	**nounours**-*m*	teddy bear
4765	**talon**-*m*	heel
4766	**porche**-*m*	porch
4767	**métaphore**-*f*	metaphor
4768	**intensité**-*f*	intensity| severity
4770	**golfe**-*m*	gulf
4772	**silhouette**-*f*	outline
4773	**kidnapping**-*m*	kidnapping
4774	**volant**-*m; adj*	steering wheel; flying
4775	**refrain**-*m*	refrain
4776	**oignon**-*m*	onion
4777	**ciment**-*m*	cement
4778	**découvert**-*adj; m*	discovered; overdraft
4780	**emprisonné**-*adj; m*	jailed; detainee
4781	**suspension**-*f*	suspension| stay
4783	**renaissance**-*f*	renaissance| reawakening
4784	**enseignant**-*m*	schoolteacher
4786	**hameçon**-*m*	hook
4787	**clochard**-*m; adj*	tramp; down-at-heel
4788	**proverbe**-*m*	proverb| saying
4789	**diplôme**-*m*	diploma
4790	**trouillard**-*adj; m*	yellow belly; yellow-livered
4791	**inférieur**-*adj; m*	lower; inferior
4792	**adultère**-*m; adj*	adultery; adulterous
4794	**mare**-*f*	pond
4796	**moelle**-*f*	marrow
4798	**offense**-*f*	offense| insult
4799	**médium**-*m*	medium
4800	**taverne**-*f*	tavern
4804	**ivresse**-*f*	drunkenness
4805	**crocodile**-*m*	crocodile
4806	**radical**-*adj; m*	radical; radical
4807	**marathon**-*m*	marathon
4808	**sérum**-*m*	serum
4809	**adoption**-*f*	adoption| passage
4810	**vingtaine**-*num*	around twenty
4811	**cactus**-*m*	cactus
4812	**abondance**-*f*	abundance
4813	**considération**-*f*	consideration| account
4814	**carrefour**-*m*	crossroads
4815	**confrérie**-*f*	brotherhood
4817	**républicain**-*adj; m*	republican; republican
4818	**dinosaure**-*m*	dinosaur
4819	**occident**-*m*	West
4822	**hygiène**-*f*	hygiene
4825	**arène**-*f*	arena
4826	**mendier**-*vb; m*	beg; sponge

4827	**pousse**-*f*	shoot	4889	**psychotique**-*adj; m/f*	psychotic; psychotic
4828	**fabrication**-*f*	manufacturing| production	4890	**mercure**-*m*	mercury
4829	**impulsion**-*f*	pulse| impetus	4891	**coréen**-*adj; m*	Korean; Korean
4832	**pi**-*m*	pi	4892	**vieillesse**-*f*	old age| old
4833	**adrénaline**-*f*	adrenaline	4893	**labyrinthe**-*m*	labyrinth
4836	**bougre**-*m*	guy	4894	**driver**-*m*	driver
4839	**succession**-*f*	succession| inheritance	4895	**roulette**-*f*	roulette| wheel
4840	**morsure**-*f*	bite	4898	**moralité**-*f*	morality
4842	**occidental**-*adj; m*	western; western	4899	**loisir**-*m*	leisure
4843	**hectare**-*m*	hectare	4902	**fouine**-*f*	weasel
4844	**pudding**-*m*	pudding	4903	**chercheur**-*m; adj*	researcher| seeker; inquiring
4845	**caramel**-*m*	caramel	4904	**médiocre**-*adj; m/f*	poor| mediocre; second-rater
4846	**asthme**-*m*	asthma			
4849	**tata**-*f*	auntie	4905	**électeur**-*m*	elector
4850	**intendant**-*m*	steward	4906	**employeur**-*m*	employer
4851	**scénariste**-*m/f*	scriptwriter	4907	**sofa**-*m*	sofa
4852	**sincérité**-*f*	sincerity| honesty	4908	**totalité**-*f*	totality| integrity
4854	**couture**-*f*	sewing	4909	**violoncelle**-*m*	cello
4855	**joint**-*adj; m*	joint; joint	4910	**planning**-*m*	schedule
4857	**forgeron**-*m*	black-smith	4911	**ferment**-*m*	ferment
4859	**courbe**-*f*	curve| bending	4914	**actionnaire**-*m/f*	shareholder
4860	**brouhaha**-*m*	hubbub	4918	**danois**-*adj; m*	Danish; Danish
4861	**junkie**-*f*	junkie	4920	**vocabulaire**-*m*	vocabulary
4862	**escadrille**-*f*	squadron	4921	**dessein**-*m*	design| plan
4864	**investisseur**-*m; adj*	investor; investing	4922	**collision**-*f*	collision| clash
4865	**fumeur**-*adj; m*	smoking; smoker	4923	**seringue**-*f*	syringe
4866	**immunité**-*f*	immunity	4924	**combustible**-*m; adj*	fuel; combustible
4867	**handicap**-*m*	handicap			
4868	**gamme**-*f*	range	4927	**arsenal**-*m*	arsenal| navy yard
4869	**étui**-*m*	case	4928	**élégance**-*f*	elegance
4870	**dévouement**-*m*	devotion	4930	**fonctionnement**-*m*	operation| running
4871	**répit**-*m*	respite| reprieve	4931	**yoga**-*m*	yoga
4872	**tirage**-*m*	drawing| print	4932	**cygne**-*m*	swan
4873	**déplacement**-*m*	shifting| displacement	4933	**successeur**-*m*	successor
4874	**morse**-*m*	morse	4934	**meeting**-*m*	meeting
4876	**firme**-*f*	firm	4935	**ampleur**-*f*	extent| magnitude
4877	**cheville**-*f*	ankle	4938	**poulette**-*f*	pullet
4878	**tuteur**-*m*	guardian	4940	**guet**-*m*	watch
4879	**humilité**-*f*	humility	4943	**excentrique**-*adj; m/f*	eccentric; eccentric
4880	**primitif**-*adj; m*	primitive; primitive			
4881	**plouc**-*m*	slob| bumpkin	4944	**ballade**-*f*	ballad
4882	**animation**-*f*	animation| liveliness	4945	**cube**-*m*	cube
4884	**gomme**-*f*	gum	4946	**préférence**-*f*	preference
4885	**trentaine**-*num*	about thirty	4947	**suspense**-*m*	suspension
4888	**escroquerie**-*f*	fraud| swindle	4948	**acompte**-*m*	down payment| installment

4949	**impératrice**-*f*	empress
4951	**colocataire**-*m/f*	room-mate
4952	**restau**-*m*	restaurant
4953	**lièvre**-*m; adj*	hare; hare's
4956	**repaire**-*m*	den
4957	**inventeur**-*m*	inventor
4958	**splendeur**-*f*	splendor
4959	**approbation**-*f*	approval| endorsement
4960	**tranquillité**-*f*	peace| quiet
4962	**infraction**-*f*	offense| infringement
4963	**chandelle**-*f*	candle
4965	**testicule**-*m*	testicle
4966	**marionnette**-*f*	marionette
4968	**élu**-*adj; m*	elected; elect
4969	**flatteur**-*adj; m*	flattering; flatterer
4970	**forge**-*f*	forge
4972	**vipère**-*f*	viper
4975	**snob**-*m/f; adj*	snob; snobbish
4976	**débat**-*m*	debate| argument
4977	**balise**-*f*	buoy| beacon
4978	**perception**-*f*	perception
4979	**virginité**-*f*	virginity
4982	**labeur**-*m*	labor| toil
4987	**brûlure**-*f*	burn
4988	**apprentissage**-*m*	learning
4990	**rodeo**-*m*	rodeo
4991	**abbé**-*m*	abbot
4993	**croc**-*m*	fang
4995	**violeur**-*m*	rapist
4996	**nickel**-*m*	nickel
4998	**relance**-*f*	revival
4999	**pénitencier**-*m*	penitentiary
5000	**prototype**-*m*	prototype
5001	**superviseur**-*m*	supervisor
5005	**ampoule**-*f*	bulb| ampoule
5007	**consentement**-*m*	consent
5008	**orientation**-*f*	orientation| guidance
5010	**pilotage**-*m; f*	control; piloting
5011	**tracé**-*m; adj*	route| course; tracing
5012	**aquarium**-*m*	aquarium
5013	**concession**-*f*	concession| dealership
5014	**rédaction**-*f*	writing| redaction
5016	**ravin**-*m*	ravine
5017	**venin**-*m*	venom
5020	**boulangerie**-*f*	bakery
5021	**maquette**-*f*	model
5023	**écharpe**-*f*	scarf
5024	**sonore**-*f; adj*	sound; acoustic
5025	**doctorat**-*m*	doctorate| phD

Verbs

Rank	French-PoS	Translation
2501	**établir**-*vb*	establish
2513	**concevoir**-*vb*	design| conceive
2517	**boucher**-*m; vb*	butcher; plug
2518	**niquer**-*vb*	fuck
2522	**épuiser**-*vb*	exhaust| drain
2523	**former**-*vb*	form| train
2524	**sucer**-*vb*	suck| suck out
2525	**considérer**-*vb*	consider
2530	**revancher**-*vb*	requite
2531	**décrire**-*vb*	describe| depict
2541	**quêter**-*vb*	take collection
2545	**évacuer**-*vb*	evacuate
2548	**atterrir**-*vb*	touch down
2560	**négocier**-*vb*	negotiate
2561	**noyer**-*m; vb*	walnut; drown
2568	**bloquer**-*vb*	block| lock
2572	**curer**-*vb*	muck out
2581	**lutter**-*vb*	fight| combat
2582	**péter**-*vb*	fart
2583	**apercevoir**-*vb*	see| perceive
2585	**réduire**-*vb*	reduce| decrease
2593	**saisir**-*vb*	seize| grasp
2596	**raccrocher**-*vb*	hang up
2597	**accorder**-*vb*	grant| award
2602	**dépenser**-*vb*	spend| outlay
2612	**mériter**-*vb*	deserve| earn
2618	**exciter**-*vb*	excite| arouse
2620	**chiffrer**-*vb*	number| cipher
2646	**balancer**-*vb*	swing
2658	**racheter**-*vb*	redeem
2661	**prétendre**-*vb*	claim| pretend
2668	**révéler**-*vb*	reveal| tell
2669	**repérer**-*vb*	spot
2671	**frire**-*vb*	fry
2677	**confirmer**-*vb*	confirm
2681	**boiter**-*vb*	limp
2684	**punir**-*vb*	punish| discipline
2693	**planquer**-*vb*	hide
2706	**rechercher**-*vb*	search| look for
2710	**hurler**-*vb*	scream| howl
2712	**augmenter**-*vb*	increase| raise
2719	**voter**-*vb*	vote
2720	**dynamiter**-*vb*	dynamite
2722	**communiquer**-*vb*	communicate| transmit
2724	**troubler**-*vb*	disturb| trouble
2730	**signaler**-*vb*	report| point out
2732	**rocher**-*m; vb*	rock; spit
2733	**cuire**-*vb*	cook
2736	**boucler**-*vb*	buckle| fasten
2758	**tester**-*vb*	test| try
2765	**fuser**-*vb*	gush
2767	**réagir**-*vb*	react
2773	**violer**-*vb*	violate| breach
2794	**accrocher**-*vb*	hang
2795	**défaire**-*vb*	undo| defeat
2796	**facturer**-*vb*	charge
2797	**intervenir**-*vb*	intervene
2804	**défoncer**-*vb*	smash
2805	**raser**-*vb*	raze| brush
2808	**aiguiller**-*vb*	switch
2810	**plonger**-*vb*	dive| plunge
2812	**carburer**-*vb*	carburize| thrive
2817	**cheminer**-*vb*	plod
2824	**traire**-*vb*	milk
2829	**cracher**-*vb*	spit| cough up
2830	**tordre**-*vb*	twist| wring
2831	**apparaître**-*vb*	appear
2834	**grimper**-*vb*	climb| soar
2842	**répliquer**-*vb*	reply
2846	**insulter**-*vb*	insult| offend
2848	**moucher**-*vb*	snuff
2852	**garantir**-*vb*	ensure| insure
2853	**reporter**-*m; vb*	reporter; postpone
2856	**glisser**-*vb*	slip| run
2864	**sacrifier**-*vb*	sacrifice
2870	**obséder**-*vb*	obsess
2879	**dénoncer**-*vb*	denounce
2882	**cheviller**-*vb*	pin
2883	**décharger**-*vb*	discharge| unload
2884	**rapprocher**-*vb*	bring closer
2885	**capturer**-*vb*	capture| take
2886	**coordonner**-*vb*	coordinate
2890	**mouiller**-*vb*	wet| anchor
2899	**défiler**-*vb*	pass
2903	**inspirer**-*vb*	inspire
2908	**fournir**-*vb*	provide| afford
2911	**graviter**-*vb*	gravitate
2917	**franchir**-*vb*	cross| pass
2919	**correspondre**-*vb*	correspond
2921	**balader**-*vb*	stroll

2923	**dépêcher**-*vb*	dispatch	3152	**prostituer**-*vb*	prostitute
2927	**habituer**-*vb*	accustom| get used to	3157	**flipper**-*m; vb*	pinball; freak out
2929	**vider**-*vb*	empty| drain	3158	**renverser**-*vb*	reverse| turn
2935	**consulter**-*vb*	consult| search	3159	**orbiter**-*vb*	orbit
2948	**déchirer**-*vb*	tear| rip	3175	**détenir**-*vb*	hold| detain
2956	**nier**-*vb*	deny	3179	**féliciter**-*vb*	congratulate
2958	**impressionner**-*vb*	impress	3180	**persuader**-*vb*	persuade
2969	**exécuter**-*vb*	execute	3181	**gêner**-*vb*	hinder
2970	**craquer**-*vb*	crack| creak	3184	**mentionner**-*vb*	mention
2982	**décoller**-*vb*	take off	3193	**maîtriser**-*vb*	control| master
2986	**photographier**-*vb*	photograph	3195	**renseigner**-*vb*	inform
2994	**grouiller**-*vb*	hurry| swarm	3196	**ficher**-*vb*	file
2998	**raccompagner**-*vb*	see off	3204	**croiser**-*vb*	cross| pass
3002	**trembler**-*vb*	tremble| shake	3210	**baigner**-*vb*	bathe| wash
3009	**séduire**-*vb*	seduce| attract	3222	**prononcer**-*vb*	pronounce
3015	**célébrer**-*vb*	celebrate	3224	**calibrer**-*vb*	calibrate| grade
3030	**dessiner**-*vb*	draw| design	3228	**empoisonner**-*vb*	poison
3035	**ruiner**-*vb*	ruin| wreck	3234	**registrer**-*vb*	register
3044	**allonger**-*vb*	lengthen	3236	**développer**-*vb; vb*	develop; adopt
3045	**exposer**-*vb*	expose| exhibit	3238	**présumer**-*vb*	assume
3048	**transmettre**-*vb*	transmit| convey	3247	**céder**-*vb*	yield| cede
3052	**explorer**-*vb*	explore	3248	**hésiter**-*vb*	hesitate
3056	**étouffer**-*vb*	stifle| smother	3250	**escorter**-*vb*	escort
3058	**honorer**-*vb*	honor	3262	**distraire**-*vb*	distract
3061	**rassembler**-*vb*	gather| collect	3267	**prévoir**-*vb*	provide| predict
3069	**fixer**-*vb*	set| fix	3275	**torturer**-*vb*	torture
3070	**transporter**-*vb*	transport| move	3281	**bavarder**-*vb*	chat| talk
3071	**racler**-*vb*	scrape	3285	**démissionner**-*vb*	resign| step down
3084	**débattre**-*vb*	discuss| debate	3298	**luire**-*vb*	gleam| glisten
3087	**échanger**-*vb*	exchange| trade	3306	**inscrire**-*vb*	enroll| list
3088	**parer**-*vb*	parry| ward off	3307	**rejeter**-*vb*	reject| dismiss
3089	**entourer**-*vb*	surround| enclose	3317	**procéder**-*vb*	proceed
3091	**jouir**-*vb*	enjoy	3323	**mater**-*vb*	stare at
3094	**tacher**-*vb*	stain| spot	3326	**comparer**-*vb*	compare| confront
3095	**réchauffer**-*vb*	warm| heat up	3335	**évader**-*vb*	escape
3103	**embarquer**-*vb*	embark	3338	**massacrer**-*vb*	massacre| murder
3105	**parcourir**-*vb*	travel| run through	3342	**trancher**-*vb*	settle| slice
3109	**choper**-*vb*	bust	3346	**doper**-*vb*	boost| dope
3114	**assembler**-*vb*	assemble	3350	**préserver**-*vb*	preserve
3118	**foirer**-*vb*	misfire	3357	**repasser**-*vb*	iron| replay
3128	**tripler**-*vb*	triple	3368	**combler**-*vb*	fill in| make up
3129	**démolir**-*vb*	demolish| destroy	3369	**débarquer**-*vb*	land| disembark
3134	**cogner**-*vb*	knock| bang	3371	**affamer**-*vb*	starve
3138	**pister**-*vb*	track	3373	**entretenir**-*vb*	maintain| nurture
3140	**publier**-*vb*	publish| publicize	3388	**assumer**-*vb*	assume
3151	**gripper**-*vb*	seize	3396	**pénétrer**-*vb*	enter| penetrate

3399	**tremper**-*vb*	soak| dip
3404	**poignarder**-*vb*	stab
3406	**comporter**-*vb*	include| have
3407	**bâtir**-*vb*	build| erect
3416	**éveiller**-*vb*	awaken
3420	**investir**-*vb*	invest
3422	**préoccuper**-*vb*	concern| preoccupy
3425	**soulever**-*vb; m*	raise; bench press
3437	**répugner**-*vb*	loathe
3438	**transférer**-*vb*	transfer| switch
3441	**pointer**-*vb*	point
3448	**accéder**-*vb*	access
3449	**emmerder**-*vb*	bother
3456	**geler**-*vb*	freeze
3467	**effrayer**-*vb*	scare| spook
3470	**coopérer**-*vb*	cooperate| club up
3474	**conquérir**-*vb*	conquer
3476	**isoler**-*vb*	isolate| separate
3477	**justifier**-*vb*	justify
3478	**clôture**-*f; vb*	closing| fence; conclude
3479	**opposer**-*vb*	oppose| put up
3488	**réfugier**-*vb*	refuge
3501	**griffer**-*vb*	scratch
3515	**fréquenter**-*vb*	patronize| frequent
3523	**enfoncer**-*vb*	push| sink
3528	**déprimer**-*vb*	depress| damp
3533	**blâmer**-*vb*	blame| censure
3534	**tabasser**-*vb*	beat up
3535	**soulager**-*vb*	relieve| alleviate
3538	**accélérer**-*vb*	accelerate| expedite
3540	**parvenir**-*vb*	get through
3546	**convenir**-*vb*	admit| agree with
3548	**verser**-*vb*	pay| pour
3552	**suspendre**-*vb*	suspend| hang
3553	**bouleverser**-*vb*	upset| shake
3554	**souffler**-*vb*	breathe| whisper
3566	**offenser**-*vb*	offend| insult
3568	**égaler**-*vb*	match
3569	**traduire**-*vb*	translate| transpose
3576	**absoudre**-*vb*	absolve
3578	**composer**-*vb*	compose| make up
3579	**garer**-*vb*	park
3585	**sécher**-*vb*	dry| cure
3586	**louper**-*vb*	miss out on
3594	**mépriser**-*vb*	despise| disregard
3597	**déterminer**-*vb*	determine
3603	**économiser**-*vb*	save| conserve
3607	**semer**-*vb*	sow
3608	**confesser**-*vb*	confess
3613	**encaisser**-*vb*	cash
3617	**percer**-*vb*	drill| pierce
3618	**emballer**-*vb*	pack| package
3623	**crâner**-*vb*	show off
3626	**consister**-*vb*	consist
3629	**repousser**-*vb*	repel| fend off
3641	**parfaire**-*vb*	perfect
3645	**reprocher**-*vb*	reproach| blame
3648	**déclencher**-*vb*	trigger| start
3652	**qualifier**-*vb*	qualify
3654	**repriser**-*vb*	darn| mend
3655	**affirmer**-*vb*	assert| assure
3656	**secouer**-*vb*	shake| rock
3657	**vouer**-*vb*	devote
3662	**corriger**-*vb*	correct| right
3664	**défier**-*vb*	challenge| defy
3666	**teindre**-*vb*	dye
3670	**exercer**-*vb*	exercise| exert
3678	**songer**-*vb*	reflect| wonder
3680	**déguiser**-*vb*	dissemble
3683	**achever**-*vb*	finish| conclude
3696	**recommander**-*vb*	recommend
3700	**passionner**-*vb*	fascinate
3708	**fantasmer**-*vb*	fantasize
3718	**générer**-*vb*	generate
3724	**couder**-*vb*	bend
3728	**revivre**-*vb*	relive
3732	**redevenir**-*vb*	become again
3740	**disposer**-*vb*	dispose| arrange
3745	**ôter**-*vb*	remove
3752	**contenter**-*vb*	satisfy
3757	**supprimer**-*vb*	remove| suppress
3758	**paniquer**-*vb*	panic
3763	**manipuler**-*vb*	handle| manipulate
3770	**lécher**-*vb*	lick
3775	**tricher**-*vb*	cheat
3784	**dater**-*vb*	date
3787	**soupçonner**-*vb*	suspect
3789	**étendre**-*vb*	extend| expand
3790	**ancrer**-*vb*	anchor
3791	**bander**-*vb*	get it up
3793	**affecter**-*vb*	affect| assign
3800	**encourager**-*vb*	encourage

3803	**endurer**-*vb*	endure| undergo	4006	**consoler**-*vb*	console
3807	**étrangler**-*vb*	strangle| choke	4008	**crisser**-*vb*	screech
3808	**larguer**-*vb*	slip	4021	**kidnapper**-*vb*	kidnap
3810	**consacrer**-*vb*	devote| spare	4036	**rôtir**-*vb*	roast
3811	**nuire**-*vb*	harm| damage	4038	**stopper**-*vb*	stop
3815	**envahir**-*vb*	invade	4051	**bronzer**-*vb*	tan| brown
3824	**hériter**-*vb*	inherit	4056	**émettre**-*vb*	emit| transmit
3826	**baser**-*vb*	base	4062	**vieillir**-*vb*	age
3829	**relâcher**-*vb*	release| relax	4063	**embaucher**-*vb*	hire| take on
3845	**lasser**-*vb*	weary| bore	4064	**éclairer**-*vb*	light| enlighten
3853	**nécessiter**-*vb*	require	4073	**envisager**-*vb*	consider
3855	**extraire**-*vb*	extract| draw	4079	**rétablir**-*vb*	restore| re-establish
3856	**approuver**-*vb*	approve| endorse	4081	**décéder**-*vb*	die
3858	**raccourcir**-*vb*	shorten	4087	**interviewer**-*vb*	interview
3860	**procurer**-*vb*	obtain	4095	**prédire**-*vb*	predict| prophesy
3861	**éprouver**-*vb*	experience| test	4097	**ruser**-*vb*	use cunning
3862	**salir**-*vb*	soil| smear	4104	**humilier**-*vb*	humiliate
3874	**dorer**-*vb*	brown	4108	**huer**-*vb*	boo| hoot
3878	**abîmer**-*vb*	spoil| ruin	4109	**heurter**-*vb*	hit| offend
3880	**aborder**-*vb*	approach| tackle	4119	**capsuler**-*vb*	cap
3890	**surmonter**-*vb*	overcome| rise above	4120	**braquer**-*vb*	shine| point
3896	**soumettre**-*vb*	submit| refer	4122	**gratter**-*vb*	scratch| strum
3900	**étiqueter**-*vb*	label| brand	4127	**reproduire**-*vb*	reproduce
3904	**adapter**-*vb*	adapt| suit	4133	**cueillir**-*vb*	pick| collect
3908	**rafraîchir**-*vb*	refresh	4143	**fraiser**-*vb*	mill
3910	**promouvoir**-*vb*	promote| instigate	4160	**timbrer**-*vb*	stamp
3913	**financer**-*vb*	finance	4169	**distinguer**-*vb*	distinguish
3914	**rassurer**-*vb*	reassure	4171	**gonfler**-*vb*	inflate| rise
3925	**planifier**-*vb*	plan| chart	4174	**détacher**-*vb*	detach| loose
3934	**dérouler**-*vb*	unwind| roll	4177	**ceinturer**-*vb*	engirdle
3937	**espionner**-*vb*	spy	4178	**réjouir**-*vb*	rejoice
3941	**appliquer**-*vb*	apply| carry out	4179	**agresser**-*vb*	attack| mug
3944	**empirer**-*vb*	worse	4186	**écrouler**-*vb*	collapse
3945	**bousiller**-*vb*	botch	4187	**exploiter**-*vb*	exploit| operate
3955	**griller**-*vb*	grill| toast	4189	**intégrer**-*vb*	integrate| include
3963	**anéantir**-*vb*	annihilate| wreck	4191	**enfreindre**-*vb*	violate| infringe
3969	**paumer**-*vb*	lose	4199	**inspecter**-*vb*	inspect| examine
3971	**acquérir**-*vb*	acquire	4201	**détourner**-*vb*	divert| deflect
3974	**écarter**-*vb*	exclude	4205	**clicher**-*vb*	stereotype
3982	**introduire**-*vb*	introduce| place	4207	**crotter**-*vb*	poop| drop
3988	**exagérer**-*vb*	exaggerate	4211	**découper**-*vb*	carve| clip
3992	**dresser**-*vb*	draw up| develop	4216	**imiter**-*vb*	imitate| mimic
3994	**contrarier**-*vb*	upset| thwart	4224	**plaider**-*vb*	plead
3997	**sonder**-*vb*	probe| sound	4225	**vanter**-*vb*	boast
4001	**éponger**-*vb*	mop up| sponge	4244	**plier**-*vb*	bend
4003	**branler**-*vb*	wobble| loose	4245	**régner**-*vb*	reign| take over

4249	**soupirer**-*vb*	sigh		4480	**graver**-*vb*	engrave| carve
4257	**répandre**-*vb*	spill| scatter		4482	**divertir**-*vb*	entertain
4258	**effondrer**-*vb*	collapse		4486	**provenir**-*vb*	result
4260	**distribuer**-*vb*	distribute| deliver		4490	**limiter**-*vb*	limit| restrict
4262	**clore**-*vb*	rule off		4494	**saliver**-*vb*	salivate
4264	**apprêter**-*vb*	ready		4501	**téter**-*vb*	suck
4267	**remuer**-*vb*	stir| move		4502	**surfer**-*vb*	go surfing
4269	**corrompre**-*vb*	corrupt| taint		4505	**fonder**-*vb*	base| set up
4274	**choquer**-*vb*	shock| hit		4510	**verrouiller**-*vb*	lock on
4279	**dominer**-*vb*	dominate| control		4511	**assommer**-*vb*	knock| stun
4280	**perturber**-*vb*	disrupt		4514	**coudre**-*vb*	sew| sew on
4281	**mariner**-*vb*	marinate		4515	**calculer**-*vb*	calculate| time
4283	**gerber**-*vb*	throw up		4518	**centrer**-*vb*	center
4293	**abuser**-*vb*	abuse| impose		4523	**interpréter**-*vb*	interpret
4304	**gaspiller**-*vb*	waste| throw away		4524	**harceler**-*vb*	harass| nag
4315	**pratiquer**-*vb*	practice| use		4525	**regagner**-*vb*	regain
4316	**frotter**-*vb*	rub| scrub		4528	**dénommer**-*vb*	name
4318	**exclure**-*vb*	exclude		4529	**dériver**-*vb*	derive| drift
4319	**naviguer**-*vb*	navigate		4532	**contourner**-*vb*	get around
4334	**dévorer**-*vb*	devour| eat up		4535	**étinceler**-*vb*	sparkle| flash
4346	**puer**-*vb*	stink| smell		4540	**infecter**-*vb*	infect
4350	**critiquer**-*vb*	criticize		4551	**reconstruire**-*vb*	rebuild| reconstruct
4352	**convoquer**-*vb*	convene| call		4560	**compliquer**-*vb*	complicate
4365	**vexer**-*vb*	vex| upset		4562	**déborder**-*vb*	overflow| spill
4367	**capter**-*vb*	capture| receive		4564	**implorer**-*vb*	implore| plead
4376	**traquer**-*vb*	track| track down		4565	**cataloguer**-*vb*	catalog| label
4379	**circuler**-*vb*	circulate		4566	**activer**-*vb*	activate
4393	**agiter**-*vb*	shake| wave		4578	**doucher**-*vb*	douche| shower
4396	**animer**-*vb*	animate| conduct		4581	**errer**-*vb*	wander
4412	**paralyser**-*vb*	paralyze| cripple		4585	**refroidir**-*vb*	cool
4413	**débuter**-*vb*	start| enter		4586	**lécher**-*vb*	lick
4420	**poster**-*vb*	post| poster		4587	**carotter**-*vb*	diddle
4429	**décorer**-*vb*	decorate		4597	**rechanger**-*vb*	change again
4432	**insoler**-*vb*	expose		4599	**arroser**-*vb*	water
4433	**terrifier**-*vb*	terrify		4604	**faciliter**-*vb*	facilitate| aid
4434	**baver**-*vb*	drool| run		4605	**applaudir**-*vb*	applaud| cheer
4441	**pincer**-*vb*	pinch| pluck		4611	**cocher**-*vb; m*	check; coachman
4452	**fracturer**-*vb*	fracture		4617	**ouvrager**-*vb*	tool
4456	**expulser**-*vb*	expel| deport		4618	**moduler**-*vb*	modulate
4460	**dégonfler**-*vb*	deflate		4622	**flatter**-*vb*	flatter| gratify
4461	**protester**-*vb*	protest		4627	**classer**-*vb*	classify| rank
4466	**caresser**-*vb*	caress| stroke		4629	**enrager**-*vb*	annoy| enrage
4472	**retarder**-*vb*	delay| postpone		4631	**rogner**-*vb*	crop| trim
4476	**télescoper**-*vb*	telescope		4633	**camper**-*vb*	camp| plant
4478	**poêler**-*vb*	fry		4634	**stupéfier**-*vb*	amaze| astound
4479	**quereller**-*vb*	quarrel		4639	**enfiler**-*vb*	put on

4641	**confondre**-*vb*	confound| mix
4643	**délivrer**-*vb*	issue| deliver
4647	**éclaircir**-*vb*	clear| lighten
4650	**liquider**-*vb*	liquidate| wind up
4656	**anesthésier**-*vb; m*	anesthetize; anesthetic
4661	**désigner**-*vb*	designate| nominate
4671	**siffler**-*vb*	whistle| hiss
4673	**évoluer**-*vb*	evolve| change
4678	**soûler**-*vb*	get drunk
4680	**miner**-*vb*	undermine
4683	**brocher**-*vb*	stitch
4686	**effectuer**-*vb*	perform| make
4690	**aspirer**-*vb*	aspire| aspirate
4692	**civiliser**-*vb*	civilize
4705	**résumer**-*vb*	summarize| resume
4706	**hausser**-*vb*	raise| increase
4709	**gifler**-*vb*	slap
4710	**ronger**-*vb*	gnaw
4719	**écouler**-*vb*	sell
4725	**endommager**-*vb*	damage
4727	**renaître**-*vb*	come back to life
4729	**trafiquer**-*vb*	traffic
4732	**ramper**-*vb*	crawl| trail
4746	**engueuler**-*vb*	shout
4750	**remporter**-*vb*	win| take
4751	**programmer**-*vb*	program
4758	**évaluer**-*vb*	assess| rate
4760	**raisonner**-*vb*	reason
4771	**préjuger**-*vb*	prejudge
4779	**renforcer**-*vb*	strengthen| reinforce
4801	**rajouter**-*vb*	add
4802	**réconforter**-*vb*	comfort
4816	**égarer**-*vb*	mislead| stray
4820	**dédier**-*vb*	dedicate
4823	**essuyer**-*vb*	wipe| dry
4826	**mendier**-*vb; m*	beg; sponge
4830	**ficeler**-*vb*	tie up
4834	**résider**-*vb*	reside| live
4835	**revendre**-*vb*	sell
4838	**préciser**-*vb*	specify| point out
4863	**trousser**-*vb*	truss
4875	**cultiver**-*vb*	cultivate| grow
4886	**tousser**-*vb*	cough
4896	**redevable**-*adj; vb*	beholden; put under stress
4900	**contraindre**-*vb*	compel| force
4913	**situer**-*vb*	locate| situate
4916	**sécuriser**-*vb*	reassure
4919	**chialer**-*vb*	blubber
4925	**constater**-*vb*	note
4929	**outrager**-*vb*	outrage| insult
4936	**prospérer**-*vb*	prosper| floor
4937	**tolérer**-*vb*	tolerate| bear
4939	**ridiculiser**-*vb*	ridicule
4942	**étoffer**-*vb*	enrich
4967	**définir**-*vb*	define
4971	**ferrer**-*vb*	shoe
4973	**négliger**-*vb*	neglect| overlook
4983	**romancer**-*vb*	romanticize
4984	**planer**-*vb*	plane
4992	**relier**-*vb*	connect
4994	**grossir**-*vb*	swell| magnify
4997	**infiltrer**-*vb*	infiltrate
5003	**manœuvrer**-*vb*	maneuver| manipulate
5009	**connecter**-*vb*	log on
5022	**greffer**-*vb*	graft| engraft

Alphabetical order

Rank	French-PoS	Translation
4954	**à bout**-*adj*	overwrought
4576	**abandon**-*m*	abandonment| surrender
4991	**abbé**-*m*	abbot
3577	**abeille**-*f*	bee
3878	**abîmer**-*vb*	spoil| ruin
4837	**abominable**-*adj*	abominable
4812	**abondance**-*f*	abundance
3880	**aborder**-*vb*	approach| tackle
2539	**absent**-*adj; m*	absent; absentee
3576	**absoudre**-*vb*	absolve
4293	**abuser**-*vb*	abuse| impose
3713	**abus**-*m*	abuse
3040	**académie**-*f*	academy
3448	**accéder**-*vb*	access
3538	**accélérer**-*vb*	accelerate| expedite
4699	**acceptable**-*adj*	acceptable| fair
4615	**accessoire**-*adj; m*	accessory| incidental; accessory
2597	**accorder**-*vb*	grant| award
4356	**accouchement**-*m*	delivery| childbirth
2794	**accrocher**-*vb*	hang
4749	**ace**-*m*	ace
3536	**achat**-*m*	purchase
4182	**acheteur**-*m*	buyer| shopper
3683	**achever**-*vb*	finish| conclude
2652	**acide**-*adj; m*	acid| sour; acid
4948	**acompte**-*m*	down payment| installment
3971	**acquérir**-*vb*	acquire
3331	**actif**-*adj; m*	active| working; assets
4914	**actionnaire**-*m/f*	shareholder
4566	**activer**-*vb*	activate
2867	**actuel**-*adj*	current
3904	**adapter**-*vb*	adapt| suit
2964	**addition**-*f*	addition| sum
4150	**adjudant**-*m*	adjutant
3844	**admirable**-*adj*	admirable
4513	**admiration**-*f*	admiration
4711	**adolescent**-*m; adj*	teenager; adolescent
4332	**ado**-*m*	teenager
4809	**adoption**-*f*	adoption| passage
4833	**adrénaline**-*f*	adrenaline
4792	**adultère**-*m; adj*	adultery; adulterous
3000	**aérien**-*adj*	air| aerial
3962	**affamé**-*adj*	starving| famished
3371	**affamer**-*vb*	starve
3793	**affecter**-*vb*	affect| assign
2954	**affiche**-*f*	poster| public notice
3894	**affirmatif**-*adj*	affirmative
3655	**affirmer**-*vb*	assert| assure
4075	**africain**-*adj; m*	African
2999	**âgé**-*adj*	old
4427	**agenda**-*m*	diary
4272	**agitation**-*f*	agitation| restlessness
4393	**agiter**-*vb*	shake| wave
2704	**agneau**-*m*	lamb
4179	**agresser**-*vb*	attack| mug
3812	**agressif**-*adj*	aggressive
3022	**agression**-*f*	aggression
3042	**aigle**-*m/f*	eagle
4226	**aiguille**-*f*	needle
2808	**aiguiller**-*vb*	switch
3574	**ail**-*m*	garlic
2952	**aîné**-*adj; m*	eldest; senior
3318	**aire**-*f*	area
3349	**alcoolique**-*adj; m/f*	alcoholic; alcoholic
4066	**alentour**-*adj*	surrounding
3871	**alias**-*adv*	alias
3627	**alimentation**-*f*	supply| food
4464	**aliment**-*m*	food
4218	**alléluia**-*int*	alleluia
3543	**allergique**-*adj*	allergic
3044	**allonger**-*vb*	lengthen
3029	**allumette**-*f*	match
2569	**allure**-*f*	look| pace
4503	**allusion**-*f*	allusion| reference
2788	**alpha**-*m*	alpha
3682	**alternative**-*f*	alternative
2836	**altitude**-*f*	altitude| height
2623	**amateur**-*adj; m*	amateur; amateur
2552	**ambassade**-*f*	embassy
2573	**ambiance**-*f*	ambience| environment
3869	**ambitieux**-*adj; m/f*	ambitious; careerist
2976	**amende**-*f*	fine| penalty
3891	**amer**-*adj; m*	bitter; bitter
4071	**amical**-*adj*	friendly
4935	**ampleur**-*f*	extent| magnitude
5005	**ampoule**-*f*	bulb| ampoule

4731	**anarchie**-*f*	anarchy	
3790	**ancrer**-*vb*	anchor	
3731	**andouille**-*f*	dummy	
3963	**anéantir**-*vb*	annihilate| wreck	
2554	**âne**-*m*	donkey	
4656	**anesthésier**-*vb; m*	anesthetize; anesthetic	
2605	**angoisse**-*f*	anguish	
4882	**animation**-*f*	animation| liveliness	
4396	**animer**-*vb*	animate| conduct	
4089	**annonce**-*f*	ad| announcement	
3958	**annuaire**-*m*	directory| yearbook	
4489	**annuel**-*adj*	annual	
4533	**anomalie**-*f*	anomaly	
3079	**anonyme**-*adj*	anonymous	
3895	**anormal**-*adj*	abnormal	
4286	**antécédent**-*adj*	antecedent	
4092	**antidote**-*m*	antidote	
4635	**antique**-*adj; m*	antique| ancient; antique	
2583	**apercevoir**-*vb*	see| perceive	
3991	**apocalypse**-*f*	apocalypse	
2831	**apparaître**-*vb*	appear	
2535	**apparence**-*f*	appearance	
3270	**apparition**-*f*	appearance	
3145	**appât**-*m*	bait	
4605	**applaudir**-*vb*	applaud| cheer	
3198	**applaudissement**-*m*	cheering	
3941	**appliquer**-*vb*	apply| carry out	
4666	**apprenti**-*m*	apprentice| novice	
4988	**apprentissage**-*m*	learning	
4264	**apprêter**-*vb*	ready	
4959	**approbation**-*f*	approval| endorsement	
3856	**approuver**-*vb*	approve| endorse	
3767	**appui**-*m*	support| rest	
5012	**aquarium**-*m*	aquarium	
3208	**arbitre**-*m*	referee	
3394	**arche**-*f*	ark	
3374	**architecte**-*m*	architect	
4114	**architecture**-*f*	architecture	
2751	**archives**-*fpl*	archives	
3130	**arc**-*m*	arc| longbow	
4825	**arène**-*f*	arena	
4458	**argument**-*m*	argument	
4383	**armement**-*m*	armament	
3161	**armure**-*f*	armor	

2947	**arrangement**-*m*	arrangement| understanding	
3921	**arrière**-*adj; m*	rear| back; back	
3726	**arrogant**-*adj*	arrogant	
4599	**arroser**-*vb*	water	
4927	**arsenal**-*m*	arsenal| navy yard	
3060	**artifice**-*m*	artifice| trick	
4754	**artificiel**-*adj*	artificial	
2894	**artistique**-*adj*	artistic	
4824	**asiatique**-*adj*	Asian	
2740	**aspect**-*m*	aspect| appearance	
4690	**aspirer**-*vb*	aspire| aspirate	
3211	**aspirine**-*f*	aspirin	
2737	**assassinat**-*m*	assassination	
3114	**assembler**-*vb*	assemble	
3246	**assistance**-*f*	assistance| audience	
2534	**assistant**-*adj; m*	assistant; assistant	
4511	**assommer**-*vb*	knock| stun	
3388	**assumer**-*vb*	assume	
4846	**asthme**-*m*	asthma	
4492	**astronaute**-*m/f*	astronaut	
4603	**athlète**-*m/f*	athlete	
3924	**atlantique**-*adj*	Atlantic	
3172	**atomique**-*adj*	atomic	
4018	**atout**-*m*	asset	
3019	**atroce**-*adj*	atrocious	
3147	**attentat**-*m*	attempt| attack| bombing	
4926	**attentif**-*adj*	attentive| careful	
2548	**atterrir**-*vb*	touch down	
2683	**atterrissage**-*m*	landing	
3584	**attraction**-*f*	attraction| pull	
3961	**audace**-*f; adj*	boldness; woodless	
4522	**audacieux**-*adj*	bold	
3113	**augmentation**-*f*	increase| rise	
2712	**augmenter**-*vb*	increase| raise	
4738	**aurore**-*f*	dawn	
2578	**aussitôt**-*adv*	immediately	
3507	**autel**-*m*	altar	
3066	**authentique**-*adj*	authentic| genuine	
3008	**autobus**-*m*	bus	
3163	**autographe**-*m*	autograph	
2807	**automatique**-*adj*	automatic	
3516	**automobile**-*adj; f*	automotive; automobile	
4098	**avancée**-*f*	progress	
3429	**aveu**-*m*	confession	

3658	**aviation**-*f*	aviation| air force	3407	**bâtir**-*vb*	build| erect
4702	**avortement**-*m*	abortion	2613	**batte**-*f*	bat
			3733	**batteur**-*m*	drummer| batter
	B		4575	**bavard**-*adj; m*	talkative; chatterbox
			3281	**bavarder**-*vb*	chat| talk
4344	**bâbord**-*m*	port	4434	**baver**-*vb*	drool| run
3430	**bac**-*m*	tray	2924	**bazar**-*m*	bazaar
3212	**bacon**-*m*	bacon	2912	**bec**-*m*	beak| spout
3155	**badge**-*m*	badge	4558	**béguin**-*m*	crush
3928	**baguette**-*f*	baguette| stick	3827	**beignet**-*m*	fritter
3210	**baigner**-*vb*	bathe| wash	2657	**bénédiction**-*f*	blessing
2641	**baignoire**-*f*	bath	3695	**bénéfice**-*m*	profit| income
3561	**baise**-*f*	fuck| sex	3593	**berceau**-*m*	cradle| bed
2921	**balader**-*vb*	stroll	2715	**berger**-*m*	shepherd
2825	**balai**-*m*	broom	4658	**bêta**-*m*	beta
2646	**balancer**-*vb*	swing	3328	**béton**-*m*	concrete
3202	**balcon**-*m*	balcony	4421	**biche**-*f*	doe
3741	**baleine**-*f*	whale	4404	**bicyclette**-*f*	bicycle
4977	**balise**-*f*	buoy| beacon	4616	**bide**-*m*	belly
4944	**ballade**-*f*	ballad	4251	**bilan**-*m*	balance sheet
3310	**ballet**-*m*	ballet	3170	**billard**-*m*	billiards
3987	**banal**-*adj*	banal	4405	**biologie**-*f*	biology
3614	**banane**-*f*	banana	3981	**biologique**-*adj*	biological
4537	**bancaire**-*adj*	banking	2770	**bip**-*m*	beep| beeper
2792	**banc**-*m*	bench| bank	2780	**biscuit**-*m*	biscuit
3791	**bander**-*vb*	get it up	3126	**bizarrement**-*adv*	oddly| peculiarly
2746	**bandit**-*m*	bandit| gangster	4232	**blaireau**-*m*	badger
2599	**Bang!**-*int*	Pow!	3799	**blâme**-*m*	blame| reprimand
3463	**banlieue**-*f*	suburbs	3533	**blâmer**-*vb*	blame| censure
3927	**banquet**-*m*	banquet	4339	**bled**-*m*	boondocks
3788	**banquier**-*m*	banker	3471	**bloqué**-*adj*	blocked
4675	**baptême**-*m*	baptism	2568	**bloquer**-*vb*	block| lock
4717	**baptiste**-*m*	baptist	4285	**blouson**-*m*	blouse| jacket
3692	**baratin**-*m*	spiel| flannel	4142	**boche**-*adj; m/f*	German; Jerry (derogative)
4506	**barbare**-*adj; m*	barbaric; barbarian			
3201	**barbecue**-*m*	barbecue	3209	**bœuf**-*m*	beef
3065	**barman**-*m*	bartender	2681	**boiter**-*vb*	limp
4500	**baronne**-*f*	baroness	4493	**bombardement**-*m*	bombardment| bombing
3673	**barque**-*f*	bark| small boat			
2782	**barrage**-*m*	dam	4237	**bombardier**-*m*	bomber
3537	**barreau**-*m*	bar	3705	**bonnet**-*m*	cap
4077	**barre**-*f*	bar	3712	**boom**-*m*	boom
3005	**barrière**-*f*	barrier| fence	3391	**borne**-*f*	terminal
3826	**baser**-*vb*	base	4682	**boucherie**-*f*	butchery
4002	**bassin**-*m*	basin| pool	2517	**boucher**-*m; vb*	butcher; plug
2909	**bataillon**-*m*	battalion	3633	**bouchon**-*m*	plug| cork
			4336	**bouclé**-*adj*	curly

2736	**boucler**-*vb*	buckle| fasten
2950	**bouclier**-*m*	shield
3866	**bouc**-*m*	goat
3055	**Bouddha**-*m*	Buddha
3671	**bouffon**-*m; adj*	buffoon; fool
2760	**bougie**-*f*	candle| spark plug
4836	**bougre**-*m*	guy
5020	**boulangerie**-*f*	bakery
4668	**boulette**-*f*	pellet
4389	**boulevard**-*m*	boulevard| parade
3553	**bouleverser**-*vb*	upset| shake
3359	**bouquet**-*m*	bouquet| bunch
3136	**bouquin**-*m*	book
3847	**bourbon**-*m*	bourbon
4481	**bourgeois**-*adj; m*	bourgeois; bourgeois
3499	**bourreau**-*m*	executioner
3945	**bousiller**-*vb*	botch
3292	**bout**-*m*	end| toe
3494	**bowling**-*m*	bowling
3156	**boxeur**-*m*	boxer
3918	**box**-*m*	box
3125	**bracelet**-*m*	bracelet| strap
4146	**brandy**-*m*	brandy
4003	**branler**-*vb*	wobble| loose
3820	**braquage**-*m*	defection
4120	**braquer**-*vb*	shine| point
4395	**bravoure**-*f*	bravery
3834	**break**-*m*	break
4055	**brebis**-*f*	sheep
4747	**brèche**-*f*	breach| gap
2591	**Brésil**-*m*	Brazil
3669	**bridge**-*m*	bridge
2666	**brillant**-*adj; m*	brilliant| bright; gloss
3796	**brin**-*m*	strand| sprig
3053	**brique**-*f*	brick
3191	**briquet**-*m*	lighter
4683	**brocher**-*vb*	stitch
4051	**bronzer**-*vb*	tan| brown
2962	**brosse**-*f*	brush
4860	**brouhaha**-*m*	hubbub
2527	**bruit**-*m*	noise| sound
4987	**brûlure**-*f*	burn
3888	**brume**-*f*	mist
3302	**brun**-*adj; m*	brown; brown
4401	**brusquement**-*adv*	suddenly| sharply
2659	**brut**-*adj; m*	gross; crude

3565	**brutal**-*adj; m*	brutal; brute
4795	**bruyant**-*adj*	noisy
2504	**budget**-*m*	budget
3761	**buffet**-*m*	buffet| dresser
4547	**buisson**-*m*	bush
4025	**bulle**-*f*	bubble| bull
3194	**bulletin**-*m*	newsletter
3939	**bunker**-*m*	bunker
3329	**butin**-*m*	booty| loot

C

4111	**cabaret**-*m*	cabaret
3942	**cacahuète**-*f*	peanut
3253	**caca**-*m*	poo
2781	**cache**-*m*	cover
3135	**cachet**-*m*	stamp| cachet
2642	**cachette**-*f; adj*	hiding place| cache; hideaway
4811	**cactus**-*m*	cactus
3875	**cadet**-*adj; m*	cadet; cadet
3500	**cafard**-*m*	cockroach
4020	**cahier**-*m*	notebook
4681	**caïd**-*m*	boss
4215	**caillou**-*m*	pebble
4515	**calculer**-*vb*	calculate| time
3642	**calcul**-*m*	calculation| calculus
4233	**caleçon**-*m*	pants| underpants
3525	**cale**-*f*	hold| wedge
3984	**calendrier**-*m*	calendar
3224	**calibrer**-*vb*	calibrate| grade
3555	**câlin**-*adj; m*	hugging; hug
3581	**calmement**-*adv*	calmly
3393	**cambriolage**-*m*	burglary
4667	**cambrioleur**-*m*	burglar
2895	**camionnette**-*f*	van
4633	**camper**-*vb*	camp| plant
4200	**camping**-*m*	camping| campsite
3166	**campus**-*m*	campus
4375	**canadien**-*adj*	Canadian
4411	**canaille**-*f*	vulgar
2609	**canal**-*m*	channel| canal
2819	**candidat**-*m; adj*	candidate; elect
4440	**cannabis**-*m*	cannabis
3021	**canne**-*f*	cane
4005	**canot**-*m*	canoe| dinghy

3353	**canyon**-*m*	canyon		3665	**cerf**-*m*	deer| stag
4007	**caoutchouc**-*m*	rubber		4357	**cerise**-*adj; f*	cherry; cherry
2647	**capacité**-*f*	capacity| ability		3115	**certificat**-*m*	certificate| degree
3122	**cape**-*f*	mantle		3573	**certitude**-*f*	certainty
3413	**capote**-*f*	hood		4707	**chalet**-*m*	chalet
4612	**capot**-*m*	hood		4688	**chaleureux**-*adj*	warm| cordial
4119	**capsuler**-*vb*	cap		3897	**chameau**-*m*	camel
4367	**capter**-*vb*	capture| receive		3439	**champignon**-*m*	mushroom
3823	**capture**-*f*	capture| catch		2798	**championnat**-*m*	championship
2885	**capturer**-*vb*	capture| take		3870	**chancelier**-*m*	chancellor
4845	**caramel**-*m*	caramel		4963	**chandelle**-*f*	candle
2509	**caravane**-*f*	caravan| trailer		3036	**chantage**-*m*	blackmail
3968	**carbone**-*adj; m*	carbon; carbon		2543	**chanteur**-*m*	singer
2812	**carburer**-*vb*	carburize| thrive		3003	**chantier**-*m*	site| yard
3754	**cardinal**-*adj; m*	cardinal; cardinal		3231	**chapelle**-*f*	chapel
4495	**caresse**-*f*	caress		3622	**chargement**-*m*	loading| charge
4466	**caresser**-*vb*	caress| stroke		4208	**chargeur**-*m*	charger
4314	**cargo**-*m*	cargo		2835	**char**-*m*	tank
4485	**carnage**-*m*	carnage		3457	**châtiment**-*m*	punishment
4718	**carnaval**-*m*	carnival		4131	**chaton**-*m*	kitten
2717	**carnet**-*m*	book		3836	**chauffage**-*m*	heating| heater
4305	**carotte**-*f; adj*	carrot; carroty		3351	**chauffé**-*adj*	heated
4587	**carotter**-*vb*	diddle		3123	**chauve**-*adj*	bald
4214	**carreau**-*m*	tile		2817	**cheminer**-*vb*	plod
4814	**carrefour**-*m*	crossroads		4903	**chercheur**-*m; adj*	researcher| seeker; inquiring
3938	**cartouche**-*f*	cartridge				
3839	**caserne**-*f*	barracks		3825	**cherry**-*f*	sherry
3341	**casquette**-*f*	cap		4877	**cheville**-*f*	ankle
4565	**cataloguer**-*vb*	catalog| label		2882	**cheviller**-*vb*	pin
4623	**catch**-*m*	wrestling		3300	**chèvre**-*f*	goat
3931	**catégorie**-*f*	category		4919	**chialer**-*vb*	blubber
2914	**cavalerie**-*f*	cavalry		2620	**chiffrer**-*vb*	number| cipher
2643	**cavalier**-*m; adj*	rider; cavalier		3818	**chimie**-*f*	chemistry
3912	**caverne**-*f*	cave		3598	**chimique**-*adj*	chemical
3986	**caviar**-*m*	caviar		4126	**chiot**-*m*	puppy
3247	**céder**-*vb*	yield| cede		2985	**chirurgie**-*f*	surgery
4177	**ceinturer**-*vb*	engirdle		4035	**chœur**-*m*	choir
3015	**célébrer**-*vb*	celebrate		2822	**chômage**-*m*	unemployment
3715	**célébrité**-*f*	celebrity| stardom		3109	**choper**-*vb*	bust
3556	**céleste**-*adj*	celestial| unworldly		4274	**choquer**-*vb*	shock| hit
3344	**cellulaire**-*adj*	cellular		4584	**choral**-*adj; m*	choral; choral
4363	**centime**-*m*	centime		2918	**chrétien**-*adj; m*	Christian; Christian
4046	**centimètre**-*m*	centimeter| tape		4311	**chronique**-*adj; f*	chronic; chronicle
4518	**centrer**-*vb*	center		3935	**chute**-*f*	fall| falling
3686	**céréale**-*f*	cereal| fruit		2940	**cicatrice**-*f*	scar
4105	**cérébral**-*adj*	cerebral		4777	**ciment**-*m*	cement

3518	**ciné-***m*	pics
2839	**cinquième-***adj*	fifth
4379	**circuler-***vb*	circulate
3459	**cire-***f*	wax
3304	**ciseau-***m*	chisel
4487	**citation-***f*	quote| summons
2799	**citron-***adj; m*	lemon; lemon
4692	**civiliser-***vb*	civilize
4627	**classer-***vb*	classify| rank
2555	**clef-***f; adj*	key; pivotal
4205	**clicher-***vb*	stereotype
4536	**clientèle-***f*	customers| clientele
3402	**climat-***m*	climate
4516	**clin-***m*	wink
4787	**clochard-***m; adj*	tramp; down-at-heel
2968	**cloche-***f*	bell
3699	**clochette-***f*	bell
3947	**clope-***f*	butt
4262	**clore-***vb*	rule off
3478	**clôture-***f; vb*	closing| fence; conclude
3142	**clou-***m*	nail
4662	**cobra-***m*	cobra
3647	**cocaïne-***f*	cocaine
4611	**cocher-***vb; m*	check; coachman
2977	**cocktail-***m*	cocktail
3265	**code-***m*	code
4698	**coffre-***m*	safe| trunk
2594	**cognac-***m*	cognac
3134	**cogner-***vb*	knock| bang
2821	**coiffeur-***m*	hairdresser| barber
2640	**coiffure-***f*	hairdressing| coiffure
2592	**coke-***m*	coke
4726	**cola-***m*	cola
2959	**colis-***m*	package
4277	**collaboration-***f*	collaboration
4384	**collecte-***f*	collection
4922	**collision-***f*	collision| clash
2757	**col-***m*	collar| pass
4951	**colocataire-***m/f*	room-mate
4431	**colombe-***f*	dove
3148	**colonie-***f*	colony
2544	**colonne-***f*	column
2611	**coma-***m*	coma
3698	**combattant-***m; adj*	fighter; fighting
4275	**combine-***f*	combination
3368	**combler-***vb*	fill in| make up
4924	**combustible-***m; adj*	fuel; combustible
4294	**comédien-***m*	actor
4439	**comète-***f*	comet
2674	**comique-***adj; m/f*	comic; comic
4713	**commando-***m*	commando
3640	**commencement-***m*	beginning| start
3165	**commentaire-***m*	comment| commentary
3509	**commode-***adj; f*	convenient| handy; chest of drawers
2722	**communiquer-***vb*	communicate| transmit
4626	**communisme-***m*	Communism
4042	**compagne-***f*	companion
4559	**comparaison-***f*	comparison
3326	**comparer-***vb*	compare| confront
4308	**compartiment-***m*	compartment
2675	**compassion-***f*	compassion
4676	**compatriote-***m/f*	compatriot
4284	**compétence-***f*	competence| skill
2749	**complice-***m/f*	accomplice
2932	**compliment-***m*	compliment
4560	**compliquer-***vb*	complicate
2875	**complot-***m*	conspiracy
3406	**comporter-***vb*	include| have
3578	**composer-***vb*	compose| make up
4340	**compositeur-***m; adj*	composer; compositive
4645	**composition-***f*	composition
4981	**compréhensible-***adj*	understandable
3590	**compréhension-***f*	comprehension
2787	**compromis-***m*	compromise
4657	**comptabilité-***f*	accounting| accounts
2689	**comptable-***adj; m/f*	accounting; accountant
3689	**comptant-***adj*	spot| cash
4084	**compteur-***m*	counter
3207	**comptoir-***m*	counter
3023	**concentration-***f*	concentration| focus
3746	**conception-***f*	design| designing
2815	**concept-***m*	concept
5013	**concession-***f*	concession| dealership
2513	**concevoir-***vb*	design| conceive
2763	**concierge-***m/f*	concierge
2809	**conclusion-***f*	conclusion

4569	**concurrent**-*m; adj*	competitor| contestant; concurrent	2872	**contrairement**-*adv*	counter
3943	**condamnation**-*f*	conviction| locking	3994	**contrarier**-*vb*	upset| thwart
3777	**conditionnel**-*adj*	conditional	4697	**contrebande**-*f*	smuggling
2663	**conducteur**-*m*	driver| conductor	4022	**contribution**-*f*	contribution| input
3608	**confesser**-*vb*	confess	4349	**contrôleur**-*m*	controller| supervisor
2946	**confession**-*f*	confession	4803	**convaincant**-*adj*	convincing
3255	**confidentiel**-*adj*	confidential	3830	**convenable**-*adj*	suitable| appropriate
3547	**confirmation**-*f*	confirmation| swearing	3546	**convenir**-*vb*	admit| agree with
2677	**confirmer**-*vb*	confirm	3821	**convention**-*f*	convention| covenant
3762	**confiture**-*f*	jam	3177	**conviction**-*f*	conviction| belief
4641	**confondre**-*vb*	confound| mix	2981	**convoi**-*m*	convoy
2546	**confortable**-*adj*	comfortable	4352	**convoquer**-*vb*	convene| call
3434	**confort**-*m*	comfort	3392	**coopération**-*f*	cooperation
4815	**confrérie**-*f*	brotherhood	3470	**coopérer**-*vb*	cooperate| club up
2937	**confus**-*adj*	confused	2886	**coordonner**-*vb*	coordinate
3271	**confusion**-*f*	confusion	2902	**copine**-*f; adj*	girlfriend; pally
3455	**connasse**-*f*	motherfucker	2837	**coq**-*m*	rooster
5009	**connecter**-*vb*	log on	4256	**coque**-*f*	hull
3857	**connexion**-*f*	connection	4687	**coquille**-*f*	shell| typo
3474	**conquérir**-*vb*	conquer	4362	**coquin**-*m; adj*	rascal; naughty
3810	**consacrer**-*vb*	devote| spare	4096	**corbeau**-*m*	raven
2567	**conscient**-*adj*	aware| conscious	4595	**cordon**-*m*	cordon
5007	**consentement**-*m*	consent	4891	**coréen**-*adj; m*	Korean; Korean
3487	**conséquent**-*adj*	consequent	4121	**corne**-*f*	horn
4813	**considération**-*f*	consideration| account	2653	**correction**-*f*	correction| patch
2525	**considérer**-*vb*	consider	4534	**correspondance**-*f*	correspondence
3626	**consister**-*vb*	consist	2919	**correspondre**-*vb*	correspond
4638	**console**-*f*	console	3662	**corriger**-*vb*	correct| right
4006	**consoler**-*vb*	console	4269	**corrompre**-*vb*	corrupt| taint
4640	**consommation**-*f*	consumption	2939	**corruption**-*f*	corruption
3946	**conspiration**-*f*	conspiracy| plot	4588	**cosmos**-*m*	cosmos
2588	**constamment**-*adv*	constantly	2840	**coton**-*m*	cotton
4573	**constant**-*adj*	constant	4176	**coude**-*m*	elbow| bend
4925	**constater**-*vb*	note	3724	**couder**-*vb*	bend
3153	**constitution**-*f*	constitution| incorporation	4514	**coudre**-*vb*	sew| sew on
4322	**consul**-*m*	consul	4271	**couillon**-*m*	sod
2935	**consulter**-*vb*	consult| search	3685	**coupure**-*f; adj*	cut; clipping
4652	**contagieux**-*adj*	contagious; communicable	4859	**courbe**-*f*	curve| bending
3752	**contenter**-*vb*	satisfy	3782	**coureur**-*m; adj*	runner; racing
4242	**contexte**-*m*	context	4016	**courtoisie**-*f*	courtesy
3291	**continent**-*adj; m*	continent; continent	4117	**coût**-*m*	cost
4532	**contourner**-*vb*	get around	3305	**coutume**-*f*	custom| practice
4900	**contraindre**-*vb*	compel| force	4854	**couture**-*f*	sewing
			3078	**couvent**-*m*	convent
			4306	**crabe**-*m*	crab
			2829	**cracher**-*vb*	spit| cough up

2987	**crack-***m*	crack| wiz
3623	**crâner-***vb*	show off
3506	**crapaud-***m*	toad
4298	**crapule-***f*	scoundrel
2970	**craquer-***vb*	crack| creak
3026	**crayon-***m*	pencil
3254	**créateur-***m*	creator
4841	**créatif-***adj*	creative
4607	**crédible-***adj*	credible
4448	**crêpe-***f*	crepe| pancake
3742	**crépuscule-***adj; m*	dusk; dusk
3239	**creux-***adj; m*	hollow| sunken; hollow
3919	**crevette-***f*	shrimp
4408	**criant-***adj*	crying
4572	**cricket-***m*	cricket
4008	**crisser-***vb*	screech
2926	**cristal-***m*	crystal
4350	**critiquer-***vb*	criticize
4993	**croc-***m*	fang
4805	**crocodile-***m*	crocodile
3311	**croisé-***adj; m*	cross; crusader
3204	**croiser-***vb*	cross| pass
3635	**croisière-***f*	cruise
3624	**croissance-***f*	growth| growing
4207	**crotter-***vb*	poop| drop
3482	**croyable-***adj*	believable
4601	**croyance-***f*	belief
3415	**croyant-***m; adj*	believer; god-fearing
3495	**cruauté-***f*	cruelty
4720	**crucial-***adj*	crucial| critical
4945	**cube-***m*	cube
4133	**cueillir-***vb*	pick| collect
3976	**cuillère-***f*	spoon
2733	**cuire-***vb*	cook
3385	**cuisinier-***m*	cook
3520	**cuisse-***f*	thigh
2520	**cuit-***adj*	cooked| baked
2922	**culot-***m*	base| nerve
3854	**culte-***m*	worship
4875	**cultiver-***vb*	cultivate| grow
2572	**curer-***vb*	muck out
3675	**cycle-***m*	cycle
4932	**cygne-***m*	swan
4323	**cynique-***adj; m*	cynical; cynic

D

4918	**danois-***adj; m*	Danish; Danish
2850	**danse-***f*	dance
2705	**danseur-***m*	dancer
3784	**dater-***vb*	date
4539	**dauphin-***m*	dolphin
3369	**débarquer-***vb*	land| disembark
4976	**débat-***m*	debate| argument
3084	**débattre-***vb*	discuss| debate
4562	**déborder-***vb*	overflow| spill
3846	**débris-***mpl*	debris
4413	**débuter-***vb*	start| enter
3289	**décédé-***adj; m*	deceased; defunct
4081	**décéder-***vb*	die
4241	**déception-***f*	disappointment
2883	**décharger-***vb*	discharge| unload
3348	**déchet-***m*	wretch
2948	**déchirer-***vb*	tear| rip
3648	**déclencher-***vb*	trigger| start
3243	**décollage-***m*	take-off
2982	**décoller-***vb*	take off
4445	**décoration-***f*	decoration
4429	**décorer-***vb*	decorate
2843	**décor-***m*	decor
4211	**découper-***vb*	carve| clip
4778	**découvert-***adj; m*	discovered; overdraft
2531	**décrire-***vb*	describe| depict
4820	**dédier-***vb*	dedicate
2566	**déesse-***f*	goddess
2795	**défaire-***vb*	undo| defeat
2584	**défaut-***m*	fault| failing
4679	**défenseur-***m*	defender
3664	**défier-***vb*	challenge| defy
2899	**défiler-***vb*	pass
4967	**définir-***vb*	define
4986	**définitif-***adj*	final
3975	**définition-***f*	definition
3051	**définitivement-***adv*	definitively
4442	**défoncé-***adj*	stoned
2804	**défoncer-***vb*	smash
3505	**défunt-***adj; m*	late; deceased person
4460	**dégonfler-***vb*	deflate
4116	**déguisement-***m*	disguise
3680	**déguiser-***vb*	dissemble

3169	**délai**-*m*	period| delay
4337	**délibérément**-*adv*	deliberately| willfully
2774	**délit**-*m*	offense| misdemeanor
4643	**délivrer**-*vb*	issue| deliver
3164	**delta**-*m*	delta
3595	**dément**-*adj*	demented| insane
3492	**démission**-*f*	resignation
3285	**démissionner**-*vb*	resign| step down
2699	**démocratie**-*f*	democracy
3129	**démolir**-*vb*	demolish| destroy
2967	**démonstration**-*f*	demonstration| proof
4528	**dénommer**-*vb*	name
2879	**dénoncer**-*vb*	denounce
4509	**dentaire**-*adj*	dental
2923	**dépêcher**-*vb*	dispatch
3296	**dépense**-*f*	expenditure| expense
2602	**dépenser**-*vb*	spend| outlay
3706	**dépit**-*m*	spite
4873	**déplacement**-*m*	shifting| displacement
2764	**dépôt**-*m*	deposit| filing
4417	**déprimant**-*adj*	depressing
4642	**déprimé**-*adj*	depressed
3528	**déprimer**-*vb*	depress| damp
3221	**député**-*m*	member| deputy
4660	**dérangement**-*m*	disturbance| inconvenience
4529	**dériver**-*vb*	derive| drift
2913	**dernièrement**-*adv*	recently| at last
3934	**dérouler**-*vb*	unwind| roll
3057	**désagréable**-*adj*	unpleasant
2690	**descente**-*f*	descent
3192	**description**-*f*	description| depiction
2855	**désespéré**-*adj*	desperate| hopeless
2800	**désespoir**-*m*	despair
4661	**désigner**-*vb*	designate| nominate
2624	**désordre**-*m*	disorder
4921	**dessein**-*m*	design| plan
3030	**dessiner**-*vb*	draw| design
4409	**détachement**-*m*	detachment
4174	**détacher**-*vb*	detach| loose
3949	**détecteur**-*m*	detector| detecting
3175	**détenir**-*vb*	hold| detain
3400	**détente**-*f*	relaxation
3358	**détention**-*f*	detention| possession
3312	**détenu**-*adj; m*	detained; inmate
4598	**détermination**-*f*	determination| fixing

3597	**déterminer**-*vb*	determine
4072	**détour**-*m*	detour| bend
4201	**détourner**-*vb*	divert| deflect
4467	**détroit**-*m*	strait
2743	**deuil**-*m*	mourning
4386	**deuxièmement**-*num*	secondly
2728	**développement**-*m*	development
3236	**développer**-*vb; vb*	develop; adopt
4334	**dévorer**-*vb*	devour| eat up
4870	**dévouement**-*m*	devotion
3218	**diabolique**-*adj*	diabolical| devilish
3877	**diagnostic**-*m*	diagnosis
4309	**dialogue**-*m*	dialogue
4644	**dictionnaire**-*m*	dictionary
2771	**différemment**-*adv*	differently
2963	**difficulté**-*f*	difficulty
3849	**diligence**-*f*	diligence
3831	**dimension**-*f*	dimension| size
2608	**dinde**-*f*	turkey
4219	**Ding!**-*int*	Ding-Dong!
4818	**dinosaure**-*m*	dinosaur
5015	**diplomatique**-*adj*	diplomatic
4789	**diplôme**-*m*	diploma
3570	**dirigeant**-*m*	leader
3735	**disciple**-*m*	disciple
4728	**disco**-*adj; m*	disco; disco
2862	**discret**-*adj*	discreet
4040	**discrètement**-*adv*	discreetly
3873	**discrétion**-*f*	discretion
2507	**disponible**-*adj; adv*	available; on call
3740	**disposer**-*vb*	dispose| arrange
4243	**dispositif**-*m*	device
2851	**disposition**-*f*	provision| disposal
4390	**dispute**-*f*	dispute| argument
4169	**distinguer**-*vb*	distinguish
4333	**distorsion**-*f*	distortion
3262	**distraire**-*vb*	distract
4260	**distribuer**-*vb*	distribute| deliver
4203	**distributeur**-*m*	distributor
3460	**distribution**-*f*	distribution| delivery
3216	**district**-*m*	district
4059	**divan**-*m*	couch
3863	**divers**-*adj*	various| several
3828	**diversion**-*f*	diversion
4482	**divertir**-*vb*	entertain

4636	**divertissement**-*m*	entertainment	
2888	**divorcé**-*adj; m*	divorced; divorcee	
3703	**dizaine**-*f*	about ten| decade	
5025	**doctorat**-*m*	doctorate| phD	
2838	**domestique**-*adj; m/f*	domestic; domestic	
2988	**domicile**-*m*	home| residence	
4279	**dominer**-*vb*	dominate| control	
4428	**donneur**-*m*	giver| dealer	
3346	**doper**-*vb*	boost| dope	
3874	**dorer**-*vb*	brown	
4330	**dortoir**-*m*	dormitory	
3653	**dot**-*f*	dowry	
4498	**double**-*adj; m*	double| twin; double	
4403	**doublure**-*f*	lining| understudy	
4578	**doucher**-*vb*	douche| shower	
2664	**douloureux**-*adj*	painful	
2601	**douzaine**-*f*	dozen	
3903	**doyen**-*m*	dean| provost	
4248	**drague**-*f*	dredge	
3028	**dramatique**-*adj*	dramatic	
2753	**drame**-*m*	drama	
3992	**dresser**-*vb*	draw up| develop	
4894	**driver**-*m*	driver	
3083	**drogué**-*adj; m*	drugged; junkie	
2844	**drôlement**-*adv*	funnily	
3127	**duchesse**-*f*	duchess	
2713	**duel**-*m*	duel	
4197	**duo**-*m*	duo	
4797	**durement**-*adv*	harshly	
2720	**dynamiter**-*vb*	dynamite	

E

3974	**écarter**-*vb*	exclude
3087	**échanger**-*vb*	exchange| trade
3376	**échantillon**-*m*	sample
5023	**écharpe**-*f*	scarf
3384	**écho**-*m*	echo
4045	**éclairage**-*m*	lighting| illumination
4647	**éclaircir**-*vb*	clear| lighten
4064	**éclairer**-*vb*	light| enlighten
3258	**éclat**-*m*	eclat| brightness
2983	**économique**-*adj*	economic| thrifty
3603	**économiser**-*vb*	save| conserve

4557	**écossais**-*adj; m: mpl*	Scottish; Scottish; Scots
4719	**écouler**-*vb*	sell
3440	**écoute**-*f*	listening
4186	**écrouler**-*vb*	collapse
3725	**écureuil**-*m*	squirrel
3840	**écurie**-*f*	stable
3080	**éditeur**-*m*	editor
2941	**édition**-*f*	edition
2536	**effectivement**-*adv*	effectively
4686	**effectuer**-*vb*	perform| make
4321	**efficacité**-*f*	efficiency
4701	**effondrement**-*m*	collapse| crash
4258	**effondrer**-*vb*	collapse
3467	**effrayer**-*vb*	scare| spook
3568	**égaler**-*vb*	match
3356	**égalité**-*f*	equality
3137	**égard**-*m*	respect
4816	**égarer**-*vb*	mislead| stray
3277	**ego**-*m*	ego
3676	**égout**-*m*	sewer| drain
4157	**égratignure**-*f*	scratch
4328	**élan**-*m*	elan| elk
4905	**électeur**-*m*	elector
2845	**élection**-*f*	election
3408	**électronique**-*adj; f*	electronic; electronics
4928	**élégance**-*f*	elegance
3390	**élégant**-*adj; m*	elegant; dandy
2904	**élite**-*f*	elite
4968	**élu**-*adj; m*	elected; elect
3618	**emballer**-*vb*	pack| package
3663	**embarquement**-*m*	boarding| shipping
3103	**embarquer**-*vb*	embark
4399	**embarras**-*m*	embarrassment
3620	**embarrassant**-*adj*	embarrassing
4589	**embauche**-*f*	hiring
4063	**embaucher**-*vb*	hire| take on
4184	**embrasse**-*f*	embrace| kiss
4437	**embrouillé**-*adj*	confused| muddled
3615	**embuscade**-*f*	ambush| fall
4086	**émetteur**-*m*	transmitter
4056	**émettre**-*vb*	emit| transmit
4023	**émeute**-*f*	riot
4542	**émissaire**-*m*	emissary
3449	**emmerder**-*vb*	bother
3944	**empirer**-*vb*	worse

3644	**emplacement**-*m*	location| site	2622	**équilibre**-*m*	balance
4906	**employeur**-*m*	employer	4419	**équipier**-*m*	team member
3228	**empoisonner**-*vb*	poison	4430	**érection**-*f*	erection| stand
4780	**emprisonné**-*adj; m*	jailed; detainee	4955	**érotique**-*adj*	erotic
4543	**emprunt**-*m*	borrowing	4581	**errer**-*vb*	wander
4507	**ému**-*adj*	affected	4862	**escadrille**-*f*	squadron
3613	**encaisser**-*vb*	cash	3933	**escadron**-*m*	squadron
3557	**enchère**-*f*	bid| raise	4651	**escalade**-*f*	climbing| escalation
3800	**encourager**-*vb*	encourage	3250	**escorter**-*vb*	escort
2887	**encre**-*f*	ink	2906	**escroc**-*m*	crook
4725	**endommager**-*vb*	damage	4888	**escroquerie**-*f*	fraud| swindle
3803	**endurer**-*vb*	endure| undergo	3906	**espionnage**-*m*	espionage
4639	**enfiler**-*vb*	put on	3937	**espionner**-*vb*	spy
3523	**enfoncer**-*vb*	push| sink	4823	**essuyer**-*vb*	wipe| dry
4191	**enfreindre**-*vb*	violate| infringe	4625	**esthétique**-*adj; f*	aesthetic; aesthetics
2634	**engagement**-*m*	commitment| engagement	2501	**établir**-*vb*	establish
2553	**engin**-*m*	machine| engine	3443	**établissement**-*m*	establishment
4746	**engueuler**-*vb*	shout	2747	**étage**-*m*	floor| stage
3917	**énigme**-*f*	enigma| puzzle	4371	**étalon**-*m*	standard| stallion
3320	**enlèvement**-*m*	removal| abduction	4058	**étang**-*m*	pond
4406	**enquête**-*f*	survey| investigation	3789	**étendre**-*vb*	extend| expand
4629	**enrager**-*vb*	annoy| enrage	3014	**éternellement**-*adv*	eternally
4784	**enseignant**-*m*	schoolteacher	3889	**éthique**-*f; adj*	ethics; ethical
3868	**enseignement**-*m*	education| teaching	4535	**étinceler**-*vb*	sparkle| flash
4017	**entente**-*f*	agreement	3900	**étiqueter**-*vb*	label| brand
3313	**enthousiasme**-*m*	enthusiasm	4942	**étoffer**-*vb*	enrich
4693	**enthousiaste**-*adj; m*	enthusiastic; enthusiast	4465	**étonnant**-*adj*	surprising| astonishing
3089	**entourer**-*vb*	surround| enclose	3056	**étouffer**-*vb*	stifle| smother
4130	**entrailles**-*f; fpl*	womb; insides	4793	**étrangement**-*adv*	strangely
4009	**entrain**-*m*	spirit| zest	3807	**étrangler**-*vb*	strangle| choke
2863	**entrepôt**-*m*	warehouse| store	3842	**étroit**-*adj*	narrow| close
3097	**entreprise**-*f*	business	4869	**étui**-*m*	case
3373	**entretenir**-*vb*	maintain| nurture	2744	**euro**-*m*	euro
3815	**envahir**-*vb*	invade	4964	**européen**-*adj*	European
4073	**envisager**-*vb*	consider	3259	**évacuation**-*f*	evacuation| draining
4291	**envoi**-*m*	sending| dispatch	2545	**évacuer**-*vb*	evacuate
3514	**épais**-*adj*	thick| heavy	3335	**évader**-*vb*	escape
3885	**épave**-*f*	wreck	4193	**évaluation**-*f*	evaluation
3186	**épicerie**-*f*	grocery	4758	**évaluer**-*vb*	assess| rate
3816	**épidémie**-*f*	epidemic	2729	**évasion**-*f*	evasion
4761	**épingle**-*f*	pin	3416	**éveiller**-*vb*	awaken
4001	**éponger**-*vb*	mop up| sponge	3694	**évêque**-*m*	bishop
3016	**épouvantable**-*adj*	terrible| appalling	4541	**évier**-*m*	sink
3861	**éprouver**-*vb*	experience| test	4673	**évoluer**-*vb*	evolve| change
2522	**épuiser**-*vb*	exhaust| drain	2789	**évolution**-*f*	evolution
			3988	**exagérer**-*vb*	exaggerate

4943	**excentrique**-*adj; m/f*	eccentric; eccentric
3688	**excepté**-*prp*	except
2966	**exceptionnel**-*adj*	exceptional
3646	**excès**-*adj; m; mpl*	excess; excess; debauchery
4078	**excitation**-*f*	excitation| anticipation
2618	**exciter**-*vb*	excite| arouse
4318	**exclure**-*vb*	exclude
2969	**exécuter**-*vb*	execute
3315	**exemplaire**-*m; adj*	copy; exemplary
3670	**exercer**-*vb*	exercise| exert
4614	**exigence**-*f*	requirement
4374	**exil**-*m*	exile
2571	**expédition**-*f*	shipment| expedition
4303	**exploitation**-*f*	exploitation
4187	**exploiter**-*vb*	exploit| operate
4468	**exploit**-*m*	feat
3052	**explorer**-*vb*	explore
2880	**explosif**-*adj; m*	explosive; explosive
3045	**exposer**-*vb*	expose| exhibit
2639	**exposition**-*f*	exposure| exhibition
2858	**express**-*m*	express
4456	**expulser**-*vb*	expel| deport
4630	**exquis**-*adj*	exquisite| delicious
4026	**extinction**-*f*	extinction
3855	**extraire**-*vb*	extract| draw
3321	**extra-terrestre**-*adj; m/f*	alien; alien
2759	**extrême**-*adj; m*	extreme; extreme

F

4828	**fabrication**-*f*	manufacturing| production
4748	**façade**-*f*	façade| front
4604	**faciliter**-*vb*	facilitate| aid
2811	**facteur**-*m*	factor| mailman
2766	**facture**-*f*	invoice| statement
2796	**facturer**-*vb*	charge
4220	**faculté**-*f*	faculty| ability
2741	**faiblesse**-*f*	weakness
3077	**faillite**-*f*	bankruptcy
5004	**faisable**-*adj*	feasible| doable
3489	**faîte**-*m*	ridge| top
3819	**falaise**-*f*	cliff
3187	**familial**-*adj*	family

3132	**familier**-*adj; m*	familiar; familiar
4359	**famine**-*f*	famine
3708	**fantasmer**-*vb*	fantasize
3160	**farce**-*f*	farce| joke
2951	**fardeau**-*m*	burden| charge
3343	**farine**-*f*	flour
4416	**fasciste**-*m/f; adj*	fascist; fascist
2813	**fauché**-*adj*	broke| hard
3405	**faucon**-*m*	falcon
4538	**favorite**-*adj*	favored
2779	**fédéral**-*adj*	federal
3504	**fédération**-*f*	federation
2721	**fée**-*f; adj*	fairy; pixy
3179	**féliciter**-*vb*	congratulate
2984	**femelle**-*adj; f*	female; female
3284	**féminin**-*adj*	female| feminine
4734	**fermement**-*adv*	firmly
4911	**ferment**-*m*	ferment
2672	**fermeture**-*f*	closing| closure
2866	**fermier**-*m*	farmer
3932	**féroce**-*adj*	fierce| savage
4971	**ferrer**-*vb*	shoe
4410	**ferry**-*m*	ferry
4310	**festin**-*m*	feast
2574	**festival**-*m*	festival| celebration
2820	**février**-*m*	February
3513	**Fi!**-*int*	Pooh!
3450	**fiable**-*adj*	reliable
3006	**fiançailles**-*fpl*	engagement
4830	**ficeler**-*vb*	tie up
3196	**ficher**-*vb*	file
3372	**fichier**-*m*	catalog| file
2874	**fiction**-*f*	fiction
3423	**fidélité**-*f*	loyalty| fidelity
4012	**file**-*f*	queue| row
2636	**filet**-*m*	net| fillet
3913	**financer**-*vb*	finance
3453	**financier**-*adj; m*	financial; financier
4876	**firme**-*f*	firm
3069	**fixer**-*vb*	set| fix
3630	**flanc**-*m*	flank
2688	**flash**-*m*	flash| flashlight
4622	**flatter**-*vb*	flatter| gratify
4969	**flatteur**-*adj; m*	flattering; flatterer
4351	**fléau**-*m*	scourge| plague
3185	**flingue**-*m*	gun| shooter

3157	**flipper**-*m; vb*	pinball; freak out	
4621	**flot**-*m*	stream| flood	
4527	**flou**-*adj; m; adv*	vague; blurring; fuzzily	
3426	**flûte**-*f*	flute	
4235	**flux**-*m*	flow| flux	
3118	**foirer**-*vb*	misfire	
4912	**follement**-*adv*	madly	
3995	**foncé**-*adj*	dark	
4128	**fonctionnaire**-*m/f*	official| officer	
4930	**fonctionnement**-*m*	operation| running	
3064	**fondation**-*f*	foundation	
3838	**fondé**-*adj*	based| founded	
4505	**fonder**-*vb*	base| set up	
3609	**fondu**-*adj*	molten	
3233	**fontaine**-*f*	fountain| spring	
4970	**forge**-*f*	forge	
4857	**forgeron**-*m*	black-smith	
3178	**formé**-*adj*	formed| trained	
2523	**former**-*vb*	form| train	
2614	**formule**-*f*	formula| form	
4252	**fortement**-*adv*	strongly	
3564	**forteresse**-*f*	fortress	
3386	**fosse**-*f*	pit| grave	
4266	**fossé**-*m*	ditch| moat	
2633	**foudre**-*f*	lightning	
2920	**fouet**-*m*	whip	
3034	**fouille**-*f*	search	
4902	**fouine**-*f*	weasel	
4571	**foulard**-*m*	scarf| foulard	
4317	**fourchette**-*f*	fork	
3567	**fourgon**-*m*	van	
3146	**fourmi**-*f*	ant	
2908	**fournir**-*vb*	provide| afford	
4039	**fourré**-*m; adj*	thicket; filled	
3428	**fourrure**-*f*	fur	
4452	**fracturer**-*vb*	fracture	
3929	**fraise**-*f*	strawberry	
4143	**fraiser**-*vb*	mill	
2917	**franchir**-*vb*	cross| pass	
3571	**frappe**-*f*	strike| striking	
4231	**fraternité**-*f*	fraternity	
3792	**frein**-*m*	brake	
2949	**fréquence**-*f*	frequency	
3515	**fréquenter**-*vb*	patronize| frequent	
4343	**frérot**-*m*	little brother	

2671	**frire**-*vb*	fry
4712	**frisson**-*m*	thrill| shivers
2961	**froc**-*m*	frock| pants
4316	**frotter**-*vb*	rub| scrub
4397	**fugitif**-*adj; m*	fugitive; fugitive
2861	**fumé**-*adj*	smoked
4865	**fumeur**-*adj; m*	smoking; smoker
4368	**furax**-*adj*	hopping mad
3781	**fureur**-*f*	fury
2765	**fuser**-*vb*	gush
3047	**fusillade**-*f*	shooting
3333	**fusion**-*f*	fusion
3124	**futé**-*adj*	smart

G

3436	**gâchette**-*f*	trigger
3074	**gâchis**-*m*	mess
3020	**gage**-*m*	pledge
4299	**gain**-*m*	gain| benefit
4234	**gala**-*m*	gala
2685	**galaxie**-*f*	galaxy
4436	**gale**-*f*	scabies
2627	**galerie**-*f*	gallery
4868	**gamme**-*f*	range
3473	**gangster**-*m*	gangster
2852	**garantir**-*vb*	ensure| insure
4163	**gardon**-*m*	roach
3579	**garer**-*vb*	park
4735	**garnison**-*f*	garrison
4304	**gaspiller**-*vb*	waste| throw away
4917	**gâté**-*adj*	spoiled| tainted
3716	**gaze**-*adj; f*	gauze; gauze
4394	**gazon**-*m*	grass| lawn
3456	**geler**-*vb*	freeze
4609	**gémissement**-*m*	groan| whine
2626	**gênant**-*adj*	embarrassing
4190	**gène**-*m*	gene
3360	**généralement**-*adv*	generally| usually
3605	**générateur**-*m; adj*	generator; generating
3718	**générer**-*vb*	generate
3545	**générosité**-*f*	generosity
3181	**gêner**-*vb*	hinder
3287	**génétique**-*adj; f*	genetic; genetics
4137	**gentilhomme**-*m*	gentleman
3149	**gentillesse**-*f*	kindness

2576	**gentiment**-*adv*	kindly| gently
4283	**gerber**-*vb*	throw up
3952	**gestion**-*f*	management
3612	**ghetto**-*m*	ghetto
4422	**gibier**-*m*	game| prey
4709	**gifler**-*vb*	slap
3833	**gigantesque**-*adj*	gigantic
3442	**gilet**-*m*	vest
2823	**gin**-*m*	gin
3102	**glace**-*f*	ice| mirror
2856	**glisser**-*vb*	slip| run
4167	**glorieux**-*adj*	glorious
4770	**golfe**-*m*	gulf
4884	**gomme**-*f*	gum
4171	**gonfler**-*vb*	inflate| rise
3283	**gonzesse**-*f*	chick
4221	**gorgée**-*f*	mouthful| gulp
3729	**gorille**-*m*	gorilla
4145	**gouvernant**-*adj*	governing
3511	**grade**-*m*	grade
3432	**graine**-*f*	seed
2769	**grain**-*m*	grain
3466	**graisse**-*f*	fat
4370	**gramme**-*m*	gram| ounce
3062	**grandeur**-*f*	size| magnitude
4301	**grandiose**-*adj*	grandiose
2682	**grange**-*f*	barn
4213	**gratis**-*adv; adj*	free; free
4122	**gratter**-*vb*	scratch| strum
3361	**gratuitement**-*adv*	free of charge
3419	**gravement**-*adv*	seriously| gravely
4480	**graver**-*vb*	engrave| carve
2911	**graviter**-*vb*	gravitate
2701	**grec**-*adj; m*	Greek; Greek
4883	**grecque**-*adj*	Greek
5022	**greffer**-*vb*	graft| engraft
2925	**grenade**-*f*	grenade
3167	**grenier**-*m*	attic| granary
3171	**grenouille**-*f*	frog
3501	**griffer**-*vb*	scratch
2992	**grillé**-*adj*	grilled
2814	**grille**-*f*	grid| gate
3955	**griller**-*vb*	grill| toast
2834	**grimper**-*vb*	climb| soar
3151	**gripper**-*vb*	seize
3611	**grossesse**-*f*	pregnancy

2916	**grossier**-*adj*	coarse| rude
4994	**grossir**-*vb*	swell| magnify
4165	**grotesque**-*adj; m*	grotesque; grotesque
2723	**grotte**-*f*	cave
2994	**grouiller**-*vb*	hurry| swarm
4312	**grue**-*f*	crane
3805	**guérison**-*f*	healing| cure
4940	**guet**-*m*	watch
3106	**gym**-*f*	gym
4110	**gymnase**-*m*	gymnasium

H

3909	**habile**-*adj*	clever| skilful
3751	**habituel**-*adj*	usual| regular
4278	**habituellement**-*adv*	usually
2927	**habituer**-*vb*	accustom| get used to
4014	**hallucination**-*f*	hallucination
3693	**hamburger**-*m*	hamburger
4786	**hameçon**-*m*	hook
3677	**hanche**-*f*	hip
4867	**handicap**-*m*	handicap
4000	**hangar**-*m*	hangar
4524	**harceler**-*vb*	harass| nag
2868	**haricot**-*m*	bean
3242	**harmonie**-*f*	harmony
4706	**hausser**-*vb*	raise| increase
4742	**hébreu**-*adj; m*	Hebrew; Hebrew
4843	**hectare**-*m*	hectare
3710	**hémorragie**-*f*	hemorrhage
3484	**herbe**-*f*	grass| herb
2547	**héritage**-*m*	heritage| legacy
3824	**hériter**-*vb*	inherit
2665	**héritier**-*m*	heir| heirdom
2526	**héroïne**-*f*	heroin
4901	**héroïque**-*adj*	heroic
3248	**hésiter**-*vb*	hesitate
4100	**hétéro**--*pfx*	hetero-
4109	**heurter**-*vb*	hit| offend
2514	**historique**-*adj*	historical
3182	**hockey**-*m*	hockey
4093	**hollandais**-*adj; mpl*	Dutch; Dutch
4355	**Hollande**-*f*	Holland
4345	**homard**-*m*	lobster
2975	**homicide**-*m; adj*	homicide; homicidal

2708	**hommage**-*m*	tribute	3075	**immobilier**-*adj*	immovable
2586	**homo-**-*pfx*	homo-	4580	**immonde**-*adj*	unclean
4887	**hongrois**-*adj*	Hungarian	5018	**immoral**-*adj*	immoral
3352	**honnêteté**-*f*	honesty	4477	**immortalité**-*f*	immortality
2537	**honorable**-*adj*	honorable	3965	**immortel**-*adj; m*	immortal; immortal
3058	**honorer**-*vb*	honor	4866	**immunité**-*f*	immunity
3381	**honteux**-*adj*	shameful| ashamed	4141	**impasse**-*f*	impasse| deadlock
3636	**horaire**-*m*	schedule	3558	**impatience**-*f*	impatience
3174	**horizon**-*m*	horizon	4129	**impeccable**-*adj*	impeccable| spotless
4696	**hormone**-*f*	hormone	4949	**impératrice**-*f*	empress
3723	**hospitalité**-*f*	hospitality	4053	**impérial**-*adj*	imperial
4628	**hostie**-*f*	host	4470	**impitoyable**-*adj*	ruthless| merciless
3979	**hostile**-*adj*	hostile| opposed	4564	**implorer**-*vb*	implore| plead
2745	**hôte**-*m*	host	4034	**impoli**-*adj*	impolite
3668	**Hou!**-*int*	Boo!	3661	**imposteur**-*m*	impostor
2841	**Hourra!**-*int*	Hurrah!	2958	**impressionner**-*vb*	impress
4108	**huer**-*vb*	boo| hoot	4254	**imprévisible**-*adj*	unpredictable
2893	**humble**-*adj*	humble	4446	**impuissant**-*adj*	powerless
3217	**humide**-*adj*	wet| damp	4829	**impulsion**-*f*	pulse| impetus
4512	**humidité**-*f*	moisture| humidity	4483	**inacceptable**-*adj*	unacceptable
4821	**humiliant**-*adj*	humiliating	4181	**inattendu**-*adj*	unexpected
4123	**humiliation**-*f*	humiliation	3227	**inconscient**-*adj; m*	unconscious; unconscious
4104	**humilier**-*vb*	humiliate	3039	**indépendance**-*f*	independence
4879	**humilité**-*f*	humility	3911	**indépendant**-*adj; m*	independent; independent
4858	**hurlant**-*adj*	howling			
2710	**hurler**-*vb*	scream| howl	4743	**indigène**-*adj; m/f*	native; native
4822	**hygiène**-*f*	hygiene	3628	**indigne**-*adj*	unworthy
4067	**hymne**-*m*	anthem| canticle	3417	**indispensable**-*adj*	essential
4739	**hypnose**-*f*	hypnosis	2698	**individu**-*m*	individual
3707	**hypothèse**-*f*	hypothesis	4348	**industriel**-*adj; m*	industrial; industrialist
4033	**hystérique**-*adj*	hysterical	3073	**inévitable**-*adj*	inevitable
			4590	**infâme**-*adj*	infamous| vile

I

			3510	**infanterie**-*f*	infantry
			4691	**infarctus**-*m*	infarct
3380	**identification**-*f*	identification	4540	**infecter**-*vb*	infect
4263	**identique**-*adj*	identical	3274	**infection**-*f*	infection
4300	**idole**-*f*	idol| goddess	4791	**inférieur**-*adj; m*	lower; inferior
3905	**ignoble**-*adj*	despicable	4637	**infidèle**-*adj*	unfaithful
3650	**ignorance**-*f*	ignorance	4997	**infiltrer**-*vb*	infiltrate
2508	**illusion**-*f*	illusion	3461	**infini**-*adj; m*	infinite; infinity
3379	**imaginaire**-*adj*	imaginary	2607	**infiniment**-*adv*	infinitely
4216	**imiter**-*vb*	imitate| mimic	4164	**infirme**-*adj*	infirm
4753	**immatriculation**-*f*	registration	3503	**infirmerie**-*f*	infirmary
3531	**immédiat**-*adj*	immediate	4737	**informateur**-*m*	informant
4091	**immigration**-*f*	immigration	3297	**informatique**-*f; adj*	data processing; paperless
4037	**immobile**-*adj*	motionless| immobile			

3957	**informe**-*adj*	shapeless| unformed	2702	**interne**-*adj; m/f*	internal; intern
4974	**informé**-*adj*	informed	3980	**interprétation**-*f*	interpretation
4962	**infraction**-*f*	offense| infringement	3899	**interprète**-*m/f*	interpreter
4268	**ingrat**-*adj*	ungrateful	4523	**interpréter**-*vb*	interpret
3324	**inhabituel**-*adj*	unusual	2896	**interrogatoire**-*m*	examination| questioning
4377	**initial**-*adj*	initial	2797	**intervenir**-*vb*	intervene
3990	**initiative**-*f*	initiative| lead	2644	**intervention**-*f*	intervention| speech
3717	**injection**-*f*	injection	4087	**interviewer**-*vb*	interview
4004	**injustice**-*f*	injustice| unfairness	2660	**intime**-*adj*	intimate
2739	**innocence**-*f*	innocence	2695	**intimité**-*f*	privacy
4054	**inoffensif**-*adj*	harmless	3591	**intrigue**-*f*	plot
4764	**inoubliable**-*adj*	unforgettable	3982	**introduire**-*vb*	introduce| place
3744	**inscription**-*f*	registration| entry	3879	**intrusion**-*f*	intrusion
3306	**inscrire**-*vb*	enroll| list	3529	**intrus**-*m; adj*	intruder; intruding
3024	**inscrit**-*m/f; adj*	registered voter/student; enrolled	2934	**intuition**-*f*	intuition
2748	**insecte**-*m*	insect	4473	**inventaire**-*m*	inventory
2791	**insensé**-*adj; m*	senseless; madman	4957	**inventeur**-*m*	inventor
4716	**insensible**-*adj*	insensitive	2790	**invention**-*f*	invention
3223	**insigne**-*m; adj*	badge| insignia; signal	2938	**inverse**-*adj; m*	reverse; reverse
4432	**insoler**-*vb*	expose	3420	**investir**-*vb*	invest
4199	**inspecter**-*vb*	inspect| examine	3378	**investissement**-*m*	investment
3278	**inspection**-*f*	inspection	4864	**investisseur**-*m; adj*	investor; investing
2903	**inspirer**-*vb*	inspire	4391	**invincible**-*adj*	invincible
3776	**instable**-*adj*	unstable| unsteady	3550	**iris**-*m*	iris
4704	**installation**-*f*	installation| plant	2621	**irlandais**-*adj; m/mpl*	Irish; Irish
4674	**instituteur**-*m*	teacher			
3621	**institution**-*f*	institution	3684	**ironie**-*f*	irony
3007	**institut**-*m*	institute	4769	**ironique**-*adj*	ironic| quizzical
2604	**instrument**-*m*	instrument| implement	4402	**irrésistible**-*adj*	irresistible
3817	**insulte**-*f*	insult	4030	**irresponsable**-*adj*	irresponsible
2846	**insulter**-*vb*	insult| offend	4027	**isolement**-*m*	isolation
3099	**insupportable**-*adj*	unbearable| insupportable	3476	**isoler**-*vb*	isolate| separate
4289	**intact**-*adj*	intact| unspoiled	4484	**itinéraire**-*m; adj*	route; itinerary
4189	**intégrer**-*vb*	integrate| include	4804	**ivresse**-*f*	drunkenness
3993	**intégrité**-*f*	integrity| honesty	2801	**ivrogne**-*m/f; adj*	drunkard; drunken
4649	**intellectuel**-*adj; m*	intellectual; intellectual			
4850	**intendant**-*m*	steward		**J**	
2915	**intense**-*adj*	intense			
4768	**intensité**-*f*	intensity| severity	2696	**jalousie**-*f*	jealousy
4425	**interdiction**-*f*	prohibition	3086	**jambon**-*m*	ham
4382	**intermédiaire**-*adj; m*	intermediate; intermediate	2610	**janvier**-*m*	January
2691	**international**-*adj; m*	international; international	3780	**jardinier**-*m*	gardener
			2832	**jazz**-*m*	jazz
			3454	**jeep**-*f*	jeep
			2726	**jet**-*m*	jet| stream
			4855	**joint**-*adj; m*	joint; joint

4700	**joker**-*m*	joker
3091	**jouir**-*vb*	enjoy
4596	**journalisme**-*m*	journalism
4041	**judas**-*m*	peephole| judas
3108	**judiciaire**-*adj; m/f*	judicial; judiciary
2615	**jules**-*m*	stud
2697	**jumeau**-*adj; m*	twin; twin
3011	**jumelle**-*adj; f*	twin; twin
4620	**jument**-*f*	mare
4861	**junkie**-*f*	junkie
2965	**jupe**-*f*	skirt
4715	**juridiction**-*f*	jurisdiction
4166	**juridique**-*adj*	legal
3477	**justifier**-*vb*	justify

K

4545	**karaté**-*m*	karate
4102	**karma**-*m*	karma
4447	**ketchup**-*m*	ketchup
4021	**kidnapper**-*vb*	kidnap
4773	**kidnapping**-*m*	kidnapping
4162	**klaxon**-*m*	horn| klaxon

L

4982	**labeur**-*m*	labor| toil
4893	**labyrinthe**-*m*	labyrinth
2955	**laid**-*adj*	ugly
2506	**lame**-*f*	blade
4239	**lamentable**-*adj*	lamentable
3018	**lard**-*m*	bacon
3704	**largement**-*adv*	widely
3808	**larguer**-*vb*	slip
3038	**laser**-*m*	laser
3845	**lasser**-*vb*	weary| bore
2876	**latin**-*adj*	Latin
4060	**lavage**-*m*	washing
3770	**lécher**-*vb*	lick
4586	**lècher**-*vb*	lick
4230	**lecteur**-*m*	reader| pickup
3697	**légalement**-*adv*	legally
4101	**légendaire**-*adj*	legendary
3397	**légèrement**-*adv*	slightly| lightly
4568	**légion**-*f*	legion
3813	**légiste**-*m*	jurist

2519	**légitime**-*adj*	legitimate
2718	**légume**-*m*	vegetable
2649	**lent**-*adj*	slow
3435	**lessive**-*f*	laundry| lye
4381	**levier**-*m*	lever
4155	**lézard**-*m*	lizard
2772	**libération**-*f*	release| releasing
4115	**librairie**-*f*	bookstore
3978	**librement**-*adv*	freely
3203	**licence**-*f*	license
4953	**lièvre**-*m; adj*	hare; hare's
2930	**ligue**-*f*	league
4490	**limiter**-*vb*	limit| restrict
3759	**limonade**-*f*	lemonade
3850	**lin**-*m*	linen
4650	**liquider**-*vb*	liquidate| wind up
3364	**littéralement**-*adv*	literally
4152	**livreur**-*m*	delivery man
2754	**local**-*adj*	local
4550	**locataire**-*m/f*	tenant| lodger
3907	**location**-*f*	hire
3604	**logement**-*m*	housing| accommodation
3915	**lointain**-*adj*	distant| far
4899	**loisir**-*m*	leisure
2785	**longueur**-*f*	length
3542	**loterie**-*f*	lottery
4624	**loto**-*m*	lotto
2889	**louche**-*f; adj*	ladle; shady
3709	**loué**-*adj*	rented| leased
3586	**louper**-*vb*	miss out on
3037	**loyal**-*adj*	loyal| fair
3822	**lueur**-*f*	glow| light
3298	**luire**-*vb*	gleam| glisten
4438	**lumineux**-*adj*	luminous
2581	**lutter**-*vb*	fight| combat

M

3779	**mâchoire**-*f*	jaw
4206	**maestro**-*m*	maestro
2667	**mafia**-*f*	mafia
2816	**maigre**-*adj*	lean| meager; lean
3117	**maillot**-*m*	shirt
3104	**mairie**-*f*	town hall
2957	**maïs**-*m*	corn

2854	**maîtrise**-*f*	control| proficiency	4443	**masse**-*f*	mass| body
3193	**maîtriser**-*vb*	control| master	4247	**massif**-*adj; m*	massive; massif
3851	**majeur**-*adj; m*	major| middle finger; major	3206	**mat**-*adj; m; abr*	matt; mate; morning
2603	**majorité**-*f*	majority	3068	**matelas**-*m*	mattress
3970	**maladroit**-*adj; m*	awkward; blunderer	4196	**matelot**-*m*	sailor
4138	**malais**-*adj; m*	Malay; Malay	4094	**maternel**-*adj*	maternal
3809	**malchance**-*f*	bad luck| misfortune	3323	**mater**-*vb*	stare at
4076	**maléfique**-*adj*	maleficient	4161	**mauviette**-*adj; f*	wimp; weakling
2752	**malentendu**-*m*	misunderstanding	4989	**maximal**-*adj*	terminal
3493	**malle**-*f*	trunk	2735	**Maya**-*m; adj*	Maya; Maya
3205	**mallette**-*f*	briefcase	4135	**mécanicien**-*m*	mechanic
2617	**manager**-*m*	manager	3303	**mécanique**-*adj; f*	mechanical; mechanics
4665	**manège**-*m*	carousel| treadmill	4052	**mécanisme**-*m*	mechanism
4552	**manie**-*f*	mania	3365	**mèche**-*f*	wick
4029	**manifestation**-*f*	event| manifestation	4904	**médiocre**-*adj; m/f*	poor| mediocre; second-rater
3916	**manifestement**-*adv*	obviously	4799	**médium**-*m*	medium
3763	**manipuler**-*vb*	handle| manipulate	4934	**meeting**-*m*	meeting
2849	**mannequin**-*m*	model| dummy	3887	**mélodie**-*f*	melody
5003	**manœuvrer**-*vb*	maneuver| manipulate	4204	**melon**-*m*	melon
3447	**manoir**-*m*	manor	4229	**mémé**-*f*	granny| nanny
3940	**manuscrit**-*adj; m*	manuscript; manuscript	4826	**mendier**-*vb; m*	beg; sponge
5021	**maquette**-*f*	model	3337	**mental**-*adj*	mental
2768	**marais**-*m*	marsh	4897	**mentalement**-*adv*	mentally
4807	**marathon**-*m*	marathon	3977	**menthe**-*f*	mint
3930	**marbre**-*adj; m*	marble; marble	3184	**mentionner**-*vb*	mention
2625	**marchandise**-*f*	commodity	3293	**menton**-*m*	chin
2577	**marchand**-*m; adj*	dealer| seller; mercantile	3594	**mépriser**-*vb*	despise| disregard
3999	**maréchal**-*m*	marshal	4890	**mercure**-*m*	mercury
3162	**marée**-*f*	tide	3316	**merdique**-*adj*	crappy| shitty
4794	**mare**-*f*	pond	2612	**mériter**-*vb*	deserve| earn
3232	**marge**-*f*	margin	5019	**merveilleusement**-*adv*	wonderfully
3144	**marijuana**-*f*	marijuana	2686	**messe**-*f*	mass
4281	**mariner**-*vb*	marinate	4496	**messie**-*m*	messiah
4966	**marionnette**-*f*	marionette	4767	**métaphore**-*f*	metaphor
3319	**marquis**-*m*	marquis	2973	**mexicain**-*adj*	Mexican
3141	**marron**-*adj; m*	brown; brown	4577	**microbe**-*m*	microbe
2662	**marteau**-*m*	hammer	3701	**miette**-*f*	crumb
3398	**martial**-*adj*	martial	4663	**milice**-*f*	militia
3458	**martini**-*m*	martini	3483	**millionnaire**-*m/f*	millionaire
4703	**martyr**-*m; adj*	martyr; martyred	3711	**milord**-*m*	milord
4194	**masculin**-*adj; m*	male; masculine	4680	**miner**-*vb*	undermine
3338	**massacrer**-*vb*	massacre| murder	3199	**mineur**-*adj; m*	minor; minor
3131	**massage**-*m*	massage	2538	**minimum**-*adj; m*	minimum; minimum
			2936	**minou**-*m*	kitty

3736	**minuscule**-*adj; f*	tiny| lowercase; minuscule
3063	**mis**-*adj*	placed
3882	**miséricorde**-*f*	mercy
2516	**missile**-*adj; m*	missile; missile
4619	**mitrailleuse**-*f*	machine gun
4618	**moduler**-*vb*	modulate
4796	**moelle**-*f*	marrow
2784	**moine**-*m*	monk
3798	**momie**-*f*	mummy
4227	**monastère**-*m*	monastery
4297	**monstrueux**-*adj*	monstrous
2651	**montage**-*m*	mounting
2742	**mont**-*m*	mount
2802	**montre**-*f*	watch
4898	**moralité**-*f*	morality
3730	**morphine**-*f*	morphine
4874	**morse**-*m*	morse
4840	**morsure**-*f*	bite
3481	**morveux**-*adj; m*	snotty; snot
4608	**motivation**-*f*	motivation
3176	**mou**-*adj; m*	soft; slack
4259	**mouchard**-*m*	sneak| informer
2848	**moucher**-*vb*	snuff
2943	**mouchoir**-*m*	handkerchief
2873	**mouillé**-*adj*	wet
2890	**mouiller**-*vb*	wet| anchor
3462	**moulin**-*m*	mill
3332	**mousse**-*f*	foam| moss
2635	**moustache**-*f*	mustache| whiskers
2631	**muet**-*adj; m*	silent; mute
3214	**mule**-*f*	mule
4324	**municipal**-*adj*	municipal
4613	**mûr**-*adj*	mature| grown
2558	**muscle**-*m*	muscle
3264	**musical**-*adj*	musical
2857	**musicien**-*m*	musician
3795	**musulman**-*adj; m*	Muslim; Muslim
4610	**mutation**-*f*	mutation
2512	**mystérieux**-*adj*	mysterious
4459	**mystique**-*adj; m/f*	mystical; mystic

N

2562	**nage**-*m*	swim
4103	**naïf**-*adj; m*	naive; babe

3143	**nain**-*adj; m*	dwarf; dwarf
4469	**natal**-*adj*	native
4606	**nausée**-*f*	nausea
2628	**navette**-*f*	shuttle
4360	**navigation**-*f*	navigation
4319	**naviguer**-*vb*	navigate
3107	**néanmoins**-*con; adv*	however; withal
3722	**néant**-*m*	nothingness
4659	**nécessairement**-*adv*	necessarily
3853	**nécessiter**-*vb*	require
4973	**négliger**-*vb*	neglect| overlook
4024	**négociation**-*f*	negotiation
2560	**négocier**-*vb*	negotiate
3111	**nettoyage**-*m*	cleaning| scrub
4250	**neutre**-*adj*	neutral| neuter
4996	**nickel**-*m*	nickel
2638	**nièce**-*f*	niece
2956	**nier**-*vb*	deny
2518	**niquer**-*vb*	fuck
4347	**noblesse**-*f*	nobility
2775	**noce**-*f*	nuptials
4593	**noces**-*fpl*	nuptials
4156	**nocturne**-*adj*	nocturnal
3588	**nœud**-*m*	node| knot
4276	**notion**-*f*	notion
3521	**nouille**-*f; adj*	noodle| dope; dumb
3560	**nounou**-*f*	nanny
4763	**nounours**-*m*	teddy bear
4600	**nourrice**-*f*	nurse
4136	**noyau**-*m*	core| kernel
2561	**noyer**-*m; vb*	walnut; drown
3811	**nuire**-*vb*	harm| damage
5006	**numérique**-*adj*	digital| numerical
3632	**nuque**-*f*	neck

O

3401	**obligation**-*f*	obligation| bond
4366	**obligatoire**-*adj*	compulsory| binding
4950	**obscène**-*adj*	obscene
3524	**obscur**-*adj*	obscure| dim
2870	**obséder**-*vb*	obsess
4648	**obsèques**-*adj; f; fpl*	obsequies; funeral
3190	**observation**-*f*	observation| comment

3268	**obstacle**-*m*	obstacle	3926	**pagaille**-*f*	mess
4090	**obus**-*m; adj*	shell; dense	3606	**paiement**-*m*	payment| payoff
4842	**occidental**-*adj; m*	western; western	3100	**paille**-*f*	straw
4819	**occident**-*m*	West	3266	**paisible**-*adj*	peaceful| quiet
3920	**occupation**-*f*	occupation| tenure	3587	**palace**-*m*	palace
4149	**odieux**-*adj*	odious| heinous	2680	**pâle**-*adj*	pale
3486	**œuvre**-*f*	work	4028	**panama**-*m*	panama
4798	**offense**-*f*	offense| insult	3758	**paniquer**-*vb*	panic
3566	**offenser**-*vb*	offend| insult	2580	**pan**-*m; int*	panel; bang!
4400	**offensif**-*adj*	aggressive	2505	**panneau**-*m*	panel| sign
3200	**office**-*m*	office| pantry	4708	**pansement**-*m*	dressing
3625	**Ohé!**-*int*	Yoo-Hoo!	2694	**papillon**-*m*	butterfly
4139	**oie**-*f*	goose	3898	**parachute**-*m*	parachute
4776	**oignon**-*m*	onion	3314	**parade**-*f*	parade
3702	**olive**-*f*	olive	4412	**paralyser**-*vb*	paralyze| cripple
4159	**omelette**-*f*	omelette	3527	**parapluie**-*f*	umbrella
3989	**opérateur**-*m*	operator	4327	**parasite**-*m; adj*	parasite; parasitic
3479	**opposer**-*vb*	oppose| put up	3105	**parcourir**-*vb*	travel| run through
3951	**opposition**-*f*	opposition	3088	**parer**-*vb*	parry| ward off
3960	**optimiste**-*adj; m/f*	optimistic; optimist	3667	**paresseux**-*adj; m*	lazy; sloth
2978	**option**-*f*	option	3641	**parfaire**-*vb*	perfect
3159	**orbiter**-*vb*	orbit	3802	**parlement**-*m*	parliament
3027	**oreiller**-*m*	pillow	4212	**parleur**-*m*	talker
2878	**organe**-*m*	organ	4549	**paroisse**-*f*	parish
3727	**organisme**-*m*	organization	2637	**parrain**-*m*	sponsor
3954	**orgasme**-*m*	orgasm	4723	**participation**-*f*	participation| contribution
3370	**orgueil**-*m*	pride			
5008	**orientation**-*f*	orientation| guidance	4694	**particule**-*f*	part| particle
2777	**orient**-*m*	east	4290	**partisan**-*adj; m*	partisan| adherent; partisan
3950	**orphelin**-*adj; m*	orphan; orphan			
3362	**orphelinat**-*m*	orphanage	3540	**parvenir**-*vb*	get through
3498	**orteil**-*m*	toe	4295	**passage**-*m*	passage| passing
2806	**osé**-*adj*	bold| racy	3700	**passionner**-*vb*	fascinate
3745	**ôter**-*vb*	remove	3033	**patate**-*f*	potato (chip)
4112	**oubli**-*m*	oversight| oblivion	3687	**pâte**-*f*	paste
3953	**ouf**-*m/f; int*	crazy person; whew	3865	**pâté**-*m*	pâté
4019	**ouragan**-*m*	hurricane	2953	**pathétique**-*adj; m*	pathetic; pathos
4929	**outrager**-*vb*	outrage| insult	3969	**paumer**-*vb*	lose
2995	**outre**-*prp; f*	besides; skin	3424	**pauvret**-*m/f*	poor looking
4617	**ouvrager**-*vb*	tool	3530	**pavillon**-*m*	flag
4140	**overdose**-*f*	overdose	3032	**paysage**-*m*	landscape
			2827	**paysan**-*adj; m*	peasant; peasant
	P		4508	**pécheur**-*m*	sinner
			3804	**pêcheur**-*m*	fisherman
			4085	**pédale**-*f*	pedal
2510	**pacifique**-*adj*	peaceful| pacific	3749	**peigne**-*m*	comb
3383	**pacte**-*m*	pact| agreement	4223	**peignoir**-*m*	robe

4373	**peine**-*f*	penalty| sentence	4721	**pion**-*m*	pawn| piece
2645	**peintre**-*m*	painter	3043	**piqûre**-*f*	sting| puncture
4209	**peinture**-*f*	painting| paint	3138	**pister**-*vb*	track
4172	**pellicule**-*f*	film	3446	**pitoyable**-*adj*	pitiful
3674	**peloton**-*m*	pack	2692	**plafond**-*m*	ceiling| plafond
3639	**pelouse**-*f*	lawn	4224	**plaider**-*vb*	plead
4364	**pendaison**-*f*	hanging| hang	3282	**plaie**-*f*	wound
3396	**pénétrer**-*vb*	enter| penetrate	3883	**planche**-*f*	board| plank
2590	**pénible**-*adj*	painful| hard	4984	**planer**-*vb*	plane
4999	**pénitencier**-*m*	penitentiary	3925	**planifier**-*vb*	plan| chart
4655	**pente**-*f; adj*	slope| incline; heavy	4910	**planning**-*m*	schedule
4567	**pépé**-*m*	grandpa	2693	**planquer**-*vb*	hide
4978	**perception**-*f*	perception	4591	**plantation**-*f*	planting
3617	**percer**-*vb*	drill| pierce	4556	**plâtre**-*m*	plaster
4741	**perdant**-*adj; m*	losing; loser	4407	**pleinement**-*adv*	fully
3766	**performance**-*f*	performance	4244	**plier**-*vb*	bend
3773	**péril**-*m*	peril| distress	4435	**plombier**-*m*	plumber
2905	**périmètre**-*m*	perimeter	2826	**plomb**-*m*	lead| plumb
2877	**perle**-*f*	pearl| jewel	2810	**plonger**-*vb*	dive| plunge
4449	**permanent**-*adj; m*	permanent; permanent	4881	**plouc**-*m*	slob| bumpkin
4361	**perroquet**-*m*	parrot	3235	**plume**-*f*	feather
3240	**perruque**-*f*	wig	2679	**pneu**-*m*	tire
3180	**persuader**-*vb*	persuade	4519	**pneumonie**-*f*	pneumonia
4280	**perturber**-*vb*	disrupt	4478	**poêler**-*vb*	fry
4065	**peso**-*m*	peso	3404	**poignarder**-*vb*	stab
3923	**pétard**-*m*	firecracker	3983	**poignard**-*m*	dagger
2582	**péter**-*vb*	fart	3244	**poignet**-*m*	wrist
4561	**pet**-*m*	fart	3441	**pointer**-*vb*	point
4475	**pharaon**-*m*	Pharaoh	3403	**pois**-*m*	pea
3549	**phare**-*m*	lighthouse| headlight	4069	**poisse**-*f*	rotten luck
3183	**pharmacie**-*f*	pharmacy| dispensary	4544	**poivre**-*m*	pepper
2974	**phénomène**-*m*	phenomenon	4426	**pôle**-*m*	pole
4329	**philosophe**-*m/f*	philosopher	2589	**poli**-*adj*	polished| polite
2786	**philosophie**-*f*	philosophy	4353	**politesse**-*f*	politeness
2551	**photographe**-*m/f*	photographer	3421	**politicien**-*m*	politician
2986	**photographier**-*vb*	photograph	4530	**polo**-*m*	polo
3230	**physiquement**-*adv*	physically	3004	**polonais**-*adj; m|mpl*	Polish; Polish
4677	**piaule**-*f*	room| pad			
3076	**pic**-*m*	peak| woodpecker	4724	**poney**-*m*	pony
4124	**piège**-*m*	trap| snare	2860	**pop**-*adj; m*	pop; pop
3786	**pieu**-*m*	stake| pale	4766	**porche**-*m*	porch
5010	**pilotage**-*m; f*	control; piloting	3334	**portail**-*adj; m*	portal; portal
2521	**pilote**-*m*	pilot	3327	**porteur**-*m; adj*	carrier| holder; supporting
4832	**pi**-*m*	pi			
4441	**pincer**-*vb*	pinch| pluck	4369	**portière**-*f*	door
4499	**pin**-*m*	pine	4757	**portier**-*m*	porter| doorkeeper
			4474	**porto**-*m*	port

2818	**positif**-*adj; m*	positive; positive
2542	**possession**-*f*	possession
4261	**postal**-*adj*	postal
4420	**poster**-*vb*	post| poster
4083	**poteau**-*m*	post| pole
2703	**potentiel**-*adj; m*	potential; potential
4488	**potion**-*f*	potion
4938	**poulette**-*f*	pullet
4424	**pou**-*m*	louse
2731	**poumon**-*m*	lung
3237	**pourboire**-*m*	tip| fee
4175	**pourcentage**-*m*	percentage
4326	**pourriture**-*f*	decay| rot
2716	**poursuite**-*f*	pursuit| prosecution
4827	**pousse**-*f*	shoot
3748	**poussin**-*m*	chick
4151	**prairie**-*f*	meadow
4315	**pratiquer**-*vb*	practice| use
4168	**précaution**-*f*	precaution
4048	**précédemment**-*adv*	previously
3154	**précédent**-*adj; m*	previous; precedent
4838	**préciser**-*vb*	specify| point out
3771	**précision**-*f*	precision| accuracy
4095	**prédire**-*vb*	predict| prophesy
3893	**préférable**-*adj*	preferable
4946	**préférence**-*f*	preference
3563	**préfet**-*m*	prefect
4771	**préjuger**-*vb*	prejudge
4113	**préméditation**-*f*	premeditation
3599	**premièrement**-*adv*	firstly
3422	**préoccuper**-*vb*	concern| preoccupy
3600	**préparation**-*f*	preparation
5002	**préparé**-*adj*	prepared
3738	**présentation**-*f*	presentation
3350	**préserver**-*vb*	preserve
3719	**présidence**-*f*	presidency
3049	**pressé**-*adj*	pressed
3290	**pressentiment**-*m*	feeling
3238	**présumer**-*vb*	assume
2661	**prétendre**-*vb*	claim| pretend
4302	**prétentieux**-*adj*	pretentious| snooty
3267	**prévoir**-*vb*	provide| predict
3551	**primaire**-*adj*	primary; primary
4880	**primitif**-*adj; m*	primitive; primitive

4714	**principalement**-*adv*	mainly| mostly
2734	**priorité**-*f*	priority| preference
3081	**privilège**-*m*	privilege
2616	**probable**-*adj*	likely
3317	**procéder**-*vb*	proceed
3860	**procurer**-*vb*	obtain
2565	**profession**-*f*	profession
2503	**profil**-*m*	profile
2783	**profondeur**-*f*	depth| hollowness
4751	**programmer**-*vb*	program
2869	**proie**-*f*	prey| decoy
4210	**projection**-*f*	projection| screening
4785	**prometteur**-*adj*	promising
3690	**promis**-*adj*	promised
3910	**promouvoir**-*vb*	promote| instigate
3222	**prononcer**-*vb*	pronounce
3964	**propagande**-*f*	propaganda
3367	**prophète**-*m*	prophet
3760	**prophétie**-*f*	prophecy
4936	**prospérer**-*vb*	prosper| floor
4444	**prospérité**-*f*	prosperity
3152	**prostituer**-*vb*	prostitute
3859	**protecteur**-*adj; m*	protective; protector
2579	**protégé**-*adj*	protected
4461	**protester**-*vb*	protest
3785	**protocole**-*m*	protocol
5000	**prototype**-*m*	prototype
4517	**provenance**-*f*	origin
4486	**provenir**-*vb*	result
4788	**proverbe**-*m*	proverb| saying
3119	**province**-*f*	province
4457	**proviseur**-*m*	principal| headmaster
3309	**provision**-*f*	provision
4011	**provisoire**-*adj*	provisional
4288	**proximité**-*f*	proximity| vicinity
3308	**prudence**-*f*	caution| prudence
2563	**psychiatre**-*m/f*	psychiatrist
3288	**psychiatrique**-*adj*	psychiatric
3872	**psychologie**-*f*	psychology
3526	**psychologique**-*adj*	psychological
4132	**psychologue**-*m/f*	psychologist
3336	**psychopathe**-*m/f*	psychopath
4889	**psychotique**-*adj; m/f*	psychotic; psychotic
4856	**puant**-*adj*	stinking

4669	**puanteur**-*f*	stench
3140	**publier**-*vb*	publish| publicize
4844	**pudding**-*m*	pudding
4346	**puer**-*vb*	stink| smell
2989	**pull**-*m*	sweater
4015	**punch**-*m*	punch
2684	**punir**-*vb*	punish| discipline
2533	**punition**-*f*	punishment
4049	**punk**-*adj; m*	punk; punk
3508	**purée**-*f*	puree
4282	**purement**-*adv*	purely
3814	**pureté**-*f*	purity
4153	**puzzle**-*m*	puzzle
3093	**pyjama**-*m*	pajamas

Q

3652	**qualifier**-*vb*	qualify
2670	**quantité**-*f*	amount| number
3252	**quarantaine**-*f*	quarantine| about forty
3092	**quarante**-*num*	forty
3085	**quasiment**-*adv*	almost
3580	**quatorze**-*num*	fourteen
2907	**quelconque**-*adj; prn*	any; some or other
4479	**quereller**-*vb*	quarrel
2541	**quêter**-*vb*	take collection
3366	**quotidien**-*adj; m*	daily; daily

R

3215	**rabbin**-*m*	rabbi
3867	**racaille**-*f*	riffraff
2998	**raccompagner**-*vb*	see off
3858	**raccourcir**-*vb*	shorten
2596	**raccrocher**-*vb*	hang up
2658	**racheter**-*vb*	redeem
3322	**racine**-*f*	root
3864	**raciste**-*adj; m/f*	racist; racist
3071	**racler**-*vb*	scrape
2859	**radar**-*m*	radar
4074	**radiation**-*f*	radiation
4806	**radical**-*adj; m*	radical; radical
4752	**radin**-*m; adj*	tightwad; mean
3908	**rafraîchir**-*vb*	refresh
4180	**ragot**-*adj; m*	dirty; gossip

4453	**ragoût**-*m*	stew
4238	**raid**-*m*	raid
3433	**rail**-*m*	rail
4010	**raisin**-*m*	grape
4760	**raisonner**-*vb*	reason
4801	**rajouter**-*vb*	add
3286	**rampe**-*f*	ramp| rail
4732	**ramper**-*vb*	crawl| trail
3219	**rançon**-*f*	ransom
3602	**rancune**-*f*	grudge| rancor
3837	**rappel**-*m*	reminder| encore
2884	**rapprocher**-*vb*	bring closer
3325	**ras**-*adj*	all clear| short
2805	**raser**-*vb*	raze| brush
2944	**rasoir**-*m*	razor
3522	**rassemblement**-*m*	gathering| rally
3061	**rassembler**-*vb*	gather| collect
3914	**rassurer**-*vb*	reassure
5016	**ravin**-*m*	ravine
4125	**réacteur**-*m*	reactor
2767	**réagir**-*vb*	react
3876	**réalisation**-*f*	realization| achievement
3229	**réaliste**-*adj; m/f*	realistic; realist
2655	**rebelle**-*m/f; adj*	rebel; rebellious
4521	**rébellion**-*f*	rebellion| rebel
4331	**récent**-*adj*	recent
2833	**recette**-*f*	recipe
4597	**rechanger**-*vb*	change again
3095	**réchauffer**-*vb*	warm| heat up
2706	**rechercher**-*vb*	search| look for
4847	**réciproque**-*adj*	reciprocal| mutual
3294	**récit**-*m*	story| recital
3041	**récolte**-*f*	harvest| crop
3696	**recommander**-*vb*	recommend
4802	**réconforter**-*vb*	comfort
3734	**réconfort**-*m*	comfort| reassurance
4551	**reconstruire**-*vb*	rebuild| reconstruct
3512	**recours**-*m*	recourse| remedy
4228	**recul**-*m*	recoil| retreat
4195	**rédacteur**-*m*	editor
5014	**rédaction**-*f*	writing| redaction
4896	**redevable**-*adj; vb*	beholden; put under stress
3732	**redevenir**-*vb*	become again
4222	**redoutable**-*adj*	formidable| dreadful
4520	**réduction**-*f*	reduction| discount

2585	**réduire**-*vb*	reduce| decrease	2532	**répétition**-*f*	repetition| rehearsal
4915	**réduit**-*adj*	reduced	4423	**re**--*pfx*	re-
3835	**reflet**-*m*	reflection	4871	**répit**-*m*	respite| reprieve
3465	**réflexion**-*f*	reflection| thinking	4526	**réplique**-*f*	replica| reply
4775	**refrain**-*m*	refrain	2842	**répliquer**-*vb*	reply
4585	**refroidir**-*vb*	cool	3643	**répondeur**-*m*	answering machine
2847	**refuge**-*m*	refuge| shelter	3150	**reportage**-*m*	report
3488	**réfugier**-*vb*	refuge	2853	**reporter**-*m; vb*	reporter; postpone
3120	**refus**-*m*	refusal| rejection	3629	**repousser**-*vb*	repel| fend off
4525	**regagner**-*vb*	regain	4335	**représentant**-*m*	representative| agent
2515	**régiment**-*m*	regiment	3480	**représentation**-*f*	representation| performance
3234	**registrer**-*vb*	register			
4245	**régner**-*vb*	reign| take over	4695	**reprise**-*f*	recovery
2898	**regret**-*m*	regret	3654	**repriser**-*vb*	darn| mend
4582	**regrettable**-*adj*	regrettable| unfortunate	3637	**reproche**-*m*	reproach| rebuke
			3645	**reprocher**-*vb*	reproach| blame
4313	**régulier**-*adj; m*	regular; regular	4653	**reproduction**-*f*	reproduction
3427	**régulièrement**-*adv*	regularly	4127	**reproduire**-*vb*	reproduce
3756	**rein**-*m*	kidney	4817	**républicain**-*adj; m*	republican; republican
3307	**rejeter**-*vb*	reject| dismiss	3437	**répugner**-*vb*	loathe
4178	**réjouir**-*vb*	rejoice	4358	**réservation**-*f*	booking| reservation
3659	**relâche**-*f*	respite	3059	**réserve**-*f*	reserve| reservation
3829	**relâcher**-*vb*	release| relax	3133	**réservoir**-*m*	tank
2928	**relais**-*m*	relay	2629	**résidence**-*f*	residence
4998	**relance**-*f*	revival	4834	**résider**-*vb*	reside| live
2996	**relevé**-*m; adj*	statement; raised	3249	**respectable**-*adj*	respectable
4992	**relier**-*vb*	connect	4497	**ressemblance**-*f*	resemblance| likeness
2979	**religieux**-*adj; m*	religious; religious	2972	**ressort**-*m*	spring| resilience
4745	**remontant**-*adj; m*	pick-me-up; tonic	2630	**ressource**-*f*	resource
2991	**rempli**-*adj; m*	filled| full; tuck	4952	**restau**-*m*	restaurant
4750	**remporter**-*vb*	win| take	4047	**restaurant**-*m*	restaurant| cafe
4170	**remué**-*adj*	stirred	4705	**résumer**-*vb*	summarize| resume
4267	**remuer**-*vb*	stir| move	4070	**résurrection**-*f*	resurrection
4783	**renaissance**-*f*	renaissance| reawakening	4079	**rétablir**-*vb*	restore| re-establish
			3985	**retardé**-*adj*	backward
4727	**renaître**-*vb*	come back to life	4472	**retarder**-*vb*	delay| postpone
2776	**renard**-*m*	fox	2557	**réussite**-*f*	success
4779	**renforcer**-*vb*	strengthen| reinforce	2530	**revancher**-*vb*	requite
3195	**renseigner**-*vb*	inform	3936	**révélation**-*f*	revelation
2678	**renversé**-*adj*	reversed	2668	**révéler**-*vb*	reveal| tell
3158	**renverser**-*vb*	reverse| turn	3973	**revenant**-*adj; m*	return| reverting; ghost
4956	**repaire**-*m*	den	4835	**revendre**-*vb*	sell
4257	**répandre**-*vb*	spill| scatter	4553	**revers**-*m*	reverse| back
4388	**réparation**-*f*	repair| satisfaction	3728	**revivre**-*vb*	relive
3357	**repasser**-*vb*	iron| replay	3753	**révolte**-*f*	revolt| mutiny
4307	**repère**-*m*	landmark	3475	**révolutionnaire**-*adj; m/f*	revolutionary; revolutionary
2669	**repérer**-*vb*	spot			

3387	**rhum**-*m*	rum
3110	**richesse**-*f*	wealth| richness
2714	**rideau**-*m*	curtain
4939	**ridiculiser**-*vb*	ridicule
4756	**rigueur**-*f*	rigor
3260	**rime**-*f*	rhyme
4385	**ringard**-*adj; m*	tacky; has-been
2778	**ring**-*m*	ring
3251	**rituel**-*adj; m*	ritual; ritual
4451	**rivage**-*m*	shore
3410	**rive**-*f*	bank| shore
2755	**robe**-*f*	dress| gown
4387	**robinet**-*m*	tap| faucet
2732	**rocher**-*m; vb*	rock; spit
4144	**roc**-*m*	rock
4990	**rodeo**-*m*	rodeo
4631	**rogner**-*vb*	crop| trim
3188	**romain**-*adj*	Roman
4983	**romancer**-*vb*	romanticize
4710	**ronger**-*vb*	gnaw
4036	**rôtir**-*vb*	roast
2901	**roue**-*f*	wheel
4372	**rouleau**-*m*	roller| roll
4895	**roulette**-*f*	roulette| wheel
4320	**roupie**-*f*	rupee
2598	**routine**-*f*	routine
3491	**ruban**-*m*	ribbon
4192	**ruelle**-*f*	alley
3072	**ruine**-*f*	ruin| doom
3035	**ruiner**-*vb*	ruin| wreck
3691	**ruisseau**-*m*	stream| creek
3090	**rupture**-*f*	break| rupture
3272	**ruse**-*f*	cunning| ruse
4097	**ruser**-*vb*	use cunning

S

3363	**sacrément**-*adv*	mighty
2864	**sacrifier**-*vb*	sacrifice
4782	**saisi**-*adj*	grasped
2593	**saisir**-*vb*	seize| grasp
3189	**saké**-*m*	sake
3862	**salir**-*vb*	soil| smear
4494	**saliver**-*vb*	salivate
4255	**saloon**-*m*	saloon
3464	**salutation**-*f*	greeting

3496	**sanctuaire**-*m*	sanctuary
4684	**sanguin**-*adj*	blood
2897	**saoul**-*adj*	drunk
3755	**sapin**-*m*	pine
4594	**sardine**-*f*	sardine
4583	**satané**-*adj*	devilish
3596	**satisfaction**-*f*	satisfaction
4414	**satisfait**-*adj*	satisfied| pleased
3330	**saucisse**-*f*	sausage
3967	**saumon**-*m*	salmon
2707	**sauvetage**-*m*	rescue| salvage
3082	**sauveur**-*m*	savior
3884	**savant**-*adj; m*	learned; scholar
4632	**scandaleux**-*adj*	scandalous| outrageous
3797	**scanner**-*m*	scanner
4851	**scénariste**-*m/f*	scriptwriter
4265	**scie**-*f*	saw
3469	**scolaire**-*adj*	school
3651	**scoop**-*m*	scoop
3263	**score**-*m*	score
4546	**scorpion**-*m*	scorpion
2511	**scotch**-*m*	Scotch tape| whisky
3922	**scout**-*m*	scout
3411	**script**-*m*	script
3225	**seau**-*m*	bucket
2654	**sèche**-*f; adj*	fag; dry
3585	**sécher**-*vb*	dry| cure
3656	**secouer**-*vb*	shake| rock
4980	**secrètement**-*adv*	secretly
4418	**secte**-*f*	sect| connection
4916	**sécuriser**-*vb*	reassure
3009	**séduire**-*vb*	seduce| attract
3301	**séduisant**-*adj*	attractive| seductive
3412	**seize**-*num*	sixteen
4354	**sélection**-*f*	selection| team
2559	**selle**-*f*	saddle
3339	**semblable**-*adj; m*	similar; fellow creature
3607	**semer**-*vb*	sow
4118	**semestre**-*m*	half
4555	**séminaire**-*m*	seminar
2828	**sénat**-*m*	senate
4471	**sensationnel**-*adj*	sensational
3168	**sensé**-*adj*	sensible
4574	**sensibilité**-*f*	sensibility
3572	**sentence**-*f*	sentence

4455	**sentier**-*m*	path| trail	3997	**sonder**-*vb*	probe| sound
4044	**sentimental**-*adj*	sentimental	3678	**songer**-*vb*	reflect| wonder
3025	**séparation**-*f*	separation	3559	**sonnerie**-*f*	ring| bell
4961	**séparément**-*adv*	separately| apart	3649	**sonnette**-*f*	doorbell| buzzer
3768	**septième**-*num*	seventh	5024	**sonore**-*f; adj*	sound; acoustic
4923	**seringue**-*f*	syringe	4454	**sorcellerie**-*f*	witchcraft| sorcery
3901	**sermon**-*m*	sermon	4672	**sordide**-*adj*	sordid| wretched
3299	**serrure**-*f*	lock	3966	**sottise**-*f*	folly| silliness
4808	**sérum**-*m*	serum	3031	**soudainement**-*adv*	suddenly
3601	**servante**-*f*	servant| maid	3554	**souffler**-*vb*	breathe| whisper
2606	**serveur**-*m*	waiter	4531	**souffrant**-*adj*	suffering| ill
2529	**serviteur**-*m*	servant	3121	**souhait**-*m*	wish
4740	**set**-*m*	set	2750	**soûl**-*adj*	drunk
4134	**seuil**-*m*	threshold| sill	3714	**soulagement**-*m*	relief| solace
3616	**sévère**-*adj*	severe| strict	3535	**soulager**-*vb*	relieve| alleviate
4158	**sexualité**-*f*	sexuality	4678	**soûler**-*vb*	get drunk
4296	**sexuellement**-*adv*	sexually	3425	**soulever**-*vb; m*	raise; bench press
3502	**sherry**-*m*	sherry	3269	**soulier**-*m*	shoe
3539	**shopping**-*m*	shopping	3896	**soumettre**-*vb*	submit| refer
4240	**short**-*m*	shorts	3354	**soupçon**-*m*	suspicion| soupcon
3418	**SIDA**-*abr*	AIDS	3787	**soupçonner**-*vb*	suspect
4671	**siffler**-*vb*	whistle| hiss	4249	**soupirer**-*vb*	sigh
3774	**sifflet**-*m*	whistle	3721	**soupir**-*m*	sigh
2730	**signaler**-*vb*	report| point out	4099	**sourcil**-*m*	eyebrow
3892	**signification**-*f*	meaning| notification	4853	**souriant**-*adj*	smiling
2676	**silencieux**-*adj; m*	silent; silencer	4985	**souterrain**-*adj*	underground
4772	**silhouette**-*f*	outline	4398	**souverain**-*adj; m*	sovereign; sovereign
4852	**sincérité**-*f*	sincerity| honesty	2891	**soviétique**-*adj*	Soviet
3226	**sinistre**-*adj; m*	sinister| grim; fire	3544	**spatial**-*adj*	spatial
4380	**sirène**-*f*	siren	2910	**spécialement**-*adv*	specially| notably
4061	**sirop**-*m*	syrup	2595	**spécialiste**-*m/f*	specialist
4913	**situer**-*vb*	locate| situate	4722	**spécimen**-*m*	specimen
3445	**sixième**-*num*	sixth	4173	**spectaculaire**-*adj*	spectacular
3575	**ski**-*m*	ski	3720	**spectateur**-*m*	spectator| onlooker
3261	**slip**-*m*	briefs| panties	4292	**spectre**-*m*	spectrum| ghost
4253	**smoking**-*m*	tuxedo	3220	**sperme**-*m*	sperm
4975	**snob**-*m/f; adj*	snob; snobbish	4958	**splendeur**-*f*	splendor
3377	**sobre**-*adj*	sober	4646	**spot**-*m*	spot| blip
4570	**socialiste**-*adj; m*	socialist; socialist	2931	**square**-*m*	square
2600	**soda**-*m*	soda	4107	**squelette**-*f*	skeleton
4907	**sofa**-*m*	sofa	3139	**stable**-*adj*	stable| steady
4730	**soigneusement**-*adv*	carefully	4217	**stage**-*m*	course
			3096	**standard**-*adj; m*	standard; standard
4185	**soixante**-*num*	sixty	3497	**stand**-*m*	stall
2997	**solaire**-*adj*	solar	4579	**statistique**-*adj; f*	statistical; statistics
3610	**solde**-*m*	balance	3395	**statut**-*m*	status

2709	**steak**-*m*	steak
3280	**stock**-*m*	stock
4038	**stopper**-*vb*	stop
2687	**stratégie**-*f*	strategy
2711	**stress**-*m*	stress
4068	**strictement**-*adv*	strictly
2738	**structure**-*f*	structure
4634	**stupéfier**-*vb*	amaze| astound
4941	**subitement**-*adv*	suddenly
3017	**sublime**-*adj*	sublime
3778	**substance**-*f*	substance| material
4755	**subtil**-*adj*	subtle
4933	**successeur**-*m*	successor
4839	**succession**-*f*	succession| inheritance
2524	**sucer**-*vb*	suck| suck out
3959	**suède**-*adj; f*	suede; suede
3737	**suédois**-*adj; m*	Swedish; Swedish
2871	**sueur**-*f*	sweat| sweating
3213	**suggestion**-*f*	suggestion
4744	**suicidaire**-*adj*	suicidal
4183	**sultan**-*m*	sultan
3241	**supermarché**-*m*	supermarket
5001	**superviseur**-*m*	supervisor
4106	**supplémentaire**-*adj*	additional
3757	**supprimer**-*vb*	remove| suppress
4502	**surfer**-*vb*	go surfing
3532	**surf**-*m*	surf
3890	**surmonter**-*vb*	overcome| rise above
2960	**surnom**-*m*	nickname
2564	**survivant**-*m; adj*	survivor; surviving
4689	**susceptible**-*adj*	susceptible
3552	**suspendre**-*vb*	suspend| hang
4947	**suspense**-*m*	suspension
4781	**suspension**-*f*	suspension| stay
3679	**sympathie**-*f*	sympathy
2942	**sympathique**-*adj*	sympathetic
3256	**symptôme**-*m*	symptom
3806	**syndrome**-*m*	syndrome

T

3534	**tabasser**-*vb*	beat up
3472	**table**-*f*	table| calculator
3583	**tâche**-*f*	task
3094	**tacher**-*vb*	stain| spot

2892	**tactique**-*adj; f*	tactical; tactics
3375	**tailleur**-*m*	tailor
4602	**talentueux**-*adj*	talented
4765	**talon**-*m*	heel
3783	**tambour**-*m*	drum
3098	**tango**-*m*	tango
3382	**tank**-*m*	tank
3541	**tapette**-*f*	pansy
3832	**tare**-*f*	stigma
4147	**tarif**-*m*	rate
4849	**tata**-*f*	auntie
2673	**tatouage**-*m*	tattoo
4378	**taudis**-*m*	slum
2993	**taupe**-*f; adj*	mole; taupe
2587	**taureau**-*m*	bull
4800	**taverne**-*f*	tavern
4342	**taxe**-*f*	tax
3389	**techniquement**-*adv*	technically
3666	**teindre**-*vb*	dye
4450	**télécommande**-*f*	remote control
3197	**téléphone**-*m*	phone
3592	**téléphonique**-*adj*	telephone
4476	**télescoper**-*vb*	telescope
3431	**temporaire**-*adj*	temporary
2528	**tendance**-*f*	trend| movement
3672	**tendresse**-*f*	tenderness| kindness
4273	**tenon**-*m*	tenon
3948	**tentant**-*adj*	tempting
3660	**tentation**-*f*	temptation
4031	**tequila**-*m*	tequila
4415	**terminal**-*adj; m*	terminal; terminal
3010	**terrestre**-*adj*	terrestrial| earthly
3681	**terrifiant**-*adj*	terrifying
4433	**terrifier**-*vb*	terrify
2758	**tester**-*vb*	test| try
4965	**testicule**-*m*	testicle
4501	**téter**-*vb*	suck
3638	**têtu**-*adj*	stubborn| headstrong
2575	**thème**-*m*	theme
2570	**thérapie**-*f*	therapy
3848	**thèse**-*f*	thesis| theory
3772	**thon**-*m*	tuna
4463	**tic**-*m*	tic
3634	**tigre**-*m*	tiger
4160	**timbrer**-*vb*	stamp

4872	**tirage**-*m*	drawing| print	3399	**tremper**-*vb*	soak| dip
2793	**tiroir**-*m*	drawer	4885	**trentaine**-*num*	about thirty
2632	**tissu**-*m*	fabric| tissue	3743	**trêve**-*f*	truce
4937	**tolérer**-*vb*	tolerate| bear	4050	**triangle**-*m*	triangle
3101	**tomate**-*f*	tomato	3519	**tribord**-*m*	starboard
3765	**tombeau**-*m*	tomb	3775	**tricher**-*vb*	cheat
3956	**tonne**-*f*	tonne	4548	**tricheur**-*m*	cheater
4148	**topo**-*m*	sketch	4654	**trimestre**-*m*	quarter
3355	**torche**-*f*	torch	2980	**triomphe**-*m*	triumph
2830	**tordre**-*vb*	twist| wring	3128	**tripler**-*vb*	triple
4338	**torpille**-*f*	torpedo	3739	**trompette**-*f*	trumpet| trumpeter
3275	**torturer**-*vb*	torture	2881	**tronche**-*f*	face
4908	**totalité**-*f*	totality| integrity	4736	**tronc**-*m*	trunk| stem
3050	**toubib**-*m*	doctor| medic	3589	**trophée**-*m*	trophy
3257	**touchant**-*adj*	touching	2900	**trouble**-*m; adj*	disorder| trouble; dim
2502	**touche**-*f*	key	2724	**troubler**-*vb*	disturb| trouble
2971	**touriste**-*m/f*	tourist	4790	**trouillard**-*adj; m*	yellow belly; yellow-livered
2727	**tournoi**-*m*	tournament	2549	**troupeau**-*m*	herd| flock
4886	**tousser**-*vb*	cough	3619	**trousse**-*f*	kit
3414	**toutefois**-*con; adv*	however; nevertheless	4863	**trousser**-*vb*	truss
3843	**toutou**-*m*	doggie| lapdog	3295	**tsar**-*m*	tsar
4188	**toux**-*f*	cough	2865	**tube**-*m*	tube| hit
4831	**toxique**-*adj*	toxic	3485	**tumeur**-*f*	tumor| growth
5011	**tracé**-*m; adj*	route| course; tracing	3794	**turc**-*adj; m*	Turkish; Turkish
4057	**trac**-*m*	stage fright	4878	**tuteur**-*m*	guardian
4664	**tracteur**-*m; adj*	tractor; towing	2990	**typique**-*adj*	typical
3569	**traduire**-*vb*	translate| transpose			
4729	**trafiquer**-*vb*	traffic			
2824	**traire**-*vb*	milk		**U**	
3517	**trajectoire**-*f*	path			
3046	**trajet**-*m*	path	2761	**ultime**-*adj*	ultimate
3342	**trancher**-*vb*	settle| slice	4341	**uni**-*adj*	united| plain
2700	**tranquillement**-*adv*	quietly	4246	**universitaire**-*adj; m/f*	university; postgraduate student
4960	**tranquillité**-*f*	peace| quiet	4032	**urine**-*f*	urine
4592	**transaction**-*f*	transaction| deal	3841	**utilisation**-*f*	use
3438	**transférer**-*vb*	transfer| switch	4080	**utilité**-*f*	utility| value
4554	**transformation**-*f*	transformation			
3048	**transmettre**-*vb*	transmit| convey			
3070	**transporter**-*vb*	transport| move		**V**	
4198	**trappe**-*f; adj*	hatch| trap; cobwebby			
4376	**traquer**-*vb*	track| track down	4670	**vaccin**-*m*	vaccine
3013	**travailleur**-*m; adj*	worker| employee; industrious	2540	**vachement**-*adv*	really
3276	**treize**-*num*	thirteen	4392	**vagabond**-*adj; m*	vagabond; vagabond
3769	**tremblement**-*m*	trembling| tremor	3409	**vagin**-*m*	vagina
3002	**trembler**-*vb*	tremble| shake	4848	**vaguement**-*adv*	vaguely
			2762	**vainqueur**-*m; adj*	winner| conqueror; winning

2550	**vaisselle**-*f*	dishes		4979	**virginité**-*f*	virginity
3112	**valable**-*adj*	valid		3852	**visible**-*adj*	visible
3116	**valet**-*m*	valet		3801	**visiblement**-*adv*	visibly
4462	**vanité**-*f*	vanity| pride		2650	**visite**-*f*	visit
4225	**vanter**-*vb*	boast		2803	**visiteur**-*m*	visitor
3067	**vase**-*m; f*	vase; mud		3279	**visuel**-*adj*	visual
2933	**vaste**-*adj*	vast| wide		4202	**vital**-*adj*	vital
3468	**vaurien**-*m*	rascal| scoundrel		3998	**vitre**-*f*	window
4759	**vautour**-*m*	vulture		3996	**vitrine**-*f*	showcase| window
3582	**veau**-*m*	calf| veal		4270	**vivement**-*adv*	deeply
3452	**véhicule**-*m; adj*	vehicle; vehicular		4920	**vocabulaire**-*m*	vocabulary
3562	**veinard**-*adj*	lucky		4236	**vocation**-*f*	vocation| call
2756	**veine**-*f*	vein| luck		3173	**voire**-*adv*	indeed
4325	**velours**-*m*	velvet		4287	**voisinage**-*m*	neighborhood| neighbors
5017	**venin**-*m*	venom				
2656	**verdict**-*m*	verdict		4774	**volant**-*m; adj*	steering wheel; flying
4013	**vérification**-*f*	verification| check		4504	**volcan**-*m*	volcano
3001	**ver**-*m*	worm		4043	**vole**-*f*	vole
3345	**vermine**-*f*	vermin		4762	**volet**-*m*	flap
4510	**verrouiller**-*vb*	lock on		3444	**volume**-*m*	volume| tonnage
3548	**verser**-*vb*	pay| pour		3012	**vomi**-*m*	vomit
4082	**vertige**-*m*	vertigo| spell		2719	**voter**-*vb*	vote
2619	**vertu**-*f*	virtue		3657	**vouer**-*vb*	devote
3886	**vestiaire**-*m*	cloakroom		3902	**voyageur**-*m; adj*	traveler| passenger; traveling
3881	**vétérinaire**-*adj; m/f*	veterinary; veterinary		2725	**vulgaire**-*adj*	vulgar
4365	**vexer**-*vb*	vex| upset		3764	**vulnérable**-*adj*	vulnerable
4088	**via**-*prp*	via				
4733	**vibration**-*f*	vibration| pulse			**W**	
3245	**vice**-*m*	vice				
3750	**vicieux**-*adj; m*	vicious; lecher		3273	**wagon**-*m*	car| wagon
2929	**vider**-*vb*	empty| drain		3747	**western**-*m*	western
2945	**vieillard**-*m*	old man		4685	**won**-*m*	won
4892	**vieillesse**-*f*	old age| old				
4062	**vieillir**-*vb*	age			**Y**	
2556	**villa**-*f*	villa				
3451	**villageois**-*m*	villager		3490	**yacht**-*m*	yacht
4810	**vingtaine**-*num*	around twenty		3054	**yankee**-*adj*	Yankee
3972	**violation**-*f*	violation| breach		4154	**yard**-*m*	yard
2773	**violer**-*vb*	violate| breach		4931	**yoga**-*m*	yoga
3631	**violet**-*adj; m*	purple; purple		4563	**yuan**-*m*	yuan
4995	**violeur**-*m*	rapist				
4909	**violoncelle**-*m*	cello			**Z**	
2648	**violon**-*m*	violin				
4972	**vipère**-*f*	viper		4491	**zombi**-*m*	zombie
3340	**virage**-*m*	turn| shift		3347	**zone**-*f*	area

Contact, Further Reading and Resources

For more tools, tips & tricks visit our site www.mostusedwords.com. We publish various language learning resources.

If you have a great idea you want to pitch us, please send an e-mail to info@mostusedwords.com.

Frequency Dictionaries

Frequency Dictionaries in this series:

French Frequency Dictionary 1 – Essential Vocabulary – 2500 Most Common French Words
French Frequency Dictionary 2 - Intermediate Vocabulary – 2501-5000 Most Common French Words
French Frequency Dictionary 3 - Advanced Vocabulary – 5001-7500 Most Common French Words
French Frequency Dictionary 4 - Master Vocabulary – 7501-10000 Most Common French Words

Please visit our website www.mostusedwords.com/frequency-dictionary/french-english for more information.

Our goal is to provide language learners with frequency dictionaries for every major and minor language worldwide. You can view our selection on www.mostusedwords.com/frequency-dictionary

Bilingual books

We're creating a selection of parallel texts, and our selection is ever expanding.

To help you in your language learning journey, all our bilingual books come with a dictionary included, created for that particular book.

Current bilingual books available are English, Spanish, Portuguese, Italian, German, and French.

For more information, check www.mostusedwords.com/parallel-texts. Check back regularly for new books and languages.

Other language learning methods

You'll find reviews of other 3rd party language learning applications, software, audio courses, and apps. There are so many available, and some are (much) better than others.

Check out our reviews at www.mostusedwords.com/reviews.

Contact

If you have any questions, you can contact us through e-mail info@mostusedwords.com.

Printed in Great Britain
by Amazon

41335098R00145